# Poverty in the United States

Ann O'Leary • Paula M. Frew
Editors

# Poverty in the United States

## Women's Voices

Springer

*Editors*
Ann O'Leary
Atlanta, GA, USA

Paula M. Frew
Emory University School of Medicine
Department of Medicine
Division of Infectious Diseases
Atlanta, GA, USA

Emory University, Rollins School of Public Health
Hubert Department of Global Health & Department of Behavioral Sciences and Health Education
Atlanta, GA, USA

ISBN 978-3-319-43831-3 ISBN 978-3-319-43833-7 (eBook)
DOI 10.1007/978-3-319-43833-7

Library of Congress Control Number: 2016960578



Printed on acid-free paper

This Springer imprint is published by Springer Nature
The registered company is Springer Science+Business Media LLC
The registered company address is: 233 Spring Street, New York, NY 10013, U.S.A.

# Foreword

I am honored to introduce *Poverty in the United States: Women's Voices* written by strong and committed HIV Prevention Trial Network investigators and coedited by Drs. Ann O'Leary and Paula M. Frew. The editors are two scholars who have dedicated their scientific journeys to advocating for the needs of women and for the design and implementation of scientifically based multilevel interventions for women in the USA and globally. If you have followed Drs. O'Leary and Frew's research as I have, you will not be surprised to learn that they have produced this unique book. *Poverty in the United States: Women's Voices* has a powerful message that although numerous biomedical and behavioral prevention and treatment approaches have been used to slow the public health crises of AIDS, without addressing poverty and food insecurity, which constitute the major drivers of HIV among women, we will not witness the end of AIDS or other public health epidemics in our country.

This book arose from an HIV-focused study whose investigators wished to contextualize the study's HIV incidence findings. One out of five new HIV infections in the USA is among women, and women of color, particularly African American women, are disproportionately affected by HIV. Unfortunately, how the social structural forces of poverty that have shaped the HIV epidemic and other health problems among women of color has been understudied. These women represent the most marginalized segments of our society in terms of economic strength, political force, social status, and access to legal systems.

While most individuals in the USA have met or learned about someone who has suffered from hunger and poverty, few of us acknowledge that this is happening in the wealthiest nation in the world. We think that hunger and poverty occurs primarily in underdeveloped countries. The reality is that the latest Census Income, Poverty, and Health Insurance Data released in September 2015 show that in 2014 about 46.7 million Americans (15.0 %) lived below the poverty line ($24,250 for a family of four in 2014). Women in America are 32 % more likely to be poor than men. Employed women are more likely to be poor than employed men, and women are more likely to be poor at every level of educational attainment than men. African Americans have been found to have the highest poverty rate. African Americans are disproportionately affected by poverty, food insecurity, and unemployment and are also more likely to receive food assistance than any other ethnic group in the USA. Women make up over 90 % of adult Temporary Assistance to Needy Families (TANF) recipients. Moreover, TANF, the country's main cash assistance program, does not provide sufficient support to prevent hunger, homelessness, and substandard living conditions, such as living with utility cut-offs. Unfortunately, the anti-poverty and safety net programs in the USA have eroded over the past two decades and continue to neglect providing sufficient provisions for helping women and their families escape poverty. Women face not only poverty but also the circumstances that cause them to remain mired in it. They cannot break the cycle of poverty despite their formidable reservoirs of resilience.

*Poverty in the United States: Women's Voices* is a timely book and one that is urgently needed. A growing number of calls to action have called for addressing structural and policy drivers, such as poverty and food insecurity, in preventing and treating the spread of HIV among women most at risk for infection who live in inner city and rural communities in the USA that have high poverty and extremely high rates of HIV.

One of the novel contributions of this book is the use of qualitative methods to capture the life experiences of such women and how poverty, food insecurity, limited educational opportunities, class, unemployment, policing, incarceration and criminal justice involvement, and community violence have shaped the HIV epidemic in this population. Each of these social structural drivers has, unfortunately, been ignored in the fight against AIDS and other diseases faced by women in the USA. This book is characterized by its rigorous research methods, strong science, and the collective voices it captures that underscore the need for changes to be made in our HIV prevention and treatment interventions and policies.

*Poverty in the United States: Women's Voices* makes clear that solutions must avoid individually oriented paradigms to resolve the AIDS crisis. Each chapter has integrated science and advocacy strategies to provide the reader with steps that need to be taken to enact large-scale societal changes to end poverty co-occurring issues.

The book forcefully argues how social and political drivers of diseases such as HIV, drug use, mental illness, and gender-based and gun violence will remain with us for many years to come, if social and structural drivers are not addressed. One must not focus on "blaming the victim" ideologies, but on ideologies and approaches that target structural drivers of diseases and social problems which are affecting a large number of women across the USA.

I couldn't agree more with the core underlying messages of the book that posit maintaining the status quo of huge and growing economic and attendant disparities that have befallen the USA over the past decades which have disproportionately affected women is fueling a public health crisis and creating an enormous risk to our nation. The book underscores that public health can be traced to the impact of poverty and social inequities and cannot be stopped with solutions that do not address the original drivers of the problems.

I urge you to read this powerful book to understand women's lives and struggles. This book will be an eye opening experience for many.

The book presents insights, suggestions for innovative and strategic policy reform, such as approaches for expanding reproductive health care, as well as primary health care in general and sexually transmitted diseases and HIV in particular. Women need to get the services they deserve. It also addresses that access to care must be guided by rights-based ideology, where social and economic rights are obtained through government commitment and public policies.

Finally, when you complete reading this book, you will not only have learned about the scope of poverty and its consequences among some of the most vulnerable populations in our society, but also have deepened your understanding about the role of poverty and food insecurity and other drivers of health and social problems. No disease can be reduced or eliminated without addressing these structural drivers.

This book is important for researchers, policy makers, advocates, and service providers. Collectively, the authors make it very clear that women who are poor are not responsible for the conditions and diseases they experience on a daily basis. The book highlights the message that the poor are not responsible for their own fates and systematically demonstrates how this belief is a major obstacle to economic redistribution, the creation of services and "safety nets" that are essential for reducing health disparities and achieving the end game of lifting women out of poverty. Each of us needs to have a better grasp of the many sorrows and stresses that poverty manifests in the daily lives of poor women who are often challenged with intersections of other marginal identities, gender and race most specifically.

This book serves as a way to engage with the life experiences of those who are often left voiceless, hearing both their traumas and their successes and resiliency. The book sends a message to politicians and policy makers to avoid blaming the women who are victims of life's poor conditions. This valuable book sends the message to people who have little experience with poverty and may not realize the degree to which Americans suffer hunger, violence, addiction, community, and gun violence.

This book calls for the reader to look for and embrace points of transformation in the systems which facilitate the attitudes, narratives, and policies that fuel the conditions of poverty.

Professor at the School of Social Work
Columbia University, New York, NY

Nabila El-Bassel, PhD

# Preface

The tendency to attribute blame to the unfortunate is very common in the case of people living in poverty (Cozzarelli, Wilkinson, & Tagler, 2001; Rice, 2015). Historically, economic status was perceived by many to be reflective of the individual's ability and industry, and many still believe this to be true. Others believe poverty to be caused by economic unfairness and discrimination. In editing this book, we were aware of the possibility that readers might take much of the content—substance use, unemployment, and violence—to be indicative that the poor participants in our study were in some way responsible for their plight. In an effort to contextualize these topics in the chapters, we asked authors to start each chapter with a sociohistorical description of how current conditions came to be and to end with a section on policy recommendations.

One personal factor that has been studied as a contributor to people's tendencies to attribute blame to the unfortunate generally and the poor specifically is the "just world" hypothesis (Lerner, 1970). This refers to the belief that the world is just and people get what they deserve. It is a specific example of the "fundamental attribution error" marked by a tendency to attribute one's own fate to external factors and those of others to internal traits (Ross, 1977). This belief system is believed to be motivated by fear that the person themselves may fall prey to the same misfortune if causes are seen as being random or systemically caused (as US poverty, by and large, is). The notion that people are responsible for their own fates is a major impediment to economic redistribution and the creation of services and "safety nets" for the disadvantaged (Lane, 2001).

A substantial body of research has documented people's tendencies to apply the just world hypothesis to victims of misfortune. These include victims of sexual assault (Patel, 2009), economic inequality following Hurricane Katrina (Belle, 2006), as well as poverty (Cozzarelli et al., 2001; Shapiro, 2003). Further, individuals who believe in a just world have been shown to have more negative attitudes toward poverty and the poor (Shapiro, 2003). Interventions have been developed that attempt to reduce these attitudes (Ioannou, Kouta, & Andreou, 2015).

These attitudes however are not, in and of themselves, a slight on the character of those who believe them; in fact, they are emblematic of the challenges of living in a diverse nation, a nation where, in order to achieve equity for all citizens, we can have no room for assumptions about the lived experiences and the status of the well-being of others. It is about competence, not character. Many Americans will never be given the opportunity to understand the crippling angst and stress that poverty manifests in the daily lives of the impoverished. Moreover, socioeconomic status is oftentimes further complicated at the intersections of other marginal identities, gender, and race most specifically. Complicated by our nation's challenges with knowledgably engaging in and navigating racial and gendered dynamics is a racial and gendered illiteracy (Stevenson, 2013). It is at these identity intersections that we can see the synergy of multiple levels of systemic oppression and insufficient public policy, policy which orients itself toward a capitalist brand of efficiency rather than a politic of humanity.

In twenty-first century America, from gentrification to water contamination and discrimination to congressional obstruction, the poor are often the victims of displacement, insecurity, and state-sponsored violence at all levels. These factors create a perfect storm of isolation and stress which is neatly tucked away from the American consciousness. This text should serve as a way to engage the narratives of those who are often left voiceless, hearing both their traumas and their triumphs. Acknowledging the resilience of their humanity and spirit despite their conditions will be instrumental in order to develop a desire to understand further the lives lived by those who are in poverty.

In the face of tragic events, "conspiracy theories" are often voiced. However, sometimes conspiracy theories have truth to them. For example, many people believe that crack cocaine—a drug that decimated inner cities in the late 1980s and early 1990s—was intentionally distributed within inner cities (where it still exists today). Cheap and highly addicting, this form of cocaine was associated with extreme behavior (for extensive descriptions of the lifestyles of women who were addicted to crack, see Sharpe, 2005; Sterk, 1999). In fact, an investigation by the U.S. Department of Justice revealed that the anti-Sandinista Contras had been smuggling crack cocaine from Central America into the Los Angeles area and returned the cash profits to pay for automatic weapons. While the role of the CIA (Central Intelligence Agency) in this situation remains controversial, the explosion of crack cocaine in the urban USA is believed to have been sparked by this process (U.S. Department of Justice, 1997).

It is our hope that this book will have the effect of preventing blaming of the victims described here by increasing awareness of the life conditions experienced by many poor women and that they will come to life for readers with their verbatim quotes. We hope that the book will be read by people who have little experience with poverty and may not realize the degree to which Americans suffer hunger, violence, addiction, and other factors that are topics of these chapters. We hope that educating the public in this way about the suffering caused by poverty will increase empathy and with it the desire to reform harmful policies and practices.

Beyond the narratives shared in this volume, developing this empathy will require that readers look both reflexively and introspectively at the conditions of poverty in relation to their own lives. For many, especially those who have little personal experience with poverty, it is very easy and quite compelling to overestimate the validity the assumptions made about opportunity, access, and ability in America. Despite this ease, we cannot neglect the emotional and psychological ramifications of poverty, wounds that can never truly be healed. We encourage our readers to probe more deeply, beyond "bootstrap" and "American Dream" narratives. We ask you to stand face to face with the historical and contemporary realities of our nation surrounding the dehumanization of our fellow citizens in our quest for wealth and power. We encourage our readers to vicariously engage with the trauma of intergenerational social exclusion, systemic inequity, and status quo deficitization that has shaped life trajectories of the poor and the common perspectives many have of their conditions.

Moreover, developing this empathy will require that readers confront the concrete realities of the vast racial, ethnic, and socioeconomic disparities in the domains of health, education, justice, and employment that affect the lived experiences of those who live in poverty. By taking a systemic and life course view of poverty, we can see that poverty is not a moment in time but is being shaped and made at all times, shaped and made by failing schools with underqualified teachers, schools which prioritize neoliberal labor-market educational aims over the concerted preparation of students to thrive in an ever-changing world. The same schools contribute most egregiously to the school to prison pipeline and school-related trauma (Nasir, 2011). Poverty results from being embedded in communities where over-policing and over-incarceration tear apart households and limits family earning potential (Alexander, 2012). It affects both the psychological and corporal experience of those in its grasp at every moment of every day.

We encourage our readers to endeavor to question their own assumptions about the nature of American life, survival, and opportunity. Are the conditions as they seem? If not, how can we even begin to blame the victim? Napier, Mandisodza, Andersen, and Jost (2006), in their analysis of reactions to the victims of Hurricane Katrina, invite us to consider where and why we attribute blame for issues which are at their root systemic. The authors note that in the wake of one of the most devastating environmental disasters of the twenty-first century, people blamed the victims of the hurricane, despite the many failures of the local and national government to respond adequately to the warnings. Ask yourself what role these "victim-blaming attributions" (p. 64) play for us psychologically and emotionally? Do we engage them as a way to cope in an inequitable world? Do we lean on them to avoid grappling with the reality of our nation's multisystemic challenges? How do we consider the role of systems and institutions in constructing and maintaining systems of poverty? These are the questions we must wrestle with. In this spirit, we also challenge our readers to look for sites of transformation in the systems which facilitate the attitudes, narratives, and policies that facilitate the conditions of poverty. It is at these sites that we will find possibility for transformation, the impetus for rehumanization, and paths out of poverty.

## References


Alexander, M. (2012). *The new Jim Crow: Mass incarceration in the age of colorblindness*. The New Press.

Belle, D. (2006). Contested interpretations of economic inequality following Hurricane Katrina. *Analyses of Social Issues and Public Policy, 6*(1), 143–158.

Cozzarelli, C., Wilkinson, A. V., & Tagler, M. J. (2001). Attitudes toward the poor and attributions for poverty. *Journal of Social Issues, 57*, 207–227.

Ioannou, S., Kouta, C., & Andreou, A. (2015). *Health Education, 115*(3–4), 392–404.

Lane, R. E. (2001). Self-reliance and empathy: The enemies of poverty—and of the poor. *Political Psychology, 22*, 473–492.

Lerner, M. J. (1970). The desire for justice and reactions to victims. In J. R. Macaulay & L. Berkowitz (Eds.), *Altruism and helping behavior.* New York: Academic Press.

Moraes, R. (2014). Decades-old CIA crack-cocaine scandal gains new momentum. *Reuters*. Retrieved February 3, 2016, from https://www.rt.com/usa/194992-cia-crack-scandal-webb/

Napier, J. L., Mandisodza, A. N., Andersen, S. M., & Jost, J. T. (2006). System justification in responding to the poor and displaced in the aftermath of Hurricane Katrina. *Analyses of Social Issues and Public Policy, 6*(1), 57–73.

Nasir, N. I. (2011). *Racialized identities: Race and achievement among African American youth*. Stanford University Press.

Patel, M. N. (2009). Why do we blame the victims of sexual assault? *Dissertation Abstracts International: Section B: The Sciences and Engineering, 70* (11-B), pp. 7218.

Rice, A. (2015, August 20). *Our perceptions about the "Unworthy Poor" haven't changed*. Retrieved August 21, 2015, from hppt://talkpoverty.org/2015/08/20/unworthy-poor/

Ross, L. (1977). The intuitive psychologist and his shortcomings: Distortions in the attribution process. In L. Berkowitz (Ed.), *Advances in experimental social psychology* (Vol. 10, pp. 173–220). New York: Academic Press.

Sharpe, T. T. (2005). *Behind the eight ball: Sex for crack cocaine exchange and poor black women*. New York: Routledge.

Shapiro, S. M. (2003). The relationships among mental health clinicians' beliefs in a just world, attitudes toward the poor, and beliefs about helping the poor. *Dissertation Abstracts International: Section B: The Sciences and Engineering, 63*(8-B), pp. 3938.

Sterk, C. E. (1999). *Fast lives: Women who use crack cocaine*. Philadelphia, PA: Temple University Press.

Stevenson, H. C. (2013). *Promoting racial literacy in schools: Differences that make a difference*. Teachers College Press.

U.S. Department of Justice, Office of the Inspector General. (1997, December). *The CIA-Contra-Crack Cocaine controversy: A review of the justice department's investigations and prosecutions*. Retrieved from https://oig.justice.gov/special/9712/ch01p1.htm



Atlanta, GA, USA

Ann O'Leary
Lloyd M. Talley
Paula M. Frew

# Acknowledgments

Support for this book was made possible by a grant from the Scholarly Writing and Publishing Fund from Emory University, The Center for Faculty Development and Excellence.

We wish to thank Drs. Evelyn Davila, Ward Cates, and Tom Coates for their review of chapter manuscripts and Ms. Lauren E. Owens for her editorial assistance. We also thank the study participants, community stakeholders, and staff from each study site.

Grant support for the HPTN 064 study was provided by the National Institute of Allergy and Infectious Diseases, National Institute on Drug Abuse, and National Institute of Mental Health [UM1 AI068619, U01-AI068613, and UM1-AI068613]; Centers for Innovative Research to Control AIDS, Mailman School of Public Health, Columbia University [5U1AI069466]; University of North Carolina Clinical Trials Unit [AI069423]; University of North Carolina Clinical Trials Research Center of the Clinical and Translational Science Award [RR 025747]; University of North Carolina Center for AIDS Research [AI050410]; Emory University HIV/AIDS Clinical Trials Unit [5UO1AI069418], Center for AIDS Research [P30 AI050409], the Clinical and Translational Science Award [UL1 RR025008], NIMH predoctoral awards (F31MH105238 and F31MH096630), and the Robert W. Woodruff Pre-Doctoral Fellowship of the Emory University Laney Graduate School; The Terry Beirn Community Programs for Clinical Research on AIDS Clinical Trials Unit [5 UM1 AI069503-07], The Johns Hopkins Adult AIDS Clinical Trial Unit [AI069465] and The Johns Hopkins Clinical and Translational Science Award [UL1 RR 25005].

## Disclaimer

The views expressed herein are solely the responsibility of the authors and do not necessarily represent the official views of the National Institute of Allergy and Infectious Diseases, the National Institute of Mental Health, the National Institutes of Health, the US Centers for Disease Control and Prevention, the HPTN, or its funders.

# Contents

# Contributors

**Adaora A. Adimora** University of North Carolina Schools of Medicine and Gillings School of Global Public Health, Chapel Hill, NC, USA

**Oluwakemi Amola** School of Medicine and Gillings School of Global Public Health, University of North Carolina at Chapel Hill, Chapel Hill, NC, USA

**Alexis Amsterdam** FHI 360, Durham, NC, USA

**Lynne Anderson** Georgia School of Public Health, Georgia State University, Atlanta, GA, USA

**Matthew Archibald** Department of Sociology, Colby College, Waterville, ME, USA

**Lauren Bishop** Division of Infectious Diseases, Department of Medicine, School of Medicine, Emory University, Atlanta, GA, USA

**Oni Blackstock** Montefiore Medical Center/Albert Einstein College of Medicine, New York, NY, USA

**Dorothy Bota** Department of Behavioral Science and Health Education, Rollins School of Public Health, Emory University, Atlanta, GA, USA

**Yunmi Chung** Division of Infectious Diseases, Department of Medicine, School of Medicine, Emory University, Atlanta, GA, USA

**Hannah L.F. Cooper** Department of Behavioral Science and Health Education, Rollins School of Public Health, Emory University, Atlanta, GA, USA

**Anna Dardick** Division of General Medicine and Clinical Epidemiology, School of Medicine, University of North Carolina at Chapel Hill, Chapel Hill, NC, USA

**Emily F. Dauria** Department of Behavioral Science and Health Education, Rollins School of Public Health, Emory University, Atlanta, GA, USA

**Dazon Dixon Diallo** SisterLove, Inc., Atlanta, GA, USA

**Wafaa El-Sadr** ICAP, Mailman School of Public Health, Columbia University, New York, NY, USA

**Paula M. Frew** Emory University School of Medicine, Department of Medicine, Division of Infectious Diseases, Atlanta, GA, USA

Emory University, Rollins School of Public Health, Hubert Department of Global Health & Department of Behavioral Sciences and Health Education, Atlanta, GA, USA

**Carol E. Golin** Cecil G. Sheps Center for Health Services Research, University of North Carolina at Chapel Hill, Chapel Hill, NC, USA

Department of Health Behavior, Gillings School of Global Public Health, University of North Carolina at Chapel Hill, Chapel Hill, NC, USA

Division of General Medicine and Clinical Epidemiology, School of Medicine, University of North Carolina at Chapel Hill, Chapel Hill, NC, USA

**Danielle F. Haley** FHI 360, Durham, NC, USA

Department of Behavioral Sciences and Health Education, Rollins School of Public Health, Emory University, Atlanta, GA, USA

**Sally Hodder** West Virginia Clinical and Translational Sciences Institute (WVCTSI), West Virginia University, Charlottesville, WV, USA

**Larissa Jennings** Bloomberg School of Public Health, Johns Hopkins University, Baltimore, MD, USA

**LaShawn Jones** FHI 360, Durham, NC, USA

**Jessica E. Justman** ICAP, Mailman School of Public Health, Columbia University, New York, NY, USA

**Irene Kuo** Milken Institute School of Public Health, George Washington University, Washington, DC, USA

**Kathryn Lancaster** FHI 360, Durham, NC, USA

**Jessie R.M. Legros** Atlanta, GA, USA

**Stephanie Lykes** ICAP, Mailman School of Public Health, Columbia University, New York, NY, USA

**Kathleen MacQueen** FHI 360, Durham, NC, USA

**Terry McGovern** Mailman School of Public Health, Columbia University, New York, NY, USA

**Brooke Montgomery** Fay W. Boozman College of Public Health, University of Arkansas for Medical Sciences, Little Rock, AR, USA

**Ann O'Leary** Atlanta, Georgia, USA

**Deirdre Oakley** Department of Sociology, Georgia State University, Atlanta, GA, USA

**Kari R. Olson** ICAP, Mailman School of Public Health, Columbia University, New York, NY, USA

**Lauren E. Owens** Division of Infectious Diseases, Department of Medicine, School of Medicine, Emory University, Atlanta, GA, USA

**Kimberly A. Parker** Department of Health Studies, Texas Woman's University, Denton, TX, USA

**Sharon Parker** The Miriam Hospital Joint Master of Social Work Program, Division of Infectious Diseases, North Carolina A&T State University, Greensboro, NC, USA

**James Peterson** Milken Institute School of Public Health, George Washington University, Washington, DC, USA

**Laura Randall** Division of Infectious Diseases, Department of Medicine, School of Medicine, Emory University, Atlanta, GA, USA

Rollins School of Public Health, Emory University, Atlanta, GA, USA

**Ilana Gabrielle Raskind** Division of Infectious Diseases, Department of Medicine, School of Medicine, Emory University, Atlanta, GA, USA

**Laura Riley** Department of Behavioral Science and Health Education, Rollins School of Public Health, Emory University, Atlanta, GA, USA

**Carlos del Rio** Hubert Department of Global Health, Rollins School of Public Health, Emory University, Atlanta, GA, USA

**Lorenna Rodriguez** Bronx Lebanon Hospital, New York, NY, USA

**Christin Root** Rollins School of Public Health and Center for AIDS Research, Emory University, Atlanta, GA, USA

**Erin Ruel** Department of Sociology, Georgia State University, Atlanta, GA, USA

**Waheedah Shabazz** Positive Women's Network-USA, Philadelphia, PA, USA

**Lydia Soto-Torres** Kelly Government Solutions, Contractor to DAIDS/NIAID/NIH, Rockville, MD, USA

**H. Spiegel** Kelly Government Solutions, Contractor to DAIDS/NIAID/NIH, Rockville, MD, USA

**Jennifer Stewart** School of Nursing, Johns Hopkins University, Baltimore, MD, USA

**Claudia Trezza** Milken Institute School of Public Health, George Washington University, Washington, DC, USA

**Melissa Turner** Infectious Diseases Section, Veterans Affairs Medical Center, Washington, DC, USA

**Sten H. Vermund** Vanderbilt Institute for Global Health, Vanderbilt University School of Medicine, Nashville, TN, USA

**Linda Vo** Division of Infectious Diseases, Department of Medicine, School of Medicine, Emory University, Atlanta, GA, USA

**Jing Wang** Fred Hutchinson Cancer Research Center, Seattle, WA, USA

**Lisa Diane White** SisterLove, Inc., Atlanta, GA, USA

**Gina M. Wingood** Mailman School of Public Health, Columbia University, New York, NY, USA

# About the Editors

**Ann O'Leary** is a psychologist living in Atlanta, Georgia. She served as a senior behavioral scientist in the Division of HIV/AIDS Prevention, Centers for Disease Control and Prevention, for 16 years. Her training included a summa cum laude undergraduate degree from the University of Pennsylvania; a Ph.D. in Psychology from Stanford University, supported by a National Science Foundation fellowship; and 1 year of postdoctoral training in Health Psychology at the University of California at San Francisco. She served on the faculty of the Psychology Department at Rutgers University from 1986 to 1999. She has conducted research on HIV prevention for the past 26 years and has also published many articles on other aspects of Health Psychology. Dr. O'Leary has published more than 165 scientific articles and chapters and has edited or coedited five books, *Women at Risk: Issues in the Primary Prevention of AIDS*; *Women and AIDS: Coping and Care*; *Beyond Condoms: Alternative Approaches to HIV Prevention*; *From Child Sexual Abuse to Adult Sexual Risk: Trauma, Revictimization, and Intervention*; and *African Americans and HIV/AIDS: Understanding and Addressing the Epidemic.* She is a fellow of the American Psychological Association and won the inaugural "Distinguished Leader" award from the APA's Committee on Psychology and AIDS. She serves on the editorial boards of several scientific journals and is a frequent consultant to the NIH and other scientific organizations.

**Paula M. Frew** Paula Frew holds a faculty appointment within the Division of Infectious Diseases in Medicine at the Emory University School of Medicine and at the Emory University Rollins School of Public Health (Global Health and Behavioral Sciences and Health Education). She holds degrees from the University of California at San Diego (BA *cum laude*), San Diego State University (MA), Emory University (MPH), and the University of Georgia (PhD). She served as the principal investigator on the HIV Prevention Trials Network women's HIV seroincidence estimation study and its companion study, "Understanding Women's HIV Risk in the United States." She has also been the principal investigator on five national HIV prevention projects in collaboration with Research Support Services, Inc., and IMPAQ International on behalf of the US Centers for Disease Control and Prevention

(CDC). She has been an investigator on the Women's Interagency HIV Study (WIHS), the HIV Prevention Trials Network (HPTN) studies, the HIV Vaccine Trials Network (HVTN), the "Involvement," the "Engagement," the EnhanceLink, and other HIV and vaccine prevention projects. Her career, community service, and lifetime achievement awards include those from the American Public Health Association, the Georgia Public Health Association, the Society for Prevention Research, and National AIDS Education & Services for Minorities She has over 100 published papers in peer-reviewed journals, book chapters, and conference presentations on HIV/AIDS clinical trial and prevention product acceptability issues, vaccine-preventable disease issues, and the role of community engagement in prevention research.

# Chapter 1
# Women and Poverty in the USA

**Sally Hodder, H. Spiegel, Lydia Soto-Torres, and Danielle F. Haley**

## Introduction

Since 1981, more than 36.9 million people globally have been infected with human immunodeficiency virus (HIV), including more than 1.2 million who have died (World Health Organization, 2016). Though it was known early in the HIV epidemic that consistent condom use prevented sexual transmission of HIV infection and highly active antiretroviral therapy has been accessible in the USA for more than 15 years, new HIV infections have been relatively stable over the past decade. The HIV Prevention Trials Network (HPTN) has conducted cutting-edge HIV prevention studies across the globe. In an effort to address HIV prevention among US women, the HPTN 064 Women's HIV Seroincidence Study was designed to assess HIV incidence among women in the USA most likely to be at risk for HIV acquisition. The HPTN 064 investigators were struck by the ubiquitous, substantive theme of poverty in the lives of women participating in the 064 study. Poverty among US women is a compelling concern that policy makers, citizens, and students of social science, politics, justice, and health outcomes need to understand. We now bring a snapshot of poverty's impact on the lives of women in the USA, in their own words.

S. Hodder (✉)
West Virginia Clinical and Translational Sciences Institute (WVCTSI),
West Virginia University, Morgantown, WV, USA
e-mail: slhodder@hsc.wvu.edu

H. Spiegel • L. Soto-Torres
Kelly Government Solutions, Contractor to DAIDS/NIAID/NIH, Rockville, MD, USA

D.F. Haley
FHI 360, Durham, NC, USA

Department of Behavioral Sciences and Health Education, Rollins School of Public Health,
Emory University, Atlanta, GA, USA



A. O'Leary, P.M. Frew (eds.), *Poverty in the United States*,
DOI 10.1007/978-3-319-43833-7_1

The purpose of this introductory chapter is to provide an overview of poverty among US women, describe current epidemiology of HIV among US women, and summarize the rationale, study design, and results of the HPTN 064 study.

## Description of Poverty Among US Women

Forty-six million persons in the USA were living in poverty in 2012, more than in the previous 54 years (National Center for Law and Economic Justice, 2007–2015). In 2013, the median household income in the USA was $51,939 (U.S. Census Bureau, 2014). Though median US income in 2013 was not significantly different from that in 2012, real median household income in 2013 was 8 % lower than that in 2007, a time point before the recent recession (U.S. Census Bureau, 2014). Critical to any discussion of poverty in the USA is an understanding of the vastly uneven distribution of income. US households in the lowest quintile had annual incomes of $20,901 or less while the highest quintile had incomes of greater than $105,910. Moreover, households in the top 5 % had incomes of more than $196,000.

Poverty is not an unbiased condition. More women than men live in poverty. Among persons aged 18–64 years, 15 % of women and 11.8 % of men live in poverty; this difference is amplified in the older age group (>64 years) where 11.6 % of women compared with 6.8 % of men live in poverty. Thirty-one percent of households headed by a single woman lived in poverty compared with 16.4 % of single male-headed households and 6.3 % of households led by married couples (National Center for Law and Economic Justice, 2015). Relevant to working persons, women have an earnings ratio of 0.78 compared with men, a ratio that has not significantly increased for the past 6 years, providing a pathetic commentary on economic inequality of the sexes in the USA.

Nearly 20 million persons in the USA live in deep poverty, defined by household incomes below 50 % of the poverty line (U.S. Census Bureau, 2014). More than twice as many black persons (12.2 %) compared with white persons (5.3 %) and more women (6.9 %) than men (5.7 %) live in deep poverty (U.S. Census Bureau, 2014).

## Epidemiology of HIV Among US Women

Historically, HIV infection in the USA has been most common among men who have sex with men. Cases of AIDS among women (as a proportion of all US AIDS cases) increased from approximately 7 % in 1985 to 25 % in 2011 (Centers for Disease Control and Prevention, 2012a). Today, women constitute approximately 20 % of individuals with newly diagnosed HIV infections in the USA (Centers for Disease Control and Prevention, 2012a). Most HIV infection in women is acquired through heterosexual contact, with 89 % of cases among black women and 75 % of cases in white women attributed to heterosexual contact (Centers for Disease Control and Prevention, 2012a, 2012b). Surveillance data demonstrate that 64 % of newly diagnosed HIV infections among US women occur among black women and 18 % among white women (Centers for Disease Control and Prevention, 2014). As black women constitute approximately 13 % of the US female population (U.S. Census Bureau, 2014), there is a marked disparity in infection rates of black compared with white women. Unfortunately, the disparity does not stop with infection rates; black women have a significantly higher risk of progression to AIDS and death (Centers for Disease Control and Prevention, 2012a).

Poverty and HIV are closely associated in the USA. In a cross-sectional study of 18,430 heterosexual participants aged 18–50 years conducted in 2006–2007 by the Centers for Disease Control and Prevention (CDC), 49 % lived in poverty. The HIV prevalence among those participants living in poverty was 2.1 %, 20 times greater than the HIV prevalence among all US heterosexuals. Moreover, HIV prevalence was 2.8 % among those with a household income less than $10,000 compared with 0.4 % for those with a household income ≥$50,000 (Denning & DiNenno, 2010).

## Summary of HPTN 064

### *Rationale for Study*

In 2008, scant HIV incidence data for US women existed, limiting the ability to design robust domestic HIV prevention trials. Therefore, before trials assessing the efficacy of any HIV prevention interventions for US women could be designed, accurate HIV incidence data were needed. To evaluate HIV incidence among US women living in geographic areas with high rates of poverty and HIV prevalence and to assess factors that may increase their risk for HIV acquisition and other health problems, the HPTN supported design and conduct of the 064 study, the Women's HIV Seroincidence Study. HPTN 064 was intended to provide better understanding of the risk of HIV infection among certain populations of US women and to provide information about risk behaviors. A qualitative substudy conducted at four of the ten HPTN 064 study sites assessed social, structural, and other contextual factors likely to affect women's sexual and other risk-related decision making as well as women's preferred recruitment and retention strategies for future studies.

### *Study Design*

HPTN 064 was a multisite, longitudinal cohort study conducted in 2009–2011 in ten urban and periurban communities in six geographic areas of the USA (Atlanta, GA; Baltimore, MD; New York, NY; Newark, NJ; Raleigh/Durham, NC; Washington, D.C.). The study was approved by institutional review boards at each of the study sites.

Eligible individuals were 18–44 years of age, self-identified as a woman (transwomen were eligible), reported at least one episode of unprotected vaginal and/or anal sex with a man in the 6 months before enrollment, and were willing to undergo

HIV rapid testing. Additional inclusion criteria were that individuals reside in census tracts (zip codes for the Bronx and Harlem) that ranked in the top 30th percentile of HIV prevalence and with >25 % of inhabitants living below the US federal poverty line. Eligible individuals also had to report ≥1 of the following in past 6 months: (a) illicit injection and/or non-injection drug use (e.g., heroin, cocaine, crack cocaine, methamphetamine, and/or use of prescription drugs apart from those prescribed by a licensed provider); (b) alcohol dependence (defined as CAGE Score ≥2), (Ewing, 1984); (c) binge drinking, defined as ≥4 drinks at one time by a woman; (d) self-reported history of sexually transmitted infections (STIs) (gonorrhea, chlamydia, or syphilis); (e) exchange of sex for commodities (e.g., drugs, money, shelter); (f) incarceration (jail and/or prison ≥24 h within past 5 years); and (g) reported male sexual partner with reported history of incarceration (within past 5 years), injection or non-injection drug use, STIs, HIV diagnosis, history of binge drinking (≥5 drinks at one time by a man), and/or alcohol dependence (CAGE Score ≥2) (Ewing, 1984).

Exclusion criteria included self-reported history of a previous positive HIV test, current HIV prevention trial enrollment, current/past participation in an HIV vaccine trial, or anticipated absence for >2 consecutive months during the follow-up period.

## *Recruitment and Study Procedures*

Venue-based recruitment using time-space sampling, a method used successfully in previous studies to obtain large, diverse samples among hard-to-reach populations (MacKellar, Valleroy, Karon, Lemp, & Janssen, 1996; Muhib et al., 2001; Stueve, O'Donnell, Duran, San Doval, & Blome, 2001), was conducted in an effort to sample women that may not have been reached using other standard recruitment methodologies. Specific venues (or locations) in which young women from the target census tracts (or zip codes) could reasonably be expected to congregate were identified and a list of potential venues (e.g., laundromats, street corners, liquor stores) was created by each study site. Venues were then evaluated by study personnel as to whether the target population (i.e., women likely to meet eligibility criteria) frequented the location and at what hours. Venues frequented by few women between 18 and 44 years of age were eliminated. In addition, feasibility of venues as appropriate recruitment locations was assessed and inappropriate venues (e.g., those frequented predominantly by women aged outside the 18–44 range or by men, where confidentiality or safety were a concern, or where study staff were barred from accessing venue attendees by owners) were eliminated from the final venue list (Haley et al., 2014). Venues for specified time periods were randomly selected each month in order to construct a sampling event calendar. To minimize selection bias, women present at a designated venue were systematically approached for prescreening when they entered a predetermined "recruitment area" (e.g., study staff designated the exact space that a potential subject must first enter before she was approached and asked about possible study participation). Women giving verbal approval for prescreening were asked a limited number of eligibility questions in a more private area within the recruitment venue (e.g., outside direct line of foot traffic). Women who met eligibility criteria and provided written consent to participate in the HPTN 064 study were subsequently enrolled in an area that provided additional privacy (i.e., the clinical research site, mobile van, or private room at venue). Enrolled participants were compensated for their time and transportation.

Participants received HIV rapid testing and audio computer-assisted self-interview (ACASI)-delivered surveys at baseline and at 6-month intervals for up to 12 months. The ACASI included questions regarding socioeconomic factors, food insecurity, mental health (depression and post-traumatic stress disorder (PTSD)), sexual behavior, history of STIs, domestic violence, health perceptions, and social support.

## *Determination of HIV Incidence*

The primary outcome of the study was a composite measure of HIV incidence that included infections acquired shortly before enrollment (recent infections), acute infections detected at study entry, and seroconversion events that occurred during study follow-up. Acute HIV infections were detected using a fourth-generation antigen/antibody assay and/or an HIV RNA test (Laeyendecker et al., 2013). Recent HIV infection was assessed at study entry using a multi-assay algorithm (Laeyendecker et al., 2013) which includes the CD4 cell count, HIV RNA viral load, the BED capture immunoassay (BED-CEIA), measuring the proportion of IgG that is HIV specific (Hall et al., 2008), and an assay that measures the avidity of anti-HIVantibodies for target antigens (Masciotra et al., 2010). HIV seroconversion during follow-up was assessed using HIV rapid test screening with Western blot confirmation. HIV incidence findings from all communities were pooled, as per a priori plans.

## *Qualitative Substudy*

The qualitative substudy was conducted at four study sites: Raleigh/Durham, Washington, D.C., the Bronx, and Atlanta. Semi-structured interviews were conducted with 130 women for purposes of identifying social, structural, and other contextual factors likely to affect women's sexual and other risk-related decision making. Additionally, 31 focus groups were held consisting of women of similar age, race, and ethnicity to discuss barriers to HIV prevention. Women participated in either the interviews or the focus groups (ineligible to participate in both activities). The rich dialogue of both the interviews and focus groups provided the basis for the theme-based content of this book.

## *Study Results*

Of the 8029 women screened, 3233 (40 %) were eligible for enrollment and 2099 (26 %) were enrolled. The majority of participants (73 %) reported both individual and partner risk factors. Eighty-six percent of participants reported ≥1 individual risk factor, 34 % reported ≥3 individual risk factors, and 87 % reported male partner risk factors. Participant retention was 93 % at 6 months and 94 % at 12 months. Ten participants died during follow-up (0.61 %/year), considerably higher than the expected age-adjusted mortality rate of 0.11 %/year (Murphy, Xu, & Kochanek, 2012). Eighty-six percent of participants were black, 7 % white, 3 % mixed, and 5 % "other" race. Hispanic ethnicity was reported by 12 % of participants. Median age was 29 years. Almost all participants (97 %) were born in the USA. Thirty-seven percent of participants had not completed high school, 37 % had a high-school diploma, and the remainder had education beyond high school. A majority (53.8 %) of participants were single and 44 % reported an annual household income ≤$10,000.

At baseline, 46 % of participants reported being concerned about having sufficient food for themselves and/or their families over the past 6 months. Although only 6 % of participants considered themselves to be commercial sex workers (CSW), 31 % of the 1885 participants who did not consider themselves to be CSW reported exchanging sex for goods (e.g., food, money, or shelter). Illicit drug use (excluding cannabis) was reported by 22 % of participants in the 6 months preceding study entry and 24 % reported at least one binge drinking episode (≥4 drinks at a time). Participants reported various types of abuse: 45 % reported a history of childhood abuse and 37 % reported some type of abuse (physical, emotional, sexual) during the 6 months before study entry. At baseline, 36 % of participants reported symptoms indicative of psychological distress or depressive symptoms and 29 % screened positive for PTSD. At baseline, the median number of sex partners reported by participants in the previous 6 months was two (mean 4.2), and 38 % reported anal sex in the 6 months before study entry. Forty-one percent and 44 % of participants at baseline reported not knowing the HIV status of their last partner with whom they had vaginal sex and anal sex, respectively. One percent reported that the partner with whom they last had vaginal or anal sex was HIV infected. Condom use was infrequent, with 18 % reporting condom use at last vaginal or anal sex. Risky behaviors decreased during follow-up: condom use at last vaginal sex increased from 18 % at baseline to 35 % at 6 months, and 37 % at 12 months. Sensitivity analyses suggest that 40–70 % of the increase in condom use was a study effect.

HIV prevalence at study entry was 1.5 %, despite the fact that prior self-reported history of HIV infection was an exclusion criterion. This suggests that, despite living in high HIV-prevalence areas of the USA, HIV testing programs or the test results did not effectively reach these participants. The overall annual HIV incidence for this cohort was 0.32 % (95 % CI: 0.14–0.74 %), which is substantially higher than the 2009 CDC national estimate for HIV incidence in the general population of US black women of comparable age (0.05 %) (Prejean et al., 2011). This suggests that the recruitment methods successfully identified women at risk for

HIV acquisition. The HIV incidence reported in this study is similar to estimated HIV incidence among the general adult population in some sub-Saharan African countries (e.g., the Congo 0.28 % [95 % CI: 0.23–035], Nigeria 0.38 [95 % CI: 0.33–0.44]).

There were no associations of either participant or partner characteristics reported at baseline with incident HIV infection, likely due to the limited number of observed incident infections. However, increasing participant age and substance use (at least weekly use of illicit drugs or binge drinking over the past 6 months) were associated with prevalent HIV infection. The only partner risk factor associated with prevalent HIV infection in participants was known HIV infection of the partner (relative risk (RR): 8.19; 95 % CI 2.64–25.42).

Medical care was often unavailable as reported by a substantial proportion of the participants. One in five women in the study who needed medical care in the previous 6 months reported that they were not able to obtain care. The majority of women (62 %) cited financial reasons for inability to access care, highlighting the critical need for reforms that improve access to healthcare for persons living in poverty. However, structural barriers other than financial need also precluded care, as 18 % of women reported not accessing needed care because they did not know where to find care, could not get an appointment, or concluded that care was unavailable.

## *Implications*

Results of the HPTN 064 study clearly highlight the enormous impact of poverty on the lives of study participants, 44 % of whom lived in households with annual incomes ≤$10,000. Mortality rates and HIV incidence rates were well above expected rates. The prevalence of PTSD was on the order of returning war veterans during the Vietnam era. Substance abuse and binge drinking were extremely high. In the pages that follow, the women who participated in the HPTN 064 study reflect their experiences regarding a number of aspects of their lives, in their own words.

## References

Centers for Disease Control and Prevention. (2012a). Estimated HIV incidence among adults and adolescents in the United States, 2007-2010. *HIV Surveillance Supplemental Report 2012, 17*(4).

Centers for Disease Control and Prevention. (2012b). *HIV surveillance in women*. Retrieved April 23, 2013, from www.cdc.gov/hiv/topics/surveillance/resources/slides/women/index.htm

Centers for Disease Control and Prevention. (2014). *HIV among women—Fact sheet*. Retrieved from www.cdc.gov/HIV/risk/gender/women/facts/index.html

Denning, P., & DiNenno, E. (2010). *Communities in crisis: Is there a generalized HIV epidemicin impoverished urban areas of the United States*? Retrieved January 23, 2016, from http://www.cdc.gov/hiv/pdf/statistics_poverty_poster.pdf

Ewing, J. A. (1984). Detecting alcoholism. The CAGE questionnaire. *Journal of the American Medical Association, 252*(14), 1905–1907.

Haley, D. F., Golin, C., El-Sadr, W., Hughes, J. P., Wang, J., Roman Isler, M., … Hodder, S. (2014). Venue-based recruitment of women at elevated risk for HIV: An HIV prevention trials network study. *Journal of Women's Health, 23*(6), 541–551.

Hall, H. I., Song, R., Rhodes, P., Prejean, J., An, Q., Lee, L. M., … Janssen, R. S. (2008). Estimation of HIV incidence in the United States. *Journal of the American Medical Association, 300*(5), 520–529.

Laeyendecker, O., Brookmeyer, R., Cousins, M. M., Mullis, C. E., Konikoff, J., Donnell, D., … Eshleman, S. H. (2013). HIV incidence determination in the United States: A multiassay approach. *Journal of Infectious Diseases, 207*(2), 232–239. doi: 10.1093/infdis/jis659.

MacKellar, D., Valleroy, L., Karon, J., Lemp, G., & Janssen, R. (1996). The Young Men's Survey: Methods for estimating HIV seroprevalence and risk factors among young men who have sex with men. *Public Health Reports, 111*(Suppl 1), 138–144.

Masciotra, S., Dobbs, T., Candal, D., Hanson, D., Delaney, K., Rudolph, D., … Owen, M. (2010). *Antibody avidity-based assay for identifying recent HIV-1 infections based on genetic systems TM½ plus O EIA*. Paper presented at the 17th Conference on Retroviruses and Opportunistic Infections, San Francisco, CA.

Muhib, F. B., Lin, L. S., Stueve, A., Miller, R. L., Ford, W. L., Johnson, W. D., & Smith, P. J. (2001). A venue-based method for sampling hard-to-reach populations. *Public Health Reports, 116*(Suppl 1), 216–222.

Murphy, S., Xu, J., & Kochanek, K. (2012). *Deaths: Preliminary data for 2010 National Vital Statistics reports* (Vol. 60). Hyattsville, MD: National Center for Health Statistics.

National Center for Law and Economic Justice. (2015). *Poverty in the United States: A snapshot.* (Original work published 2007) Retrieved November 14, 2014, from www.nclej.org/poverty-in-the-us.php

Prejean, J., Song, R., Hernandez, A., Ziebell, R., Green, T., Walker, F., … Group, H. I. S. (2011). Estimated HIV incidence in the United States, 2006-2009. *PLoS One, 6*(8), e17502. doi: 10.1371/journal.pone.0017502.

Stueve, A., O'Donnell, L. N., Duran, R., San Doval, A., & Blome, J. (2001). Time-space sampling in minority communities: Results with young Latino men who have sex with men. *American Journal of Public Health, 91*(6), 922–926.

U.S. Census Bureau. (2014). Current Population Reports, P60-249, *Income and Poverty in the United States*: 2013. U.S. Government Printing Office, Washington, DC.

World Health Organization. (2016). *Global summary of the AIDS epidemic—2014.* Retrieved January 23, 2016, from http://www.who.int/hiv/data/epi_core_july2015.png?ua=1

# Chapter 2
# Qualitative Methodological Approach

**Danielle F. Haley, Linda Vo, Kimberly A. Parker, Paula M. Frew, Carol E. Golin, Oluwakemi Amola, Sally Hodder, Irene Kuo, Alexis Amsterdam, Kathryn Lancaster, LaShawn Jones, Adaora A. Adimora, Ann O'Leary, Oni Blackstock, Lydia Soto-Torres, and Kathleen MacQueen**

## Introduction

Many large-scale studies and clinical trials, particularly those with biological endpoints, require the enrollment of hundreds, if not thousands, of participants across multiple sites (HPTN, 2012). There is a growing interest in large-scale, multisite qualitative data collection, as this approach has the potential to provide valuable insight into the broader social and structural factors that influence behaviors but may not be captured using quantitative data instruments. However, the collection of qualitative data in large, multisite trials presents challenges, such as determining what, how much, and where data will be collected, coded, and analyzed; ensuring stakeholder involvement throughout the process; standardization of study procedures across sites; managing large volumes of qualitative data; identification and training of staff with qualitative research skills; and, in some settings, translation of transcripts. While these challenges are not unique to qualitative research designs,

D.F. Haley (✉)
FHI 360, Durham, NC, USA

Department of Behavioral Sciences and Health Education, Rollins School of Public Health, Emory University, Atlanta, GA, USA
e-mail: dfhaley@emory.edu

L. Vo
Division of Infectious Diseases, Department of Medicine, School of Medicine, Emory University, Atlanta, GA, USA

K.A. Parker
Department of Health Studies, Texas Woman's University, Denton, TX, USA

P.M. Frew
Emory University School of Medicine, Department of Medicine, Division of Infectious Diseases, Atlanta, GA, USA

Emory University, Rollins School of Public Health, Hubert Department of Global Health & Department of Behavioral Sciences and Health Education, Atlanta, GA, USA

 
A. O'Leary, P.M. Frew (eds.), *Poverty in the United States*,
DOI 10.1007/978-3-319-43833-7_2

they are often magnified in the clinical research context and may hinder widespread use of qualitative methods in the setting of large trials (Guest & MacQueen, 2008). In this chapter, we describe approaches to collecting, managing, coding, and analyzing qualitative data, as well as lessons learned, in the HIV Prevention Trials Network (HPTN) 064 (the Women's HIV SeroIncidence Study), a large, multisite observational study in the USA.

## Study Methods

### *Study Design*

As described in Chap. 1, HPTN 064 was a multisite, prospective cohort study designed to estimate HIV incidence among 2099 women living in communities with prevalent HIV and poverty in New York (the Bronx and Harlem), New Jersey (Newark), Maryland (Baltimore), North Carolina (Durham and Raleigh), Georgia (Atlanta and Decatur), and Washington, D.C. (Hodder et al., 2013). Study

C.E. Golin
Cecil G. Sheps Center for Health Services Research, University of North Carolina at Chapel Hill, Chapel Hill, NC, USA

Department of Health Behavior, Gillings School of Global Public Health, University of North Carolina at Chapel Hill, Chapel Hill, NC, USA

Division of General Medicine and Clinical Epidemiology, School of Medicine, University of North Carolina at Chapel Hill, Chapel Hill, NC, USA

O. Amola
School of Medicine and Gillings School of Global Public Health, University of North Carolina at Chapel Hill, Chapel Hill, NC, USA

A. A. Adimora
University of North Carolina Schools of Medicine and Gillings School of Global Public Health, Chapel Hill, NC, USA

S. Hodder
West Virginia Clinical and Translational Sciences Institute (WVCTSI), West Virginia University, Charlottesville, WV, USA

I. Kuo
Milken Institute School of Public Health, George Washington University, Washington, DC, USA

A. Amsterdam • K. Lancaster • L. Jones • K. MacQueen
FHI 360, Durham, NC, USA

A. O'Leary
Atlanta, GA, USA

O. Blackstock
Montefiore Medical Center/Albert Einstein College of Medicine, New York, NY, USA

L. Soto-Torres
Kelly Government Solutions, Contractor to DAIDS/NIAID/NIH, Rockville, MD, USA

**Table 2.1** HPTN 064 qualitative component key activities, contributors, and timelines

| | | | Phase 3: Qualitative coding and analysis | | |
|---|---|---|---|---|---|
| Study phase | Phase 1: Pre-implementation | Phase 2: Implementation | Stage 1: *Structural coding* | Stage 2: *Member checking* | Stage 3: *Advanced systematic analysis* |
| Key activities | • Site selection | • Study management | • Structural coding and codebook development | • Review of structurally coded data | • Constant comparative content coding and analysis (see Fig. 2.1) |
| | • Instrument development | • Data collection | • Intercoder agreement assessment | • Preliminary data summary and theme generation | |
| | | • Transcription | | | |
| Key contributors | • Protocol team | • Central data-coordinating center | • Central data-coordinating center | • Central data-coordinating center | • Central data-coordinating center |
| | • Community working group | • Protocol team | • Protocol team | • Protocol team | • Protocol team |
| | | • Community working group | • Community working group | • Community working group | • Advanced systematic analysis team |
| | | • Study sites | • Study sites | • Study sites | • Qualitative steering committee |
| | | • Qualitative working group | • Qualitative working group | • Qualitative working group | |
| Activity timeframe | 2 years | 1 year | 9 months | 1 year | 2 years |

participants were self-identified women aged 18–44 years who reported unprotected vaginal or anal sex with a man in the past 6 months and who resided within a geographic area with prevalent HIV and poverty. In addition, women reported at least one additional personal risk within the past 6 months (e.g., illicit substance use) and/or male partner within the past 6 months with characteristics associated with greater risk of HIV acquisition (e.g., HIV infection) (Haley et al., 2014). Women were recruited from community venues (e.g., shopping centers, well-traveled streets) using venue-based sampling (Haley et al., 2014; Hodder et al., 2013).

Our study design included a substantial qualitative component. Four study sites (the Bronx, NY; Washington, D.C.; Raleigh/Durham, NC; and Atlanta/Decatur, GA) conducted semi-structured interviews and focus groups between June 2009 and August 2010 designed to explore social, structural, and contextual factors related to HIV risk among participants. In this chapter, we describe the activities for each of the three phases of the qualitative research process: (1) pre-implementation, (2) implementation, and (3) coding and analysis (Table 2.1). These study activities spanned from May 2007 to September 2013.

## Phase 1: Pre-implementation

Site Selection. We selected the four study sites (the Bronx, New York; Washington, D.C.; Raleigh/Durham, North Carolina; and Atlanta, Georgia) because they had existing expertise in qualitative research methods and represented a geographically diverse sample of HPTN 064 study sites.

Instrument Development and Stakeholder Involvement. We developed semi-structured interview and focus group guides with suggested probes, which aligned with the qualitative aims of the study, with input from study investigators (including several with expertise in qualitative research) and community members. The majority of questions/topic areas in the interview and focus group guides were the same. Interviews focused on individual-level experiences or perspectives, whereas focus groups explored community perspective and norms. Highly sensitive questions about personal experiences (e.g., trauma or victimization) were included only in the interview guide. We developed the qualitative guides in parallel with the quantitative behavioral audio computer-assisted survey instrument (ACASI) to allow for both quantitative and qualitative exploration of constructs.

## Phase 2: Implementation

Sampling. We conducted a total of 120 interviews (30 per site) and 32 focus groups, based on prespecified age and race/ethnicity strata (Table 2.2). This total number of interviews and focus groups was determined to ensure saturation, explore geographic variation, and allow for additional analysis within and across sites (Guest, Bunce, & Johnson, 2006; Guest & MacQueen, 2008; Onwuegbuzie & Leech, 2007).

We used sequential sampling to identify potential interview participants and quota sampling for the focus groups. For interviews, women with an odd participant identification number, beginning with the first participant enrolled, were invited to participate in an interview. After completing the interviews, each site moved on to quota sampling for focus groups, inviting 8–12 women who were not enrolled in the individual interviews and met the predefined age and race/ethnicity focus group strata.

We chose this approach to sampling in an effort to balance representativeness of the interviews and minimize the possibility of bias that could be introduced from ongoing participation in the HPTN 064 study. To reduce such bias, we conducted the interviews and focus groups as close to enrollment as possible. Pre-enrollment random selection of women was not feasible because focus groups included predefined race/ethnicity and demographic strata. A comparison of the overall study cohort and the qualitative interview and focus group cohorts on select characteristics (Table 2.3) indicated that women participating in a semi-structured interview or focus group tended to be slightly younger, more likely to be financially responsible for a child under 18, and more likely to be living with friends or family, but less likely to be homeless than women who did not participate in the qualitative component of the study.

**Table 2.2** HPTN 064 focus groups and participants by site

| Strata | Geographic location | | | | |
|---|---|---|---|---|---|
| | The Bronx, NY | Washington, DC | Raleigh, NC | Atlanta, GA | Total |
| *Black Women 18–24 years old* | | | | | |
| Number of focus groups | 2 | 2 | 3 | 2 | 9 |
| Number of participants per group | 6, 5 | 6, 4 | 6, 4, 5 | 4, 9 | – |
| Total number of participants | 11 | 10 | 15 | 13 | 49 |
| *Black Women 25–35 years old* | | | | | |
| Number of focus groups | 2 | 2 | 2 | 2 | 8 |
| Number of participants per group | 6, 7 | 6, 8 | 5, 5 | 6, 4 | – |
| Total number of participants | 13 | 14 | 10 | 10 | 47 |
| *Black Women 36 years plus* | | | | | |
| Number of focus groups | 2 | 2 | 3 | 2 | 9 |
| Number of participants per group | 4, 3 | 7, 4 | 6, 4, 4 | 5, 4 | – |
| Total number of participants | 7 | 11 | 14 | 9 | 41 |
| *Hispanic Women 18–24 years old* | | | | | |
| Number of focus groups | 2 | N/A | N/A | N/A | 2 |
| Number of participants per group | 9, 6 | | | | – |
| Total number of participants | 15 | | | | 15 |
| *Hispanic Women 25–35 years old* | | | | | |
| Number of focus groups | 2 | N/A | N/A | N/A | 2 |
| Number of participants per group | 6, 3 | | | | – |
| Total number of participants | 9 | | | | 9 |
| *Hispanic Women 36 years plus* | | | | | |
| Number of focus groups | 2 | N/A | N/A | N/A | 2 |
| Number of participants per group | 5, 3 | | | | – |
| Total number of participants | 8 | | | | 8 |
| Total number of focus groups | 12 | 6 | 8 | 6 | 32 |
| Total number of participants | 63 | 35 | 39 | 32 | 169 |

N/A: Insufficient number of enrolled HPTN 064 participants at sites in specified strata for focus group

Study Management. We formed a Qualitative Working Group (QWG) to provide ongoing oversight and input on study implementation, structural coding, and preliminary data analysis (e.g., codebook development, prioritization of data analysis topics). HPTN 064 investigators with behavioral science expertise and experience in qualitative methodologies as well as community representatives comprised the QWG. We reviewed the progress of the qualitative component during bimonthly site team meetings and monthly QWG meetings.

To maximize consistency and quality assurance across sites, we managed the qualitative component activities and data through a central data-coordinating center. The data-coordinating center employed a number of steps to ensure standardization of

**Table 2.3** HPTN 064 participant baseline characteristics, including a comparison of participants who did and did not participate in the qualitative component

| Variable | Did not participate in qualitative component ($n$=1811)<br>$n$ (%)<br>Median (IQR) | Participated in qualitative component ($n$=288)<br>$n$ (%)<br>Median (IQR) | $p$-value |
|---|---|---|---|
| Age (years) | 29 (23–38) | 27 (23–36) | **0.0407** |
| Black race | 1601 (88 %) | 250 (87 %) | 0.4350 |
| Hispanic ethnicity | 201 (11 %) | 44 (15 %) | **0.0402** |
| Relationship status | | | 0.9650 |
| Single/Widowed/Divorced/Separated | 1086 (60 %) | 172 (60 %) | |
| Married or living as married | 552 (30 %) | 86 (30 %) | |
| Other | 130 (7 %) | 22 (8 %) | |
| Missing | 43 (2 %) | 8 (3 %) | |
| Household income | | | 0.2614 |
| $10,000 or less | 799 (45 %) | 134 (47 %) | |
| $10,001–$20,000 | 191 (11 %) | 34 (12 %) | |
| $20,001 or more | 166 (9 %) | 31 (11 %) | |
| Don't know | 536 (30 %) | 80 (28 %) | |
| Missing/Refused | 119 (7 %) | 9 (3 %) | |
| Financially responsible for at least one child | 934 (51 %) | 175 (61 %) | **0.0147** |
| Missing | 14 (1 %) | 2 (<1 %) | |
| Food insecurity | 841 (46 %) | 130 (45 %) | 0.2659 |
| Missing | 26 (1 %) | 1 (<1 %) | |
| Drug and alcohol use | | | 0.1001 |
| No use | 424 (23 %) | 71 (25 %) | |
| Non-frequent use (as less than weekly use of illicit drugs and/or | 662 (36 %) | 121 (42 %) | |
| Frequent use (daily to weekly use of any illicit drug and/or weekly | 689 (38 %) | 92 (32 %) | |
| Missing | 36 (2 %) | 4 (1 %) | |
| Symptoms of depression[a] | 608 (36 %) | 84 (31 %) | 0.8698 |
| Missing | 141 (8 %) | 16 (6 %) | |
| Symptoms of PTSD[b] | 515 (28 %) | 85 (29 %) | 0.1097 |
| Missing | 50 (3 %) | 2 (1 %) | |
| Social support | | | |
| Number of people that provide financial support | 3 (2–4) | 3 (2–4) | 0.3869 |
| Missing | 30 (2 %) | 1 (<1 %) | |
| Number of people that provide emotional support | 4 (3–4) | 4 (3–4) | 0.6024 |

(continued)

**Table 2.3** (continued)

| Variable | Did not participate in qualitative component ($n=1811$)<br>$n$ (%)<br>Median (IQR) | Participated in qualitative component ($n=288$)<br>$n$ (%)<br>Median (IQR) | $p$-value |
|---|---|---|---|
| Missing | 21 (1 %) | 1 (<1 %) | |
| Housing | | | **0.0071** |
| Place participant rents/owns | 733 (40 %) | 119 (41 %) | |
| Place male partner rents/owns | 159 (9 %) | 19 (7 %) | |
| Place friend/family rents/owns | 608 (34 %) | 120 (42 %) | |
| Homeless[c] | 266 (15 %) | 28 (10 %) | |
| Missing | 45 (2 %) | 1 (1 %) | |
| No condom used at last vaginal sex | 1468 (81 %) | 230 (80 %) | 0.8320 |
| Missing | 22 (1 %) | 3 (1 %) | |
| Self-reported sexually transmitted infection | 198 (11 %) | 34 (12 %) | 0.8804 |
| Missing | 29 (2 %) | 4 (1 %) | |

[a] A score of ≥7 out of 24 was indicative of psychological distress or depressive symptoms (DiClemente et al., 2001)

[b] A score of 3 or greater on the Primary Care PTSD Scale (Prins et al., 2004)

[c] Living in shelter, on the street, motel, boarding house/single-room occupancy unit (SRO), half-way house

procedures across the sites, such as file-naming conventions, milestones and tracking of each step of the process (e.g., time from interview to transcription), and outlining these processes in study procedural manuals.

Focus Group and Interview Conduct. Site research staff conducted interviews and focus groups in settings that ensured adequate privacy and confidentiality, such as the study clinical site, a mobile van, local community-based organizations, or another appropriate public venue (e.g., library). Trained interviewers and focus group facilitators were matched to interviewees by race, ethnicity, and gender when possible. We compensated participants for their time and effort, and all participants provided written consent for participation.

Transcription and De-identification. Interviews and focus groups were recorded and transcribed by research staff at each study site. Each site reviewed transcripts for accuracy and removed geographic and personal identifiers. All transcripts were then reviewed by the central data-coordinating center for quality assurance (e.g., confirmation of de-identification, consistency with tracking logs) prior to upload into NVivo 8 software (QSR International, Australia) for coding.

## *Phase 3: Qualitative Coding and Analysis*

As depicted in Table 2.1, coding and analysis of study transcripts took place in three stages: (1) structural coding, (2) member checking, and (3) advanced systematic analysis.

### Stage 1: Structural Coding

All transcripts were structurally coded by the central data-coordinating center using NVivo 8 software. In qualitative research, structural coding is generally intended to identify text associated with a particular question in the interview/focus group guide. We selected this approach because it allowed for quick identification of text associated with questions in the interview and focus group guides, and was a helpful method for coding and organizing large data sets generated from semi-structured guides (Guest & MacQueen, 2008).

Structural Coding, Codebook Development, and Intercoder Agreement Assessment. Structural codes were based on each of the questions and associated prompts in the interview and focus group guides. Through this process, we developed one structural codebook for the interviews and one for the focus groups. In the codebook, each code included a definition, when to use the code, when not to use the code, and dates of any changes to the code. The conversational nature of the interviews and focus groups meant that structural coding was not a straightforward linear process clearly aligned with the structure of the guide, but rather required attention to conversational shifts in the ordering and overlapping of guide questions and topics. Coding was conducted as an iterative process. First, all coders independently coded one interview transcript and one focus group transcript from each site. Next, the coding of these transcripts was reviewed and compared line by line; discrepancies were discussed and resolved until consensus was achieved by both coders. We designated one person as the primary coder of transcripts for each of the four study sites. Throughout the structural coding phase, all of the coders met weekly to review findings and revise the codebook as needed based on group consensus. We selected 20 % of all transcripts to assess the intercoder agreement between the two independent coders for each structural code using the NVivo 8 intercoder reliability (ICR) function. For codes with an ICR below 90 % agreement, the designated primary coder for that transcript reviewed, resolved discrepancies, and recoded the transcript. The structural codebook was revised as needed with updated definitions and examples.

### Stage 2: Member Checking

After we completed structural coding, HPTN 064 investigators from each of the four study sites, members of the HPTN 064 Community Working Group (CWG), and QWG were invited to review a randomly selected subsample of interview and focus group transcripts in preparation for future analysis. This "interpretative community" was constructed in order to facilitate active participation in qualitative data interpretation by those who were most familiar with participants, community, and data at each site (Guest, MacQueen, & Namey, 2012).

Review of Structurally Coded Data. Preliminary data summarization and member checking took place over two in-person meetings. The first 4-h meeting involved group discussion of text from a randomly selected set of transcripts. This meeting was followed by a 5-day member checking meeting. In preparation for this 5-day meeting, the QWG identified structural codes to be explored using the HPTN 064 study objectives as a framework for prioritization of topics for exploration.

To facilitate review of massive amounts of data in advance of the 5-day meeting, we assembled four teams approximately four months before the meeting. Each team was responsible for reviewing and summarizing data from one site. Each site team consisted of site representatives, at least one member from the protocol team, community members from that site, a coder, and content experts. One person from each site served as the site team facilitator and each team member was assigned at least one structural code. Each site team member reviewed the interview and focus group data associated with the assigned codes, summarized these data, and suggested emerging themes using a standardized presentation template. The site team facilitator presented this information to their team in advance of the meeting to ensure that each member arrived at the meeting well informed. Site team facilitators attended an in-person, half-day training on presentation skills. Prior to receiving any data, all of the team members completed human subjects training and signed data confidentiality agreements.

Preliminary Data Summary and Theme Generation. During the 5-day meeting, the site team facilitator and a community member representative copresented on each of their assigned structural code topic areas. Meeting participants collectively reviewed data for each of the structural codes across all sites, described themes, and developed corresponding conceptual frameworks within and across structural codes. Following this meeting, we agreed that the richness and depth of the data merited additional content coding of the interviews and focus group data. The themes generated from this process were used to inform the advanced systematic analysis.

### Stage 3: Advanced Systematic Analysis

Due to the large number of transcripts collected in HPTN 064 and the extensive time and resources required for advanced systematic analysis, we randomly selected 30 % of interviews ($n = 36$), and 50 % ($n = 16$) of focus group transcripts for this Stage. For the interviews, we enumerated the transcripts, and randomly selected 9 per site. For the focus groups, we randomly selected one focus group per stratum per study site. In addition, we randomly selected one additional focus group from a study site that had a large number of focus groups. We selected the constant comparative technique (Boeije, 2002) for advanced systematic coding and analysis (Table 2.1, Step 3) because this approach was compatible with both the systematic team-based structural coding already applied to the transcripts (Guest et al., 2012; Guest & MacQueen, 2008) and a grounded theory approach. Grounded theory approach utilizes an iterative, inductive, and deductive process, and places great emphasis on simple systematic procedures to allow emergence of theory (Strauss & Corbin, 1998).

We conducted the advanced systematic analysis in four steps as depicted in Fig. 2.1. During the initial coding phase (Step 1), analysts reviewed transcripts to develop and identify codes, and emerging themes, building on previous structural codes. We applied open coding to code larger segments of text to codes. Next, we noted possible relationships between codes and groups based on geographical location, and developed descriptive subcodes and categories, also known as axial coding (Step 2). We then conducted selective coding (Step 3), to further define and develop the subcode. This step involved reviewing the code categories and coding specific information relating to that category. Steps 1 through 3 were highly iterative; analysts constantly revisited and refined codes until saturation was reached. Saturation was assessed in real time, and was defined as the point in the coding process where new codes or themes no longer emerged. In Step 4, we conducted our final analyses by reviewing code clustering and performed axial analyses to develop theoretical models.

The advanced systematic process was conducted centrally at a study site with expertise in qualitative data analysis, with support and oversight from the central data-coordinating center and the Qualitative Steering Committee (QSC). The QSC was first developed in November 2011 to provide scientific oversight throughout the advanced systematic analysis process. The team was carefully selected to ensure a range of perspectives and experience, including community expertise. The QSC convened by conference call on a monthly basis between January and June of 2012. During this time, the advanced systematic analysis team generated coding status reports and shared them with QSC weekly for feedback.

As depicted in Fig. 2.1, advanced coding analysis occurred in four iterative steps. Codes were organized hierarchically using the structural codes developed in previous

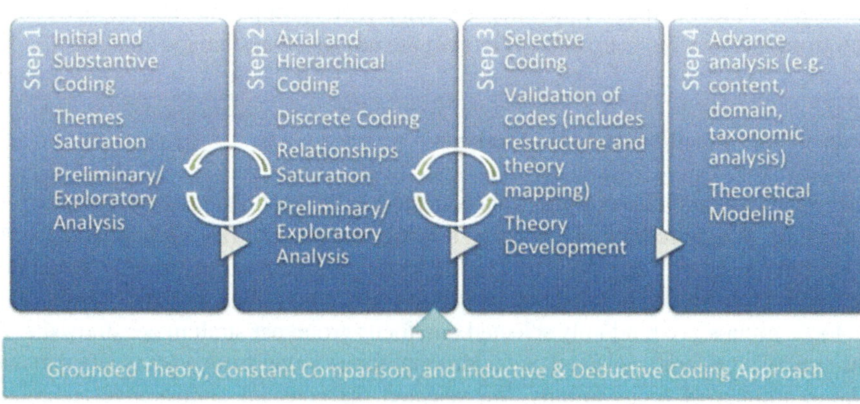


**Fig. 2.1** HPTN 064 advanced systematic analysis process

stages as the parent node. This facilitated rapid assessment of source and reference frequencies for each code. To allow for emergence of themes, we developed the content codebooks separately for the interviews and focus groups. We later then compared the content and structural codebooks, and harmonized the codes and definitions across codebooks.

*Initial and Substantive Coding (Step 1).* We coded the interview and focus group transcripts in parallel. We randomly selected three interview transcripts and three focus group transcripts for initial codebook development. For both the interviews and focus groups, the initial transcript was used primarily for codebook development, the second for identifying additional themes, and the third for assessing analysts' comfort and clarity with the codebooks. After the codebooks were developed, we ensured alignment with the structural codebook and themes generated from the member checking process. We then independently coded remaining transcripts. During this step we openly coded large segments of the text to codes, and continued to identify inductively and add codes for emerging themes. Each transcript was independently coded by two analysts. The codes and themes for each codebook were reviewed for consensus and updated accordingly through out this inductive process. One analyst, who coded both interview and focus groups, led codebook harmonization.

*Axial and Hierarchical Coding (Step 2).* The intent of Step 2 was to further develop codes and emerging themes within the data, including relationships within and across codes. This axial coding process involved a combination of inductive and deductive thinking to allow for emergence of codes based on the data and based on logical top-down approach, respectively. We reviewed code definitions and used the NVivo cluster analysis procedure to assess relationships between codes, and codes to demonstrate those relationships. For each structural code, we further segmented data into similar categories (hierarchical codes), and distinctly coded descriptive information (discrete coding). The items were then grouped together (chunked) based on similar characteristics. All of these new codes were added to the existing interview and focus group codebooks. During the coding process, we discussed the addition of codes during weekly meetings, and revised the codebook with updated codes, definitions, and categories based on consensus.

*Harmonization of interview and focus group datasets.* At the end of Step 2, the NVivo databases for the interview and focus groups were combined so that additional axial coding could be conducted across all of the data. We used vigorous constant comparative techniques to synchronize the interview and focus group data in the combined dataset (Boeije, 2002). We reviewed each group of codes, merged similar codes, and grouped associated codes as appropriate. The interview and focus group codebooks were then compared and synchronized by combining codes that had the similar definitions. We then reviewed the coded data to further identify relationships, distinct items, and similar items. We added and refined codes as necessary, and applied the codes. We further reviewed and repeated the axial, hierarchical, and discrete coding described above. We completed a final review of the codes to ensure that the lowest level (most discrete) code was included in its hierarchical code (larger category), and that the hierarchical code was further coded into discrete codes. Any additional codes were added to the final codebooks. As part of this harmonization process, we refined definitions and rules for each code, resulting in the more refined codebooks for the focus group and interview as well as a combined codebook. As discussed previously, because the interview and focus group guides varied, some codes were not applied to both the interviews and focus groups, but were included in all of the codebooks to allow for future analysis.

*Selective Coding (Step 3).* We assigned each of the major categories in the combined dataset to an analyst for selective coding. The analysts independently reviewed each code to ensure that the coded texts in each codes fit the definitions, and that they were appropriately applied to other relevant codes. The team further refined the code definitions and parameters in the final codebook as needed to make them more clear and operational for further analysis, especially those who have not been a part of this advanced systematic analysis process. The combined database was separated into an interview dataset and a focus group dataset to generate frequencies of codes, assess intercoder agreement, and resolve any discrepancies. All of the codebooks were updated as needed. The final datasets were then merged into a final combined dataset, and all of the datasets and codebooks were locked and stored for further analysis and synthesis. The dataset included a total of 1139 codes (10 structural and 1129 content). Coding saturation was assessed in real time, and was achieved in Step 3 (Selective Coding) of coding and analysis, and by that time 90 % of the data were coded, indicating that limiting this phase of the analysis to a subsample of transcripts was appropriate.

*Intercoder Agreement Assessment.* All of the transcripts randomly selected for advanced systematic analysis were coded independently by two analysts. Intercoder agreement was randomly assessed throughout the constant comparative coding process for 20 % of transcripts using the NVivo 8 ICR function. Using percent agreement and disagreement generated by NVivo 8 ICR function, we calculated the final ICR manually using traditional calculation methods. For transcripts with a Kappa below 0.80, the two analysts who coded them reviewed, reconciled, and revised any coding discrepancies. The final ICR was a combined average Kappa score of 0.91 for the random sample of the focus groups and the ICR for the random sample of interviews was a combined average Kappa score of 0.92.

*Focused Qualitative Analysis (Step 4).* The aforementioned process resulted in a systematically coded dataset. We analyzed data using conceptual mapping of the research question accompanied by a review of the thematic domains and categorical codes, and systematic descriptive analyses, e.g., matrix queries of the codes of interest.

## Lessons Learned and Considerations for Future Research

The processes described in this chapter resulted in a richly coded dataset that will contribute to a broader understanding of the social and structural factors which contribute to women's health behaviors in the USA, and provided the foundation needed for the chapters included in this book. This success is clearly a reflection of significant time and effort across many stakeholders, to include the funders, sites, and the participants themselves. Based on our experience, we present our successes, challenges, and recommendations for collecting, managing, coding, and analyzing qualitative data, as well as lessons learned, for a large, multisite clinical trial in the USA.

*Multisite Study Management*. The multisite nature of HPTN 064 necessitated the development of a number of manuals and standard operating procedures to ensure consistency across sites prior to study implementation. Documentation in all stages of the process was necessary to ensure that all contributors were informed and that the research process was clearly outlined. In addition, geographic variation necessitated the development of additional tools for use in coding, analysis, and interpretation. For example, each site created its own local "terminology list"; some sites had similar terms with different meanings.

*Advance Resource Planning*. As described, we developed the quantitative and qualitative data collection instruments in parallel, allowing for triangulation of data to validate our findings and for mixed-method analysis. However, we did not adequately anticipate the sheer volume and richness of data and the amount of subsequent advanced systematic analysis that would be needed to analyze these data. A number of strategies could be implemented in future studies which would streamline the process going forward, including using one institution for all coding and analysis, data reduction strategies, and planning for analysis support during the manuscript development process. Although we benefited from the insights of many team members and advisory committees, we would have benefited from the formation of the QSC earlier in the planning process. The QSC consisted of both internal and external members with expertise in multisite, large, mixed-method approaches and provided a number of insights, which may have focused analyses and reduced timelines.

*Timelines and Staffing*. As with many elements of clinical research trials, each step of the qualitative component was contingent on completion of previous steps. As a result, any delays resulted in trickle-down effects for the overall timeline. Qualitative data coding is labor intensive and, for a project of this size and complexity, required multiple analysts. Staffing was also an important consideration; coders needed to be team-oriented, well versed in qualitative methods and software, and the topic area under study. Coders and analysts worked on the study on a part-time basis. Disruptions in timelines made staff planning difficult (e.g., some staff were pulled into other projects during initial delays which resulted in time conflicts for later coding). Future studies might consider hiring full-time coders if funding allows. It may be advisable to identify and contract with a group to code and analyze all data up-front to the point of focused qualitative analysis, both as a means to enhance efficiency and because groups which exclusively manage qualitative data may be better able to adapt to changes in timelines.

*Software Selection and Data Sharing*. Software selection was an essential component of qualitative data management and analysis, as some software packages are more suitable for large quantities of data than others. The multisite nature of HPTN 064 introduced additional software considerations, to include the purchase of licenses across institutions and compatibility of software versions. While NVivo offered capacity to conduct in-depth coding of large volumes of data, it was provided by few participating institutions free of cost and licenses were subsequently purchased by each site. Future studies should consider not only the capacity of the software package, but also preexisting availability across sites, how often licenses will need to be renewed over the course of the study, the potential for negotiating bulk pricing, and version compatibility. In addition, multiple data collection sites introduced the need for additional data security measures and software environments for sharing and storing these data. This may be particularly relevant for qualitative data, since transcripts include distinct, rich "stories" which cannot be entirely de-identified. In addition to each institution's own data security policy, we implemented a number of measures to securely share and store data, to include the development of a password-protected portal for registered users.

*Community Engagement*. It may be difficult to engage community members and other stakeholders in the data interpretation process remotely, particularly when making connections within and across data, and in developing theoretical frameworks to describe these connections. We found the face-to-face member checking meeting a successful and relatively efficient approach to identify themes within the data and generate increased understanding of the data among a large and diverse group. More regular, shorter meetings discussing less data may facilitate early and ongoing discussions; however, these meetings will need to be budgeted for accordingly. Alternatively, other technologies for remote review and discussion may be explored.

## Recommendations

Based on the lessons learned described above, we recommend the following:

1. Develop standardized study procedures for all study elements.
2. Develop detailed research questions and manuscript development timelines utilizing qualitative data early in implementation.
3. Develop contingency plans to address delays likely to occur in implementation and results dissemination.
4. House all coding and analysis within one institution and select coding and analytic strategies conducive for both the research aims and large data sets.
5. Integrate community feedback into the analysis process (member checking).

Although each research study presents its own unique challenges, we hope that our experience can inform future implementation of qualitative research in clinical trial settings and help ensure a rich qualitative data that will contribute to a broader understanding of the social and structural determinants of women's health.

## References

Boeije, H. (2002). A purposeful approach to the constant comparative method in the analysis of qualitative interviews. *Quality and Quantity, 36*, 391–409.

DiClemente, R. J., Wingood, G. M., Crosby, R. A., Sionean, C., Brown, L. K., Rothbaum, B., … Davies, S. (2001). A prospective study of psychological distress and sexual risk behavior among black adolescent females. *Pediatrics, 108*(5), E85.

Guest, G., Bunce, A., & Johnson, L. (2006). How many interviews are enough? An experiment with data saturation and variability. *Field Methods, 18*(1), 59–82.

Guest, G., & MacQueen, K. M. (2008). *Handbook for team-based qualitative research*. Altamira: Lanham.

Guest, G., MacQueen, K. M., & Namey, E. E. (2012). *Applied thematic analysis*. Los Angeles: Sage.

Haley, D. F., Golin, C., El-Sadr, W., Hughes, J. P., Wang, J., Roman Isler, M., … Hodder, S. (2014). Venue-based recruitment of women at elevated risk for HIV: An HIV prevention trials network study. *Journal of Women's Health, 23*(6), 541–551.

Hodder, S. L., Justman, J., Hughes, J. P., Wang, J., Haley, D. F., Adimora, A. A., … Women's HIV SeroIncidence Study Team. (2013). HIV acquisition among women from selected areas of the United States: A cohort study. *Annals of Internal Medicine, 158*(1), 10–18.

HPTN. (2012). *HPTN studies: HIV prevention trials network*. Retrieved August 14, 2013, from http://www.hptn.org/research_studies/hptn_research_areas.asp

Onwuegbuzie, A., & Leech, N. (2007). A call for qualitative power analyses. *Quality & Quantity, 41*, 105–121.

Prins, A., Ouimette, P., Kimerling, R. P., Hugelshofer, D. S., Shaw-Hegwer, J., Thrailkill, A., … Sheikh, J. I. (2004). The primary care PTSD screen (PC-PTSD): Development and operating characteristics. *Primary Care Psychiatry, 5*.

Strauss, A. L., & Corbin, J. M. (1998). *Basics of qualitative research: Techniques and procedures for developing grounded theory*. Thousand Oaks: Sage.

# Chapter 3
# The Intersection of Women's Health and Poverty

**Paula M. Frew, Kimberly A. Parker, Linda Vo, Danielle F. Haley, Terry McGovern, Lauren E. Owens, Lisa Diane White, Ann O'Leary, Carol E. Golin, Irene Kuo, Sally Hodder, and Laura Randall**

*"There is more to life than the little box you live in. There's a whole other world."*

## Introduction

Poverty is a persistent problem faced by many in the USA. Despite efforts taken starting in 1964 with President Lyndon Johnson declaring war on poverty, the recent results from the U.S. Census Bureau's American Community Survey show that the overall poverty level in the USA for 2013 was steady at 15.8 % (after an average of 14.3 % from 2007 to 2011), which is approximately 48.8 million people (Bishaw & Fontenot, 2014; U.S. Census Bureau, 2014). Black/African Americans experience poverty at a rate of 27.6 % and Hispanic Americans at 24.8 % (U.S. Census Bureau, 2013a). These census data also indicate that while women overall experience a higher rate of poverty compared to men (14.5 % vs. 11.0 %, respectively), black/

P.M. Frew (✉)
Emory University School of Medicine, Department of Medicine, Division of Infectious Diseases, Atlanta, GA, USA

Emory University, Rollins School of Public Health, Hubert Department of Global Health & Department of Behavioral Sciences and Health Education, Atlanta, GA, USA
e-mail: pfrew@emory.edu

L. Randall
Division of Infectious Diseases, Department of Medicine, School of Medicine, Emory University, Atlanta, GA, USA

Rollins School of Public Health, Emory University, Atlanta, GA, USA

K.A. Parker
Department of Health Studies, Texas Woman's University, Denton, TX, USA

L. Vo • L.E. Owens
Division of Infectious Diseases, Department of Medicine, School of Medicine, Emory University, Atlanta, GA, USA



A. O'Leary, P.M. Frew (eds.), *Poverty in the United States*,
DOI 10.1007/978-3-319-43833-7_3

African Americans have the highest rates of poverty regardless of gender (25.1 % for women compared to 20.6 % for men (U.S. Census Bureau, 2013b).

In this book, we seek to contextualize women's lives in relation to poverty. The book is organized according to the socioecological model (Bronfenbrenner, 1994), moving from individual-level factors to those at the overall community level. Each chapter explores social factors affecting women that were identified from the study data, told time and again by each woman's story. In this introduction, we provide an overview of the myriad of multilevel factors that place women at risk of HIV by conceptualizing these factors within a socioecological framework. In the first four subsections of this chapter we provide background information regarding four broad areas that affect women living in poverty. We then provide the theoretical framework for our analyses of qualitative data we present in this chapter to create an overarching picture of a multilevel model of factors associated with living in poverty. The socioecological model serves as the foundation for the other chapters, which explore specific issues in more depth.

The "mesosystem" and "microsystem" issues associated with community challenges—poverty, unemployment, and the sociocultural environment—include greater sexual concurrency (overlapping sexual partnerships) among persons living in defined geographic areas resulting from neighborhood gender imbalances (Ferguson, Quinn, Eng, & Sandelowski, 2006; Newsome & Airhihenbuwa, 2013). For example, in predominantly black/African-American communities, the impact of our nation's disproportionate incarceration of black men and the associated mortality from community violence creates an imbalanced female-to-male ratio. Such imbalances thereby reduce

D.F. Haley
FHI 360, Durham, NC, USA

Department of Behavioral Sciences and Health Education, Rollins School of Public Health, Emory University, Atlanta, GA, USA

T. McGovern
Mailman School of Public Health, Columbia University, New York, NY, USA

L.D. White
SisterLove, Inc., Atlanta, GA, USA

A. O'Leary
Atlanta, Georgia, USA

C.E. Golin
Cecil G. Sheps Center for Health Services Research, University of North Carolina at Chapel Hill, Chapel Hill, NC, USA

Department of Health Behavior, Gillings School of Global Public Health, University of North Carolina at Chapel Hill, Chapel Hill, NC, USA

Division of General Medicine and Clinical Epidemiology, School of Medicine, University of North Carolina at Chapel Hill, Chapel Hill, NC, USA

I. Kuo
Milken Institute School of Public Health, George Washington University, Washington, DC, USA

S. Hodder
West Virginia Clinical and Translational Sciences Institute (WVCTSI), West Virginia University, Morgantown, WV, USA

women's opportunities to negotiate sexual monogamy in these circumstances (Ferguson et al., 2006; Hankins, 2008; Newsome & Airhihenbuwa, 2013). Managing such relationship challenges, which are often coupled with the stress of providing for children without financial and social support, has been independently linked to individual-level risk factors. These risk factors include coping with antecedent childhood and/or adolescent sexual trauma, substance abuse, depression and mental health disorders, intimate partner violence (IPV), and acquisition of sexually transmitted infections (STIs) (Ferguson et al., 2006; Hankins, 2008; Hodder et al., 2013; Newsome & Airhihenbuwa, 2013). These themes are explored in depth in subsequent chapters. The individual-level factors of food insecurity, personal experience with violence and trauma, and substance abuse are covered in Chaps. 4–6. The social-level factors—social support, partner concurrency and relationship dynamics, and sex exchange—follow in Chaps. 7–9. Finally, Chaps. 10–12 cover community-level factors of physical safety and neighborhood issues, housing, and gun violence, and overall policy implications are discussed in the Afterword.

## Poverty and Income Inequality

The disproportionate impact of poverty on women of color is rooted in historical and political discrimination. As mentioned above, in the USA poverty rates are higher among women than men, and higher among black/African Americans than whites. Among women, blacks have one of the highest poverty rates (25 %) compared to women of other racial/ethnic groups, rates disproportionately higher than either race or gender alone (Bishaw & Fontenot, 2014; Entmacher, Gallagher Robins, Vogtman, & Frohlich, 2013; U.S. Census Bureau, 2013b). Poverty in urban cities is even greater. The percentage of black women living in poverty in D.C., Georgia, New York, and North Carolina is 24.9 %, 26.3 %, 21.7 %, and 26.7 %, respectively (Entmacher et al., 2013). In New York City, the Bronx has the highest concentration of women and children living in poverty compared to the other boroughs (Mason, Salas, Ebanks, & Bowser, 2013).

There are many structural factors that place black women at a high risk of poverty. Income inequality disproportionately affects women; while the gender wage gap narrowed between 2000 and 2012, it did so by only three cents (Mason et al., 2013). Black women experience a higher wage gap compared to white, non-Hispanic women. In 2012, black women in New York City earned just 64 % of what black men earned for working full-time year round, while white, non-Hispanic women earned 78 % of the median earnings of white, non-Hispanic men (Mason et al., 2013). Nationally, higher poverty rates and higher gaps in income place a high burden on black women, especially among the 43 % of black households that are headed by single women (National Alliance of State & Territorial AIDS Directors, 2008). Unemployment rates among black women are about 1.5 times higher in 2013 than they were in 2007 (National Women's Law Center, 2013b). Sixty percent of women who have gained back their jobs since the start of the 2007 recession have gained back jobs in one of the ten largest low-wage job sectors that earn less than $10.10 an hour. These low-wage jobs account for only 20 % of men's job growth (National Women's Law Center, 2013a).

Economic poverty goes beyond income inequality and unemployment rates; it is also rooted in wealth gaps (Ms. Foundation for Women, 2013). Wealth includes the accumulation of assets and investments that can be sold for cash (Ms. Foundation for Women, 2013). On average, single black/African-American women have a median wealth of $100 and half of all single black/African-American women have zero or negative wealth, whereas single white women have a median wealth of $41,500 (Ms. Foundation for Women, 2013).

Institutional discrimination also contributes to the high rates of racial economic inequality. Numerous studies show that black/African-American citizens experience greater scrutiny. They often have to deal with stereotyping, thereby needing to display a higher level of productivity than whites to get the same favorable assessment when applying for a promotion, making it more difficult for them to move up in the workplace (Bell & Nkomo, 2003; Hall, Everett, & Hamilton-Mason, 2012; National Women's Law Center, 2000; U.S. Equal Employment Opportunity Commission, 2013). Educational attainment does not necessarily overcome these levels of discrimination. Even though the mean annual income for adults 25 years and older increases at the same rate per level of schooling, whites continue to earn more than blacks at every level of education gained (Harris, 2010) This disparity does not diminish but rather increases among adults with a professional degree, with whites earning $20,000 more than blacks per year (Harris, 2010).

## Housing Inequality and Insecurity

Black/African American women experience housing discrimination which makes them vulnerable to housing segregation and poverty (Lipsitz, 2011). The U.S. Department of Housing and Urban Development (HUD) provides housing assistance to low-income households; however, the program only services about 25 % of those households that are eligible and in need of assistance (National Low Income Housing Coalition, 2012). Blacks who receive public housing assistance are about three times more likely to live in a high-poverty neighborhood than their white counterparts (National Low Income Housing Coalition, 2012). Individuals living in high-poverty neighborhoods tend to experience heightened police scrutiny and arrests compared to individuals living in lower poverty neighborhoods (Lipsitz, 2011). Blacks also experience higher rates of homelessness than their white counterparts in New York City, where more than half (57 %) of homeless shelter residents are black/African American and less than 10 % are white.

## Incarceration Rates, Sexual Concurrency, and Intimate Partner Violence

Housing insecurity and segregation increase the risk of incarceration or re-incarceration (recidivism) among black/African Americans and also contribute to high rates of sexual concurrency and IPV. Black men are incarcerated at a rate six times higher than white men and 2.6 times higher than Hispanic men (National Minority AIDS Council & Housing Works, 2013). Convictions and imprisonments for drug charges also disproportionately affect blacks (National Minority AIDS Council & Housing Works, 2013). These convictions do not reflect heightened drug use or drug dealing among the black population compared to other populations (Lipsitz, 2011). In fact, studies show comparable drug use among all racial groups, and some studies show heightened use among whites (Lipsitz, 2011).

There is an inequality with how people of color are entering the criminal justice system. A three-city study found no difference among racial groups in drug use or dealing among women; yet 86 % of women arrested for drug convictions were women of color (Lipsitz, 2011). Incarceration is also a risk factor for HIV infection due to a lack of condoms, high rates of unprotected sex, and tattooing with unsafe needles (National Alliance of State & Territorial AIDS Directors, 2008). A study in the Georgia Department of Corrections found that all 88 male inmates who entered as HIV negative were HIV positive upon release, and two-thirds of these men were black (National Alliance of State & Territorial AIDS Directors, 2008). New York State has one of the highest HIV rates among state inmates (National Minority AIDS Council & Housing Works, 2013). A lack of housing security upon release is associated with prison reentry. One-third of inmates released from a New York State prison who entered a homeless shelter ended up back in prison (National Minority AIDS Council & Housing Works, 2013). Incarceration is also a risk factor for HIV infection outside of prison. High rates in which black men are incarcerated create an imbalance in the male-to-female sex ratio, which contributes to high sexual concurrency among black women (National Alliance of State & Territorial AIDS Directors, 2008). There are more black females for every black male, which reduces their sense of power in a relationship and limits their ability and willingness to negotiate condom use (National Alliance of State & Territorial AIDS Directors, 2008).

Violence is also linked to an increased risk for HIV infection and transmission (National Alliance of State & Territorial AIDS Directors, 2008). Safer-sex practices such as condom negotiation, number of sexual partners, and getting tested are usually controlled by the batterer and any negotiation could be dangerous for the person experiencing violence (National Coalition Against Domestic Violence, 2014). Black/African-American women experience high rates of IPV; almost one-third of black American women experience IPV in their lifetime (Women of Color Network, 2006). In New York City, women living in the Bronx have the highest IPV hospitalizations and emergency room visits than women from the other boroughs (Stayton et al., 2008).

## *Theoretical Orientation*

To examine intersecting factors that describe women's lives in poverty, we adopted a socioecological framework to analyze the dynamic interactions across individual, dyadic, network, and community levels in society. Our resulting adaptation of the seminal Bronfenbrenner ecological model (Fig. 3.1) illustrates that individual

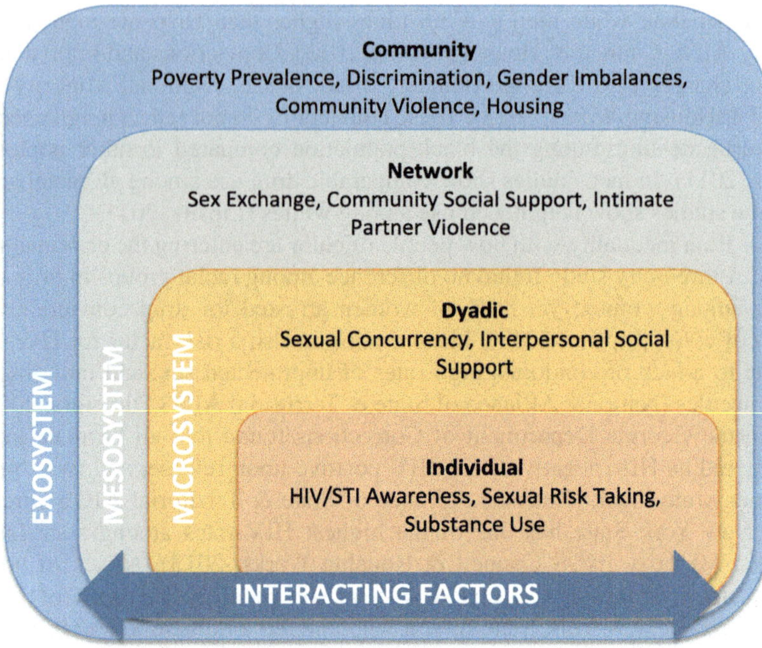


**Fig. 3.1** Adapted Bronfrenbrenner Conceptual Model

women's behaviors are influenced and defined by surrounding ecology, environment, and systems (Bronfenbrenner, 1994).

From a conceptual standpoint, HIV risk (the basis for the HPTN 064 study) likely arises from influencers at all four of these levels. Our study introduces evidence of the intersections across levels and how these factors operate in a similar manner among women living in discrete geographic areas of the USA. The individual-level factors include women's beliefs, feelings, perceptions, and attitudes. Risk-taking behavior and awareness of disease vulnerability are examples of these individual-level factors. The second level, the microsystem, is theorized to have a strong impact on an individual's decision making due to strong interpersonal dynamics. Due to the dyadic nature of many personal relationships, an individual often belongs to several microsystems, which intersect based on affiliations among these relationships. The third level, the mesosystem, represents the intersection and linkage an individual has within multiple microsystems (e.g., partnership connections or perceived degree of social support in a network). This is how phenomena such as sexual concurrency may arise when men have multiple female partners (Adimora et al., 2004; Aral, 2010). At the exosystem level, individuals may be affected by indirect forces beyond their direct control. Examples might be housing relocation, poverty, and racial discrimination. Finally, a macrosystem (societal) level represents the external system, which influences behavior through policies, laws, and regulations that influences larger cultural and social norms.

## Methods

As explained in Chap. 2, the HPTN 064 project was a multisite observational study to determine HIV incidence among women living in communities with a high prevalence of HIV infection and high rates of poverty. Details of the HPTN 064 study have been previously reported (Eshleman et al., 2013; Hodder et al., 2013). Inclusion criteria included women, aged 18–44 years, residing in census tracts or zip codes (New York, NY) in the top 30th percentile of HIV prevalence and more than 25 % of inhabitants living in poverty, reporting at least one episode of unprotected sex with a man in the 6 months before enrollment, and also reporting at least one additional HIV risk behavior (either personal or partner). Using venue-based sampling, eligible women were enrolled between May 2009 and July 2010 from ten communities in six geographic areas of the USA (Atlanta, GA; Baltimore, MD; New York, NY; Newark, NJ; Raleigh/Durham, NC; Washington, D.C.). The study was approved by institutional review boards at each site and collaborating institutions, and a certificate of confidentiality was obtained. Routine HIV testing and counseling were performed at baseline and at 6-month intervals, with 6 or 12 months of follow-up. Additionally, participants completed an audio computer-assisted self-interview (ACASI) at all visits that provided for collection of socioeconomic data, alcohol and substance use, mental health symptoms (depression and post-traumatic stress disorder [PTSD]), social support, and sexual behaviors.

To contextualize the participants' vulnerability to HIV and better explore the nuances of the women's lived experiences, four of the ten study communities (New York, New York; Washington, D.C.; Raleigh/Durham, North Carolina; and Atlanta, Georgia) also participated in a qualitative substudy. Each site conducted 30 semi-structured interviews with study participants and two to three focus groups per age and race/ethnic stratum of women. Women were divided according to age group (e.g., 18–25, 26–35, and 36–44 years) and assigned to groups by race and ethnicity (i.e., black/African American or other race and Hispanic/non-Hispanic ethnicity). We first selected women for interviews based on their alternating participant identification numbers assigned at enrollment and used the same methodology to identify women eligible for focus groups after the interviews were completed.

The interviews and focus groups explored social, structural, and contextual factors that influence women's HIV risk. Example questions included the following: "Who do you turn to when you are going through a rough time?" "What are some things that you believe make a women have a greater chance of getting HIV or an STD?" "What can women do to protect themselves from getting HIV/STDs?" Highly sensitive questions about personal experiences (e.g., trauma or victimization) were included in the interview guide only. Focus groups focused on community-level factors.

## Overview of Qualitative Findings

As described in previous publications, coding and analysis took place in two steps, resulting in a total of 1139 nodal and subnodal codes for women (10 structural and 1129 content) (Eshleman et al., 2013; Hodder et al., 2013). We developed a total of three codebooks and corresponding NVivo databases. Saturation was assessed in real time, and was achieved in Phase 3 (Advanced Systematic Analysis) of coding and analysis by the time that 90 % of the data were coded. The final ICR was a combined average Kappa score of 0.91 and the ICR for the random sample of interviews was a combined average Kappa score of 0.92.

Our descriptive research yielded themes that described similar linked patterns of HIV risk experience among women. With evidence of multilevel directionality of independent/dependent variable relationships (e.g., poverty driving willingness to remain in a concurrent relationship for partner's income), variable strength (e.g., thematic magnitude emergent from data), and observed reciprocal factor relationships across levels (e.g., violence and perceived social (non)support), we examined conceptual structures that may align with established behavioral models (Fawcett, 1999).

We mapped these major themes to the individual, microsystem, mesosystem, and exosystem levels proposed by Bronfenbrenner's ecological model. The themes within this rubric consist of (1) Individual level: lack of HIV/STI awareness/vulnerability; sexual risk-taking, and substance abuse; (2) microsystem: social support, sex exchange, and IPV; (3) mesosystem: concurrency and social support; and (4) exosystem: poverty, discrimination, gender imbalances, and community violence. An overarching theme emerged on the fundamental role of financial insecurity driving an array of factors contributing to risk-taking behaviors.

We present the thematic content according to the Bronfenbrenner model that reflects effects observed on factors contributing to women's HIV risk, with the overarching theme of poverty that inspired this book. We present our findings going from the broadest to the narrowest factors, walking through the community-, social-, and individual-level factors.

## *Exosystem: Community*

A growing body of literature suggests that issues such as poverty, perceived discrimination, housing policies and insecurity, community-level gender imbalances, and crime and violence contribute to HIV risk (Aral & Wasserheit, 1995; Bogart, Landrine, Galvan, Wagner, & Klein, 2013; Ferguson et al., 2006; Hankins, 2008; Inciardi & Surratt, 1998; Kidder et al., 2007; Newsome & Airhihenbuwa, 2013; Riley, Gandhi, Hare, Cohen, & Hwang, 2007; Soto, Komaie, Neilands, & Johnson, 2013; Su et al., 2013). Women in our study described these issues and provided insight into how these issues potentially interact.

### Poverty Pervasiveness

Women explained the toll of financial hardship in their lives and communities and the extent to which individuals will go to procure resources and money for themselves and their children. Many indicated that women often lack enough money or food stamps to obtain food and other household and family necessities for daily living (e.g., diapers, clothing). Such challenges present women with few options to remedy the situation despite having accessible neighborhood food pantries that often place limits on given items to eligible persons and households. A woman summed the desperation experienced by many:

> I know a couple of people around our way that don't really eat like that or their mother might be on drugs or something and she'll leave for the whole week and just have them in there. So they got to come over my house and eat dinner or my mother make sure we go take the food over there.
>
> —*Interviewee, Washington, D.C.*

Issues of food insecurity are examined in-depth in Chap. 4.

In addition, participants explained that the level of education in their communities directly corresponds with financial challenges. They reasoned that a lack of formal education results in less marketable knowledge and skill base to gain employment with decent income potential. Respondents detailed how difficult it is on women who function as heads of households as they are often the (nonvolitional) sole provider to their children. Many are also faced with few options for affordable childcare and have the added challenge of not being recipients of child support from fathers.

> I mean, a lot of people there ain't got no education, period, you know. That's why they ain't got no money, because ain't nobody got no high school diploma or GED trying to make no money.
>
> —*Focus Group Participant, Raleigh/Durham, NC*

> What I do, I just start making phone calls … Talk to some guys … it drives me nuts that I have to do it. To get what my girls need, you know, so. I mean I'm a single mom; I'm by myself. Pops, they don't want to help, so …
>
> —*Interviewee, Atlanta, GA*

Many women explained that if they had an opportunity to achieve more education and acquire employment, they would be motivated to work.

> So, yeah it's hard for when them check and food stamps. That's why I got myself into little programs and I'm going to program it out too until the country or whoever don't have no more programs. They pay you $50.00 to go to this program. I'm going for my GED and I'm going for my, I'm going for anything they got so I can get certified. I'm going for food handler license. I'm going for computer, basic computer training.
>
> —*Focus Group Participant, Washington, D.C.*

A woman in Atlanta summarized that for her, and her children, the attainment of education would inspire hope for a better future.

> There is more to life than the little box you live in. There's a whole other world. There's different things to strive for and you can do anything you want to do …
>
> —*Focus Group Participant, Atlanta, GA*

## Perceived Discrimination

Among those women who explained that they did perceive distinct differences in HIV vulnerability across communities, they felt that this stemmed from fundamental problems like a lack of access to educational and informational opportunities often found in higher income parts of their cities and suburbs. They mentioned that they often felt left behind and left out of knowing important health information that could help them to protect themselves against HIV. Women perceived that educational disparities (more direct effects of racial discrimination) did not give certain groups, including black/African-American women, equal opportunity to engage in preventive health behavior, thereby rendering them vulnerable to HIV and other diseases.

> Yeah. It's a lot different especially for people who have money and stuff. They're more educated. They're more like getting pamphlets at their doorstep, but in the black community it's like we have to go out and get the information or people—I mean we have some people who come door-to-door, but at the same time it's like that information is not easy access for us.
> —*Focus Group Participant, Raleigh/Durham, NC*

Another woman described how she dealt with the lack of education in her neighborhood for her daughters in order to protect them and to foster their independence.

> And with them going so far out, to different schools that's not in your area, it's hard to get to them and be involved in their schoolwork … It's being there, and making sure they get that education. Letting them know that without that, it's gonna be harder. All that stuff comes into play. Drugs. Unprotected sex. Pregnancy too young. All that stuff—without that education. Because with that, they know, regardless of what happens in their life, they can take care of themselves. They can be independent—do what they want.
> —*Focus Group Participant, Raleigh/Durham, NC*

## Housing Policies and Insecurity

Women described how poverty reduced their options and kept them in housing they did not like or feel safe in. Others described run-down locations, poorly maintained or filled with pests, like this woman:

> My apartment, for instance. It's just falling apart. The pipes is a mess. The heat is too hot. I have bugs now. I've never had bugs, you know, the cockroaches, spiders. I clean my house and it gets right back dusty like I ain't touched it. You know, I just hate the apartment … I was grateful to get it 'cause I had to get out of my parent's house. I had to. But then once I got over there I'm like "oh, God. Why did I move here," you know?
> —*Interviewee, Raleigh/Durham, NC*

Some women described how an improvement in a housing situation ushered in an almost instant sense of calm and comfort to their lives. These women from New York relayed how happy moving from a shelter to well-kept public housing made them feel:

> Participant 1: Right now, it's good. It's a brand new building, a brand new apartment. It's beautiful. I know. I was blessed with that, but I'm coming from the shelter for five years. I love it, where I am now.
>
> Participant 2: It's now, like, when you go out stairs, you walk out and you think you're someplace else. I just feel, oh my goodness, so clean, and you don't got to step in—it's a total relief … Like I said, it's better now, but at first I wouldn't even let nobody come visit me. No one ever—in the three months I've been there, no one ever came and visited me. Now I am going to have somebody come visit me.
> —*Focus Group, New York, NY*

The discussion on housing is continued in Chap. 11.

## Gender Imbalances

Many women described challenges with dating and keeping men as exclusive sexual partners given the considerably low ratio of men to women in the community. Women often attributed this phenomenon to more men in jail or prison, higher male mortality, and having more "undercover men" (i.e., men who have sex with men) available as sexual partners in the community. Men's records of incarceration did not function as a deterrent to sexual relationships with women in the community. In fact, even among the women in the study, a notable 55 % of them reported that they were in jail or prison in the past 5 years ($n = 159$); the broader HPTN 064 study population experienced higher rates of incarceration (59 %, $n = 1233$). One woman stated that she observed women becoming less "particular" about their partners given these challenges. Another focus group participant summarized why she thought there were fewer male partners available to women:

> I'm telling you, if they are not on Rikers, they are gay ... And coming here, the first—when I first came here and having to talk, I just really was like ... And I was on the computer doing that little thing, like, "If you are having sex with such and such"—like, all right: one. But how many people is he having sex with? I don't know.
>
> —*Focus Group Participant, New York, NY*

In another focus group, some fear was expressed about women who were knowingly or unknowingly partnered with "undercover men" who could make them vulnerable to HIV and STIs.

> It happens a lot. It's happening a lot more for some reason. But they men really got it over their head and it's five women to one man so they, you know, it's enough to go around. And it's a lot more undercover brothers out here now that are just leading double lives. So it's really scary now because I've come to the realization that it's a lot more undercover brothers out here claiming to be thorough and thug and gangster or whatever. And those be the ones so it is, it's very scary.
>
> —*Interviewee, Washington, D.C.*

Gender imbalances are further explored in Chap. 8, along with sexual concurrency and relationship dynamics.

## Community Violence

Community violence is of major concern in these communities. Conversation focused on the role of drugs and gangs, which are a source of income for the communities, as major contributors to the issues of crime and violence in the neighborhoods.

> Mmm mmm, alcohol use and you know street walking and everything, shooting, gun shots, people beating each other up, people hollering, jumping fences and shooting cats with the BB gun and just everything. It's just everything. They just want to kill everything that's walking. So, it's just a very like I said destructive, depressing neighborhood.
>
> —*Focus Group Participant, Washington, D.C.*

Community gun violence is discussed in Chap. 12.

Many women indicated that they had a difficult time coping with the extent and magnitude of violence in their neighborhoods. In an effort to protect themselves and their children, some stated that they would like to leave the neighborhood to avoid becoming crime victims, and yet many were financially unable to move. Their immobility often transpired into self-isolation as a key coping mechanism.

> So we've got—we've got each project against each other. So you've got the shooting, you've got the fighting, you've got the gangs. And, you know, so it's too much. I have a two-year-old, you know, so it's not too much that I want him to see.
>
> —*Focus Group Participant, New York, NY*

Physical safety and neighborhood issues for the women in the study are covered in Chap. 10.

## *Mesosystem: Social*

Individuals are connected to and operate in many social systems and networks that constitute the "mesosystem," a level representing intersections across contexts. At this level, we identified themes including how sexual concurrency and (lack of) community social support function to promote women's HIV vulnerability.

### Sexual Concurrency

Our quantitative data revealed that a substantial proportion of our study sample reported being a partner to a man with multiple relationships (38 %, $n = 110$). The qualitative data offered many perspectives on the subject of sexual concurrency. Within this domain, we learned that women tolerate their male partners' sexual concurrency with other women as involvement with that partner privileges their relationship. By having an elevated status as "main partner" to her man, women indicated that they felt validated. Often she knew that other women were simultaneously competing for his interest. One woman summarized the situation for women in "committed" relationships who knew of their partner's "external" sexual relations:

> Or they look at it like, "I'm wifey, he is getting what he wants, and I'm going to be his number one. No matter what, he's going to come home to me tonight."
>
> —*Focus Group Participant, New York, NY*

Elsewhere, a woman commented that other women may experience a boost of self-esteem when they feel that they are elevated socially, sexually, and emotionally by the way a man treats her even if she knows or suspects that he has other female partners:

> I guess 'cause they feel like they're getting treated like a queen at the time and nobody else can probably do or say—I don't know, I guess, I mean I really don't know. I mean maybe I guess because they're not getting treated the way they want to get treated with other people. Maybe he's just saying and doing stuff that's making her feel good.
>
> —*Interviewee, Raleigh/Durham, NC*

Similarly, participants explained that most people, especially women, remained in concurrent relationships with men because they did not want to suffer from loneliness. This woman stated:

> A lot of women can't be by themselves. They have to be with a man because they don't want to be alone. How is that? If you really—when you go through a problem and you let him go, you can work on yourself. You can try to do things better for yourself, but to say, "I can't live without him" or "I can't live without a man," knowing that he did this is, no no.
>
> —*Focus Group Participant, New York, NY*

For some women, financial reasons factor into their willingness to stay with a male sexual partner who they know to have other female sexual partners. In Atlanta, one woman summarized what she perceived to be the reasons many women tolerate his relationships with other women:

> I think it's that comfort and security that they have with that person. Okay, well, he's paying my bills; I'll just deal with this. I'm going to tolerate what he's done, if it's right or wrong…
>
> —*Focus Group Participant, Atlanta, GA*

Overall, many women believed that people, both women and men in their communities, engage in high frequency of overlapping sexual partnerships. They described that women are often aware or have strong intuition of their partners' indiscretions and they have direct knowledge of their friends' or the friends' partners' concurrent sexual behaviors. Yet, it is important to note that only a few women reported concurrency or suspected concurrency in their own relationships. A woman commented on women's tendencies to emotionally and socially protect themselves when making social comparisons:

> I think women know when a man is cheating on them. They just don't want to admit it. They don't want to know 'cause they don't want to be embarrassed around their friends that they're fronting for and they make them think they've got the perfect relationships.
>
> —*Interviewee, Raleigh/Durham, NC*

As mentioned above, sexual concurrency and relationship dynamics, along with gender imbalances, are discussed in Chap. 8.

## Community Social Support

We observed important distinctions on actual and perceived social support at the community level. Women explained that instrumental support such as food, shelter, clothing, and healthcare services was available in their communities. They felt that such services were necessary for their survival, especially as many indicated that family, friends, and neighbors could not be trusted to offer any instrumental or emotional support. Thus, the women described turning to caseworkers, community-based organizations, rescue missions, and women's health clinic staff for any type of support. As one woman from Raleigh stated, she turned to community-based organization staff, "…'Cause I feel like they can help you, answer your questions and stuff." Another woman from New York explained the critical role of formal organizations to be leaders on developing needed support groups for women in the neighborhood. Such opportunities provide women with emotional support, social connection, and access to information and coping strategies that help them to protect their health and well-being:

> I have a support group, you know, I have a support group, I go to therapy. You know, because when you're raised in neighborhoods like this, you know, and you've been here all your life, you know, you're subjected to a lot of things. You know? You're subjected to abuse, you're subjected to violence, subjected to domestic violence, you know?
>
> —*Focus Group Participant, New York, NY*

Importantly, social support organizations hold trust with these women. They connect with the staff and volunteers of the organizations and form trusting relationships with the individuals who can help them work through difficult problems such as staying in recovery, addressing homelessness, and other critical needs. Finally, women described the importance of having other female volunteers deliver educational support to children in the community. An Atlanta interviewee explained the importance of having homework and childcare support present in her apartment complex recreational facility as it addresses vital needs of many women for their children, especially as men are not around and able to assist with after-school activities.

> Okay, where I stay at, they have a breakout center. They keep your kids from 2:30 [in the] afternoon to 6 o'clock in the afternoon. They help the kids with their homework and everything so I mean, it's women doing that. So I think that's one way they helping the children out in the community because they … I mean it's a program, a free program … A lot of people need that sometimes. Free!
>
> —*Interviewee, Atlanta, GA*

The social support structures and voids in these communities are discussed in Chap. 7.

## *Microsystem: Social*

The effects observed at this level included three major factors directly affecting women's vulnerability—sex exchange in the community, varying peer and familial social support, and IPV.

### Sex Exchange

To survive, many participants reported that they and/or people in their communities turn to any means necessary to obtain money or food for themselves or their families. They may turn to selling sex or exchanging their bodies for drugs, housing, food, or other living needs. During a focus group, one woman stated:

> There's girls out here that I know that you would never imagine in your wildest dreams that they would do the type of things they do. But crunch times, you got your kids, you got to feed your baby. You got to feed yourself. They out here streaking or whatever you want to call it just to make sure that they good and they baby good, because at the end of the day, if

> they ain't watching out for their kids, ain't nobody else gone do it. I mean, people is resorting to any and everything at the end of the day, just to make sure they're getting—they're gonna eat, and their baby's gonna eat.
>
> —*Focus Group Participant, Raleigh/Durham, NC*

Sex exchange is further discussed in Chap. 9.

## Dyadic Social Support

Women reported receiving some personal social support from their mothers or friends. Yet the majority of women stated that they felt a general lack of instrumental (or physical "resource-based") and emotional support. Instead, they perceived more negative support from family, friends, and peers (e.g., disapproval of life choices). Many of the women reported having very few people they could turn to in times of need (some referred to having only one person they could claim in their support system, i.e., mother or friend). Those who reported little or no emotional or instrumental support (e.g., childcare for employability) also explained that too often the women in their communities are simply disingenuous and have hidden motivations if they extend offers to help. An example of this type of behavior is described in a quote by a woman who described what happened after she confided in a "friend." According to this woman, the acquaintance betrayed her confidence to gain material support (or money) from a man with whom she shared the story:

> So she goes back and tells him all my business, because she might need a three-piece—$1.99 for Church's or some money or some toilet paper … So that's why I say I really don't turn to nobody no more. But I keep her real close to me. Because if something happens to me, she gonna get hurt first.
>
> —*Interviewee, Raleigh/Durham, NC*

Women stated that they were often distrustful of family members, friends, and neighbors, especially those who previously were or currently are critical of their lifestyle or life circumstances. Women therefore implemented self-isolation in response to negative social support and withdrawal from social circles often came at some hidden cost. Reasons why women would not want to confide in others were summarized by this woman:

> So you can't tell everything to anyone, because you don't know who they're going to tell or if they're going to tell this person and that person's going to tell another person.
>
> —*Interviewee, New York, NY*

Dyadic social support is also covered in Chap. 7.

## Intimate Partner Violence

The women in our study chronicled a considerable amount of traumatic experiences associated with domestic violence and IPV. Detailed accounts emerged on past and current physical and emotional partner abuse episodes, both witnessed within families and experienced personally. As victims and household bystanders to partner violence, women echoed how this type of violence fostered their strong distrust of men. In North Carolina, a woman described her history:

> Well, growing up, my mother used to get beat up on a regular—um, I been around my mother getting her tail beat most of my life, all the way up till I was 18 when I left home. Then I'd be around my sister, the one up there, she's just like—her boyfriend all the time. Then I got into a bad relationship where it won't like he was hitting on me. He just was yelling and screaming all the time, playing with guns, putting guns out and stuff like that. But pretty much all the time.
>
> —*Interviewee, Raleigh/Durham, NC*

Another woman from Washington, D.C., described her experience with a jealous husband of whom she suffered his abuse for some time that became a norm in their household:

> My husband used to beat me and I did not, you know, me living up in D.C., I wasn't raised like that, men beating on you or nothing. My husband was jealous...
>
> —*Focus Group Participant, Washington, D.C.*

Typically, women detailed that their male partners either exhibited violent behavior against them or ended up being incarcerated for some time. An Atlanta woman stated:

> He's been incarcerated now for, like, three years now and I felt unsafe 'cause he use to abuse me ... I don't know why he started abusing me and stuff.
>
> —*Interviewee, Atlanta, GA*

Those who survived violent acts perpetrated by male partners described other ways out of these relationships. Many stated that men took advantage of their low self-esteem and exploited their vulnerabilities. Yet they described their resiliency and process of transformation to stand up to the abuses experienced after some catalytic event such as going to jail or prison, losing their children, or some other major life change. A woman in Washington, D.C., spoke of her attitude shift toward her partner and her desire to move past her history of abuse:

> ... can't nobody touch me. And if you do, there's consequences. That's where I was. I went from there to there in 1996. From 1996 until now, I'm here. My tolerance—everything—process of elimination. I went through that whole process myself. I have to pinch myself. I have to get my mind right. I have to get my body right. I have to get my head right. Spiritually, emotionally, everything. I have to do all of that myself ...
>
> —*Interviewee, Washington, D.C.*

Personal experience with IPV and trauma is explored in Chap. 5.

## *Individual Level*

Major themes emerged on the interdependent roles of risk-taking behaviors and substance use that linked to themes observed at the micro-, meso-, and exosystems.

## Sexual Risk-Taking Behaviors

Most participants reported the lack of condom use, having multiple previous and/or current sexual partners, and having a lack of knowledge of partners' history as major risk factors for HIV/AIDS. Many participants explained that they do not use condoms with partners whom they consider to be in a steady or long-term relationship.

> Yeah, I mean we have them in the house. But it's not like I'm going to go and grab one, you know, every time we get ready. 'Cause I guess, 'cause I've been around him for so long, it's just, it doesn't even come up in our conversations … I guess 'cause I've been around him for so many years, you know. I guess I just fell into that comfortable mode as far as not using protection.
>
> —*Interviewee, Washington, D.C.*

Although the majority of women indicated that they were not in a "non-partnered" relationship (67 %, $n=194$), a woman from New York described that relationship duration is a criterion for determining if condoms are used.

> I'm going to be honest with you. If I'm with this man for ten years, I'm not going to be using a condom, if I'm with this one man for ten years. If I'm with this man for one year, yeah, we going to be using condoms.
>
> —*Interviewee, New York, NY*

Another facet of risk-taking behavior involved the association of substance use to condom decision making. They offered many accounts of women they knew who engaged in more risky sexual behaviors under the influence of drugs and alcohol.

> It might, you might be in the heat of the moment, might be on some alcohol anything, like boom! You know it might not happen. You might think, you might not think about it, oh darn, get a condom. You know, you could be in the heat.
>
> —*Focus Group Participant, Atlanta, GA*

## Substance Use

Many women described a personal history of substance use, including crack, alcohol, marijuana, ecstasy, and other hallucinogens that they used to cope with other life factors such as a lack of social support, partner violence, and other negative life circumstances. In Washington, D.C., one woman summarized why she began using:

> Okay, well, it started in [name of state] you know what I mean, 'cause I kept saying, "oh I need my," I used to say it was self-medicating. 'Cause I was going through like a lot and then it was like I got depressed real bad and my son went to live with his father. So I just my attitudes like, I just couldn't cope. So it's just when I got high I didn't think about nothing. I didn't care pretty much, I used to say it was self-medicate. But then it was like when I removed myself from the domestic violence part of it, it was like I just started seeing a different outlook.
>
> —*Interviewee, Washington, D.C.*

Women reported that their consistent use of substances rendered them vulnerable to HIV, having impaired their judgment especially with respect to sexual partners.

One woman stated that she did not even think about using condoms with male partners while she binged on alcohol:

> Oh, I came from the club that's what happened, I came from the club and probably was drunk. That's how I got my first daughter. I was drunk and it was too late, too late.
>
> —*Interviewee, Raleigh/Durham, NC*

The quantitative data indicated that, on a weekly basis, women in our sample consumed fewer drugs (15 %, $n=42$, $p=0.004$) and were less likely to engage in binge drinking (24 %, $n=69$) compared to the larger study sample's drug (22 %, $N=2099$) and alcohol use (24 %, $n=498$). This suggests that women were cognizant of the role of substance abuse on their risk of acquiring HIV or STIs. Several described their substance abuse experiences in the past tense, indicating personal journeys with recovery. By reducing or eliminating use of substances, they recognized that they could avoid acquiring HIV. One woman spoke of her personal struggle with crack addiction and that of her male partner who was living with HIV. This raised concern for her about her vulnerability to HIV as they shared drugs, of which their paraphernalia was also shared with his wider social network. She explained how using drugs placed her directly at risk of contracting HIV from her partner whom she remained with for more than 10 years. With treatment for crack addition, she was able to liberate herself from a challenging relationship with a man living with HIV.

> Because he's sick. He has the virus, so … Yeah, everybody was on crack, everybody was on crack. Except for the wheelchair; he was a weed head. It was all about getting high. 'Cause today I'm working and I can wait for the next paycheck to get what I need. I don't have to go out because I'm not using anymore not under the influence. So I'm thinking more clearly now.
>
> —*Interviewee, Raleigh/Durham, NC*

Substance abuse at a social level is discussed in Chap. 6.

## Discussion

Findings from HPTN 064 qualitative data from 288 women selected from the HPTN 064 study provide unprecedented insight into the effects of poverty on women's lives in the USA, as a precursor to the aim of exploring HIV risk. This study is among the first multilevel analyses that qualitatively explores nested and interacting factors contributing to women's HIV risk in the USA. The findings correspond with quantitative studies that examine the role of poverty, such as homelessness, disintegration of neighborhoods, and overall lack of social capital in geographically defined areas, and how these factors may facilitate HIV transmission (Adimora et al., 2013; Cene et al., 2011; Frumence et al., 2010; Gillies, Tolley, & Wolstenholme, 1996; Gregson et al., 2011). Our findings support the fundamental role that poverty and financial insecurity play in HIV risk among women in certain communities in the USA (Adimora et al., 2006; Aral, Adimora, & Fenton, 2008; Schwartz et al., 2011). Participants indicated that their reported high-risk behaviors, including unprotected anal or vaginal intercourse with concurrent partners, stemmed from challenges related to acquiring food, housing, and other necessary provisions for themselves and their children.

This study offers further evidence of important structural considerations at the exosystem level—that women in poverty experience stress due to large forces exerting power on the social and built environment (Kidder et al., 2007; Sumartojo, Doll, Holtgrave, Gayle, & Merson, 2000). Women described conditions of poorly managed, unstable housing conditions, and unsafe neighborhoods characterized by violence and substance abuse issues, all previously correlated with HIV risk behavior (Corneil et al., 2006; Elifson, Sterk, & Theall, 2007; Marshall et al., 2009; Riley et al., 2007). They describe living in these environments as chaotic and stressful, with many women unable to escape their neighborhoods due to financial constraints. Economic immobility experienced by women offers little or no choice in housing and physical environment. This aspect alone contributes to the psychosocial stressors they experience on a daily basis (Ezzy, de Visser, & Bartos, 1999). Consequently, personal or witnessed risk-taking behaviors are described as being induced by increased stress and anxiety associated with unsafe and unstable housing environments.

Additionally, there was consensus that the prevalence of substance abuse—both as a coping mechanism and as a social issue—in neighborhoods contributed to risk-taking behavior and fueled unnecessary crime and violence. Sex exchange was also described both in terms of personal means to obtain financial and in-kind resources. Trading sex for money, housing, food, drugs, or gifts is a manifestation of coping with living in an area characterized by high unemployment, incarceration, and poverty (Bolton, 1992). Thus, as we (and others) have identified, overall financial difficulties and poor living conditions exacerbate overall stress endured by women which pose significant barriers for HIV risk reduction (Konkle-Parker, Erlen, & Dubbert, 2008).

At the micro- and mesosystem levels, women described key issues that reciprocally interact with other upper- and lower-level socioecological factors including a prevalence of community-wide sexual concurrency and IPV, as well as a lack of perceived social support and, relatedly, self-imposed alienation from others stemming from distrust (Denning & DiNenno, 2010). Yet, important information emerged on the vital role of social support from community agencies. Women expressed a moderately high level of trust in the staff and volunteers of these organizations who lent tangible support to them as well as emotional comfort in times of distress and need. Thus, leveraging the role of community-based organizations will facilitate the development of effective multilevel interventions to reduce HIV risk among women living in these communities (Frew, Archibald, Hixson, & del Rio, 2011; Kakietek et al., 2013; Mayer et al., 2012).

With a substantial number of women reporting being a partner to a man with multiple relationships, women described it as a more widespread phenomenon constituting a community norm (Adimora et al., 2004; Adimora & Schoenbach, 2005). This norm is driven by exosystem issues such as violence and criminal laws associated with substance abuse, resulting in greater incarceration rates compared to other neighborhoods and thereby constraining sexual partner options (Aral, 2010; Drumright, Gorbach, & Holmes, 2004; Flom et al., 2001; Garnett & Johnson, 1997).

They explained that they are very aware of the role of men's sexual concurrency with multiple women in the community on HIV risk. They reported this from direct observation of men and women entering and leaving residences for sexual activity, having conversations with others about "stepping out" (deliberate sexual encounters outside of a relationship), and experiencing or knowing people living with HIV and STIs (Drumright et al., 2004).

Sexual concurrency, also linked to experiences with IPV, is also associated with women's HIV risk (El-Bassel et al., 2007). Women detailed their personal experiences with physical and mental abuse inflicted by partners, often explaining IPV as a multigenerational cultural norm witnessed or experienced by mothers, grandmothers, sisters, and female cousins who may not necessarily offer social support to them (Bhandari et al., 2012). Traumatic IPV experiences with male partners often arose through confrontations about his "stepping out" on her or about sexual liaisons with other women.

Similar to other studies that report on women who experience PTSD following IPV (El-Bassel et al., 2007; Renzetti, 2013), our participants also signaled their inability to effectively address concurrency or walk away from partners who offer financial support (Perez, Johnson, & Wright, 2012). In these circumstances, financial dependency reduced women's independence and her power to advocate for herself and her children's health and well-being. Thus at these levels, trust and dependency issues emerge as significant challenges. Women see themselves as being "in debt" to others. These factors directly restrict women's ability to confront partners for fear of violent retaliation, to negotiate condom use, or to identify those she can trust to identify instrumental resources to navigate away from these risk circumstances (Okechukwu, El Ayadi, Tamers, Sabbath, & Berkman, 2012; Sweet, Nandi, Adam, & McDade, 2013). Given the importance of these issues, integrated HIV-related interventions featuring partner communication and financial empowerment may offer great promise for addressing these challenges.

Finally, at the individual level women described substance use and sexual risk-taking despite having observed a high prevalence of those living with HIV in the community. Women described the use of drugs and alcohol by members of their community as a common coping mechanism to their socioenvironmental challenges including sexual partner norms (i.e., concurrency), IPV, and living environment violence (Gonzalez-Guarda, Vasquez, Urrutia, Villarruel, & Peragallo, 2011; Saylors & Daliparthy, 2005). Thus, although the linkage between substance abuse and HIV risk-taking behavior is well known at the individual level (Meader et al., 2013), our qualitative analyses identified that these community challenges influence their willingness to engage in social relationships with others in their community for fear of violence, harmful gossip, and/or some other form of retribution inflicted on themselves, their children, or people close to them. Often choosing to withdraw from social interactions with others beyond one or two persons (usually a child or other family member), women describe that they have turned to sex with men who may have behavioral risk characteristics (e.g., living with HIV) and/or use substances, thereby altering their own risk for HIV acquisition in spite of having a relatively high HIV/STI awareness and knowledge of how HIV is transmitted (Golden,

Perreira, & Durrance, 2013; Jones-Webb & Karriker-Jaffe, 2013). Our findings corroborate those that link more distal factors, such as disadvantaged neighborhoods to proximate health behaviors and outcomes, including negative drinking norms, sexual risk-taking, stress reactivity, depression, and lower condom use (Bauermeister, Zimmerman, & Caldwell, 2011; Golden et al., 2013; Hackman, Betancourt, Brodsky, Hurt, & Farah, 2012; Haines, Beggs, & Hurlbert, 2011; Jones-Webb & Karriker-Jaffe, 2013; Karriker-Jaffe et al., 2012). Integrated prevention services for persons who use drugs are therefore extremely needed and useful for the reduction of HIV in these communities.

## Policy Implications

A full analysis and summary of the policy implications that are a result of this study are included in the Afterword. The interventions include topics ranging from revisions to drug policies and reductions in police profiling that contribute to high incarceration rates among men coming black communities, and unlinking school funding from property taxes so that poorer neighborhoods are not further disadvantaged by underfunding education, to microfinance solutions that empower women as community leaders while improving their social capital, to name a few. Other interventions include changes and improvements to housing, substance use, and gun control policies.

## References


Adimora, A. A., Ramirez, C., Auerbach, J. D., Aral, S. O., Hodder, S., Wingood, G., ... HIV Prevention Trials Network Women at Risk Committee. (2013). Preventing HIV infection in women. *Journal of Acquired Immune Deficiency Syndromes, 63*(Suppl 2), S168–S173. doi: 10.1097/QAI.0b013e318298a166.

Adimora, A. A., & Schoenbach, V. J. (2005). Social context, sexual networks, and racial disparities in rates of sexually transmitted infections. *Journal of Infectious Diseases, 191*(Suppl 1), S115–S122. doi:10.1086/425280.

Adimora, A. A., Schoenbach, V. J., Martinson, F. E., Coyne-Beasley, T., Doherty, I., Stancil, T. R., & Fullilove, R. E. (2006). Heterosexually transmitted HIV infection among African Americans in North Carolina. *Journal of Acquired Immune Deficiency Syndromes, 41*(5), 616–623. doi: 10.1097/01.qai.0000191382.62070.a5.

Adimora, A. A., Schoenbach, V. J., Martinson, F., Donaldson, K. H., Stancil, T. R., & Fullilove, R. E. (2004). Concurrent sexual partnerships among African Americans in the rural south. *Annals of Epidemiology, 14*(3), 155–160. doi:10.1016/S1047-2797(03)00129-7.

Aral, S. O. (2010). Partner concurrency and the STD/HIV epidemic. *Current Infectious Disease Reports, 12*(2), 134–139. doi:10.1007/s11908-010-0087-2.

Aral, S. O., Adimora, A. A., & Fenton, K. A. (2008). Understanding and responding to disparities in HIV and other sexually transmitted infections in African Americans. *Lancet, 372*(9635), 337–340. doi:10.1016/S0140-6736(08)61118-6.

Aral, S. O., & Wasserheit, J. N. (1995). Interactions among HIV, other sexually transmitted diseases, socioeconomic status, and poverty in women. In *Women at risk: Issues in the primary prevention of AIDS* (pp. 13–42). New York, NY: Plenum Press.

Bauermeister, J. A., Zimmerman, M. A., & Caldwell, C. H. (2011). Neighborhood disadvantage and changes in condom use among African American adolescents. *Journal of Urban Health, 88*(1), 66–83. doi:10.1007/s11524-010-9506-9.

Bell, E. L. J. E., & Nkomo, S. M. (2003). *Our separate ways: Black and white women and the struggle for professional identity*. Boston: Harvard Business Review Press.

Bhandari, S., Bullock, L. F., Bair-Merritt, M., Rose, L., Marcantonio, K., Campbell, J. C., & Sharps, P. (2012). Pregnant women experiencing IPV: Impact of supportive and non-supportive relationships with their mothers and other supportive adults on perinatal depression: A mixed methods analysis. *Issues in Mental Health Nursing, 33*(12), 827–837. doi: 10.3109/01612840.2012.712628.

Bishaw, A., & Fontenot, K. (2014). Poverty: 2012 and 2013. In U.S. Census Bureau (Ed.), *American community survey briefs* (pp. 9). Washington, DC: U.S. Department of Commerce—Economics and Statistics Administration, U.S. Census Bureau.

Bogart, L. M., Landrine, H., Galvan, F. H., Wagner, G. J., & Klein, D. J. (2013). Perceived discrimination and physical health among HIV-positive Black and Latino men who have sex with men. *AIDS and Behavior, 17*(4), 1431–1441. doi:10.1007/s10461-012-0397-5.

Bolton, R. (1992). AIDS and promiscuity: Muddles in the models of HIV prevention. *Medical Anthropology, 14*(2–4), 145–223. doi:10.1080/01459740.1992.9966072.

Bronfenbrenner, U. (1994). *Ecological models of human development* (International encyclopedia of education 2nd ed., Vol. 3). Oxford, UK: Elsevier.

Cene, C. W., Akers, A. Y., Lloyd, S. W., Albritton, T., Powell Hammond, W., & Corbie-Smith, G. (2011). Understanding social capital and HIV risk in rural African American communities. *Journal of General Internal Medicine, 26*(7), 737–744. doi:10.1007/s11606-011-1646-4.

Corneil, T. A., Kuyper, L. M., Shoveller, J., Hogg, R. S., Li, K., Spittal, P. M., … Wood, E. (2006). Unstable housing, associated risk behaviour, and increased risk for HIV infection among injection drug users. *Health Place, 12*(1), 79–85. doi: 10.1016/j.healthplace.2004.10.004.

Denning, P., & DiNenno, E. (2010). *Communities in crisis: Is there a generalized HIV epidemic in impoverished urban areas of the United States*? Center for Disease Control and Prevention.

Drumright, L. N., Gorbach, P. M., & Holmes, K. K. (2004). Do people really know their sex partners? Concurrency, knowledge of partner behavior, and sexually transmitted infections within partnerships. *Sexually Transmitted Diseases, 31*(7), 437–442.

El-Bassel, N., Gilbert, L., Wu, E., Chang, M., Gomes, C., Vinocur, D., & Spevack, T. (2007). Intimate partner violence prevalence and HIV risks among women receiving care in emergency departments: Implications for IPV and HIV screening. *Emergency Medicine Journal, 24*(4), 255–259. doi: 10.1136/emj.2006.041541.

Elifson, K. W., Sterk, C. E., & Theall, K. P. (2007). Safe living: The impact of unstable housing conditions on HIV risk reduction among female drug users. *AIDS and Behavior, 11*(6 Suppl), 45–55. doi:10.1007/s10461-007-9306-8.

Entmacher, J., Gallagher Robins, K., Vogtman, J., & Frohlich, L. (2013). *Insecure and unequal: Poverty and income among women and families 2000-2012*. Washington, DC: National Women's Law Center.

Eshleman, S. H., Hughes, J. P., Laeyendecker, O., Wang, J., Brookmeyer, R., Johnson-Lewis, L., … Hodder, S. (2013). Use of a multifaceted approach to analyze HIV incidence in a cohort study of women in the United States: HIV Prevention Trials Network 064 Study. *Journal of Infectious Diseases, 207*(2), 223–231. doi: 10.1093/infdis/jis658.

Ezzy, D., de Visser, R., & Bartos, M. (1999). Poverty, disease progression and employment among people living with HIV/AIDS in Australia. *AIDS Care, 11*(4), 405–414.

Fawcett, J. (1999). *The relationship of theory and research* (3rd ed.). Philadelphia, PA: FA Davis Company.

Ferguson, Y. O., Quinn, S. C., Eng, E., & Sandelowski, M. (2006). The gender ratio imbalance and its relationship to risk of HIV/AIDS among African American women at historically black colleges and universities. *AIDS Care, 18*(4), 323–331. doi:10.1080/09540120500162122.

Flom, P. L., Friedman, S. R., Kottiri, B. J., Neaigus, A., Curtis, R., Des Jarlais, D. C., … Zenilman, J. M. (2001). Stigmatized drug use, sexual partner concurrency, and other sex risk network and behavior characteristics of 18- to 24-year-old youth in a high-risk neighborhood. *Sexual Transmitted Diseases, 28*(10), 598–607.

Frew, P. M., Archibald, M., Hixson, B., & del Rio, C. (2011). Socioecological influences on community involvement in HIV vaccine research. *Vaccine, 29*(36), 6136–6143. doi:10.1016/j.vaccine.2011.06.082.

Frumence, G., Killewo, J., Kwesigabo, G., Nystrom, L., Eriksson, M., & Emmelin, M. (2010). Social capital and the decline in HIV transmission—A case study in three villages in the Kagera region of Tanzania. *SAHARA J, 7*(3), 9–20.

Garnett, G. P., & Johnson, A. M. (1997). Coining a new term in epidemiology: Concurrency and HIV. *AIDS, 11*(5), 681–683.

Gillies, P., Tolley, K., & Wolstenholme, J. (1996). Is AIDS a disease of poverty? *AIDS Care, 8*(3), 351–363. doi:10.1080/09540129650125768.

Golden, S. D., Perreira, K. M., & Durrance, C. P. (2013). Troubled times, troubled relationships: How economic resources, gender beliefs, and neighborhood disadvantage influence intimate partner violence. *Journal of Interpersonal Violence, 28*(10), 2134–2155. doi:10.1177/0886260512471083.

Gonzalez-Guarda, R. M., Vasquez, E. P., Urrutia, M. T., Villarruel, A. M., & Peragallo, N. (2011). Hispanic women's experiences with substance abuse, intimate partner violence, and risk for HIV. *Journal of Transcultural Nursing, 22*(1), 46–54. doi:10.1177/1043659610387079.

Gregson, S., Mushati, P., Grusin, H., Nhamo, M., Schumacher, C., Skovdal, M., … Campbell, C. (2011). Social capital and women's reduced vulnerability to HIV infection in rural Zimbabwe. *Population and Development Review, 37*(2), 333–359.

Hackman, D. A., Betancourt, L. M., Brodsky, N. L., Hurt, H., & Farah, M. J. (2012). Neighborhood disadvantage and adolescent stress reactivity. *Frontiers in Human Neuroscience, 6*, 277. doi:10.3389/fnhum.2012.00277.

Haines, V. A., Beggs, J. J., & Hurlbert, J. S. (2011). Neighborhood disadvantage, network social capital, and depressive symptoms. *Journal of Health and Social Behavior, 52*(1), 58–73. doi:10.1177/0022146510394951.

Hall, J. C., Everett, J. E., & Hamilton-Mason, J. (2012). Black women talk about workplace stress and how they cope. *Journal of Black Studies, 43*(2), 207–226.

Hankins, C. (2008). Gender, sex, and HIV: How well are we addressing the imbalance? *Current Opinion in HIV and AIDS, 3*(4), 514–520. doi:10.1097/COH.0b013e32830136b4.

Harris, A. L. (2010). The economic and educational state of Black Americans in the 21st century: Should we be optimistic or concerned? *The Review of Black Political Economy, 37*(3–4), 241–252. doi:10.1007/s12114-010-9065-z.

Hodder, S. L., Justman, J., Hughes, J. P., Wang, J., Haley, D. F., Adimora, A. A., … Women's HIV SeroIncidence Study Team. (2013). HIV acquisition among women from selected areas of the United States: a cohort study. *Annals of Internal Medicine, 158*(1), 10–18. doi: 10.7326/0003-4819-158-1-201301010-00004.

Inciardi, J. A., & Surratt, H. L. (1998). Children in the streets of Brazil: Drug use, crime, violence, and HIV risks. *Substance Use & Misuse, 33*(7), 1461–1480.

Jones-Webb, R., & Karriker-Jaffe, K. J. (2013). Neighborhood disadvantage, high alcohol content beverage consumption, drinking norms, and drinking consequences: A mediation analysis. *Journal of Urban Health, 90*(4), 667–684. doi:10.1007/s11524-013-9786-y.

Kakietek, J., Geberselassie, T., Manteuffel, B., Ogungbemi, K., Krivelyova, A., Bausch, S., … Gar, S. (2013). It takes a village: Community-based organizations and the availability and utilization of HIV/AIDS-related services in Nigeria. *AIDS Care, 25*(Suppl 1), S78–S87. doi: 10.1080/09540121.2012.740158.

Karriker-Jaffe, K. J., Zemore, S. E., Mulia, N., Jones-Webb, R., Bond, J., & Greenfield, T. K. (2012). Neighborhood disadvantage and adult alcohol outcomes: Differential risk by race and gender. *Journal of Studies on Alcohol and Drugs, 73*(6), 865–873.

Kidder, D. P., Wolitski, R. J., Royal, S., Aidala, A., Courtenay-Quirk, C., Holtgrave, D. R., … Housing and Health Study Team. (2007). Access to housing as a structural intervention for homeless and unstably housed people living with HIV: Rationale, methods, and implementation of the housing and health study. *AIDS and Behavior, 11*(6 Suppl), 149–161. doi: 10.1007/s10461-007-9249-0.

Konkle-Parker, D. J., Erlen, J. A., & Dubbert, P. M. (2008). Barriers and facilitators to medication adherence in a southern minority population with HIV disease. *Journal of the Association of Nurses in AIDS Care, 19*(2), 98–104. doi:10.1016/j.jana.2007.09.005.

Lipsitz, G. (2011). "In an avalanche every snowflake pleads not guilty": The collateral consequences of mass incarceration and impediments to women's fair housing rights. *UCLA Law Review, 59*, 1746–1809.

Marshall, B. D., Kerr, T., Shoveller, J. A., Patterson, T. L., Buxton, J. A., & Wood, E. (2009). Homelessness and unstable housing associated with an increased risk of HIV and STI transmission among street-involved youth. *Health & Place, 15*(3), 753–760. doi:10.1016/j.healthplace.2008.12.005.

Mason, C. N., Salas, D., Ebanks, J., & Bowser, K. (2013). *Economic security and well-being index for women in New York City*. New York, NY: The New York Women's Foundation.

Mayer, K. H., Pape, J. W., Wilson, P., Diallo, D. D., Saavedra, J., Mimiaga, M. J., … Farmer, P. (2012). Multiple determinants, common vulnerabilities, and creative responses: Addressing the AIDS pandemic in diverse populations globally. *Journal of Acquired Immune Deficiency Syndromes, 60*(Suppl 2), S31–S34. doi: 10.1097/QAI.0b013e31825c16d9.

Meader, N., Semaan, S., Halton, M., Bhatti, H., Chan, M., Llewellyn, A., & Des Jarlais, D. C. (2013). An international systematic review and meta-analysis of multisession psychosocial interventions compared with educational or minimal interventions on the HIV sex risk behaviors of people who use drugs. *AIDS and Behavior, 17*(6), 1963–1978. doi: 10.1007/s10461-012-0403-y.

Ms. Foundation for Women. (2013). *More to do: The road to equality for women in the United States*. Brooklyn, NY: Ms. Foundation for Women.

National Alliance of State and Territorial AIDS Directors. (2008). *The landscape of HIV/AIDS among African American women in the United States* (Issue Brief No. 1 ed.). Washington, DC: National Alliance of State and Territorial AIDS Directors.

National Coalition Against Domestic Violence. (2014). *Intimate partner violence and HIV/AIDS quick facts*. Retrieved from http://www.ncadv.org/files/Quick_Facts_About_Domestic_Violence_and_HIV_AIDS.doc

National Low Income Housing Coalition. (2012). Who lives in federally assisted housing? In M. Bolton (Ed.), *Housing spotlight* (Vol. 2, p. 6). Washington, DC: National Low Income Housing Coalition.

National Minority AIDS Council, & Housing Works. (2013). *Mass incarceration, housing instability and HIV/AIDS: Research findings and policy recommendations*. In G. Shubert (Ed.), National Minority AIDS Council.

National Women's Law Center. (2000, June 30). *Sex discrimination in the American workplace: Still a fact of life*. Retrieved December 8, 2014, from http://www.nwlc.org/resource/sex-discrimination-american-workplace-still-fact-life

National Women's Law Center. (2013a, July 23). *60 Percent of women's job gains in the recovery are in the 10 largest low-wage jobs*. Retrieved 2014, from http://www.nwlc.org/resource/60-percent-women%E2%80%99s-job-gains-recovery-are-10-largest-low-wage-jobs

National Women's Law Center. (2013b, August). *Women sharing in slow job growth, but full recovery is a long way off*. Retrieved 2014, from http://www.nwlc.org/resource/women-sharing-slow-job-growth-full-recovery-long-way

Newsome, V., & Airhihenbuwa, C. O. (2013). Gender ratio imbalance effects on HIV risk behaviors in African American women. *Health Promotion Practice, 14*(3), 459–463. doi:10.1177/1524839912460869.

Okechukwu, C. A., El Ayadi, A. M., Tamers, S. L., Sabbath, E. L., & Berkman, L. (2012). Household food insufficiency, financial strain, work-family spillover, and depressive symp-

toms in the working class: The Work, Family, and Health Network study. *American Journal of Public Health, 102*(1), 126–133. doi:10.2105/AJPH.2011.300323.
Perez, S., Johnson, D. M., & Wright, C. V. (2012). The attenuating effect of empowerment on IPV-related PTSD symptoms in battered women living in domestic violence shelters. *Violence Against Women, 18*(1), 102–117. doi:10.1177/1077801212437348.
Renzetti, C. M. (2013). Identified intimate partner violence (IPV) as a risk for women in contracting HIV/AIDS and other sexually transmitted disease. *Violence Against Women, 19*(7), 811–813.
Riley, E. D., Gandhi, M., Hare, C., Cohen, J., & Hwang, S. (2007). Poverty, unstable housing, and HIV infection among women living in the United States. *Current HIV/AIDS Reports, 4*(4), 181–186.
Saylors, K., & Daliparthy, N. (2005). Native women, violence, substance abuse and HIV risk. *Journal of Psychoactive Drugs, 37*(3), 273–280.
Schwartz, R. M., Bruno, D. M., Augenbraun, M. A., Hogben, M., Joseph, M. A., Liddon, N., … Wilson, T. E. (2011). Perceived financial need and sexual risk behavior among urban, minority patients following sexually transmitted infection diagnosis. *Sexually Transmitted Diseases, 38*(3), 230–234. doi: 10.1097/OLQ.0b013e3181f41b81.
Soto, T., Komaie, G., Neilands, T. B., & Johnson, M. O. (2013). Exposure to crime and trauma among HIV-infected men who have sex with men: Associations with HIV stigma and treatment engagement. *Journal of the Association of Nurses in AIDS Care, 24*(4), 299–307. doi:10.1016/j.jana.2012.11.008.
Stayton, C., Olson, C., Thorpe, L., Kerker, B., Henning, K., & Wilt, S. (2008). *Intimate partner violence against women in New York City, 2008.* Report from the New York City Department of Health and Mental Hygiene (pp. 1–21). New York, NY: New York City Department of Health and Mental Hygiene.
Su, X., Lau, J. T., Mak, W. W., Chen, L., Choi, K. C., Song, J., … Cheng, J. (2013). Perceived discrimination, social support, and perceived stress among people living with HIV/AIDS in China. *AIDS Care, 25*(2), 239–248. doi: 10.1080/09540121.2012.701713.
Sumartojo, E., Doll, L., Holtgrave, D., Gayle, H., & Merson, M. (2000). Enriching the mix: Incorporating structural factors into HIV prevention. *AIDS, 14*(Suppl 1), S1–S2.
Sweet, E., Nandi, A., Adam, E. K., & McDade, T. W. (2013). The high price of debt: Household financial debt and its impact on mental and physical health. *Social Science & Medicine, 91*, 94–100. doi:10.1016/j.socscimed.2013.05.009.
U.S. Census Bureau. (2013a). *2013 American community survey 1-year estimates, table S1701.* Retrieved from http://factfinder2.census.gov/faces/tableservices/jsf/pages/productview.xhtml?pid=ACS_13_1YR_S1701&prodType=table
U.S. Census Bureau. (2013b). *Current population survey, annual social and economic supplement—Poverty status in 2012.* Retrieved from http://www.census.gov/cps/data/cpstablecreator.html
U.S. Census Bureau. (2014). *Poverty: The history of a measure.* In U.S. Census Bureau (Ed.). Washington, DC: U.S. Department of Commerce—Economics and Statistics Administration, U.S. Census Bureau.
U.S. Equal Employment Opportunity Commission. (2013). *African American workgroup report.* Washington, DC: U.S. Equal Employment Opportunity Commission.
Women of Color Network. (2006). *Domestic violence: Communities of color.* Harrisburg, PA: Women of Color Network.

# Chapter 4
# Food Insecurity Experienced by Women Living in Poverty

**Ann O'Leary, Ilana Gabrielle Raskind, and Melissa Turner**

*"I learned that you could drink water and still be all right."*

## Introduction

The United States Department for Agriculture (USDA) estimated that in 2013 over 14 % of US households were food insecure, which is defined as having occurred when "the food intake of one or more household members was reduced and their eating patterns were disrupted at times during the year because the household lacked money and other resources for food" (Coleman-Jensen, Nord, & Singh, 2013; USDA, 2014). Significant disparities in the prevalence of food insecurity exist by race, ethnicity, gender, household structure, and economic status. Black (non-Hispanic) and Hispanic households are disproportionately affected by food insecurity with a prevalence of 26.1 % and 23.7 %, respectively. Strikingly, single female–headed households with children under the age of 18 have a food insecurity prevalence of 34.4 %, and over 42 % of households with incomes below the federal poverty line (FPL) are food insecure (USDA, 2014). While poverty and food insecurity are not synonymous, they are integrally connected (Gundersen, 2013). In 2008, at the height of the Great Recession, the prevalence of food insecurity increased by over 30 %. This was the largest increase in prevalence since food insecurity was first measured in 1995; minimal improvement has occurred since this time (Gundersen, 2013).

A. O'Leary (✉)
Atlanta, GA, USA
e-mail: aoleary@cdc.gov

I.G. Raskind
Department of Behavioral Science and Health Education, Rollins School of Public Health, Emory University, Atlanta, GA, USA

M. Turner
Infectious Diseases Section, Veterans Affairs Medical Center, Washington, DC, USA

 
A. O'Leary, P.M. Frew (eds.), *Poverty in the United States*,
DOI 10.1007/978-3-319-43833-7_4

Existing research has identified associations between food insecurity and numerous short- and long-term academic, social, and health consequences. Academic performance and social functioning (Jyoti, Frongillo, & Jones, 2005), depressive disorders (Alaimo, Olson, & Frongillo, 2002), nutritional deficiencies (Skalicky et al., 2006), and chronic disease (Seligman, Laraia, & Kushel, 2010) have all been identified as correlates of food insecurity. A rapidly growing body of literature is investigating the seemingly paradoxical association between food insecurity and obesity. A review of the literature conducted by Larson and Story (2011) identified consistent and complex associations between food insecurity and weight status. In the studies reviewed, food-insecure women were more likely to be obese than their food-secure counterparts. Evidence suggests that food-insecure households may consume more highly palatable, unhealthy foods to cope with the stress of food insecurity, and may overeat at the beginning of each month upon receipt of Supplemental Nutrition Assistance Program benefits (SNAP; formerly the Food Stamp Program), which typically run out toward the end of the month (Laraia, 2013; Leung, Epel, Ritchie, Crawford, & Laraia, 2014).

The federal SNAP is the nation's primary tool for mitigating food insecurity and hunger (Gundersen, 2013). The history of government food assistance to low-income families dates to the 1930s. Following the Great Depression, surplus commodities had accrued as a result of government attempts to stabilize farm prices; rather than disposing of the surplus, commodities were distributed to those in need. During this period and the decades that followed, a tension could be observed between the prioritization of food assistance programs as a way to dispose of agricultural surplus versus as a tool for providing nutritional assistance to individuals and families living in poverty (Ohls & Beebout, 1993). While nutrition assistance remains linked to agricultural policy today, President Lyndon B. Johnson's War on Poverty and the passage of the Food Stamp Act of 1964 solidified government food assistance as a key feature of poverty alleviation strategies (Oliveira, Tiehen, & Ver Ploeg, 2014).

Food insecurity and hunger were reintroduced into public dialogue with the airing of the 1969 CBS documentary "Hunger in America." The footage depicted a deeply impoverished Mississippi Delta where African-American sharecroppers were struggling to put food on the table and were unable to acquire the funds necessary to purchase food stamps. Many Americans were deeply shocked and disturbed by what they saw, and an antihunger movement burgeoned from this sentiment (Poppendieck, 1999). Advocacy efforts ultimately led to federal expansion of the Food Stamp Program and the phasing out of the purchase requirement. Today, the USDA administers 15 federal food assistance programs including SNAP, the Special Supplemental Nutrition Assistance Program for Women, Infants, and Children (WIC), and the National School Lunch Program (NSLP). Approximately 47 million people receive SNAP benefits, at an average amount of $133 per person per month (USDA, 2014). In 2009, in the context of rising food insecurity, unemployment, and poverty rates, the American Recovery and Reinvestment Act temporarily increased the maximum monthly benefit amount by 13.6% (Oliveira et al., 2014). However, this increase ended in November 2013, resulting in an average benefit reduction of 5.6 % for a family of four receiving the maximum benefit (Oliveira, 2014). It is important to note that the data reported below were collected prior to the 2013 benefit reduction.

Despite the successes of SNAP and other federal food assistance programs, food insecurity persists. As a result of insufficient benefit amounts, administrative barriers, incomplete participation rates, and various other factors unrelated to income, many individuals and families rely on emergency food sources, such as food banks and soup kitchens, as well as more informal channels, such as the sharing of resources between family, friends, and neighbors, to acquire food. Prior research has catalogued the numerous coping strategies people employ to manage food insecurity (Ahluwalia, Dodds, & Baligh, 1998; Anater, McWilliams, & Latkin, 2011; Kempson, Keenan, Sadani, & Adler, 2003; Swanson, Olson, Miller, & Lawrence, 2008; Wood, Shultz, Edlefsen, & Butkus, 2006), many of which may pose nutritional, legal, food safety, physical, and financial risks (Anater et al., 2011; Kempson et al., 2003), ranging from the consumption of expired or spoiled foods to the exchange of sex for money. Further, households experiencing a higher degree of food insecurity may be more likely to use more and riskier strategies (Chilton, Rabinowich, Breen, & Mouzon, 2013; Wood et al., 2006).

Given the significant disparities that exist in the prevalence of food insecurity, listening to the voices, experiences, and expertise of those most affected can facilitate the identification of factors salient to effectively addressing the causes and consequences of food insecurity. Viewing the issues of food insecurity and hunger from within a human rights framework can also assist in this endeavor. Such an approach requires consideration of the social and economic processes that underlie food insecurity, and poverty more generally, such as poor educational and employment opportunities, lack of access to health care, and housing instability (Chilton & Rose, 2009). The following section details, in their own words, how women living in poverty experience and cope with food insecurity and hunger.

## Interview and Focus Group Results

HPTN 064 participants experienced food insecurity and hunger as ongoing daily struggles. Yet, women described a variety of coping strategies they employed for mitigating the effects of such experiences. Women reported making trade-offs between eating and other necessities; using formal and informal food assistance resources, such as SNAP, food pantries, and borrowing food from family members; and engaging in high-risk behaviors, such as theft and the exchange of sex for money. As one woman explained, while there were many times when she was hungry and did not have enough money for food:

> … [I] end up thinking of something you know to survive. That's just how I've been raised so I'll end up thinking of something.
>
> —*Interviewee, Washington, D.C.*

## *Trade-Offs*

Women reported coping with food insecurity by making trade-offs between eating and other necessities. Mothers reported skipping meals in order to feed their children. As one woman shared:

> I mean it's not really a decision to be made. It's either they're going to be hungry or I'm going to be hungry. And, I'd rather for myself to be hungry.
>
> —*Interviewee, Washington, D.C.*

Women also described needing to prioritize and assist other family members who were challenged by their own limited incomes:

> … I got to give to my mother you know what I'm saying. She on a fixed income you know what I'm saying. She can only afford like to pay her phone bill so I have to get her first … so, yeah it's hard …
>
> —*Focus Group Participant, Washington, D.C.*

Sometimes women were forced to choose between basic necessities, such as eating and obtaining feminine hygiene products. One woman explained how the need to make this trade-off taught her about her body's ability to survive without food:

> Either I could go get something to eat or I could get me some pads. So, the pads come first, you know … feminine [products] comes before me eating because I learned that you could drink water and still be all right, you know. I know … how many meals I can skip and be all right as long as I drink water and don't get dehydrated.
>
> —*Interviewee, Raleigh/Durham, NC*

## *Food Assistance*

Women described using a variety of formal and informal food assistance resources when faced with food insecurity and hunger. When discussing the use of formal resources, such as SNAP, women described several problems such as administrative barriers to obtaining benefits and receiving insufficient benefits. Women also reported that they, and others in their communities, frequently used a variety of emergency food resources, such as food pantries and soup kitchens. Finally, women discussed the need to rely on informal assistance, such as borrowing food from family members. Women reported relying on family when in need, as well as giving to those whom they viewed as less fortunate than themselves.

### SNAP

Women described the insufficiency of SNAP benefits, including how administrative rules do not take into consideration that recipients may be assisting other adults in their households. As one woman explained:

> It's terrible! I get food stamps but I used to get like two something and now I get like $83.00 [per month]. That's not enough to feed me and my two [children].
>
> Like, I run out of food so quick, it's not even funny … but I think the only reason why it went down to $83.00 is because I stay with my mom and my step-dad. And I'm looking like, OK, well, sometimes they don't have money to go get food, you know. I had the money to actually, you know, help out …. to put food in the house so everyone could eat.
>
> —*Interviewee, Raleigh/Durham, NC*

Women also discussed the difficulties associated with obtaining SNAP benefits to begin with:

> But it's the point of how they make the process go … I tried to go get me some food stamps, and [the office] had me in there for like, six hours. I left. But I want some food stamps.
>
> —*Focus Group Participant, New York, NY*

Women who were receiving SNAP benefits discussed the challenges associated with budgeting and planning ahead to try to make the benefit last for the entire month. One woman explained:

> You have to sit on your food stamps … You have to buy enough food, you know how I do with my food stamps I … buy four meats because it's four Sunday's in a month. I can buy four meats for Sunday … so, you got to go home and cook and prepare the food and all of that, so yes it's hard.
>
> —*Focus Group Participant, Washington, D.C.*

## Emergency Food Resources

Women discussed using emergency food resources, such as soup kitchens and food pantries, as part of their regular routines and weekly schedules. As one woman shared:

> I've done that, you know, I've done it. I used to go every Wednesday to [the soup kitchen] … I used to tell my daughter … "come on, we're going here today, I'm not cooking today." Every Wednesday I used to hit the church and I used to eat. You know, go to the … food pantries every Saturday, you know?
>
> —*Focus Group Participant, New York, NY*

Not only did women describe using emergency food resources themselves, but they also described the high demand for these resources in their communities. One woman explained:

> Because especially in that neighborhood, there's food pantries, because there is one downstairs in my mother's building … and they be so deep, it's like—my mom's building is a courtyard building, and they will be blocking the entrance, and the super will be like, "Y'all cannot stand here. Like, move." Then they got churches over there. Yeah. There's like, three churches over that do food pantries. Food stamps, everybody get food stamps right now.
>
> —*Focus Group Participant, New York, NY*

Another woman reinforced the prevalence of hunger in her community and the need for emergency food resources:

> That's why they have these soup kitchens and pantries and places for people to go, because people are hungry. I have friends that come to my house starving, so I know. It's like that.
>
> —*Focus Group Participant, New York, NY*

However, despite reliance on these resources, the food available was described as being of poor quality. One woman described her experience as a volunteer with a food distribution service:

> They may have like a food shuttle come around on certain days of the week that drop off food, but the thing is … Their food is old. They go from different stores, like, you know how the grocery store might say, "This is not appropriate to put on our shelf"? They throw it to the back, food shuttle come around and get it, they go to restaurants and get their old leftover food. They try to freeze 'em, but then they still hand it out in the 'hood to the black folks and people actually fight over the food.
>
> *—Focus Group Participant, Raleigh/Durham, NC*

However, this food was very much in demand and people were willing to go to extreme lengths to acquire it:

> Like today my mama staying on the [place of residence]. I was over at her house and a little truck come at 1:00. Oh, people out there, they knocking the old folks down, and they know better. These people are getting $600 off of food stamps, selling food stamps so they can be fly, and you're gonna knock this old lady down 'cause she can't get food stamps. She don't have no social security benefits and she need these little collard greens and these potatoes and you're gonna knock her down? And your home girl working in there distributing the food, she's taking all the snacks and stuff and giving it to her friend down the yard. I mean it's just not right. There's people that actually need that stuff and there's people that don't really care and they're just trying to be greedy, or they get food stamps and they put it in the house, "Girl, I might need me a little snack too, girl. I'm gonna go get this too." Kitchen pantry, refrigerator, bottom cabinets and everything be full, but they're still being greedy and it's sad.
>
> *—Focus Group Participant, Raleigh/Durham, NC*

## Informal Support

Women discussed the need to reach out to family members for support when they did not have enough money or SNAP benefits to feed themselves and their children. As one woman explained:

> But if I do go without food, I probably … it would be for a week but I'd go to my mother or my sister house and stay over there for a week until well…I get food stamps … I was kind of short this month, they didn't come so … [I] just bring [child] over here or my mama will send some food.
>
> *—Interviewee, Raleigh/Durham, NC*

Despite the extreme poverty reported by the HPTN 064 participants, many women described sharing their limited resources with others in their community who they perceived of as worse off than they were. One woman shared:

> Yes. They knock, and they try to borrow stuff, and I always make sure I give it to them, because I don't like to see nobody in need or whatever. I like to always help out the next person … You never know when we're going to be like that. So … always help out.
>
> *—Focus Group Participant, New York, NY*

Another woman explained that because she lives next to a supermarket, people in her community frequently ask her if she can provide them with money for food.

> People in general, I know that people in my neighborhood, they've asked me for money … because there's a supermarket right next to my house, and they've asked me for money for food, you know? And they've said that they needed food for their kids and I said, "Well, I'm not going to give you money, but if you tell me what you need, I'll get it for you." You know? And I've done that.
>
> —*Focus Group Participant, New York, NY*

## *High-Risk Coping Strategies*

Women reported engaging in several high-risk behaviors in order to obtain food, or money for food, for themselves and their families. Exchanging sex for money, theft, and selling plasma were all reported as coping strategies.

### Sex Exchange

Women described exchanging sex for money as a last resort when they were hungry and needed money for food. Women discussed their own actions as well as observing the actions of other women in their communities. One woman described her actions as a source of shame:

> … I can always call somebody if I'm hungry. You know what I'm saying? You know there's alternative ways too, you know, that I'm not so proud of … but I do, do them … It ain't nothing to call one of my little friends and tell them, you know what I'm saying? You know, I'll do this for you and you know, they'll give me some money.
>
> —*Interviewee, Atlanta, GA*

Other women also highlighted this sense of desperation:

> You got grown women still do it. You got a grown woman out here claiming to go to school and somebody supposed to be giving them money and at the same time they running around sucking dick for $20 just so that they can have something to eat.
>
> —*Focus Group Participant, Washington, D.C.*

While exchanging sex for money was discussed as a last resort, it was also described in the context of an obligation to ensuring the health of oneself and one's children. One woman reflected on her community:

> There's girls out here that I know that you would never imagine in your wildest dreams that they would do the type of things they do. But crunch times, you got your kids, you got to feed your baby. You got to feed yourself. They out here streaking or whatever you want to call it just to make sure that they good and they baby good, because at the end of the day, if they ain't watching out for their kids, ain't nobody else gone do it. I mean, people is resorting to any and everything at the end of the day, just to make sure they're getting—they're gonna eat, and their baby's gonna eat.
>
> —*Focus Group Participant, Raleigh/Durham, NC*

Overall, the need to exchange sex for money was discussed as closely tied to the experience of living in poverty.

> I think that's why we're poor and that's why women are selling they asses in my [location]! Because we poor! We cannot feed our kids!
>
> —*Focus Group Participant, New York, NY*

## Theft

Similar to discussions of sex exchange, engaging in theft was also described as a last resort. Women described their willingness and commitment to do whatever was necessary to take care of themselves and their families. One woman discussed theft in the context of increased desperation experienced by families during the economic downturn.

> Tricking, selling drugs. I mean, last resort, stealing. I mean, anything. It's—I done seen some that are the worst-case scenarios in the past two years than I ever seen just with, you know, the economy being the way that it is. Like people will steal—I mean, your—right in front of your face, like that you see every day, they will steal and do whatever, just to make sure that they are good. Like [other participant] said, it's all for them. Like crunch time, it's all about you and yours. It's forget everybody else. It don't matter. You ain't doing—you can't benefit me, I'm gonna make sure I'm fine before the end of the day. I don't really care about you.
>
> —*Focus Group Participant, Raleigh/Durham, NC*

Even if women did not report currently engaging in theft, it was discussed as a viable option—particularly if children were involved—when no alternative solutions existed.

> Participant 1: I just go to my baby father. But if he ain't got it, because we're going to eat, girl I would go to the Giant and steal, hmmm. It ain't actually stealing but I'd take it back to the Giant and let them eat … My kids will never be homeless. Not saying that I did that before you all but I'm just saying. If I ever had to, yes I would.
>
> Participant 2: Go to Giant and steal. I don't; actually, people do be stealing though.
>
> —*Focus Group, Washington, D.C.*

> Five-finger discount. [Laughing]
>
> —*Focus Group Participant, Atlanta, GA*

## Selling Plasma

Sex was not the only commodity that could be transformed into money. One woman reported regularly selling her blood:

> As I say, we're both out of work and both of them are still in pampers. So, it's kind of hard … to … buy pampers for the babies. We're making ends meet at that right now 'cause we're both out donating plasma just to get the little money we can to just get pampers for them … [We can get] about $60 a week … twice. We can't donate over two times a week.
>
> —*Interviewee, Raleigh/Durham, NC*

### *Empathy and Generosity: Sharing with Others*

One woman felt so sorry for a neighbor's children on Thanksgiving that she fed them and inadvertently deprived her own son of his dinner—whatever else was going on in her life, she surprised herself by being extra generous:

> Before it was more not that sharing, but now it's a little bit more consideration for the next person that they don't have. And for Thanksgiving, I don't know people in the building, but it was kids and the young lady kids in the hallway and I know she got a couple of them. And I'm so mean at times, Lord forgive me, but I was just like, listening to them, so I just made plates—and what I didn't realize that I made so much plates for her kids, that there was no leftovers and my son was more like—but Thanksgiving was over. His attitude was really—I was like, you have to look at it that we had enough, and I didn't know—OK, I should have made you a plate but I forgot. Like, caught up in the mix of it, and there's no more. But you can't get upset with them.
>
> —*Focus Group Participant, New York, NY*

## Policy Implications

Hunger is a significant problem globally. In fact, the eradication of extreme poverty and hunger is the first Millennium Development Goal of the United Nations (United Nations General Assembly, 2001). That close to 16 million children under the age of 18 in the USA should live in households incapable of supplying adequate nutrition for health (Coleman-Jensen et al., 2013) is cruel and unjust. It is imperative that we sustain and expand food assistance programs such as SNAP, WIC, and the National School Lunch Program. Food availability is affected by many factors, including the public transportation infrastructure, employment policies, and, as mentioned above, taxation policies. Efforts to help farmers' markets to accept food stamps are also helpful. No one should have to worry about where their own, or their children's, next meal is coming from.

Based on the information contained in this chapter, we recommend:

- Expanding federal assistance, e.g., increasing SNAP benefit amount.
- Expanding food access, e.g., placement of affordable and healthy grocery stores in neighborhoods.
- New initiatives that fall under the blanket of "community food security," which include farmers' market incentive programs, urban gardening, etc.
- Recognition that food provision and market-based solutions (e.g., emergency food, community food security initiatives) to food insecurity cannot be relied on to the exclusion of addressing the root causes of food insecurity, namely structural issues related to poverty, such as educational and employment opportunities and access to health care.
- Addressing factors less related to financial resources/income that have found to be associated with food insecurity, such as mental health, childhood trauma, and

violence. Including addressing high-risk behaviors associated with poverty and food insecurity like sex exchange.

## References


Ahluwalia, I. B., Dodds, J. M., & Baligh, M. (1998). Support and coping behaviors of low-income families experiencing food insufficiency in North Carolina. *Health Education and Behavior, 25*(5), 599–612.

Alaimo, K., Olson, C. M., & Frongillo, E. A. (2002). Family food insufficiency, but not low family income, is positively associated with dysthymia and suicide symptoms in adolescents. *The Journal of Nutrition, 132*(4), 719–725.

Anater, A. S., McWilliams, R., & Latkin, C. A. (2011). Food acquisition practices used by food-insecure individuals when they are concerned about having sufficient food for themselves and their households. *Journal of Hunger & Environmental Nutrition, 6*, 27–44.

Chilton, M., Rabinowich, J., Breen, A., & Mouzon, S. (2013). *When the systems fail: Individual and household coping strategies related to child hunger*. Retrieved from http://sites.nationalacademies.org/DBASSE/CNSTAT/DBASSE_081775

Chilton, M., & Rose, D. (2009). A rights-based approach to food insecurity in the United States. *American Journal of Public Health, 99*(7), 1203–1211. doi:10.2105/AJPH.2007.130229.

Coleman-Jensen, A., Nord, M., & Singh, A. (2013). *Household food security in the United States in 2012*. Washington, DC: U.S. Department of Agriculture, Economic Research Service.

Gundersen, C. (2013). Food insecurity is an ongoing national concern. *Advances in Nutrition, 4*(1), 36–41. doi:10.3945/an.112.003244.

Jyoti, D. F., Frongillo, E. A., & Jones, S. J. (2005). Food insecurity affects school children's academic performance, weight gain, and social skills. *The Journal of Nutrition, 135*(12), 2831–2839.

Kempson, K., Keenan, D. P., Sadani, P. S., & Adler, A. (2003). Maintaining food sufficiency: Coping strategies identified by limited-resource individuals versus nutrition educators. *Journal of Nutrition Education and Behavior, 35*(4), 179–188.

Laraia, B. A. (2013). Food insecurity and chronic disease. *Advances in Nutrition, 4*(2), 203–212. doi:10.3945/an.112.003277.

Larson, N. I., & Story, M. T. (2011). Food insecurity and weight status among U.S. children and families: A review of the literature. *American Journal of Preventive Medicine, 40*(2), 166–173.

Leung, C. W., Epel, E. S., Ritchie, L. D., Crawford, P. B., & Laraia, B. A. (2014). Food insecurity is inversely associated with diet quality of lower-income adults. *Journal of the Academy of Nutrition and Dietetics, 114*(12), 1943–1953.e1942. Retrieved from http://dx.doi.org/10.1016/j.jand.2014.06.353

Ohls, J., & Beebout, H. (1993). *The food stamp program: Design tradeoffs, policy, and impacts*. Washington, DC: The Urban Institute Press.

Oliveira, V. (2014). *The food assistance landscape: FY 2013 annual report, EIB-120*. Economic Research Service: USDA.

Oliveira, V., Tiehen, L., & Ver Ploeg, M. (2014). USDA's food assistance programs: Legacies of the war on poverty. *Amber Waves*. Retrieved August 21, 2015.

Poppendieck, J. (1999). *Sweet charity? Emergency food and the end of entitlement*. London: Penguin.

Seligman, H. K., Laraia, B. A., & Kushel, M. B. (2010). Food insecurity is associated with chronic disease among low-income NHANES participants. *The Journal of Nutrition, 140*(2), 304–310.

Skalicky, A., Meyers, A. F., Adams, W. G. et al. (2006). *Matern Child Health J 10, 177*. doi:10.1007/s10995-005-0036-0.

Swanson, J. A., Olson, C. M., Miller, E. O., & Lawrence, F. C. (2008). Rural mothers' use of formal programs and informal social supports to meet family food needs: A mixed methods study. *Journal of Family Economic Issues, 29*, 674–690.

United Nations General Assembly (2001). *Road map towards the implementation of the United Nations Millennium Declaration: Report of the Secretary-General. A/56/326.* United Nations

USDA. (2014). *Food insecurity in the U.S., 2015*. Retrieved from http://www.ers.usda.gov/topics/food-nutrition-assistance/food-security-in-the-us.aspx

Wood, D. K., Shultz, J. A., Edlefsen, M., & Butkus, S. N. (2006). Food coping strategies used by food pantry clients at different levels of household food security status. *Journal of Hunger & Environmental Nutrition, 1*(3), 45–68.

# Chapter 5
# Poverty, Personal Experiences of Violence, and Mental Health: Understanding Their Complex Intersections Among Low-Income Women

**Carol E. Golin, Oluwakemi Amola, Anna Dardick, Brooke Montgomery, Lauren Bishop, Sharon Parker, and Lauren E. Owens**

*"Oh God, I hate to talk about this ..."*

**A Case Study** *Outpatient therapist (OPT) arrived at client's home; the client was engaging and welcoming throughout the session. OPT informed client about the therapeutic process. OPT and client discussed her previous experience with counseling and clarified her expectations for future sessions. Client is currently under the care of a psychiatrist at [local community mental health center]. Client shared that she did not feel listened to or understood by her previous counselor; instead she felt judged. Client reported a diagnosis of bipolar disorder (prescribed Risperdal) and a history of substance use (powder cocaine). Client reported achieving sobriety in 2008 and 2011. Client also shared that she is concerned that she may test positive for marijuana by her probation officer because she uses marijuana to cope with the stress in her life. She was convicted of felony check fraud, which she used to obtain food and other necessities for the children in her home. Currently, there is no air-conditioning in the home, which adds to her stress. In the middle of the session,*

C.E. Golin (✉)
Cecil G. Sheps Center for Health Services Research, University of North Carolina at Chapel Hill, Chapel Hill, NC, USA

Department of Health Behavior, Gillings School of Global Public Health, University of North Carolina at Chapel Hill, Chapel Hill, NC, USA

Division of General Medicine and Clinical Epidemiology, School of Medicine, University of North Carolina at Chapel Hill, Chapel Hill, NC, USA
e-mail: carol_golin@med.unc.edu

O. Amola
School of Medicine and Gillings School of Global Public Health, University of North Carolina at Chapel Hill, Chapel Hill, NC, USA



A. O'Leary, P.M. Frew (eds.), *Poverty in the United States*,
DOI 10.1007/978-3-319-43833-7_5

*client's children returned home; OPT observed communication styles and relational dynamics between siblings and parent. Client displayed care and concern for the other children in the house whose mother had not been home in 3 days. Client was concerned that the other woman's children may not have eaten. Client allowed the children to go in her car trunk to get a pack of ramen noodles. She has to keep her food in her trunk to make sure that it will last through the month and not be eaten by the other people in the household or contaminated by roaches. OPT normalized client's concerns as she discussed feeling overwhelmed by overcrowding (the client, her children and grandchildren, and at least three other families are living in the three-bedroom apartment); limited resources; transportation trouble; worries about her adolescent daughter; worries about her other children (children are performing poorly in school; three of them have been held back, they also have poor behavior, they are frequently suspended and sent home); and dealing with the temptation to drink alcohol, which she believes will lead back to substance use. OPT explained the concept of triggers and worked with client to explore and identify triggers for substance use. OPT and client developed strategies for preventing relapse (i.e., identifying community resources to address unmet needs; walking, or otherwise getting out of the house, when she feels crowded; spending more time with people who support her desire for recovery, like her mother; and avoiding people who facilitate alcohol/substance use). Client felt optimistic that the plans would be helpful. OPT facilitated a deep-breathing exercise. During the deep-breathing exercise, the client's 8-year-old son came in cursing and yelling because he had just gotten into a physical altercation with a kid in the neighborhood. The child went in the kitchen to grab a knife and tried to go back outside. OPT intervened as others in the house were "hyping" up the situation. Client became very upset and wanted to go and confront the other child's mother. OPT helped the client to think through that decision. OPT assisted with deescalating the incident and ensured that the situation was under control. At session close, OPT thanked client and confirmed next meeting.*

---

A. Dardick
Division of General Medicine and Clinical Epidemiology, School of Medicine, University of North Carolina at Chapel Hill, Chapel Hill, NC, USA

B. Montgomery
Fay W. Boozman College of Public Health, University of Arkansas for Medical Sciences, Little Rock, AR, USA

L. Bishop • L.E. Owens
Division of Infectious Diseases, Department of Medicine, School of Medicine, Emory University, Atlanta, GA, USA

S. Parker
The Miriam Hospital Joint Master of Social Work Program, Division of Infectious Diseases, North Carolina A&T State University, Greensboro, NC, USA

## Introduction

The real-case example above is taken from the redacted clinical notes of a mental health therapist's home visit with a female client living in one of the HPTN 064 communities. This case illustrates the complex and myriad challenges that women living in poverty face to maintain good psychological well-being and to receive mental health treatment. Women living in poverty in the USA experience extremely high rates of mental illness, particularly depression (including major depressive disorder), anxiety disorders (including generalized anxiety disorder), and post-traumatic stress disorder (PTSD) compared with the general population (Blazer, Kessler, McGonagle, & Swartz, 1994; Gapen et al., 2011; Gillespie et al., 2009; Goodman, Smyth, Borges, & Singer, 2009; Levy & O'Hara, 2010; Lorant et al., 2003; Parto, Evans, & Zonderman, 2011; Watson, Roberts, & Saunders, 2012). Not only are rates of each of these *individual* conditions especially high among low-income women, but they also often coexist. For example, studies have recorded high rates of comorbid depression and substance abuse in individuals diagnosed with PTSD (Breslau, Davis, Andreski, Peterson, & Schultz, 1997), conditions that further complicate an individual's ability to attain psychological well-being.

Many interrelated factors contribute to high rates of psychological distress among low-income women. In addition to anxiety and depression stemming from the stress of having highly constrained financial resources, other factors that occur at disproportionate rates among low-income individuals (e.g., exposure to personal and neighborhood violence) also lead to anxiety, depression, and PTSD. Studies suggest that the negative effects of exposure to personal violence and poverty may synergistically impair low-income women's mental health. Furthermore, women's roles, both traditionally and often in actuality, add to the stressors that women face, as they carry the primary responsibility for parenting and, increasingly, as primary breadwinners. Under such circumstances, low-income women confront difficult and stressful choices between low-wage employment that may minimally enhance their families' economic resources or having more personal resources (time and attention) available for parenting. The neighborhood environment, childcare and financial responsibilities, lack of educational and employment opportunities, and stressful interpersonal encounters many low-income women experience on a daily basis conspire to interfere with their abilities to maintain positive mental health and well-being, creating a downward spiral that can be extremely difficult to address (Goodman et al., 2009). Studies show that many of the factors affecting the mental health of low-income women interact in complex and nuanced ways, presenting challenges to researchers who seek to identify a clear causal pathway to address through prevention or treatment programs.

## Mental Health of Low-Income Women

Low-income women have over twice the risk for depression as "nonpoor" women (Blazer et al., 1994; Grote, Bledsoe, Larkin, Lemay, & Brown, 2007; Watson et al., 2012). Among young minority women who are economically disadvantaged, 25 % meet the criteria for major depressive disorder (Grote, Zuckoff, Swartz, Bledsoe, & Geibel, 2007) whereas 16 % of the general population will experience this at least once in their entire lifetime (Mojtabai & Jorm, 2015). Low-income women are also significantly more likely to experience both extreme depression and anxiety than the general population (Farr, Bitsko, Hayes, & Dietz, 2010; Watson et al., 2012). PTSD is a cluster of symptoms (i.e., emotional numbing, hyperarousal, sleep disturbances, difficulty concentrating and irritability) that develop after experiencing or witnessing a traumatic, often life-threatening event. Among low-income women, reported rates of PTSD are 22–46 %, which is substantially higher than estimated in the general population (6–8 %) in epidemiologic studies and comparable to or higher than those experienced by postwar veterans (Gill, Szanton, Taylor, Page, & Campbell, 2009).

Women develop PTSD at twice the rate of men (Breslau et al., 1997; Gill et al., 2009), even in studies in which men and women have experienced exactly the same traumatic event, suggesting that women have increased vulnerability to PTSD compared with men, or are more attuned to report such symptoms (Baker et al., 2005; Norris, Murphy, Baker, & Perilla, 2004; Pulcino et al., 2003). Hence, it is believed that both women's susceptibility to develop symptoms following trauma and low-income women's increased exposure to violence and other trauma likely contribute to the high level of PTSD prevalence found among low-income women (Breslau et al., 1997, 1998; Bryant-Davis, Ullman, Tsong, Tillman, & Smith, 2010; Galea et al., 2007; Kessler, Sonnega, Bromet, Hughes, & Nelson, 1995; Taylor, Budescu, & McGill, 2011).

## Identified Reasons for the Connection Between Poverty and Poor Mental Health Among Low-Income Women

The link between mental health and income is complex with bidirectional causal pathways. Several factors, such as substance abuse, childhood abuse, and joblessness, are related to having a low income and can contribute to impaired mental health. In addition, mental illness can impair an individual's ability to maintain stable employment, leading to worsening financial stability for those suffering from psychological distress. Among women, these links must be considered in the context of recent historical trends.

A number of scholars have shown that in the last 20 years, due to policy changes, economic trends, and evolving family structures, women's incomes and employment have become progressively instrumental to the financial and social stability of low-income families (Coley & Lombardi, 2014; Corcoran, Danziger, & Tolman, 2004). Since the 1960s, the percent of families with female heads of households has nearly doubled from about 10 to 19 % (U.S. Census Bureau, 2014); among the poor (as defined by the census as those living below the census methodology-determined poverty threshold), that rate increased even more steeply from 23 % to just over 50 % (U.S. Census Bureau, 2014). Moreover, poverty levels have been rising among single-mother families over the last several years, with many female heads-of-household at low education levels (U.S. Census Bureau, 2014). Thirty-one percent of families headed by women are living in poverty, nearly three times the national poverty rate (U.S. Census Bureau, 2014). Despite the 1996 Welfare Reform Act and earned income tax credits, which have increased the job-associated incomes of single women living in poverty, the number of women living in poverty has increased due to the complex interplay of several factors, including fewer low-skilled employment opportunities for men (Coley & Lombardi, 2014) and the reduced availability of stable, long-term jobs for women with low education (Zabkiewicz, 2010).

Goodman et al. (2009) identify three main mechanisms by which poverty leads low-income women to experience increased elevated levels of anxiety and depression compared with the general population of women: (1) increased levels of chronic and acute stress experienced by poor women due to their attempts to manage multiple stressors without adequate resources to do so successfully; (2) powerlessness that women living in poverty experience due to lacking control over significant aspects of their lives; and (3) social isolation due to the lack of strong social support networks. As Goodman et al. (2009) explains, "when network members themselves are equally economically stressed and in dire need of resources, they can become conduits of stress rather than conduits of assistance." Beyond the immediate effects of stress, chronic stress can contribute to a "weathering" process, where those who experience and accumulate stress have an increased risk of disease over their lifetime, including experiencing chronic conditions earlier in life than other populations and accelerated aging (Geronimus, 2013).

A robust body of evidence has documented mental health benefits of employment, as well as the harmful effects of job loss among the general population (Zabkiewicz, 2010). However, the relationship between employment and mental health among low-income women appears to be more complex (Zabkiewicz, 2010). As family structure and work patterns evolved since the initiation of Temporary Assistance for Needy Families (TANF) for single mothers, welfare reform was conducted in 1996 to enhance the well-being of low-income single women and their families by removing legal entitlements based on need and requiring women to work based on a 5-year lifetime limit on benefits (Coley & Lombardi, 2014; Goodman et al., 2009). It was theorized that employment would enhance both women's financial resources and their self-esteem, social capital, sense of self-sufficiency, and ultimately their and their families' emotional well-being (Coley & Lombardi, 2014; Pavetti & Acs, 2001). Others contended, however, that without the education and skills needed to obtain stable and fulfilling jobs, particularly in an unstable economy, employment of poor mothers single-handedly raising children could pose added stress that would thwart psychological well-being (Coley & Lombardi, 2014). Little empirical evidence is available to settle this debate but a few studies illuminate the matter. In a recent longitudinal study among a representative sample of over 1500 mothers living in poverty in three US cities, when employment led to a significant increase in women's weekly wages, it increased economic stability, well-being, and functioning (Coley & Lombardi, 2014) but lowered levels of family routines, and depended on job quality. Similarly, a study by Zabkiewicz (2010) among single mothers showed that while employment enhanced many women's mental health, this improvement was dependent on the availability of stable, full-time, long-term jobs. An experimental study of welfare reform in New Jersey found that welfare reform reduced women's anxiety levels by 40 % but increased their levels of depression (Jagannathan, Camasso, & Sambamoorthi, 2010); however, findings were limited only to short-term welfare recipients. Results of these studies suggest that lack of adequate employment is an essential ingredient that can degrade the mental health of low-income women but that the relationship is nuanced and related to the quality of available jobs (Coley & Lombardi, 2014).

Other structural and community factors have been identified as important in the relationship between mental health and low income. For example, studies among the general population have found that having a low income (Bryant-Davis et al., 2010; Parto et al., 2011), living in a low-income neighborhood (Gapen et al., 2011), and living in a disordered neighborhood (Cutrona et al., 2005) all independently increase the risk of PTSD, above and beyond the effects of having a history of exposure to violence or ongoing violence. In addition, several studies assessing factors that contribute to resiliency among low-income women exposed to violence have shown the protective effect that access to strong social support can provide (Galea et al., 2008; Glass, Perrin, Campbell, & Soeken, 2007; Schumm, Briggs-Phillips, & Hobfoll, 2006).

## Intimate Partner Violence Among Low-Income Women

Nearly a quarter of all US women have been physically or sexually assaulted by an intimate partner (Goodman et al., 2009; Tjaden & Thoennes, 2000). Women living in poverty are disproportionately burdened by intimate partner violence (IPV) (Vest, Catlin, Chen, & Brownson, 2002). Although the efforts of early domestic violence activists to frame IPV as a classless issue of gender oppression impeded researcher and policy makers from carefully considering the complex interrelationships that exist between IPV and poverty, data are now clear that poverty and IPV are very closely linked (Goodman et al., 2009). In fact, household income is now known to be one of the strongest factors associated with IPV (Cunradi, Caetano, & Schafer, 2002; Goodman et al., 2009; Vest et al., 2002). In a multistate study by Vest et al. (2002), among a sample of 19,000 US women, those with household incomes less than $25 thousand per year were nearly twice as likely to experience IPV as those with higher incomes. Moreover, studies have shown that 30–75 % of women on

TANF have experienced IPV (cites from Goodman et al., 2009, p. 308). Only a few longitudinal studies have disentangled some of the causal pathways between IPV and poverty. Like poverty and mental illness, the pathways are bidirectional: aspects of poverty can predispose women to experience IPV and IPV can contribute to poverty. Evidence from several longitudinal as well as qualitative studies shows that women with a history of IPV are predisposed to unemployment, employment instability, and poverty by its interference with women's capacity to get and keep jobs, often due to activities by the abusive partner that directly sabotage their job status (Browne, Salomon, & Bassuk, 1999; Bybee & Sullivan, 2005; Moe & Bell, 2004; Raphael, 2000; Staggs, Long, Mason, Krishnan, & Riger, 2007).

## Effect of Intimate Partner Violence on Mental Health

As described above, exposure to all types of traumatic violence can lead to PTSD, as well as to depression and anxiety. IPV in particular is further compounded by the fact that violence is perpetrated directly against the woman, and it is carried out by an individual with whom she has an ongoing relationship. Often women in relationships involving domestic violence experience coercive psychological, physical, and economic control by their abusive partner, which leads to feelings of extreme powerlessness that result in poor mental health (Goodman et al., 2009). Moreover, due to embarrassment, shame, stigmatization, lack of understanding of others regarding their abusive situation, and in some cases fixed isolation of the women from others by their abusers, women in abusive relationships often experience social isolation (Goodman, Dutton, Vankos, & Weinfurt, 2005; Goodman et al., 2009). The combination of the trauma, stress, powerlessness, and lack of social support put women in abusive relationships at particularly high risk for poor mental health. In fact, in a large meta-analysis of prospective studies it was found that women who experienced IPV were twice as likely to suffer subsequent incident symptoms of depression (Devries et al., 2013).

## The Role of Resilience on the Mental Health of Low-Income Women

As discussed above, women living in low-income neighborhoods, particularly minority women, are confronted with a myriad of stress-evoking issues, such as experiencing personal violence and trauma, balancing home and life demands, managing personal relationships, nurturing identity development, and coping with experiences of racism and sexism that often compromise their mental and emotional health. Despite these threats to maintaining their emotional and mental health, many women living in poverty display remarkable resilience that enables them to create a purpose in life that motivates them to move themselves and their families forward toward positive goals (Holden, Bradford, Hall, & Belton, 2013).

Researchers have defined the term "resilience" in many ways (Singh, Garnett, & Williams, 2013). Some researchers examine resilience as a strategy of "bouncing back" from a specific adverse event (Masten, 2001; Werner, 2005), with characteristics that center on the individual, including an internal locus of control, hardiness, problem-solving skills, and relationship development abilities (Zautra, Arewasikporn, & Davis, 2010). Other scholars, however, observe resilience as an extended, lifetime process with characteristics that change over time and are influenced by culture and the larger social world (Williams & Mickelson, 2004). Overall, "resilience" refers to a class of phenomena characterized by the ability to maintain normal functioning despite adverse events, histories, environments, and threats to adaptation or development (Windle & Bennett, 2012). Research on resilience aims to understand the processes that account for these good outcomes. Individuals are not considered resilient if a significant current or past hazard judged to have potential to derail their normative development has never the occurred (Masten, 2001). Resilience has close ties to other concepts, such as active coping (Stevens-Watkins, Sharma, Knighton, Oser, & Leukefeld, 2014) and "John Henryism," a long-term, high-effort psychological response to stressors, such as social discrimination, coupled with strong determination to succeed through adversity (Bronder, Speight, Witherspoon, & Thomas, 2013; Flaskerud, 2012).

Some scholars relate resilience or John Henryism to the internalization of the image of the "Strong Black Woman" (Bronder et al., 2013; Romero, 2000). For some African-American women, a "Strong Black Woman" exhibits great psychological and emotional strength, manages many tasks, exhibits leadership within her family and community, and grapples with racism and sexism without complaint (Romero, 2000). Women may internalize this concept and in turn deal with depression or anxiety by burying psychological distress, preventing them from seeking clinical or psychological services (Bronder et al., 2013). This theory has been postulated to partially account for the severe disparities in mental health treatment between African-American women and other groups.

Among low-income minority women, researchers have found that several characteristics play key roles in resilience and related coping mechanisms (Banks-Wallace & Parks, 2004; Laditka, Murray, & Laditka, 2010; Stevens, 1996; Stevens-Watkins et al., 2014). Such characteristics include religious and spiritual beliefs (Laditka et al., 2010), self-esteem (Stevens, 1996), and social support (Banks-Wallace & Parks, 2004; Stevens-Watkins et al., 2014). Scholars have found that the individual components of resilience protect low-income women from the symptoms of psychological distress associated with acute and chronic stressors of poverty (Grote, Bledsoe, et al., 2007).

Spirituality refers to one's belief in the existence of a higher power that transcends space and time (Bryant-Davis et al., 2010; Yick, 2008). This concept is often described as an internalization and expression of key values, including acceptance, guidance, purpose, coping, and managing adversity (Stevens-Watkins et al., 2014). Research has shown that, among African-American women, spirituality has consistently been a significant culturally relevant aspect of resilience. In a study by Watlington and Murphy (2006), spirituality has been a protective factor associated with fewer depressive and PTSD symptoms in a sample of minority women survivors of domestic violence (Watlington & Murphy, 2006). In addition, Paranjape and Kaslow (2010) found that increased spirituality was related to improved mental health, after controlling for family violence among a sample of minority women recruited from a community health care clinic.

In addition to spirituality, self-esteem has also been found to moderate the relationship between stress and mental health outcomes (Fischer & Shaw, 1999). Self-esteem has been conceptualized as the level of global regard that one has for the self as a person. Studies suggest that African-American women generally have higher self-esteem than other groups despite racial, sexist, and economic oppression (Twenge & Campbell, 2002). Patterson (2004) found that African-American women are able to maintain high levels of self-esteem from sustained favorable social and familial ties. For this group of women, self-esteem is fundamentally community based, so that family and friendship ties contribute to building and maintaining self-esteem (Defrancisco & Chatham-Carpenter, 2000). A qualitative study by Stevens's (1996) on coping of minority women survivors of child sexual abuse found that individual components of self-esteem and the ability to develop successful agency in life were salient components of resilience. The women in this study described that finding a sense of self-worth and value played a significant role in making meaning of their experiences of sexual trauma (Singh et al., 2013). The reverse has often been shown as well: impaired self-esteem has been linked to increased anxiety (Williams & Mickelson, 2004).

Minority groups have been shown to place a greater value on interdependence and collectivism than other populations (Sue & Sue, 2008), perhaps explaining the connection of social support to resilience. Social support is a multidimensional construct generally described as the structure of a social network, the functions of the support, and the perception of support provided to an individual (Hogan, Linden, & Najarian, 2002). Overall, research demonstrates that social support is valuable in the lives of low-income women as a protective factor against stressors. Studies have shown that greater social support is significantly associated with fewer symptoms of depression (Bronder et al., 2013; Bryant-Davis, Ullman, Tsong, & Gobin, 2011; Schumm et al., 2006). Research also suggests that social support has been associated with recovery from trauma (Utsey, Bolden, Lanier, & Williams, 2007), and may buffer against PTSD (Thompson, Kaslow, Short, & Wyckoff, 2002). In addition, among women with a history of interpersonal trauma, social support may serve as an essential source for emotional well-being (Banks-Wallace & Parks, 2004).

Resilience as a whole is associated with fewer depressive symptoms in HIV+ women and those at risk for HIV who are survivors of trauma or abuse (Banks-Wallace & Parks, 2004; Dale et al., 2014; Stevens-Watkins et al., 2014). Impaired resilience leads to higher levels of anxiety in poor women (Williams & Mickelson, 2004), and greater resilience facilitated by social support, self-esteem, and spirituality leads to fewer symptoms of depression and anxiety in low-income women (Mitchell & Ronzio, 2011). Further research on the impact of spirituality, self-esteem, and social support's facilitation of resilience has the potential to positively influence the overall well-being of low-income women. Interventions designed to promote resilience are needed to assist in improving the mental health functioning of low-income women.

## The Role of Treatment on the Mental Health of Low-Income Women

Despite elevated levels of psychological distress, people of color, including women, have significant unmet needs for mental health treatment (Wang et al., 2005). They are less likely to seek treatment, less likely to be prescribed antidepressants, and less likely to stay in treatment once they begin (Conner et al., 2010; Ward & Heidrich, 2009). In a systematic review, Buser (2009) showed differences in diagnoses and prescriptions for people of color with mental illness. Symptoms of mental illness in people of color are inadequately detected and recognized, leading to improper diagnosis (Hines-Martin, Malone, Kim, & Brown-Piper, 2003; Williams & Williams-Morris, 2000). For mental health care, people of color are much more likely to go to primary care physicians (Conner et al., 2010) who are more likely to underdiagnose and undertreat mental illness (Buser, 2009). When African Americans do go to mental health professionals, they report microaggressions from white counselors, including color-blind attitudes and less empathy, resulting in feelings of powerlessness and of having to represent their racial group (Buser, 2009; Nicolaidis et al., 2010). Santiago, Kaltman, and Miranda (2013) also reported that health care professionals lack formal training with issues that often concern low-income people, such as trauma.

In addition to medical barriers, low-income women of color seeking care face several structural barriers to care, including the inability to afford it and lack of insurance, childcare, transportation, and availability of services (Nadeem et al., 2007; Ward & Heidrich, 2009). Low-income women may be sole caretakers, work "shift jobs," or rely on public transportation with fixed schedules that may not fit with inflexible treatment plans (Miranda & Green, 1999; Santiago et al., 2013). They also have more competing obligations, need to travel longer distances, or may believe that they are ineligible for services (Santiago et al., 2013). In focus groups of 30 low-income women of color with histories of major depression and interpersonal violence, women reported several factors that contributed to not seeking mental health care and not taking antidepressants (Nicolaidis et al., 2010). African-American women believed that the health care system was a white system and the myth of the "Strong Black Woman" precluded them from seeking care or sharing with others. Some women also identified interpersonal violence as a barrier to care. Many women of color had negative views of antidepressants: fear of addiction and being "doped up," a desire for self-care and self-coping, mistrust of prescribers, and fear of side effects (Nicolaidis et al., 2010).

Stigma associated with seeking mental health care has also been shown to present a barrier to treatment. In his review, Buser (2009) found that African-American participants perceived disgrace, embarrassment, and isolation associated with seeking mental health services. Indeed, African-American women are more likely to report concerns with mental-illness-associated stigma and are less likely to want treatment than other groups (Nadeem et al., 2007; Santiago et al., 2013). Women of color also fear losing custody of their children if they reveal what they perceive to be stigmatizing mental health concerns. Women respond to these perceived disapproving social norms by accessing alternative support through informal circumstances and self-reliance (Santiago et al., 2013).

## Interrelationships Among Poverty, Personal Violence Experiences, and Mental Health for Low-Income Women

Given that poverty and IPV independently can lead to poor mental health, and that poverty and IPV often covary, data indicate they may even work synergistically to place low-income women at particularly increased risk of psychological distress. Because IPV and poverty are closely linked, however, few studies have extricated their various independent effects. The National Violence Against Women Study, however, is a population-based study in which residents from all 50 states and D.C. selected by random digit dialing were surveyed about risk and protective factors for PTSD symptoms (Coker, Weston, Creson, Justice, & Blakeney, 2005). In this study, researchers were able to assess, among the female IPV victims, the relative effects of socioeconomic status, and found that lower socioeconomic status was a critical predictor of being at higher risk for more severe PTSD symptoms, demonstrating clearly that poverty had its own negative effect on mental health beyond its association with IPV. As Goodman and colleagues argue convincingly, IPV and poverty each results in elevated levels of stress, powerlessness, and social isolation; in turn, these two factors act synergistically to increase women's risk for poor mental health outcomes by amplifying their feelings of incapacity and aloneness. Consequently, in a situation of reciprocal causality (Bandura), while poverty and IPV both impair mental health; they also influence each other and impaired mental health can exacerbate them, creating a downward spiral that resiliency may buffer but likely not resolve (Fig. 1).

## Understanding the Intersection of Poverty, Personal Violence Experiences, and Mental Health of the HPTN 064 Cohort: Survey, In-Depth Interview, and Focus Group Results

As described in Chap. 1, women enrolled in HPTN 064 lived in areas with high levels of poverty. For those participating in the qualitative component specifically, which included a sample of women from four of the ten study communities ($n = 488$), at the beginning of the HPTN 064 study, 69 % of women participating in the qualitative component reported annual household incomes of below $20,000. Forty-five

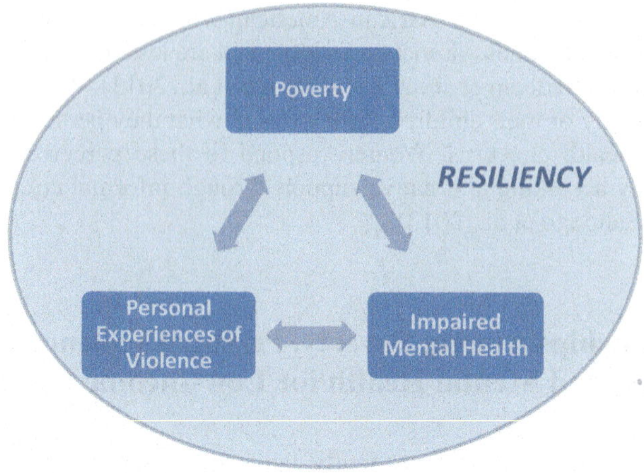


**Fig. 1** Interrelationships among poverty, personal experiences of violence, and impaired mental health and the buffering role of resiliency

percent reported not having enough food for themselves or their family in the past 6 months and 69 % were financially responsible for at least one child under 18.

## Prevalence of Personal Violence Experiences and Mental Health of the HPTN 064 Cohort

At the beginning of the study, 46 % of women reported a history of having been abused physically, emotionally, or sexually as a child and 37 % reported that they had experienced physical, emotional, or sexual abuse in the 6 months prior to study entry. At study onset, 31 % of the women in the qualitative study cohort screened positive for a high level of depressive symptoms on the Center for Epidemiologic Studies Depression (CES-D) Scale short form and 30 % of women screened positive (three of four symptoms) for PTSD symptoms on the Primary Care PTSD screener. As found in other studies among low-income women, mental health comorbidities tended to covary. For example, women in HPTN 064 who screened positive for depressive symptoms were nearly 2.5 times as likely to screen positive for symptoms of PTSD compared with those who were not depressed, even after controlling for a history of childhood abuse, ongoing abuse, food insecurity, and binge drinking. Similarly, women who reported binge drinking at least 2 times per week had about 1.5 times the odds of screening positive for PTSD symptoms.

The qualitative aspects of these experiences and their combined effect on the mental health of low-income women participating in the interviews and focus groups are outlined in the text that follows. As illustrated below, a complex interplay exists among women's various experiences of neighborhood-level violence, sexual assault, ongoing intimate partner violence, and financial stress, intrapersonal resilience, and interpersonal resources. These factors work synergistically to determine the effects these experiences have on their mental health and emotional well-being. In fact, many participants talked about the tremendous toll that a lifetime of exposure to several different types of violence had taken on their emotional well-being.

## Neighborhood Violence-Induced Stress

Many women described experiencing a general sense of stress and lack of ease due to living conditions they perceived to be unsafe as a result of neighborhood-level crime and violence. In some cases, women described a specific event in their neighborhood that resulted in their feeling vulnerable.

> I don't really feel that safe now that about a week, two weeks ago my back door was kicked in at 3:00 in the morning and they had a hammer and gloves because they tried to kidnap my sister's baby out of the house at 3:00 in the morning. So, since I've seen how easy it was to get inside my back door, I don't feel safe. But I'm more aware and I'm more on point, I know I have children, so ... I'm paying attention. My awareness is really, really — that can happen that quick. It can happen, you know.
>
> —*Interviewee, Raleigh/Durham, NC*

> ... or like in my building, throughout the whole building it's been break-ins. So that's a fear that I have if they was to come back to my house and break in again. And just, I guess the bullets, they scare me, the shots sometimes, you know. And that's why I prevent my son to really go outside' cause you never know and it don't matter now if it's daytime or nighttime.
>
> —*Interviewee, Washington, D.C*

In other cases, women described the stress and worry created by living with a constant, general exposure to gun violence, particularly the sounds of gunfire, which gave a sense of unpredictable danger, such as that experienced in a war zone.

> ... when I go to [neighborhood] to my family's house, I could look up at the sky and it's all quiet and I just like, I'll just take a deep breath and I just feel so calm. Even the air smells different, you know, and coming back over here it's like detention. It's like boom, boom, boom. And it's the stress, and you — it's like, I just get tense all over again because you've got to be on your p's and q's, you've got to make sure there ain't no shootout, or you know, people aren't rumbling in front of your house. And it's just very (sigh).
>
> –*Focus Group Participant, New York, NY*

> Yeah, where I live is, there's a spot right across the street from my house and there's always shootouts, everything. Every single day, there's fights every single day. I hear it every day, and it makes — you know, sometimes I even find drugs, I even find drugs on the — on the floor, you know? I want to get out, I really want to get out, and I feel kind of miserable there because I'm tired of sirens — this is what I hear every day. That, that noise.
>
> –*Focus Group Participant, New York, NY*

> ... any time of the day, I just feel like anything could happen, and then it's like, it's worrying. It's -- that's the only thing I have a problem with: that somebody start shooting, my kids -- something like that. So that's my problem with where I live. (laughter)
>
> –*Focus Group Participant, New York, NY*

## Experiences of Sexual Abuse and Rape

Many participants talked about having experienced sexual abuse, often more than one time by different perpetrators. Some talked about the trauma of these experiences and their resultant feelings of severe emotional distress, including reliving past traumas when episodes of revictimization occurred. Women often described not receiving support from family or the criminal justice system to help them address their sexual assault. Some women attributed their inability to heal emotionally to such lack of a supportive reaction from others.

> By my [step]brother. My father's son, if you really get what I mean. That's a nightmare that will never ever go away. He molested me when I was 13 and when I went to [country name], he did it again. I was 20 and my father didn't believe me, so that will never ever go away .... I froze, when I had real sex with my ex. I felt scared. I didn't want him to touch me, because I got molested. He eventually stayed with me and eventually, I opened myself up. Can't let that go.
>
> *–Interviewee, New York, NY*

In some cases, fear of an unsupportive reaction from the police kept women from reporting the traumatic criminal events or seeking medical care.

> I didn't call the police on none of them, not even the first one my mother did … I just wanted to die that's how I felt. But did I want to [call the police]? Yeah, I wanted to when I was up in age because I know that I'm a victim even though whatever I was doing I was still a victim, it doesn't matter. Um, I wanted to but then I thought, you know, 'cause quote some police officers, they'll be like "well, you was out there doing what you was doing so you get what you get." You know, so I didn't want to be rejected, so.
>
> *–Interviewee, Washington, D.C.*

One woman's description of her experiences indicated that she recognized that the negative judgment and lack of support she received from others when she was raped stemmed from inadequacies in those around her and did not represent an appropriate reaction to something wrong with her.

> I've been raped twice. So, the first time it was a boyfriend and he used to abuse me and I would tell my mom and my dad about it and they would say that's what I get because I shouldn't be out here being fast. But they didn't realize I was scared of this dude and he would just handcuff me to stuff and closets and just do what he want. And the second time I was coming to work and the dude snatched me off the train. It was like twelve or one o'clock in the morning; took everything out of my purse, did what he had to do, and left me in the woods and this man found me and called the police. And, I really didn't want to deal with that because the police said that I gave it up willingly and I didn't want to go to the hospital. I didn't want to do none of that, I just felt like in the moment I just wanted to go home and they were upset with me because I didn't want to pursue it. But they didn't understand how I was feeling like some man just out of the blue, because I stabbed the man in the eye because all I had was a pen. … while he was taking my clothes off I grabbed the pen and he got off of me.
>
> *–Interviewee, Washington, D.C.*

One participant described the experience of disassociation paralyzing her and preventing her from protecting herself and her children during an attempted revictimization after previous sexual assault. Eventually, she was able to regain lucidity and call the police.

> When that happened to me in my apartment, I called the police. My daughter was shaking like a washing machine, 'cause he reminded me the person who raped me when I was young, so when I first saw his face I froze, and this man is taking my shirt off in front of my daughter, and I was froze. When I heard my baby screaming that's when I woke up. I yoked him up, I got him out the apartment, I called the cops.
>
> *–Focus Group Participant, New York, NY*

## Intimate Partner Violence

In addition to neighborhood and sexual violence, many participants talked about being treated abusively by one or more of their intimate partners. Reactions to the violence varied, including extreme fear, dependence on their partner, sympathy, anger, and rejection. Many described a pattern of violence within the families of origin of their abusive partners. Women described horrific experiences of extreme violence, torture, and abuse.

> He was horrible — he was psychotic. He — I think it's a pattern with domestic violence. If you see it in the home, you're most likely going to do it yourself. I guess once I got pregnant — he got — I was kicked out of my parents' home. I guess he felt like, "You know, OK, well, I can control her." Because I felt like he was the only person I had to depend on. But, through the course of me being pregnant and being with him, which was really over like a two year span because we were coming out of high school. He was just horrible. He was very abusive. He would wake up out of his sleep, punch me in the chest, broke my tooth. Permanently indented my chest bone. He — he ripped my hair out. He did so many — so many things.
>
> *–Interviewee, New York, NY*

Another woman described a situation in which her abuser felt remorse over expressing anger and being verbally abusive toward her but explains that when he became physically abusive, she left him.

> Yeah, this boy I went with. I guess he was like that 'cause his daddy used to hit on his mama. So, he used to get mad and want to have a reaction [of] shock, disappointment, and then he'd be like "I'm sorry," but I don't got time for that. … towards the end he started getting violent on me. At first it was just the arguing. And when he put his hands on me, it was the end. So, I was in that relationship for a long time until he started acting violent.
>
> *—Interviewee, Raleigh/Durham, NC*

Some participants described life-threatening episodes related to their partners' paranoia and jealousy as exemplified by the statement of one woman below.

> Oh, God. I hate to talk about this because I've never been in any kind of violence or anything. But I was dating this guy. His name was [name of person]. For some reason, he was just so insecure and always thought I was doing something. And one day I actually came from my best friend's house, my first best friend's house. And I was getting accused of something I didn't do. And he actually put his hands on me. And I'm sitting here amazed like "I know you just didn't do that." But then I thought about it and I turned around again and he started choking me. And at the time I thought I was going to really die because my nose started bleeding and I couldn't breathe and I've got asthma. So, I had like an anxiety

> attack as well as the asthma attack 'cause I couldn't breathe. And I really thought I was going to die. I'd never been in a relationship like that before. My first and last.
>
> *–Interviewee, Raleigh/Durham, NC*

While some women described choosing to end an abusive relationship on their own, others talked about their need to use more formal mechanisms, such as police interventions, to protect themselves from life-threatening violence from their abuser. In the extreme example below, when a woman tried to stick up for herself to her partner, she was tortured for an extended period of time by her abuser until the police finally intervened.

> Yeah. He was like using my phone to call other women and just keep telling me "I'll do what I want to do." So I was like "no, not in here, this is my house, you know what I mean. So I'm asking you, you need to get off my phone and leave." And then he jumped up in my face "I ain't going no m.f'ing where." And then it's like before I knew it when I said "oh, yes you are" to stand my ground and say this is my place. You know what I mean. And before I knew it he just shoved me real hard. So I had hardwood floors and then when I hit the floor it's like my back, I couldn't even get up. And then he wound up the whole day just pretty much verbal and to torture me. And I'm hollering for help he snatched the phones out the walls. So it was like the first time it just kept on and on and on but I got out. And it's like he went to jail, the police finally came … I think it was like twenty-four hours here or forty-eight hours or something the police finally came. And when they came and it was like I was shaking like leaf you know. And I kept telling the cops 'cause he had put the shotgun under my chin and threatened to kill me and everything and this was all … in one setting … 'Cause it lasted like from that morning, I thought it would never end.
>
> *–Interviewee, Washington, D.C*

Other women talked about feeling trapped in what they experienced as a terrifying situation. As one woman explained,

> And I guess I didn't leave 'cause I was scared. I really was scared … Like it be to a point where the person make you so scared that you don't want to leave. You just stay there and take the abuse.
>
> *–Interviewee, Atlanta, GA*

As Coker et al. explain, battered women do not learn to be helpless, as had been previously espoused by some researchers; rather their perceptions reflect the reality of the powerlessness that exists in their situations despite attempts to protect themselves and those they love (Coker et al., 2005).

## Effects of Neighborhood, Sexual and Interpersonal Violence on Emotional Well-Being

### *Fear, Anxiety, and Constant Worry*

Many women experience severe and persistent fear and anxiety as a result of their exposure to many types of violence. When asked whether they ever worried for their safety, several women described a constant sense of foreboding.

> Yeah, all the time. I have panic attacks … I always feel like someone wants to shoot me or I'm going to get hit by a car, I'm going to get kidnapped, I'm going to get raped, somebody is going to kill me or somebody is going to cut me or there's going to be something. That's been, like I said, off and on now for like two years, them thoughts. I think it's because so many people keep fussing about stupid stuff, dramas, always dramas.
>
> *–Interviewee, Raleigh/Durham, NC*

> [I worry about safety] all the time. I know every night before I lay down and before I wake up I'm praying to make sure everything is all right with everybody…
>
> *–Focus Group Participant, Raleigh/Durham, NC*

> I worry about my safety every day 'cause you never know who's plotting on you, who want to do something to you. Certain people don't know when it's coming but it comes but you just don't know it. … You never know you have someone that's out here very hatred of you that you're not aware of.
>
> *–Interviewee, Washington, D.C.*

Other women described symptoms of extreme fear and post-traumatic stress (e.g., reexperiencing events, irritability, difficulty concentrating) that they related to a specific traumatic event in their lives, such as a sexual assault or domestic violence:

> Ever since that date it's very hard for me to, oh you don't know where you're going, oh what we about to do, what, what, tell me the plan I need to know what's happening. You know what I'm saying, because that day took a lot from me, you know what I'm saying, and it was like he was in control of me, power. After that I was real nervous. I was scared to tell somebody because I thought he was going to come back and get me. But that day never left me. That never left me how he overpowered me and stuff like that, that just blew me. I'm always worried about that.
>
> *–Focus Group Participant, Washington, D.C.*

> When he went to jail they let him out after forty-eight hours. And he immediately came back to my house. So I wanted him to move. … When he came back to the house he was banging on the door. And then I started calling the cops but every time they would come he would run off. … From the time he got out it was a restraining order. Yep and I never looked back or took him back or anything. But he just was persistent and wouldn't stop.
>
> *–Interviewee, Washington, D.C.*

## *Silence, Avoiding, and Withdrawal*

Many participants found it too difficult to think or talk about their experiences with others.

> … but I really, the only person that really know all of them things is my ex-boyfriend. I really don't tell too many people about it because a lot of men look at you different when you've been raped. Like you traumatized or something like that and I'm not traumatized because it happened…"
>
> *–Interviewee, Washington, D.C.*

> Yeah, my uncle [made me feel unsafe]. Because he threatened to burn down the house with us in it. About 2002. It was right after I had my son. 2002. I don't even want to get into that one. That's a negative vibe right there. Because every time I think about him and his trying to burn everybody in the house down, even his sister and his nieces and nephews. He's just — no, don't go there.
>
> *–Interviewee, New York, NY*

Some women described avoidance as a way to escape the extreme feelings of vulnerability they experienced, as exemplified by the comments below from a woman who had been hit and strangled by a man she had dated.

> I've never told my mom about it, but I did tell my kid's father. And later on, come to find out he knew him and they almost got into it. And they just — I don't know. I've never been in nothing like that. I don't even like to even talk about it though I remember it like it was yesterday. Like, why would he even do something like that. I was scared to go to sleep. I couldn't close my eyes. I didn't feel like — I didn't feel safe in my own house.
>
> *– Interviewee, Raleigh/Durham, NC*

## *Anger*

For others, a lifetime of violence led to chronic feelings of anger. As one woman put it, "And it's so much anger and hostility in me because I've been through so much," *Interviewee, Washington, D.C.* Another participant sought therapy to address the severe anger she experienced: *"You know, I know what I'm capable of doing to somebody. I see a therapist because of that. Strictly anger is inside of me. And I — that, I don't like for that to come out. You understand, because if it do, I'd … We know what would happen, OK?" Interviewee, New York, NY.* One woman talked about turning to drinking to address the anger she felt over her lack of economic resources which she perceived to only exacerbate her precarious financial situation.

> I get mad. And then, you know, I start drinking. And then I just get mad, because I don't have no more money. And I start drinking, and I be like, damn, yo, I want to — I want to — I want money, you know? 'Cause I love money in my pocket. And then I get so upset and I start drinking, then I'm wasting money in drinking, like — you know, I'll be like, damn man, it's crazy.
>
> *–Interviewee, New York, NY*

## Fatalism and Weariness

Several participants described becoming "used to" violence after a lifetime of exposure to it within their neighborhood and among their own friends and family.

> I don't know. Maybe it just kind of messed with my head up just a li'l bit. 'Cause growing up up north, you could just walk around the corner and there's a dead body laying there. And some days the Bloods were shooting at Crips, Crips shooting at Bloods and people cutting off people's fingers. And then some of my family are just crazy.
>
> *–Interviewee, Raleigh/Durham, NC*

> I'm from [southern state] and back home I've seen a lot of violence, a lot of violence throughout my life, you know what I'm saying? It's not nothing new to me, you know what I'm saying? Yeah, it scares me a little but it doesn't put fear in my heart like that. … I've seen my uncle get shot and killed in my face.
>
> *–Interviewee, Raleigh/Durham, NC*

When discussing her feelings about the violence and stressful conditions in her neighborhood, one woman described becoming numb to their effects, "*You know what, to be quite honest with you, I'm beginning to get … to get numb to it already. I'm getting numb to it, you know, it's like a part of my life already. You know, and that's sad to say, you know?" Focus Group Participant, New York, NY.* Similarly, another participant explained it this way: "*Yeah, back then it's scared me. But to it, the then you just become immune, cussing, the smells, the shooting, the stabbings, the fights. It just doesn't bother you anymore," Interviewee, Raleigh/Durham, NC.*

## Financial Stress

Many of the women described similar feeling of anxiety, fear, anger, and sadness due to the constraints of their economic circumstances.

> So, it's struggling. There's some things you got to think about, it's either the rent or do you feed the kids. It's very difficult. For me I want to move from this community but right now this all I can afford right now.
>
> *–Focus Group Participant, Washington, D.C.*

> I don't ever feel like I'm getting by money-wise. As a mother, we sacrifice and we just do without, you know. As long as my kids, they don't complain and they don't ask me for nothing. So, my life is pretty much, we don't dwell about money.
>
> *–Interviewee, Raleigh/Durham, NC*

> It [financial stress] hurts. It hurts because, you know, having things at one time and now — 'cause my oldest son, he came to me. He's like, "mom," I was like "what?" He said "what's going on?" "What do you mean what's going on?" "At one time we had it and I don't care what we asked for, we got it." I said you know "It's a part of life. It happens all the time." Constantly. I tell him, "we're not the only ones going through it. You know, somebody else is going through rougher than we are." But it's just stressful.
>
> *–Interviewee, Raleigh/Durham, NC*

> What can I do? It's just gonna run out. We don't have to worry about foods. We have food stamps. Yeah, we have soaps and stuff. That's no problem. But yeah, it's like when you want to spend it on yourself. You never have anything for extra stuff like new clothes, this, that, getting your hair and nails done. Just gives you an extra reason to be hateful all the time.
>
> *–Interviewee, Raleigh/Durham, NC*

> That's what keeps me — when it feels like you're frustrated and you're angry, and you're just saying to yourself, "What the fuck! Oh my god, how the hell am I going to get this bill

paid? Oh what am I going to do, I can't call this one, I can't call this one. If I call this one I'll have to hear a conversation. I'm going to have to do this..."

*–Interviewee, New York, NY*

## The Effect of Poor Mental Health on Poverty

I suffer from anxiety. I tried a multitude of jobs. I worked. I had my own cell phone place. I mean, I had — I've worked in supermarkets, I've worked in daycares, I've worked in preschools, I've worked in all of that, and it's like — I can't find the job where like, because of the up and down, the manic and the depressive, one day I'm fine and the next minute I'm not, and it's hard to keep a job.

*–Focus Group Participant, New York, NY*

## Resilience and Overcoming Abuse, Violence, and Financial Stress

Despite enormous burdens and substantial trauma, women demonstrated tremendous resiliency and hope to continue on. The quotes that follow demonstrate how both intrapersonal and interpersonal resources buffered the negative effects of violence and financial stress on their mental health.

### *Intrapersonal Resilience*

Women demonstrated various types of insight into an inner strength that allowed them to heal from traumatic events or maintain an optimistic attitude in the face of severe economic constraints. For some, forgiving the person who perpetrated their victimization was a key step toward healing.

And I looked and I dropped my soda and my son said "Ma, what's wrong with you?" And I just kept pointing, I couldn't say nothing. And then when the man looked at me, he seen me, he start running. [Son's name] say "what he running for?" I said "'cause that's him, that's the one rape me!" And my son just started chasing him. But when I was chasing behind him "no, leave him alone, leave him alone, I forgave him for it!" You know what I'm saying because if I can't forgive him for it then I wouldn't be able to move on in my life because I'd still be stuck. So I still have a little anger with it but I have to forgive him. But I told him I'm still going to still feel the way that I feel but.

*–Interviewee, Washington, D.C.*

Others demonstrated an ability to maintain a positive outlook despite facing adverse circumstances, such as the incarceration and job loss described by the women below.

> It's hectic. It's very frustrating. But um, I just keep moving forward. I just try to see if I can find me something. I mean, I don't let it get the best of me because sometimes I do. I just have little sad moments, and little times where I just be like, OK, why do I have to go through something like that? It used to be very easy for me to get a job back in the days when I actually had — I came across an issue back in … 2005 or 2006 and, you know, when people look at your background it's like, OK, that's why. But I don't let that be my downfall. I really don't.
>
> *–Interviewee, Raleigh/Durham, NC*

Often maintaining a positive attitude seemed to come at least partially by avoiding self-blame and protecting oneself from outside blame for not having enough money, recognizing that the problem was external to the individual as exemplified below.

> The bill going to be there whether I pay it or don't. I'm not going to stress myself, whatever happens, happens. The Lord will see fit — see fit that whatever is going to be will be. I'm not going to stress myself over it, causing more problems and headaches on top of worrying about a bill. That really, really doesn't really mean that I have to actually go out there and pull my hair out to worry about how to pay for it. Fuck it. Let it go, whatever happens, happens. I'm going stress free, I'm not getting no more gray hairs … Listen, they are not — no one is going to take me there, no one, I meant it.
>
> *–Interviewee, New York, NY*

Like the woman above, another participant discussed not only a refusal to accept outside blame, but also a tremendous trust that she will be okay financially. She used her optimism and trust as a way to prevent herself from suffering from anxiety about her finances or from worrying about her ability to provide for her son:

> Well, I watched this movie called *The Secret*. And so they said whatever you envision you just say it and you have to believe it and it comes you know. And so that's what I just do now. 'Cause you see you know how we get upset and depressed and 'cause money running low and he might got a field trip coming the next day or something, you know. And I don't know where the money was coming from but no, I don't get stressed out, I just say okay well, it's going to come from somewhere. And the opportunity will come it will show itself. And like I do hair so if it come in the form of a client wanting their hair done that's where my money is going to come from so I can pay for my son's picture or whatever needs to be done. So that's how I go through it now 'cause I just can't get stressed out anymore … I have no energy for it.
>
> *–Interviewee, Washington, D.C.*

Some women who experienced domestic violence demonstrated resiliency by refusing to accept the abuse, finding formal mechanism to protect themselves, or rejecting the fear that can come from such abuse.

> Oh, he hit me. We got into a — we got into a big fight, we had four streets blocked off, we had the police, the fire department, the ambulance, the street was shut down from corner to corner. Like I said, three streets over. Yea, we threw down [date], 2001. Police reports and everything. I got a restraining order against him, everything. Yes. First and last, never again.
>
> *–Interviewee, New York, NY*

> But, I don't — I don't hate him. I feel sorry him and I feel sorry for the person that's with him now. I don't — I don't look at him the same way — I don't look at him with fear. Because I'll be damned, I dare you. I've grown up. I'm getting older, so—I mean it was horrible. But, I'm — I'm good now.
>
> *–Interviewee, New York, NY*

> And that evening when my daughter came home from school, my middle daughter told my oldest daughter the argument word for word. And I told my husband right then and there we will never argue, have a heated discussion, have an adult conversation in front of them. Because for her to replay all of that back to her sister like that, that mean all of it stuck in her head like that. Which means this is how she's going to view relationships or whatever. So we don't do, we don't do — I didn't grow up with no, with abuse or anything like that in my family with my mother or anything like that and neither did he. So we don't have that in my house, we don't, Mm-Mm, Mm-Mm (no).
>
> *–Interviewee, Washington, D.C.*

## *Interpersonal Resilience*

In addition to drawing on their own inner resources, women relied on neighbors, family, and friends to maintain resiliency in the face of painful and challenging circumstances. Several women described tight-knit social networks within their neighborhoods that functioned to assist and support its members. People looked out for each other to provide protection from outsiders and the potential violence of others. Those who felt the safest seemed to be women who described their neighborhood networks as serving a protective function.

> … so that's why we try to stick together. Even though [friend's name] stays a couple of doors down, it's all still the same little vicinity. You couldn't be the wrong person coming into our parking lot and one of us don't call the other. [Laughter] And that didn't come from the office. That came from us.
>
> *–Focus Group Participant, Raleigh/Durham, NC*

> No, for the most part we all take care of each other. We all make sure that if it does come to a point, if — let's say if someone wants to get themselves into that kind of predicament, we try to handle it the most before it gets any further, before, you know, God forbid something really bad happens, so…I say we always, we all look out for each other.
>
> *–Interviewee, New York, NY*

Several women also talked about the support they derived from their families, such as expressed by this woman whose family supported her through a difficult time when she was incarcerated, *"I actually got in trouble. I had to face my consequences. But I mean I got through it 'cause I had my family for support," Interviewee, Raleigh/Durham, NC.*

Others focused on the love of their family over worries about economic circumstances. As one woman expressed it:

> If it [money] comes, it comes. We don't really make that be a sadness of our joy, you know, 'cause we make each other happy. Once you got food and a roof over your head, then that's what it is 'cause that's how my kids is. They're kind of like me. They're not choicey. They don't complain, don't do none of that stuff. As long as we got our health and we're together, that's all that counts at the end.
>
> *–Interviewee, Raleigh/Durham, NC*

## Conclusions: Clinical and Policy Implications: Recommended Changes to Improve Mental Health and Psychological Well-Being of Low-Income Women

An increasing recognition exists of the critical link between poverty and health. Especially for minority women living in poverty, myriad factors, including exposure to violence and limited educational and employment opportunities, intertwine to impede maintenance of good mental health, which places such women at additional risk of poverty and violence. While the factors that contribute to this potential negative spiral are numerous and linked to each other in complex ways, as research has been able to tease apart their different roles and our understanding of the mechanisms by which these factors interact has grown, strategies that are likely to intercept and reverse such patterns become clearer. Novel approaches to domestic violence advocacy that account for the unique conditions of poverty, mental health treatments for low-income women that build on their resilience without promoting John Henryism, resources to reduce stressors that have been shown to contribute to health disparities in the USA, and structural interventions to enhance access to mental health services are examples of interventions that have the potential to significantly improve the mental health of low-income women exposed to poverty and violence. Such improvements can lead to additional benefits of reducing entrenchment in poverty and exposure to interpersonal violence. While research has identified numerous factors that threaten the psychological well-being of minority women living in poverty and substantial barriers to accessing mental health care for low-income minority women, these findings and other studies point to several noteworthy options for overcoming the barriers:

- Greater recognition of the role that stress induced by various aspects of living in poverty, including financial strain, structural and interpersonal violence, and lesser educational and employment opportunities plays in the mental and physical health of minorities is needed. Increasingly, health programs are being developed that seek to address health disparities by reducing stress through addressing poverty and other structural causes.
- Domestic violence advocacy must become more-client focused and need-based, taking into consideration the real constraints that exist in the daily lives of women living in poverty. Similarly, social service systems that provide services for low-income persons must take into account the needs of women experiencing IPV and modify programs to empower women rather than placing them at increased risk. A system that could provide respectful wraparound services that would enhance provider awareness and integrate mental health services and domestic violence advocacy with educational, employment, and welfare policy is called for. Interventions focusing on empowerment of women in communities may also be effective (Pronyk, IMAGE study).
- Culturally specific models of mental health interventions must be developed, adapted, and tested with diverse people of color. Such programs benefit by

including diversity among the staff delivering programs, as women identified that they would prefer mental health programs staffed by women of color who had experienced similar personal struggles as opposed to trained mental health professionals (Nicolaidis et al., 2010).

- Treatment planning needs to be flexible and address the needs of transportation and child care. Increased access to psychotherapy conducted in the home or community would assist in overcoming structural barriers, such as transportation and child care.
- Intensive outreach is needed to overcome stigma and gain initial trust and engagement in services.
- The lack of representation of people of color in treatment-outcome research and psychiatric epidemiological studies must continuously be addressed by research grant funding organizations.
- Increased multicultural counseling competency training for practitioners: such trainings would include discussion and awareness of the racism and microaggressions present in mental health treatment. Counseling programs need to work harder to develop ethical, culturally competent practitioners.
- Because women of color are more likely to seek mental health treatment from primary care providers, increased training on the unique mental health needs of this population as well as education on low-cost referral options for mental health treatment are necessary for primary care providers.
- Mental health practitioners must become advocates for the low-income, underserved populations they serve. This can be achieved through social political lobbying or membership in a social action coalition while maintaining a balanced focus on individual change and societal reform.
- As expressed by the poem written by the HPTN 064 participant below, in response to the attention, respect, and caring she received as a study participant, this woman was empowered to make significant changes in her life that significantly improved her mental health and psychological well-being.

ISIS

By Yashika Dickerson
You reached out to me and gave me hope,
you showed me
that somebody cared about my welfare,
by just being there ....
You exemplified the meaning of ISIS,
which is Protector,
Goddess of women and children from which all beginnings arose,
Exceptionally wise with the knowledge and understanding to the highest degree .....
Universal Mother which made me believe and discover
that I could recover
from low self-esteem and always dismissing
the fact that I am a queen with every ounce of my being ....
Your symbol means life
which I was slowly taking away from myself
by risking suicidal decisions to my health ....

You educated and empowered me on the facts about HIV
and how 50 % of the ones infected look like me ....
You gave me an outlet in which I could speak and tell my story on how things came to be
in my community ....
You listened, intently, and gave me information
facilities, testing, counseling, even contacted me monthly
just to see how I was
Coping ....
Even compensated me monetarily to show you valued my time and opinion,
treated us all with confidentiality, fairness, and equality ....
"ISIS"
You revived my soul and re-birthed my spirit by nurturing
and releasing my captive mind
that longed to be freed ...
And now, I can teach my seed,
and tell everyone how
ISIS has been immeasurably PRICELESS

## References


Baker, C. K., Norris, F. H., Diaz, D. M., Perilla, J. L., Murphy, A. D., & Hill, E. G. (2005). Violence and PTSD in Mexico: Gender and regional differences. *Social Psychiatry and Psychiatric Epidemiology, 40*(7), 519–528. doi:10.1007/s00127-005-0921-2.

Banks-Wallace, J., & Parks, L. (2004). It's all sacred: African American women's perspectives on spirituality. *Issues in Mental Health Nursing, 25*(1), 25–45. doi:10.1080/01612840490248911.

Blazer, D. G., Kessler, R. C., McGonagle, K. A., & Swartz, M. S. (1994, July). The prevalence and distribution of major depression in a national community sample: The national comorbidity survey. *The American Journal of Psychiatry, 151*(7), 979–986.

Breslau, N., Davis, G. C., Andreski, P., Peterson, E. L., & Schultz, L. R. (1997). Sex differences in posttraumatic stress disorder. *Archives of General Psychiatry, 54*(11), 1044–1048.

Breslau, N., Kessler, R. C., Chilcoat, H. D., Schultz, L. R., Davis, G. C., & Andreski, P. (1998). Trauma and posttraumatic stress disorder in the community: The 1996 Detroit Area Survey of Trauma. *Archives of General Psychiatry, 55*(7), 626–632.

Bronder, E. C., Speight, S. L., Witherspoon, K. M., & Thomas, A. J. (2013). John Henryism, depression, and perceived social support in Black women. *Journal of Black Psychology, 40*(2), 115–137. doi:10.1177/0095798412474466.

Browne, A., Salomon, A., & Bassuk, S. S. (1999). The impact of recent partner violence on poor women's capacity to maintain work. *Violence Against Women, 5*, 393–426.

Bryant-Davis, T., Ullman, S. E., Tsong, Y., Tillman, S., & Smith, K. (2010). Struggling to survive: Sexual assault, poverty, and mental health outcomes of African American women. *The American Journal of Orthopsychiatry, 80*(1), 61–70. doi:10.1111/j.1939-0025.2010.01007.x.

Bryant-Davis, T., Ullman, S. E., Tsong, Y., & Gobin, R. (2011). Surviving the storm: The role of social support and religious coping in sexual assault recovery of African American women. *Violence Against Women, 17*(12), 1601–1618. doi:10.1177/1077801211436138.

Buser, J. K. (2009). Treatment-seeking disparity between African Americans and Whites: Attitudes toward treatment, coping resources, and racism. *Journal of Multicultural Counseling and Development, 37*(April), 94–104.

Bybee, D. I., & Sullivan, C. M. (2005). Predicting revictimization of battered women 3 years after exiting a shelter program. Theoretical and methodological innovations in research on intimate partner violence [Special issue]. *American Journal of Community Psychology, 36*, 85–96.

Coker, A. L., Weston, R., Creson, D. L., Justice, B., & Blakeney, P. (2005, December). PTSD symptoms among men and women survivors of intimate partner violence: The role of risk and protective factors. *Violence and Victims, 20*(6), 625–643.

Coley, R. L., & Lombardi, C. M. (2014). Low-income women's employment experiences and their financial, personal, and family well-being. *Journal of Family Psychology, 28*(1), 88–97. doi:10.1037/a0034998.

Conner, K. O., Lee, B., Mayers, V., Robinson, D., Reynolds, C. F., Albert, S., & Brown, C. (2010). Attitudes and beliefs about mental health among African American older adults suffering from depression. *Journal of Aging Studies, 24*(4), 266–277. doi:10.1016/j.jaging.2010.05.007

Corcoran, M., Danziger, S. K., & Tolman, R. (2004). Long term employment of African-American and white welfare recipients and the role of persistent health and mental health problems. *Women & Health, 39*(4), 21–40.

Cunradi, C., Caetano, R., & Schafer, J. (2002). Socioeconomic predictors of intimate partner violence among White, Black, and Hispanic couples in the United States. *Journal of Family Violence, 17*, 377–389.

Cutrona, C. E., Russell, D. W., Brown, P. A., Clark, L. A., Hessling, R. M., & Gardner, K. A. (2005). Neighborhood context, personality, and stressful life events as predictors of depression among African American women. *Journal of Abnormal Psychology, 114*(1), 3–15. doi:10.1037/0021-843X.114.1.3.

Dale, S. K., Weber, K. M., Cohen, M. H., Kelso, G. A, Cruise, R. C., & Brody, L. R. (2014). Resilience moderates the association between childhood sexual abuse and depressive symptoms among women with and at-risk for HIV. *AIDS and Behavior*, Advance online publication. doi:10.1007/s10461-014-0855-3.

Defrancisco, V. L., & Chatham-Carpenter, A. (2000). Self in community: African American women's views of self-esteem. *Howard Journal of Communications, 11*(2), 73–92.

Devries, K. M., Mak, J. Y., Bacchus, L. J., Child, J. C., Falder, G., et al. (2013). Intimate partner violence and incident depressive symptoms and suicide attempts: A systematic review of longitudinal studies. *PLoS Medicine, 10*(5), e1001439. doi:10.1371/journal.pmed.1001439.

Farr, S. L., Bitsko, R. H., Hayes, D. K., & Dietz, P. M. (2010). Mental health and access to services among US women of reproductive age. *American Journal of Obstetrics and Gynecology, 203*(6), 542.e1–9. doi:10.1016/j.ajog.2010.07.007.

Fischer, A. R., & Shaw, C. M. (1999, July). Af self-esteem and socioeconomic status: A meta-analytic review. *Journal of Counseling Psychology, 46*(3), 395–407.

Flaskerud, J. H. (2012). Coping and health status: John Henryism. *Issues in Mental Health Nursing, 33*(10), 712–715. doi:10.3109/01612840.2012.673695.

Galea, S., Ahern, J., Nandi, A., Tracy, M., Beard, J., & Vlahov, D. (2007). Urban neighborhood poverty and the incidence of depression in a population-based cohort study. *Annals of Epidemiology, 17*(3), 171–179. doi:10.1016/j.annepidem.2006.07.008.

Galea, S., Ahern, J., Tracy, M., Hubbard, A., Cerda, M., Goldmann, E., & Vlahov, D. (2008). Longitudinal determinants of posttraumatic stress in a population-based cohort study. *Epidemiology, 19*(1), 47–54. doi:10.1097/EDE.0b013e31815c1dbf

Gapen, M., Cross, D., Ortigo, K., Graham, A., Johnson, E., Evces, M., … Bradley, B. (2011). Perceived neighborhood disorder, community cohesion, and PTSD symptoms among low-income African Americans in an urban health setting. *Am J Orthopsychiatry, 81*(1), 31–37. doi:10.1111/j.1939-0025.2010.01069.x

Geronimus, A. T. (2013). Deep integration: Letting the epigenome out of the bottle without losing sight of the structural origins of population health. *The American Journal of Public Health, 103*(Suppl 1), S56–S63. doi:10.2105/AJPH.2013.301380.

Gill, J. M., Szanton, S., Taylor, T. J., Page, G. G., & Campbell, J. C. (2009). Medical conditions and symptoms associated with posttraumatic stress disorder in low-income urban women. *Journal of Women's Health (Larchmt), 18*(2), 261–267. doi:10.1089/jwh.2008.0914.

Gillespie, C. F., Bradley, B., Mercer, K., Smith, A. K., Conneely, K., Gapen, M., … Ressler, K. J. (2009). Trauma exposure and stress-related disorders in inner city primary care patients. *Gen Hosp Psychiatry, 31*(6), 505–514. doi:10.1016/j.genhosppsych.2009.05.003

Glass, N., Perrin, N., Campbell, J. C., & Soeken, K. (2007). The protective role of tangible support on post-traumatic stress disorder symptoms in urban women survivors of violence. *Research in Nursing and Health, 30*(5), 558–568. doi:10.1002/nur.20207.

Goodman, L. A., Dutton, M. A., Vankos, N., & Weinfurt, W. (2005). Women's resources and use of strategies as risk and protective factors for re-abuse over time. *Violence Against Women, 11*(3), 311–336.

Goodman, L. A., Smyth, K. F., Borges, A. M., & Singer, R. (2009). When crises collide: How intimate partner violence and poverty intersect to shape women's mental health and coping? *Trauma, Violence & Abuse, 10*(4), 306–329. doi:10.1177/1524838009339754.

Grote, N. K., Bledsoe, S. E., Larkin, J., Lemay, E. P., & Brown, C. (2007). Stress exposure and depression in disadvantaged women: The protective effects of optimism and perceived control. *Social Work Research, 31*(1), 19–33. doi:10.1093/swr/31.1.19.

Grote, N. K., Zuckoff, A., Swartz, H., Bledsoe, S. E., & Geibel, S. (2007). Engaging women who are depressed and economically disadvantaged in mental health treatment. *Social Work, 52*(4), 295–308. Retrieved from http://www.pubmedcentral.nih.gov/articlerender.fcgi?artid=3025777&tool=pmcentrez&rendertype=abstract.

Hines-Martin, V., Malone, M., Kim, S., & Brown-Piper, A. (2003). Barriers to mental health care access in an African American population. *Issues in Mental Health Nursing, 24*(3), 237–256. doi:10.1080/01612840390160775.

Hogan, B. E., Linden, W., & Najarian, B. (2002, April). Social support interventions: Do they work? *Clinical Psychology Review, 22*(3), 383–442.

Holden, K. B., Bradford, L. D., Hall, S. P., & Belton, A. S. (2013). Prevalence and correlates of depressive symptoms and resiliency among African American women in a community-based primary health care center. *Journal of Health Care for the Poor and Underserved, 24*(4), 79–93. doi:10.1353/hpu.2014.0012.

Jagannathan, R., Camasso, M. J., & Sambamoorthi, U. (2010, July). Experimental evidence of welfare reform impact on clinical anxiety and depression levels among poor women. *Social Science & Medicine, 71*(1), 152–160. doi: 10.1016/j.socscimed.2010.02.044. Epub 2010 Mar 27.

Kessler, R. C., Sonnega, A., Bromet, E., Hughes, M., & Nelson, C. B. (1995). Posttraumatic stress disorder in the National Comorbidity Survey. *Archives of General Psychiatry, 52*(12), 1048–1060.

Laditka, S. B., Murray, L. M., & Laditka, J. N. (2010). In the eye of the storm: Resilience and vulnerability among African American women in the wake of Hurricane Katrina. *Health Care for Women International, 3*(11), 1013–1027.

Levy, L. B., & O'Hara, M. W. (2010). Psychotherapeutic interventions for depressed, low-income women: A review of the literature. *Clinical Psychology Review, 30*(8), 934–950. doi:10.1016/j.cpr.2010.06.006.

Lorant, V., Deliège, D., Eaton, W., Robert, A., Philippot, P., & Ansseau, M. (2003). Socioeconomic inequalities in depression: A meta-analysis. *American Journal of Epidemiology, 157*(2), 98–112.

Masten, A. S. (2001). Ordinary magic: Resilience processes in development. *American Psychologist, 56*(3), 227–238. doi:10.1037//0003-066X.56.3.227.

Miranda, J., & Green, B. L. (1999). The need for mental health services research focusing on poor young women. *The Journal of Mental Health Policy and Economics, 2*(2), 73–80. Retrieved from http://www.ncbi.nlm.nih.gov/pubmed/11967411.

Mitchell, S. J., & Ronzio, C. R. (2011). Violence and other stressful life events as triggers of depression and anxiety: What psychosocial resources protect African American mothers? *Maternal and Child Health Journal, 15*(8), 1272–1281. doi:10.1007/s10995-010-0668-6.

Moe, A. M., & Bell, M. (2004). Abject economics: The effects of battering and violence on women's work and employability. *Violence Against Women, 10*, 29–55.

Mojtabai, R., & Jorm, A. F. (2015, March 15). Trends in psychological distress, depressive episodes and mental health treatment-seeking in the United States: 2001–2012. *Journal of Affective Disorders, 174*, 556–61. doi: 10.1016/j.jad.2014.12.039. Epub 2014 Dec 18.

Nadeem, E., Lange, J. M., Edge, D., Fongwa, M., Belin, T., & Miranda, J. (2007). Does stigma keep poor young immigrant and U.S.-born Black and Latina women from seeking mental health care? *Psychiatric Services, 58*(12), 1547–1554. doi:10.1176/appi.ps.58.12.1547.

Nicolaidis, C., Timmons, V., Thomas, M. J., Waters, A S., Wahab, S., Mejia, A., & Mitchell, S. R. (2010). "You don't go tell White people nothing": African American women's perspectives on the influence of violence and race on depression and depression care. *American Journal of Public Health, 100*(8), 1470–1476. doi:10.2105/AJPH.2009.161950

Norris, F. H., Murphy, A. D., Baker, C. K., & Perilla, J. L. (2004). Postdisaster PTSD over four waves of a panel study of Mexico's 1999 flood. *Journal of Traumatic Stress, 17*(4), 283–292. doi:10.1023/B:JOTS.0000038476.87634.9b.

Paranjape, A., & Kaslow, N. (2010, October) Family violence exposure and health outcomes among older African American women: Do spirituality and social support play protective roles? *Journal of Women's Health, 19*(10), 1899–1904.

Parto, J. A., Evans, M. K., & Zonderman, A. B. (2011). Symptoms of posttraumatic stress disorder among urban residents. *Journal of Nervous and Mental Disease, 199*(7), 436–439. doi:10.1097/NMD.0b013e3182214154.

Patterson, K. L. (2004). A longitudinal study of African American women and maintenance of healthy self-esteem. *Journal of Black Psychology, 30*, 307–328.

Pavetti, L., & Acs, G. (2001). Moving up, moving out, or going nowhere? A study of the employment patterns of young women and the implications for welfare mothers. *Journal of Policy Analysis and Management, 20*, 721–736.

Pulcino, T., Galea, S., Ahern, J., Resnick, H., Foley, M., & Vlahov, D. (2003). Posttraumatic stress in women after the September 11 terrorist attacks in New York City. *Journal of Women's Health (Larchmt), 12*(8), 809–820. doi:10.1089/154099903322447774.

Raphael, J. (2000). *Saving Bernice: Battered women, welfare, and poverty*. Boston: Northeastern University Press.

Romero, R. E. (2000). The icon of the strong Black woman: The paradox of strength. In L. C. Jackson & B. Greene (Eds.), *Psychotherapy with African American women: Innovations in psychodynamic perspectives and practice* (pp. 225–238). New York, NY: Guilford Press.

Santiago, C. D., Kaltman, S., & Miranda, J. (2013). Poverty and mental health: How do low-income adults and children fare in psychotherapy? *Journal of Clinical Psychology, 69*(2), 115–126. doi:10.1002/jclp.21951.

Schumm, J. A., Briggs-Phillips, M., & Hobfoll, S. E. (2006). Cumulative interpersonal traumas and social support as risk and resiliency factors in predicting PTSD and depression among inner-city women. *Journal of Traumatic Stress, 19*(6), 825–836. doi:10.1002/jts.20159.

Singh, A., Garnett, A., & Williams, D. (2013). Resilience strategies of African American women survivors of child sexual abuse a qualitative inquiry. *The Counseling Psychologist, 49*(8), 1093–1124.

Staggs, S. L., Long, S. M., Mason, G. E., Krishnan, S., & Riger, S. (2007). Intimate partner violence, social support, and employment in the postwelfare reform era. *Journal of Interpersonal Violence, 22*, 345–367.

Stevens, D. B. (1996). A phenomenological study of women who have overcome childhood abuse. *Dissertation Abstracts International: Section A. Humanities and Social Sciences, 57*(01), 11-A (UMI No. AAM9713010.1997-95009-138).

Stevens-Watkins, D., Sharma, S., Knighton, J. S., Oser, C. B., & Leukefeld, C. G. (2014). Examining cultural correlates of active coping among African American female trauma survivors. *Psychological Trauma: Theory, Research, Practice and Policy, 6*(4), 328–336. doi:10.1037/a0034116.

Sue, D. W., & Sue, D. (2008). *Counseling the culturally diverse: Theory and practice* (5th ed.). New York: Wiley.

Taylor, R. D., Budescu, M., & McGill, R. K. (2011). Demanding kin relations and depressive symptoms among low-income African American women: Mediating effects of self-esteem and optimism. *Cultural Diversity & Ethnic Minority Psychology, 17*(3), 303–308. doi:10.1037/a0024189.

Thompson, M. P., Kaslow, N. J., Short, L. M., & Wyckoff, S. (2002, August). The mediating roles of perceived social support and resources in the self-efficacy-suicide attempts relation among African American abused women. *Journal of Consulting and Clinical Psychology, 70*(4), 942–949.

Tjaden, P., & Thoennes, N. (2000). *Full report of the prevalence, incidence, and consequences of violence against women*. Washington, DC: U.S. Department of Justice.

Twenge, J. M., & Campbell, W. K. (2002). African Americans' mental health and perceptions of racist discrimination: The moderating effects of racial socialization experiences and self-esteem. *Personality and Social Psychology Review, 6*(1), 59–71.

U.S. Census Bureau. (2014). *Current population reports, P60-249, income and poverty in the United States: 2013*. Washington, DC: U.S. Government Printing Office.

Utsey, S. O., Bolden, M. A., Lanier, Y., & Williams, O. (2007). *Examining the role of culture-specific coping as a predictor of resilient outcomes in African Americans from high-risk urban communities. Journal of Black Psychology*, 33(1), 75–93.

Vest, J., Catlin, T., Chen, J., & Brownson, R. (2002). Multistate analysis of factors associated with intimate partner violence. *American Journal of Preventive Medicine, 22*, 156–164.

Wang, P. S., Lane, M., Olfson, M., Pincus, H. A., Wells, K. B., & Kessler, R. C. (2005). Twelve-month use of mental health services in the United States. *Archives of General Psychiatry, 62*, 629–640.

Ward, E. C., & Heidrich, S. M. (2009). African American women's beliefs about mental illness, stigma, and preferred coping behaviors. *Residential Nursing Health, 32*(5), 480–492. doi:10.1002/nur.20344.African.

Watlington, C. G., & Murphy, C. M. (2006, July). The roles of religion and spirituality among African American survivors of domestic violence. *Journal of Clinical Psychology, 62*(7), 837–857.

Watson, K. T., Roberts, N. M., & Saunders, M. R. (2012). Factors associated with anxiety and depression among African American and White women. *ISRN Psychiatry, 2012* (Article ID 432321), 1–8. doi:10.5402/2012/432321

Werner, E. E. (2005). Resilience research: past, present, and future. In R. D. Peters, B. Leadbeater, & R. J. McMahon (Eds.), *Resilience in children, families, and communities: Linking context to practice and policy* (pp. 3–11). Berlin: Springer.

Williams, S. L., & Mickelson, K. D. (2004). The nexus of domestic violence and poverty: Resilience in women's anxiety. *Violence Against Women, 10*(3), 283–293. doi:10.1177/1077801203262519.

Williams, D. R., & Williams-Morris, R. (2000). Racism and mental health: The African American experience. *Ethnicity & Health, 5*(3-4), 243–268. doi:10.1080/713667453.

Windle, G., & Bennett, K. M. (2012). Caring relationships: How to promote resilience in challenging times. In M. Ungar (Ed.), *The social ecology of resilience: A handbook of theory practice* (pp. 219–231). New York, NY: Springer. doi:10.1007/978-1-4614-0586-3.

Yick, A. (2008, September). A metasynthesis of qualitative findings on the role of spirituality and religiosity among culturally diverse domestic violence survivor. *Qualitative Health Research, 18*(9), 1289–1306.

Zabkiewicz, D. (2010). The mental health benefits of work: Do they apply to poor single mothers? *Social Psychiatry and Psychiatric Epidemiology, 45*(1), 77–87. doi:10.1007/s00127-009-0044-2.

Zautra, A. J., Arewasikporn, A., & Davis, M. C. (2010). Resilience: Promoting well-bring through recovery, sustainability, and growth. *Research in Human Development, 7*(3), 221–238.

# Chapter 6
# Substance Use Among Women in Poverty

**Irene Kuo, Melissa Turner, Claudia Trezza, and James Peterson**

*"... it's crazy how, how, you know, the drugs take you out there, and do things that you never ever thought you would do ..."*

## Introduction

Substance use and abuse is a significant public health problem for women. Substance abuse occurs more often among men than women and therefore for many years was historically not considered a problem. However, in recent years, the estimated prevalence of substance abuse among women appears to be increasing. According to the Centers for Disease Control and Prevention (CDC), the prevalence of illicit drug use among women rose from 6.4 % in 2002 to 6.9 % in 2012 and the prevalence of alcohol use among women rose from 44.9 % in 2002 to 47.9 % in 2012 (National Center for Health Statistics, 2014). Similarly, in 2009–2011, 6.7 % of women aged 18 years and older reported using illicit drugs within the past month. Drugs most commonly used by women today are marijuana and nonmedical use of psychotherapeutic drugs (U.S. Department of Health and Human Services, 2013). Alcohol use among women also continues to be a problem. In 2012, almost half of females aged 12 or older were current drinkers. That same year, an estimated 57 % of females between the ages of 18 and 25 were current drinkers, 33 % were binge drinkers, and 8.5 % of pregnant women aged 15–44 reported current alcohol use (SAMHSA, 2013).


I. Kuo (✉) • C. Trezza • J. Peterson
Milken Institute School of Public Health, George Washington University, Washington, DC, USA
e-mail: ikuo@email.gwu.edu

M. Turner
Infectious Diseases Section, Veterans Affairs Medical Center, Washington, DC, USA




A. O'Leary, P.M. Frew (eds.), *Poverty in the United States*,
DOI 10.1007/978-3-319-43833-7_6

Women drug and alcohol users have a different etiology than men users, and therefore possess different treatment needs. Although men are more likely than women to become addicted (Nelson-Zlupko, Kauffman, & Dore, 1995), women tend to progress quickly from using an addictive substance to dependence (Hernandez-Avila, Rounsaville, & Kranzler, 2004), develop medical or social consequences of addiction faster than men (Nelson-Zlupko et al., 1995), and often find it harder to quit addictive substances and are more susceptible to relapse (Ward, Klesges, Zbikowski, Bliss, & Garvey, 1997). Women typically consume less alcohol than men, drink alcohol less frequently, and are less likely to develop alcohol-related problems than men (Green, 2006). Women's drug and alcohol use is more likely to be triggered by negative experiences and stress and motivated by anxiety and depression than by a desire to experiment or conform to social expectations (Finkelstein, 1994). Compared to men, women experience a higher rate of emotional, physical, and sexual violence (Acierno, Resnick, & Kilpatrick, 1997). These events have been found to be triggers for drug and alcohol use among women. Experiences with sexual and physical abuse often play a fundamental role in the substance abuse process of women. Established correlates of female substance use are being abused as a child, being a caretaker responsible for siblings and other relatives, having rigid and regular domestic responsibilities, and early parenthood (Anderson, 2001). In addition, alcohol abuse is often linked to childhood trauma, sexual assault, unwanted pregnancies, child abuse and neglect, and spread of HIV and AIDS (Carter, 2002; Chasnoff, Neuman, Thornton, & Callaghan, 2001).

These challenges are exacerbated for women living in poverty like the women interviewed for the HPTN 064 study. We found discussions in the literature about the structural challenges to access integrated and effective health services faced by poor women who use drugs and alcohol, as well as the effects of poverty, gendered relations of power, and daily violence that women experience at home and in the streets, all of which limit the options for health management (Bungay, Johnson, Varcoe, & Boyd, 2010; Shannon et al., 2006). These were echoed in our discussion with the women interviewed for the study.

## *Drug and Alcohol Treatment for Women: Challenges Persist*

Although drug treatment options for women have multiplied since the 1980s across the USA, and research on the need for drug treatment for women has considerably advanced, drug-using women in this country still find many obstacles in dealing with their drug use including looking for appropriate treatment (Greenfield, Back, Lawson, & Brady, 2010). The problem is even greater for pregnant women and for women of color. Of all women in treatment, 62 % are white, 24 % are African-American, and 13 % are Latino (U.S. Department of Health and Human Services—Substance Abuse and Mental Health Services Administration—Office of Applied Studies, 2005).

The reasons for the lack of appropriate drug treatment options remain the same: the absence of childcare or family-centered treatment is a major limitation in a woman's decision to get into care. Similar to drug treatment programs, alcohol treatment programs have been largely focused and modeled after programs meant to treat men (Bastek-Karasow, 2007), despite the differing epidemiology and etiology of substance abuse among women compared to men. For example, treatment programs are often modeled after the 12-step programs that emphasize disclosure and personal responsibility, which tend to be less effective among women, especially those marginalized (Lapidus et al., 2005). If women are pregnant, their chances of seeking treatment are even more reduced because of the stigma attached to pregnant women who use drugs and because of the fear of the legal retaliations (Orentlicher, 1990).

These issues can prevent women from seeking treatment unless the program offers services and counseling geared specifically to these barriers. In general, women are more likely to seek and remain in care when treatment programs are tailored specifically to them and address a broad range of issues, including childcare, counseling for violence, and life-management skills (Wilsnack, 1991).

Many of the women we interviewed for HPTN 064 provided us with the stories to support these numbers and described the numerous challenges they and the women in their communities face regarding substance use and recovery.

## Methods

As part of HPTN 064, a series of individual in-depth interviews and focus groups were conducted with women affected by poverty in select geographical areas of the country (Washington, D.C.; New York, New York; Raleigh/Durham, North Carolina; and Atlanta, Georgia). We asked women to talk about HIV and other STDs, about their experiences accessing health care, and about their perceptions of the neighborhoods they lived in, as well as their social and sexual networks and subsistence.

We read the excerpts looking to identify the narratives surrounding drugs and alcohol in the women's lives, paying particular attention to the coping mechanisms and strategies that women developed to survive in their circumstances.

### *Data Analysis Process*

Data analysis was conducted using NVIVO 9.0 qualitative data analysis software. Coded excerpts of text from the HPTN 064 qualitative interview narratives were examined to identify the participants' experiences and involvement with drugs and alcohol. The inquiry sought to examine the socioecological factors contributing to drugs and alcohol use and involvement among women in poor communities.

The HPTN 064 interview guides (focus group and individual) did not ask directly about substance abuse; therefore, the issue was explored broadly within the available data. The authors examined coded summaries of text for references to drugs and alcohol or other related terms. Specific terms and colloquialisms used in the interviews and focus groups to refer to drugs, alcohol, and associated activities were identified in the transcripts, such as "crack cocaine," "hoeing," "gang bangers," and "getting high."

The resulting terms were used to run additional queries to identify appropriate categories and themes that developed from the summaries. Four domains were selected from the queries and review of the text by the authors and included (1) social norms around substance use; (2) violence related to substance use; (3) financial drivers; and (4) resilience and hope among those who were able to recover from substance-use problems. Resilience is defined here as a dynamic process encompassing positive adaptation within the context of significant adversity (Luthar & Cicchetti, 2000). This definition assumes the presence of significant threat and positive adaptation despite risks (Luthar & Cicchetti, 2000). In addition to resilience, activity in pursuit of substance-abuse recovery was explored to include efforts by the women to overcome addiction. Recovery is defined here as used in the medical model—a term that connotes a return to health following trauma or illness; in this case, the term recovery is applied broadly to refer to movement (thoughts, actions, feelings) toward a healthier life and aspirations of the women with histories of addiction to transform their lives. Lists of terms were then generated for each category and queries were run within the drugs and alcohol node.

Finally, additional queries were run for each of the four domains within the drug and alcohol node. The resultant data were thoroughly reviewed to identify themes and associations that define the identified domains. The excerpts were reorganized for contextually coherent definitions of the domains and thematic relationships within each domain. Analyses of the reorganized text segments were conducted to generate emergent themes that descriptively defined categories of data. Main themes that arose from each domain of interest were summarized and interpreted.

## Results

Substance use (both drugs and alcohol) was consistently identified by the women interviewed as a pervasive problem in their lives. For many of the women interviewed, drugs were ubiquitous in most aspects of their lives—from the environmental/neighborhood level to their social, sexual, and family networks. As described by the women in the study, the multifaceted aspects of the drug culture in these communities were a stark reality of life in the "hood" or their communities. Their stories conveyed the experiences that involved the threat of physical harm, actual physical violence from fights and altercations, stabbings, and often shootings as a result of drug selling and drug using in homes and on the streets. In addition, financial hardships experienced by these women, or the people with whom they interact, exacerbated the persistence of drugs in their lives, resulting in engagement in risky behaviors to either distribute or obtain drugs. However, despite these stories and feelings, we also observed examples of optimism, hope, and resilience among these women that seemed to uplift them to overcome and/or cope with these challenges. All of these issues have a substantial toll on these women's lives, which is often exacerbated by acute economic insecurity in low-income households. Below are their stories.

## *Ubiquity of Drugs and Alcohol in Neighborhoods and Social Networks*

When the women described their neighborhoods, some reported positive aspects of where they lived, such as being convenient to public transportation and affordability. The participants also provided comments about relationships established within the neighborhood that contributed to the important friendships and interactions. However, many participants spoke of their neighborhoods negatively, mostly as places they wanted to get away from and not places they wanted to continue to live in without some changes. Although the participants were not asked directly about drugs in their neighborhoods, women from the various study sites described drug activity and violence taking place on the streets and on the corners of the neighborhoods. For them, this drug activity detracted significantly from the positive aspects of the neighborhoods. As one woman described:

> Oh. (laughter) Out the window? I see everything. It's not a good neighborhood, so you see a lot of...You could tell that there's drug activity. A lot of – and this type of thing, you see a lot of women there, like, in drugs ...
>
> *–Interviewee, New York, NY*

Her comment explicitly states that what she sees "out the window" is a negative attribute of the neighborhood. The participant included specific characteristics as she continued to describe what she observed out the window—"drug activity" and "a lot of women." Another woman described her neighborhood the following way, suggesting a similar sentiment about the presence of drug activity in the immediate area:

> It is ghetto and drug infested and prostitute land and, I mean, it's a lot going on there.
>
> *–Interviewee, Raleigh/Durham, NC*

The use of the term "ghetto" suggests an inherent sense of economic isolation and marginalization. The participant makes the point of rendering her perception of the neighborhood as "drug infested." The participants provided examples of observations of kids and young adults engaging in the visible drug culture on neighborhood corners, and suggested that these behaviors are pervasive in the neighborhood:

> And they drink their alcohol, whether it's beer, wine, might be a soda, you know; smoke their cigarettes or whatever else they smoke ... Weed, you know, out there at the corner at the store.
>
> *–Interviewee, Raleigh/Durham, NC*

A sense of frustration was expressed regarding the pervasiveness of drugs and the consequences they posed on their daily lives, even in carrying out simple chores like going to the corner grocery store:

> I don't really go to the store because basically that's where the drugs are, the gang members are, and a lot of the kids is out there fighting, people down there begging for money and I feel like you should be able to go in your neighborhood and you should be able to walk to the store without somebody begging you for money …
>
> *–Focus Group Participant, Raleigh/Durham, NC*

The exchange, sales, use, and concomitant use of drugs and alcohol in these neighborhoods seemed to impact the people who live there in complex ways. Substance use was not only pervasive in the surrounding neighborhoods and in the immediate environment, but was present in the social and familial networks of the women we interviewed. Many women described how they were affected by family members who succumbed to drug addiction, potentially leading to a protective effect, as expressed below:

> My uncle was a crack head, so I watched him and another one of my uncles with the heroin and that was little too much. Like I just always thought that's too much. I don't want to get that high.
>
> *–Interviewee, Washington, D.C.*

They also observed their friends, peers, and partners being involved with drugs, and the subsequent results:

> Yeah, everybody was on crack, everybody was on crack. Except for the wheelchair [referring to one's partner at the time]; he was a weed head.
>
> *–Interviewee, Washington, D.C.*

> Then he [person's partner] started to hang with his cousins, drinking, taking E[cstasy]-pills behind my back that I didn't know about.
>
> *–Interviewee, Raleigh/Durham, NC*

Women also talked about their own personal substance use and the factors influencing their use. As described previously, the ubiquity of drugs in the neighborhood and their social circles seemed to be associated with personal use. Some women attributed their personal drug use to living in drug-infested neighborhoods and being surrounded by people who did drugs, describing their drug use as an inevitable result of their surroundings:

> […] and if you are in a bad neighborhood or whatever the case may be, it's – you are – you become a product of your environment. Some people that never smoked – like I started smoking when I was 13, so I don't now. But when I was young, chilling in [name deleted] Projects, I was smoking, like for no apparent reason, when I didn't have to. Like do my homework and go outside and smoke, rather than do my homework and go to the library. We was using the library – it wasn't even peer pressure, because I was smoking.
>
> *–Focus Group Participant, New York, NY*

In the previous excerpt, the participant suggested that the environment was a central element driving people to become involved in the drug culture. Interestingly, this woman alluded to making choices, opting to smoke (marijuana) "rather than do my homework," emphasizing the environmental influence for her.

For some women, substance use seemed to have been the result of coping with major disruptions to their family or social structure, such as incarceration, substance use, and/or family illness. Having little or no family support was often cited as a reason or explanation for their personal drug use. As one woman described:

> [...] my mother passed away when I was nine years old, my father got incarcerated, my brother got taken away. I literally had to drop out of school in the fifth grade because I had no place to live ... I was hustling, I was doing my thing, I was making my money, and I had my man that was doing for me, as well, too, I just needed an address to go back to school, and nobody in my family would even do that, and I don't blame them now. When I was younger I couldn't stand them for it, I hated them, like you know I don't have nobody and y'all my family and y'all don't want to do it? But now as a parent I'm like – I was 11 years old. I was selling drugs. I was sexually active. I was already living my life like a fucking adult.
>
> *–Focus Group Participant, New York, NY*

The experiences conveyed by the participants about how the drugs and alcohol influenced life in the neighborhoods and among their networks were compelling. For some participants, efforts to redirect or change the circumstances brought on by illicit drugs in the neighborhoods seemed hopeless, and women described seeking solutions to these problems both in the formal and informal systems, often leading to a vicious cycle of involvement in the drug trade or one's own drug use.

## *Violence Associated with Drugs and Alcohol*

Another domain repeatedly mentioned in the context of substance use and other issues among women in poor neighborhoods was violence. The conventional understanding is that the presence of drugs very often comes hand in hand with violence, whether it is violence experienced in their homes ("my father used to be an alcoholic – I used to get beaten," *Interviewee, New York, NY*) or in their neighborhoods ("... you know he strung out on drugs and you know he just want to hit women, take their money and stuff," *Focus Group Participant, Washington, D.C.*).

As one woman described, the presence of drugs and violence made people feel unsafe in their neighborhoods. Another woman explained that she would be moving from one neighborhood that she called "safe" to another one which she defined as being "unsafe" due to the drugs and violence found there:

> Well, for me, right now, where I'm at—the neighborhood that I live in, is safe, but ... when I move, I know I'm not going to a safe neighborhood. I know it's going to be drugs, and violence, and everything, when I move ...
>
> *–Focus Group Participant, New York, NY*

For many of the respondents, the parallel circumstances of drugs and violence resonated throughout the neighborhoods where they lived. When talking about the violence and drugs in communities, women most often pointed to the youth and street gangs in these neighborhoods as the main perpetuators of drug dealing and associated violence in the neighborhood. Gang members were usually characterized as both male and female local youth, but the respondents mainly discussed young males as the most menacing and having the predominant influence, making the neighborhood feel unsafe as a result of the drugs and violence. As exemplified in the following excerpt, the respondent pointed to a specific age group as being responsible for the violence in the neighborhood :

> I – in my – what I see from my neighborhood, it's mainly teenagers or young adults that either dropped out of school, don't go to school, either selling drugs or is in a gang. Mostly of it is just gang-affiliated people that's doing all the violence.
>
> *–Focus Group Participant, Raleigh/Durham, NC*

Drugs and alcohol were seen both as causes and consequences of violence. In one interview, a woman described experiencing domestic violence by her husband who was an alcoholic and possibly a drug addict or user. This participant explained how the consequence of substance use and the associated violence in her life had contributed to what seems to culminate into a vicious cycle of substance use and violence. The participant's comment revealed the insidious and progressive nature of substance use and how it is characterized by the volatility and violence it causes on the lives of families such as hers. This participant suggests that her own drug use is a coping mechanism to deal with the violence perpetrated against her:

> [...] That's the only person I'm scared of is my husband, you know. He hangs around the drug area and comes by, like I said. He'll get drunk and he do drugs. I've never seen him do drugs but he's an alcoholic. I've got so many warrants on my husband 'cause he keeps beating me. And I'm scared. I'm afraid for my life because he's now already killed somebody. I just can't take it. So, I don't have no other choice but to do drugs because I be so scared .
>
> *–Interviewee, Raleigh/Durham, NC*

The ambiguity of the day-to-day existence of those who are subject to the ubiquity of drugs in these resource-deprived neighborhoods was continuously described during the interviews. For many of the study participants—"using drugs" and "drug using"—had negative effects within the neighborhood and within their lives. The harsh reality of life affected by drugs and violence was a constant theme in our interviews.

> ...'cause if you wasn't smoking or you wasn't doing what you doing you wouldn't be out here doing no fighting or none of that. [R 4: I was smoking PCP boo.] Yeah, no that what I was saying though that's why a lot of people out here fight because of the violence. Is start off of the drugs I meant.
>
> *–Focus Group Participant, Washington, D.C.*

In the previous excerpt, on the one hand, the respondent suggests that using drugs is a direct effect of the violence that took place "out here." Being "under the influence" or "intoxicated" instigates some of the violence and "fighting" in the neighborhood. On the other hand, the relationship between drugs and violence also goes in the other direction. These respondents revealed experiences when consequences of drug use led to situations that involved owing money to dealers and created dangerous circumstances that resulted in violence. Many women described violence experienced from the consequences of their partners' behaviors in transactions where women were violently forced to engage in behaviors to replace the money for drugs:

> [...] When I was at my apartment, the drug dealer, he used to go over. He wanted – he – I had a boyfriend, he was telling me that my boyfriend didn't come and this and that. And then he made me do things I ain't want to do to him, and he was hitting – he made me do things I ain't want to do. So I was just – I was just stupid, and it – all of it for the drugs, they – ever since that – that – it was it. That was it.
>
> *–Interviewee, New York, NY*

The study participants articulated their experiences and how they understood the confluence of violence perpetrated as a result of drug use and the drug use as a consequence of violence in their neighborhoods and among their networks. Their shared experiences brought forth a better understanding of the complexities that defined the association of drugs and violence in the lives of these women .

## Financial Implications and Drugs and Alcohol

In the tough environments described above, resources were scarce and people found various means to provide for the basic needs of their families and to maintain their drug habits. The study participants talked about their disadvantaged financial situations. Some had lost their homes and were left with very little money, while others described not having money to pay for basic needs. One woman explained how she needed the compensation earned from her participation in the study to pay her rent:

> I wouldn't even be at this meeting right now if you didn't say nothing about no $50 because my rent due and [...] I got to take the money order around the corner.
>
> *–Focus Group Participant, Washington, D.C.*

This participant's comment embodies the general experiences and daily struggles of these women to make ends meet. One woman explained how her financial situation had pushed her to have to decide between paying rent and feeding her children:

> So, it's struggling. There's some things you got to think about; it's either the rent or do you feed the kids.
>
> *–Interviewee, Washington, D.C.*

Substance use was mentioned as a common and significant theme in many of these women's lives and the lives of the people in their networks. Many of the women interviewed struggled with substance abuse themselves or staying clean from drug abuse. Poverty represented an additional challenge in the already difficult lives of women interviewed in the study. And, as one woman put it, when multiple layers of challenges, including economic ones, are "stacked against you," women sometimes engage in exchange sex as a way to make ends meet and obtain drugs.

Some women did not necessarily do drugs themselves but had been caught up at some point in their lives in a high-risk transaction in order to obtain drugs and make ends meet. The following passage provides a picture of the challenges some women faced and the choices they were forced to make to survive financially, sometimes driven by addiction:

> […] I mean I know a couple of 'em that they gotta do what they gotta do in order to feed their families so they go out there and they sell their body to get money. A lot of 'em, some do it for drugs and stuff like that. I know a couple of them that they gotta do that.
>
> –*Focus Group Participant, Raleigh/Durham, NC*

Similarly, another woman observed:

> […] if a woman ain't got no money to get drugs, she's going to prostitute her body to get drugs or sex to get drugs, take it in her anus to get drugs. Whatever that man want to do to get her that piece of drug, she's gonna do it.
>
> –*Interviewee, Raleigh/Durham, NC*

Other women reported engaging in the drug culture as an economic opportunity, in which they sold drugs for money, or they exchanged sex for money and drugs. Drugs, money, and sex were consistently mentioned and were almost always discussed simultaneously in conversations with those women. Interestingly, many of the women talked about these transactions, mostly in reference to other women they knew, rarely reporting personal engagement in these activities, as exemplified below:

> […] Some women sleep around for money, you know, I have girlfriends that used to do that. They sleep around to support their kids or, you know, pay their bills. That's about drugs and money. That's about, that's it.
>
> –*Interviewee, Raleigh/Durham, NC*

In some cases, partners in these women's lives facilitated or encouraged the exchange of sex for drugs or for money to buy drugs for both of them. One woman explained the specific term used for this transaction:

> That's the – that's, that's the word for it when your own man will send you to "hook," or he knows that you're going to go "hook" to get money so the both of you can get high.
>
> –*Focus Group Participant, New York, NY*

The comment in the previous excerpt highlights the vulnerability that the women experienced that for the most part compromised not only their quality of life, but also their moral values directly. Some women expressed judgment toward other women who exchanged sex for money and/or drugs, as described by these participants:

> I see women disrespecting themselves a lot on this side of town. I don't know if it's for money, for drugs.
>
> –*Interviewee, Raleigh/Durham, NC*

> I'm saying I don't do neither, but I'm saying before I lay down and open my legs for money, I'll sell drugs.
>
> –*Focus Group Participant, Raleigh/Durham, NC*

Another woman expressed unfavorable judgment regarding women who exchanged sex for drugs that were ultimately used by their partners. She suggested that exchanging sex for drugs for one's personal drug use is more respectable than exchanging sex for someone else's drug use:

> But see, when I sold my body, I never sold my body for no man. I sold my body for me. 'Cause the girls that – the girls that's out here, they have they boyfriends, you know they – going – you know, they sell their body for their boyfriends. I was selling my body for getting my – my drugs. That's what I sell my body for, but – you messing up my body, and got money to a man? No, ain't no way in hell! I wasn't having that …
>
> *–Interviewee, New York, NY*

Other women expressed self-awareness and were critical of their own actions. Specifically, one woman who blamed her drug use for doing "crazy" things that she would "never [do] again," which was not consistent with who she was:

> I'll be honest, you know, me, when I was out drugging and I was with my boyfriend one time and we needed money … And he actually watched my bag while I went and, you know, trick with a guy. You know, and it's crazy how, how, you know, the drugs take you out there, and do things that you never ever thought you would do. Because that's not me, you know what I mean? And I did that one time and never again – I was so scared. But, you know, it took me there, you know?
>
> *–Focus Group Participant, New York, NY*

Some of the women also expressed disdain toward other women's addiction and, in some cases, how it led them to bypass financial responsibilities:

> And, they you know they get their food stamps and their welfare checks and they're selling their food stamps to make sure they got their drugs and whatever else they need and you know they're taking their welfare checks and they're not spending it on the kids, they're spending on their self and you know drugs, I mean I'm going through that right now with my daughter's father.
>
> *–Interviewee, Washington, D.C.*

As demonstrated in the following quote, one woman judged the desperation of a substance user on the street regarding the situation the user was in:

> Because they're on these drugs and this and that the kids, I had one lady at the store, at the carry-out had her daughter say could she have a dollar so she could get something to eat. So, I give her the dollar and then I see the mother and her going towards the liquor store. So, what I kind of did, went on by the liquor store and took the dollar right on back. I don't care what else she had I took what I gave her and took the little girl right across the street and got some French fries because you taking money to buy alcohol whatever your drugs this and that. I mean, it's just not fair.
>
> *–Focus Group, Washington, D.C.*

The stories we heard about the women's lives and the lives of the women in their networks referred to a high level of social and economic distress. Although women expressed frustration about the pervasiveness of drugs, violence, and exchange sex, there seemed to be much ambivalence about their own involvement in drug use and the involvement of other people who would engage in these behaviors and how they related to their individual financial situations.

## *Hope, Resilience, and Recovery*

> I got clean cause I got sick and tired of living the way I was living.
>
> –*Interviewee, Washington, D.C.*

In addition to witnessing addiction among others, the participants described their own personal challenges with addiction to alcohol and other drugs. In the midst of the suffering and recounting of struggles, women expressed resilience and strength when it came to quitting or sustaining recovery from their personal drug use.

The stories that the participants told about quitting or attempting to quit drug use were very much in line with the strength-based perspective which emphasizes assets and inner strength of individuals, families, and communities toward positive change (Rapp, 2002; Todd & Worell, 2000). In interviews, we often noted a great capacity of women to recognize their difficulties, however brutal and chaotic, and to aspire to overcome adversity in their lives. Highlighting their capabilities to form solutions to their own problems is an essential part of fully understanding and appreciating their narratives. It was apparent from the interviews that the women possessed unique attributes, traits, and resources upon which to build solutions to improve their own lives.

The women described tools they used to avoid personal and environmental relapse triggers. They talked about the efforts they made to achieve and sustain recovery, which sometimes included taking part in formal, structured treatment programs and learning strategies to protect against relapse. The passage below highlights problem solving, effective use of mutual aid, and pursuit of healthy alternatives to insulate oneself from relapse. In the following quote, one participant shared her journey in early recovery, receiving feedback and mutual aid within an informal network of other women:

> Well, I was staying at a recovery center … for on drug and alcohol. I have a year clean ….um, it was, it was a um, sober community, I was, um, surrounded with ten, ten females … Um, every day we'll go to group, and talk about different way to prevent for relapsing … And um, finding out other way and means to occupy our time.
>
> –*Interviewee, Atlanta, GA*

The capacity to reflect upon and gain wisdom from life experience is highlighted in the excerpt above and is a marker of adaptation to circumstances, a basic tenet of resilient behavior (Luthar & Cicchetti, 2000; O'Leary & Ickovics, 1994). With the clear intention to avoid known pitfalls (idle time) and to incorporate new coping strategies (talking in a group format), this woman was looking for and creating safe places to share, give, and receive support, reinforcement, and recognition for accomplishments in recovery. The importance of having a social support system to rely on while attempting to quit or staying clean became evident in the stories of some women who lacked or had lost such support system (Seccombe, 2002).

Although the women interviewed for this study expressed a fair amount of personal strength, resilience, and potential to build on existing capacities to cope, manage, and navigate the difficulties they faced, we also heard about the dangers and risks that the women encounter in their lives. Recognition of the difficulties in self-managing one's addiction and maintaining sobriety was a significant feature of the resiliency activity observed among the women (Rapp, 2002).

The following passages highlight participants' addiction concerns including the honest recognition of personal vulnerabilities that could possibly lead them to relapsing especially when being surrounded by people, places, and things that increase the temptation to use. We also heard about some of the women's concerns regarding their efforts to sustain clean time during early recovery as well as the risks they face when posed by inadequate social support.

> [...] And detox helped and going to meetings down there. And just I came up here but it's like the environment where I'm in, I'm not going to lie, it's a struggle every day. And then not to have the support group when I'm going through something or a mentor to call to say, so this is hard I'm not going to lie.
>
> *–Interviewee, Washington, D.C.*

> "[...] I have a family who is heavily into alcohol and drugs you know and me being a product of that as well, I don't really wanna be around you know what, I'm trying to stay away from, you know. I'm in recovery right now and being clean is something that I really, really love, you know.
>
> *–Focus Group Participant, Raleigh/Durham, NC*

The comments expressed here give insight into the willingness of these women to make some changes in their lives. As previously suggested, these excerpts provide examples of the struggles these women had to contend with: the people—"*I don't really wanna be around*"; the places—*it's like the environment where I'm in ... it's a struggle every day*; and the things—"*every time I get a little money, I want to go the drug man.*" Without specifically identifying motivation, the participants' statements imply positive motivation, a strong desire to sustain small change, and resolve to move forward productively toward a substance-free life.

The women demonstrated an abundance of accumulated knowledge over the course of their lifetime. Their wisdom and a clear understanding and acceptance of how past addictive behavior posed a risk to their health and safety were evidenced. This insight, awareness, and capacity for self-analysis and self-correction are made clear by one woman in the following passage:

> Now that I don't get high you couldn't pay me to do half of the stuff I did when I was getting high like jumping in and out of people cars, strangers. So that's what I mean about it. There're no, then again I ain't even going to say 'cause I know some people that's doing it now don't get high so. But you couldn't pay me to do it.
>
> *–Interviewee, Raleigh /Durham, NC*

Recognizing past mistakes as opportunities to learn and become better, stronger, and wiser is a key component to successful recovery. Women described learning from past mistakes and demonstrated understanding of how past behavior in the pursuit of illicit substances posed a risk to their very lives. The participant in the above statement recognized the danger of drug-seeking behavior to her life and articulated strong resolve to avoid this risk behavior in the future—knowing that the possibility of relapse is ever-present.

The presence of self-help support groups such as Narcotics Anonymous and Alcohol Anonymous in recovery from substance abuse has been helpful, although the need for gender-specific programming within these groups still exists. The women in our study described varying levels of participation in recovery processes from contemplating change in addictive patterns, participation in self-evaluation, self-management, and self-help groups to formal participation in structured treatment programs. Reliance on the support of other women in recovery was a prominent theme in the participants' narratives, through building a sisterhood of mutual support and effectively utilizing mutual aid as a fundamental prerequisite to progress toward recovery goals. Many women described the value of surrounding themselves with a support network of other women seeking recovery from addiction and verbalized recognition of the need to connect with others, particularly other women, to build close bonds that allows for sharing freely on all topics:

> I got one girlfriend that's in the fellowship; we came through treatment, we went to transition. And we got eight years together, we celebrate together and me and her we like sisters. I can talk to her about anything and she can talk to me about anything. I have a sponsor I'm not even really comfortable with talking about everything to. So this is one person that I can talk to anything about, condoms, yeah condoms, whatever, HIV. She got a daughter that's eighteen just had a baby supposed to be my God daughter. You know we talk about everything.
>
> I have some girlfriends that live in that area that's in the fellowship. Yeah, I have girlfriends in that area that's in the fellowship with me that's NA and AA. And we go to meetings they'll come and get me we go to meetings. And we might go to NA and AA dances where's there's no drugs, no alcohol, and that's it.
>
> *–Interviewee, Raleigh /Durham, NC*

Utilizing connectedness with other women as a foundation for recovery is a core strength identified by the narratives from the women in HPTN 064. Willingness to own personal vulnerabilities, and the courage to share vulnerabilities openly and completely with others, is a cornerstone to meaningful change and building the capacity to withstand assaults to sobriety experienced in everyday life.

The capacity to relate to others and to make personal and emotional connections, and the acknowledgement of the need for other like minds in one's life in order to sustain recovery, is reflected here and reinforces the importance of mutual support among women. When the participant states "I have girlfriends in the area," she is affirming the importance of women in recovery making linkages with other women from within the community in which they both live. Women pursuing recovery need other like-minded women from within their own community who can understand the world from which they both come and in which they both live. A significant feature of the strength-based perspective (Bandura, 2000; Saleebey, 1996) is harnessing assets existing within the individual's own community to facilitate the preservation of positive gains in recovery.

For anyone aspiring to recover from an addiction to substances, it is important to explore intrinsic, personal drivers of addictive behaviors in addition to environmental contributors to addiction risks. Women articulated "lessons learned," "wisdom," and/or new insights concerning substance abuse and the maladaptive role of addiction in their lives due to personal mental health issues and linked those issues to problematic, addictive behaviors.

As one woman put it:

> [...] You know I have suffered with chronic depression believe it or not and I medicated it in ways, you know crack, ways to keep me up and upbeat and stuff ...
>
> *–Focus Group Participant, Washington, D.C.*

Hopefulness that their own children, other youth in the community, and future generations would have access to better opportunities was a common theme in the narratives. Fear that their children would succumb to the temptations of substance abuse and addiction was a common concern among women. Women verbalized realistic, pragmatic concerns about the risks faced by their children and often expressed optimism and hope that their children would follow a different path and would learn from their example:

> ... and I would just tell my son you know he's 22 now but he like that weed, it's too late for him you know pretty much. But he likes the weed and everything but if I had it to do all over again I think I would have kept him a little closer just so he can learn a lesson sooner...So, but right now he's incarcerated doing federal time, he should be home in January but I hope he's learned a valuable lesson being away from home."
>
> *–Focus Group Participant, Washington, D.C.*

Learning from past mistakes, reflecting on wisdom gain over a lifetime, and acknowledgement of regret were documented in the group narratives.

## Policy Implications

Addressing the problem of substance use and abuse among women in the USA requires urgent policy interventions. As articulated by the voices of these women, most women had low levels of financial independence and most were inextricably tied to substance use, whether through personal use, engaging in risky sexual behaviors to finance personal use, and/or being engaged in drug distribution as a means of income. The women described a cycle of poverty that was both a result and/or fueled substance use among themselves and within their communities.

### *Improving Their Financial Situations*

It is critical to improve the economic situation of these women, so they may be financially empowered to avoid making choice from a vulnerable position. Being able to provide for themselves and their dependents is a critical step in repairing relationships and gaining social support from friends and family members to facilitate substance-use recovery.

The larger problem stems from how to empower these women so that they can become financially independent. Traditional government social welfare programs to deal with poverty have centered around financial assistance programs to help women and families achieve self-sufficiency, such as the Supplemental Nutrition Assistance

Program (SNAP) and Temporary Assistance for Needy Families (TANF). While SNAP provides nutrition assistance to both individuals and families, TANF provides assistance to families rather than individuals. TANF helps to support education and training for beneficiaries; yet neither TANF nor SNAP fully focuses on teaching practical skills on becoming financially independent.

In response to this gap, new policies should be developed to generate training and microfinance opportunities for impoverished women in order to move beyond the cycle of financial dependence. For example, economic empowerment or micro-enterprise programs have been found to be successful in developing countries in reducing financial dependence and concurrently reducing HIV sexual risk (Dunbar et al., 2010; Kim et al., 2009; Pronyk et al., 2008), and could be considered in the USA. However, the impact of microfinance programs on substance-use behaviors would still need to be explored. These programs should also include topics on financial literacy, management skills in addition to vocational skill building, as well as building social support networks.

## *Dealing with High Prevalence of Drugs and Associated Violence*

The ubiquity of drugs in the neighborhoods in which these women lived was widely discussed in our interviews. The federal response to drug addiction has focused mainly on supply reduction rather than demand or treatment-based reduction. Approximately two-thirds of the federal budget is allocated toward interdiction, law enforcement, and supply reduction, and only one-third toward prevention, treatment, and other demand-reduction strategies. This approach has had limited success in the original goal of curtailing drug use and sale and reducing drug trade-related violence, and the drug economy and violence persist in US communities, as described vividly in the narratives of these women. In addition, many of the practices involved in this approach have had the unintended consequences of deepening the economic and the racial divide in cities across the country. Harsh criminal penalties for drug offenders are expensive and have not decreased illegal drug use, abuse, and addiction. The benefit in public safety and health for which such policies were intended have not yet been realized, and families are disrupted by imprisoned or addicted partners and children, and neighborhoods continue to be threatened by drug dealers and gangs. As a result, the criminalization of drug use is one of the driving factors of racial and ethnic health disparities in the USA. The recent trend of legalization and decriminalization of marijuana use across the country is an example of a policy change that can potentially reduce the devastating effect of the trickle-down effects of criminalization of drug use.

Rather than focusing on criminalizing drug use and sale, policy responses should focus more on drug education, substance-abuse treatment, and increased medical assistance, which have been found to be more effective to reduce drug use. Spending should shift from detention to prevention and treatment. Prevention efforts should include programs to educate the public about the dangers of misusing prescribed medications, monitor prescription drug prescribers, and emphasize safe storage and proper disposal of unused medications (White Jr, 2008). To effectively create change in neighborhoods like those described by the women in the HPTN 064 interviews, policy makers need to develop interventions that go beyond strictly curtailing drug availability and that address the harms and causes of drug misuse which have to do with the multitude of barriers that individuals are facing at the community level, including the provision of more economic opportunities for both women and men.

## *Capitalizing on Resiliency*

The women participating in HPTN 064 consistently verbalized an innate desire to move forward and overcome their circumstances, and a review of their narratives revealed resiliency traits and efforts to cope that deserves further study to determine best strategies to build upon the existing potential for these women to problem-solve, adapt positively, and overcome the limitations of their living situations. To tap into this potential, the following policy initiatives are recommended to support sustained change for the study participants, their families, and communities.

It has long been postulated that substance-abuse recovery programs based on models designed for addicted men seeking sobriety fail to meet the needs of women (Meyer, Springer, & Altice, 2011; Mulia, Schmidt, Bond, Jacobs, & Korcha, 2008). Due to their roles as primary caretakers for minor children and other family members, their orientation toward connectedness with other women, and mental health needs and motivations for recovery, programs especially designed for substance-dependent women are indicated. Programs that recognize unique pathways to addiction common among women, their need for parenting support, job training housing, and support services can help these women reach their potential.

Strength-based perspectives that build upon existing capacities of these women and that honor their connectedness with others and capacity to bond and promote womanhood are key to harnessing their best assets. The capacity of this cohort to find value and triumph in connections with other women and hopefulness for a better future are critically important components for self-efficacy that builds self-esteem, a sense that one can impact the world around them and promote healthier families and communities.

The narratives emphasized the importance of environmental context on individual and familial functioning in the community. The women articulated positive and negative aspects of their neighborhood and varying levels of social networks operating that can both facilitate and negate positive functioning. Community-based resiliency is achieved by providing safe, affordable housing opportunities; developing and strengthening productive schools and self-help recovery networks; building intolerance for drug culture; and strengthening community-oriented policing, churches, and businesses. Gainful employment and strong social support networks facilitates community-wide resilience and builds collective self-efficacy and reduced neighborhood toxicity (Cutrona, Russell, Hessling, Brown, & Murry, 2000; German & Latkin, 2012; Latkin & Curry, 2003; Windsor, Benoit, & Dunlap, 2010).

## Conclusion

The analysis of the HPTN 064 narratives reveals the heartbreaking human struggle faced by the women attempting to confront the ravages of substance abuse in their day-to-day lives. Given the widespread scourge of illegal substances embedded in local neighborhoods, participants described conditions akin to feeling immersed or trapped in living situations where contact with illicit substances, directly or indirectly, was virtually inescapable. The study participants described their personal experiences and observations of the influence of drugs in their lives and in so doing articulated the multidimensional, systemic nature of substance use and abuse in impoverished neighborhoods and the impact of larger structural forces within local communities, neighborhoods, families, and individuals. Substance abuse for this cohort can be understood more completely by examining the individual within his or her environments, which are complex spheres of multiple levels of influence.

Structural racism, sexism, and classism allow illicit drug use in open-air markets, minimal access to gainful employment, or advanced education opportunities in the study communities. The presence of an active, visible, and violent illicit drug economy creates an atmosphere of pervasive tension and stress experienced overpoweringly by the women in the study. Lack of meaningful activities for youth and inadequate preparation for success in the legal marketplace fuel drug trade as an available, income-producing activity within a very limited scope for economic self-sufficiency using legal means. Criminality exists as a means to satisfy day-to-day survival such as the exchange of sex for money and drugs in the context of the absence of access to education, safe affordable housing, and health services that include effective gender-informed drug treatment intervention. These factors facilitate a neighborhood culture of violence fueled by desperate efforts to feed an addiction, innate drive to survive abject poverty. The women described stressful, demanding life circumstances and efforts to break the continuous cycle of drug involvement for themselves, their family, and future generations.

## References

Acierno, R., Resnick, H. S., & Kilpatrick, D. G. (1997). Health impact of interpersonal violence. 1: Prevalence rates, case identification, and risk factors for sexual assault, physical assault, and domestic violence in men and women. *Behavioral Medicine, 23*(2), 53–64. doi:10.1080/08964289709596729.

Anderson, T. L. (2001). Drug use and gender. In C. E. Faupel & P. M. Roman (Eds.), *Encyclopedia of criminology and deviant behavior. Volume IV: Self-destructive behavior and dis-valued identity* (Vol. IV, pp. 286–289). Philadelphia, PA: Taylor & Francis Publishers.

Bandura, A. (2000). Exercise of human agency through collective efficacy. *Current Directions in Psychological Science, 9*(3), 75–78.

Bastek-Karasow C, Davis R. (2007) Gender-Responsive Treatment for Women With Substance Use Diorders. WATCH, revised March 2010.

Bungay, V., Johnson, J. L., Varcoe, C., & Boyd, S. (2010). Women's health and use of crack cocaine in context: Structural and 'everyday' violence. *The International Journal on Drug Policy, 21*(4), 321–329. doi:10.1016/j.drugpo.2009.12.008.

Carter, C. S. (2002). Perinatal care for women who are addicted: Implications for empowerment. *Health and Social Work, 27*(3), 166–174.

Chasnoff, I. J., Neuman, K., Thornton, C., & Callaghan, M. A. (2001). Screening for substance use in pregnancy: A practical approach for the primary care physician. *American Journal of Obstetrics and Gynecology, 184*(4), 752–758.

Cutrona, C. E., Russell, D. W., Hessling, R. M., Brown, P. A., & Murry, V. (2000). Direct and moderating effects of community context on the psychological well-being of African American women. *Journal of Personality and Social Psychology, 79*(6), 1088.

Dunbar, M. S., Maternowska, M. C., Kang, M.-S. J., Laver, S. M., Mudekunye-Mahaka, I., & Padian, N. S. (2010). Findings from SHAZ!: A feasibility study of a microcredit and life-skills HIV prevention intervention to reduce risk among adolescent female orphans in Zimbabwe. *Journal of Prevention & Intervention in the Community, 38*(2), 147–161.

Finkelstein, N. (1994). Treatment issues for alcohol- and drug-dependent pregnant and parenting women. *Health and Social Work, 19*(1), 7–15.

German, D., & Latkin, C. A. (2012). Social stability and health: Exploring multidimensional social disadvantage. *Journal of Urban Health, 89*(1), 19–35.

Green, C. A. (2006). Gender and use of substance abuse treatment services. *Alcohol Research and Health, 29*(1), 55.

Greenfield, S. F., Back, S. E., Lawson, K., & Brady, K. T. (2010). Substance abuse in women. *Psychiatric Clinics of North America, 33*(2), 339. doi:10.1016/j.psc.2010.01.004.

Hernandez-Avila, C. A., Rounsaville, B. J., & Kranzler, H. R. (2004). Opioid-, cannabis-and alcohol-dependent women show more rapid progression to substance abuse treatment. *Drug and Alcohol Dependence, 74*(3), 265–272.

Kim, J., Ferrari, G., Abramsky, T., Watts, C., Hargreaves, J., Morison, L., … Pronyk, P. (2009). Assessing the incremental effects of combining economic and health interventions: the IMAGE study in South Africa. *Bulletin of the World Health Organization, 87*(11), 824–832.

Lapidus, L., Luthra, N., Verma, A., Small, D., Allard, P., & Levingston, K. (2005). *Caught in the net: The impact of drug policies on women and families*. New York, NY: American Civil Liberties Union.

Latkin, C. A., & Curry, A. D. (2003). Stressful neighborhoods and depression: A prospective study of the impact of neighborhood disorder. *Journal of Health and Social Behavior, 44*, 34–44.

Luthar, S. S., & Cicchetti, D. (2000). The construct of resilience: Implications for interventions and social policies. *Development and Psychopathology, 12*(4), 857–885. doi:10.1017/S0954579400004156.

Meyer, J. P., Springer, S. A., & Altice, F. L. (2011). Substance abuse, violence, and HIV in women: A literature review of the syndemic. *Journal of Women's Health, 20*(7), 991–1006.

Mulia, N., Schmidt, L., Bond, J., Jacobs, L., & Korcha, R. (2008). Stress, social support and problem drinking among women in poverty. *Addiction, 103*(8), 1283–1293.

National Center for Health Statistics. (2014). *Health, United States, 2013: With special feature on prescription drugs*. Hyattsville, MD: National Center for Health Statistics.

Nelson-Zlupko, L., Kauffman, E., & Dore, M. M. (1995). Gender differences in drug addiction and treatment: Implications for social work intervention with substance-abusing women. *Social Work, 40*(1), 45–54.

O'Leary, V. E., & Ickovics, J. R. (1994). Resilience and thriving in response to challenge: an opportunity for a paradigm shift in women's health. *Women's Health (Hillsdale, NJ), 1*(2), 121–142.

Orentlicher, D. (1990). Legal interventions during pregnancy - court-ordered medical treatments and legal penalties for potentially harmful behavior by pregnant-women. *Journal of the American Medical Association, 264*(20), 2663–2670.

Pronyk, P. M., Kim, J. C., Abramsky, T., Phetla, G., Hargreaves, J. R., Morison, L. A., … Porter, J. D. (2008). A combined microfinance and training intervention can reduce HIV risk behaviour in young female participants. *Aids, 22*(13), 1659–1665.

Rapp, R. C. (2002). The strengths perspective and persons with substance abuse problems. *Social Work, 52*(2), 185–186.

Saleebey, D. (1996). The strengths perspective in social work practice: Extensions and cautions. *Social Work, 41*(3), 296–305.

SAMHSA. (2013). *Results from the 2012 National Survey on Drug Use and Health: Summary of national findings* (No. NSDUH Series H-46, HHS Publication No.(SMA) 13–4795) (C. f. B. H. S. a. Quality, Trans.). Rockville, MD: Substance Abuse and Mental Health Services Administration.

Seccombe, K. (2002). "Beating the odds" versus "changing the odds": Poverty, resilience, and family policy. *Journal of Marriage and Family, 64*(2), 384–394.

Shannon, K., Ishida, T., Morgan, R., Bear, A., Oleson, M., Kerr, T., & Tyndall, M. W. (2006). Potential community and public health impacts of medically supervised safer smoking facilities for crack cocaine users. *Harm Reduction Journal, 3*, 1. doi:10.1186/1477-7517-3-1.

Todd, J. L., & Worell, J. (2000). Resilience in low-income, employed, African American women. *Psychology of Women Quarterly, 24*(2), 119–128.

U.S. Department of Health and Human Services - Substance Abuse and Mental Health Services Administration - Office of Applied Studies. (2005). *Treatment episode data set (TEDS) highlights - 2003, Substance Abuse Treatment Admissions by primary substance of abuse, according to sex, age group, race, and ethnicity*. From http://wwwdasis.samhsa.gov/teds03/2003_teds_highlights.pdf

U.S. Department of Health and Human Services, Health Resources and Services Administration, Maternal and Child Health Bureau. (2013). *Women's Health USA 2013*. Rockville, MD: U.S. Department of Health and Human Services.

Ward, K. D., Klesges, R. C., Zbikowski, S. M., Bliss, R. E., & Garvey, A. J. (1997). Gender differences in the outcome of an unaided smoking cessation attempt. *Addictive Behaviors, 22*(4), 521–533.

White Jr, D. (2008). The failure of the war on drugs: Charting a new course for the commonwealth. Report of the Massachusetts Bar Association Drug Policy Task Force. Electronically published.

Wilsnack, S. (1991). Barriers to treatment for alcoholic women. *Addiction and Recovery, 11*(4), 10–12.

Windsor, L. C., Benoit, E., & Dunlap, E. (2010). Dimensions of oppression in the lives of impoverished black women who use drugs. *Journal of Black Studies, 41*(1), 21–39.

# Chapter 7
# The Role of Social Support for Women Living in Poverty

**Matthew Archibald, Jennifer Stewart, Linda Vo, Dazon Dixon Diallo, Waheedah Shabazz, Lauren E. Owens, and Laura Randall**

*"In our community, though, we all look out for each other."*

## Introduction

Across all racial and ethnic groups, women in the USA are more likely to live in poverty than men. Although women also bear the disproportionate costs of care giving for children and older adults, they are often segregated into low-paying occupations.

M. Archibald (✉)
Department of Sociology, Colby College, Waterville, ME, USA
e-mail: marchiba@colby.edu

J. Stewart
School of Nursing, Johns Hopkins University, Baltimore, MD, USA

L. Vo • L.E. Owens
Division of Infectious Diseases, Department of Medicine, School of Medicine, Emory University, Atlanta, GA, USA

D.D. Diallo
SisterLove, Inc., Atlanta, GA, USA

W. Shabazz
Positive Women's Network-USA, Philadelphia, PA, USA

L. Randall
Division of Infectious Diseases, Department of Medicine, School of Medicine, Emory University, Atlanta, GA, USA

Rollins School of Public Health, Emory University, Atlanta, GA, USA

 
A. O'Leary, P.M. Frew (eds.), *Poverty in the United States*,
DOI 10.1007/978-3-319-43833-7_7

As society's chief caregivers, many women, especially those living in poverty, find their work and educational opportunities demonstrably limited (Greenberg, Dutta-Gupta, & Minof, 2007). As a result, the social and economic conditions women face are vastly different from those of men, which negatively impacts the health of, and healthcare options for, them and their families.

## Poverty and the Family

Decreases in real wages, burgeoning unemployment, increases in single-family households, an eviscerated public safety net, and other changes in socioeconomic conditions have exacerbated poverty in the USA during the last few decades. Socioeconomic changes in conjunction with shifts in cultural and familial supports are making it difficult to reduce family poverty.

Poverty directly impacts women's and their children's nutritional status, among other things, and alters health outcomes. Socioeconomic status (SES) and diabetes-related mortality, for example, tend to be strongly correlated (Saydah & Lochner, 2010). The relationship is even stronger among families of African Americans and other racial and ethnic minorities (Juon, Evans-Polce, & Ensminger, 2014). Indirect effects of poverty, like unsafe locations for women to engage in physical activity, also impact women's and their children's health outcomes (DeGuzman, Merwin, & Bourguignon, 2013).

Culturally, we in the USA tend to place the responsibility on individuals for their plight (Berlin, 2007) and therefore favor reducing social services through promotion of family-based coping techniques, which are thought to ameliorate individual stressors (Wadsworth & Santiago, 2008). Some of these family-based coping techniques are devised with children in mind. For example, research shows that poverty affects the quality of parenting behavior and reduces nurturing and support necessary for children's development. The more a parent is under financial or emotional strain, the less investment, responsiveness, and warmth are shown children, ultimately hindering their growth (Evans & Kim, 2013). The promotion of coping techniques aims to eliminate the impact of these kinds of stressors on children growing up in impoverished homes.

Women in poverty, who are frequently single mothers, experience a range of pressures that limit their ability to feed their families and/or make ends meet. Monroe, Tiller, O'Neil, and Blalock (2007) describe common coping skills women are forced to utilize to adapt to such stressors (Monroe et al., 2007). For example, respondents in Monroe et al.'s (2007) study noted that deprivation was second nature to them and often not a matter of choice—they would go without food or electricity when they had to. For these women, social networks of family and friends helped with seemingly small things like babysitting, doing hair, or cleaning the house. Still, for all the help that social support provided, these women noted that government assistance in the form of food stamps and other social services was essential if they were to meet their basic needs and those of their families.

## Poverty and Social Support

What kinds of social support provide assistance for women confronted with limiting social and economic conditions? Social networks of family and friends are critical for women, especially single mothers, trapped in the struggle to keep fragile families afloat during declines in government support for the poor and destitute (House, Landis, & Umberson, 1988; Kalil & Ryan, 2010; Rabkin, Ferrando, Jacobsberg, & Fishman, 1997). Most research assumes that social support in the form of family, relatives, neighbors, friends, and coworkers fills gaps left by declining social services in the USA. Family literacy courses, for example, provide a space not only for intellectual achievement but also for building social networks. Literacy courses "enable women to leave the house, establish supportive social relationships with teacher and peers, and pursue self-discovery and development" (Prins, Toso, & Schafft, 2009). However, poor and working-class women who are living paycheck to paycheck lack economic stability and face barriers that restrict their ability to form these beneficial social networks.

Cohen and Wills (1985) distinguish between "structural" and "functional" social support, and argue that while structural social support tends to be associated with improved well-being, it is functional support—support to provide for specific needs—that tends to buffer stressors like those associated with poverty (Cohen & Wills, 1985). Strong social relationships tend to provide support in general, but when it comes to extreme poverty or problematic situations, social support does not always have the expected beneficial effect. For instance, marriage, although often shown to have a protective effect against distress because of the social support the spouse offers (House, Williams, & Kessler, 1985), is unlikely to buffer the stresses of poverty. Some studies find little relationship between marriage and stress (at least at the neighborhood level) (Moskowitz, Vittinghoff, & Schmidt, 2013; Mulia, Schmidt, Bond, Jacobs, & Korcha, 2008). Other research shows that social support buffers do not have much of an impact on the stresses of daily life until the highest level of stress is reached. Only those individuals dealing with high-level stressors, covering the most problematic life events (and extending to neighborhood disorder), benefited from strong social networks of family and friends.

The ameliorating effects of social support might not be pronounced because individuals living in poverty also lack material resources that perpetuate stress regardless of supportive networks. Moreover, given scarce material resources, women in poverty might experience an additional source of stress when assistance has "strings attached" (Moskowitz et al., 2013). Moskowitz et al. (2013) suggest that social networks, which could be a source of stress reduction, may also be a source of stress for women living in poverty. In general, they show that a public safety net consisting of well-run social programs can provide more reliable support than the unpredictable private safety net of family and friends.

## Poverty and Community

Individuals living in poverty are often transient due to inability to pay rent. For communities experiencing marked poverty, length of residence may determine strength of social bonds, since long-term residence should lead to greater familiarity with others in the community, greater social cohesion, and thus greater community and social support among individuals and families (Keene, Bader, & Ailshire, 2013). However, other research, particularly in minority communities, finds that another positive attribute like enhanced SES does not necessarily protect against the everyday stresses of discrimination or incursions of neighborhood disorder (Keene et al., 2013; Schulz et al., 2006). Furthermore, although length of residence has a positive effect on the social ties and psychological well-being of individuals living in affluent neighborhoods, it has no effect on those living in impoverished areas (Ross, Reynolds, & Geis, 2000). In fact, neighborhood stability might even worsen the conditions in a resource-deprived neighborhood because of the continual prevalence of problems such as gang activity, violence, and unemployment, which could only change if the residents participating in them were to move out.

Community disorder and instability can contribute to poor mental health. People who move from poor neighborhoods to more affluent neighborhoods experience less stress and depressive symptoms than those who remain (Schulz et al., 2006). Increasing women's social support can bring about a decrease in depression symptoms (Mair, Roux, & Morenoff, 2010). Parental perceptions of neighborhood disorder positively correlate with children's current depression symptoms. Neighborhood disorder most often results in social isolation and lack of safety, which increase the risk of childhood depression (Ford & Rechel, 2012). Moreover, for low-income women, the greater the neighborhood disorder, the lower the levels of social support, resulting in lower self-esteem (Hill, Burdette, Jokinen-Gordon, & Brailsford, 2013). Low self-esteem limits the formation of social support with friends, neighbors, and other residents. Similarly, those living in neighborhoods with disorganized and unsafe public spaces, dirty and noisy surroundings, and high crime rates experience higher levels of psychological stress than those living in areas absent those stressors. Some research shows that social support does not mediate these effects of poverty because neighborhood disorder precludes formation of stable social groups (Haney, 2007). In impoverished communities, individuals may not feel safe and therefore isolate themselves. By isolating, residents limit the formation of social groups, since they must interact with the people living in close proximity to form those bonds. Threats, general disorder, and adversity abound in unstable communities inhibit social ties, thus fostering conditions that result in greater mental health problems (Kim, 2010).

## Themes in the Data

Many themes pertaining to social support were revealed by the women in the study through the qualitative individual and focus group interviews. The participants discussed the fact that women have multiple roles in the community. In addition to being mothers, they often also serve as the father, educator, and role model to children—both to their own children and to other children in the community. Many women acknowledged being overburdened with this responsibility and sometimes experience a lack of support from friends and family. There also appeared to be a balance between the negative and positive aspects of the women's neighborhoods. Because of the high drug and crime rates, the community tended to stick together and the participants mentioned that people looked out for one another.

Many women described their family members as the support system on which they rely in difficult times. The women described intergenerational living situations and caring for both their parents and children, like this woman:

> My mother has six kids. Two of my brothers live with me and one of my sisters, the youngest, and then my mother stay with me when she don't spend the night over her boyfriend house but she basically staying with me. 'Cause she a leave and always come back.
>
> *—Interviewee, Washington, D.C.*

Carrying on the tradition of family support was an important theme brought up by some of the participants. Remembering the feeling of support from having an involved family as a child inspired this woman to try to be there for her own children:

> And I know that with people, they just concentrate on what they're doing, not their whole family. But I remember growing up, and my aunts was there all the time—my uncles, my grandmother. You know, I just lost her recently … And thinking about my kids not really being around her, and the things that she brought to my life—so that's why I just try to be there for my family, period, let them know I'm there for them. Because in the long run, that's gonna help. You know?
>
> *—Focus Group Participant, Raleigh/Durham, NC*

These women described the differing levels of support expected from various family members:

> It's only two people that I go to when I honestly need help financially or anything like that and that's my sister and my grandmother. My sister help me with no problem. If she got it she'll give it to me with no problem. My grandmother's the one who got it but she just choose not to do for me. I don't know what it is about me but she just, I guess because she figure I'm the one with the husband or whatever that I shouldn't need any extra assistance or anything like that. But at the same token I wouldn't ask if I didn't need it.
>
> *—Interviewee, Washington, D.C.*

Interviewer: Okay, now are they the same people who you would turn to financially?
Participant: Yes, I turn; I'd be quick to turn to my sister, before I'd turn to my Mom … for as financially, um, but when it come down to it, if I really, really, really, really need it, I call my Mom … If it's like, I really don't need or I just want it, I ask my sister.

*—Interviewee, Atlanta, GA*

Similarly, these women described being able to turn to family when facing difficulties:

I think I get by very well like all the time. Because if it's not nothing I can get there's always a family member that can help me out, but I don't want to depend on nobody really to do nothing for me that I can't do for myself. Because I know if I don't have it then grandma will.

*—Interviewee, Washington, D.C.*

My mom helps out a whole lot.

*—Focus Group Participant, Raleigh/Durham, NC*

But if I do go without food, I probably … it would be for a week but I'd go to my mother or my sister house and stay over there for a week until well … I get food stamps so I was kind of short this month, they didn't come so … just bring [name of child] over here or my mama will send some food … Or my sister-in-law will come and say "go spend $50 on my card."

*—Interviewee, Atlanta, GA*

Other women described being distant from their families and instead relied upon their friends and neighbors for social support:

Interviewer: Okay, now who do you turn to when you are going through a rough time? Like do, you turn to friends or family?
Participant: I turn mostly turn to my friends.
Interviewer: Um-hum. Now, why them?
Participant: 'Cause me and my family aren't close … So, I really I haven't talked to my family in some years now actually …. So, I'm more or less, you know my adopted family, which are my friends, I go to …. Like, their advice when I'm going through, you know, certain situations, or even in relationships or even how I should deal with my family that I'm estranged from.

*—Interviewee, Atlanta, GA*

The women also described greater neighborhood cohesion, families, and networks working together for the greater good. This woman described a network of peers helping each other get through school while simultaneously the grandparent generation looked after the grandchildren to further facilitate obtaining an education:

In my community we have quite a few mothers such as myself and we're—most of us stick together and whatever and just trying to finish up school and our parents keep our children, so we're more focused on getting our degrees and getting out and going back home and moving on, taking them with us, so most of the mothers that I know in school, they're focus', and they still have fun and go clubbing and stuff like that, but we focus.

*—Focus Group Participant, Raleigh/Durham, NC*

These women told similar stories of helping the person in need or being the person in need:

> Well, just supposedly be just me and my son but you know I support many people. I guess who ever need support at that time whether it be my brother or a friend who just lost her place and she got an infant child or something, you know. So it just depends on the situation, I have a habit of helping people. So, you, that's just in my nature but it's just basically me and my son that's my main focus though.
>
> —*Interviewee, Washington, D.C.*

> People in general, I know that people in my neighborhood, they've asked me for money, they've stood in front of the—because there's a supermarket right next to my house, and they've asked me for money for food, you know? And they've said that they needed food for their kids and I said, "Well, I'm not going to give you money, but if you tell me what you need, I'll get it for you." You know? And I've done that, I've done that.
>
> —*Focus Group Participant, New York, NY*

> Friends, family, that's about the only place you can get it for free.
>
> —*Focus Group Participant, Atlanta, GA*

> I mean, I support myself and then it's just I've always had help to raise the kids, my mama did. And my baby brother and sister, like those are my heart so I have to look after them.
>
> —*Interviewee, Raleigh/Durham, NC*

> We help each other out 'cause we stick together. It's hard. Sometimes if somebody wanna go back home to see their children or whatever, give 'em a little gas money, that's it.
>
> —*Focus Group Participant, Raleigh/Durham, NC*

The support provided by the government, church, or other groups was also described in the interviews. In these women's neighborhoods, soup kitchens and public assistance provided needed support:

> That's why they have these soup kitchens and pantries and places for people to go, because people are hungry. I have friends that come to my house starving, so I know. It's like that.
>
> —*Focus Group Participant, New York, NY*

> Financially, I'm comfortable. I get public assistance, which helps, and I'm in the supportive housing building. I also get food stamps, so I am—it's—it's comfortable.
>
> —*Interviewee, New York, NY*

While in these women's neighborhoods, clubs and after-school care for children were the most notable assets of the community:

> Participant 1: Well, financially if the household isn't situated we do have help that we can turn to like Participant 2 was saying, the kids club that we have over there. They have people who comes around and picks up the kids and give you a peace of mind for a little bit and also helps them with their homework, and I know for a fact if we're ever in need we can turn to them, but as far as that if you ain't got it yourself it's hard. It's real hard.
>
> Participant 2: The school that they go to, they help out a lot too, a whole lot.
>
> Moderator: How?
>
> Participant 2: Sometimes it might be like [name of shopping center] cards or they got like a clothing closet that kids go to, stuff like that.
>
> Moderator: Okay, so you all feel like there's a lot of different resources to tap into?
>
> Participant 1: Yeah, if we really need it we have different resources in our neighborhood, in our community.
>
> —*Focus Group, Raleigh/Durham, NC*

In other neighborhoods, women described the church as a source of support:

> The only thing I like about my neighborhood is, well, the churches and stuff goin' help us out. That's the only thing.
>
> —*Focus Group Participant, Raleigh/Durham, NC*

> Researcher: All right … what do you do when you feel like the money might be running out?
> Interviewee: I go to the ministries … Honestly, I mean, I'm with God. I mean, I don't worry about nothing.
>
> —*Interview, Atlanta, GA*

Neighborhood cohesion was also a strong theme in the women's stories. Women would look out for their neighbors and receive the same treatment. In some cases, this resulted in a stronger community and social network:

> Once we started—instead of being with the outsiders and we started being as a community I think it got better that way.
>
> —*Focus Group Participant, Raleigh/Durham, NC*

> What I do like about where I live is that a lot of my neighbors I do know and that we always looking out for each other, you know … If someone's not home we know if they're not home and we know to … Watch their place and everything like that and I haven't had any problems with break-ins or anything like that, but I think that's due to the fact that even though it's an apartment complex it's just like a few group of us, you know, almost have like our own little neighborhood watch since it's been taken over by a new place and they cut out the security that we use to have 24/7 but, you know, it's still well lighted, and, like I said, we just look out for each other.
>
> —*Focus Group Participant, Atlanta, GA*

> I guess I feel … I feel safe, because being that I know a majority of the people, everyone looks out for one another … So it's not like if I'm isolated and by myself, you know, I wouldn't feel so safe, but being that everyone socializes with each other, you know, I feel safe in my neighborhood.
>
> —*Interviewee, New York, NY*

Women also described community gatherings as events that improved neighborhood cohesion and support:

> Participant 1: They have a community parties and stuff that we go to over there, yeah.
> Participant 2: Yeah, they have big community parties. They give away a lot of stuff.
>
> —*Focus Group, Atlanta, GA*

> As it gets hotter we'll probably do that; if somebody come out with a grill, the building a probably pitch in and put some food on the grill, and maybe put on the radio, and if it's a nice day have the kids run out and play outside like that. Yeah so, I hope it a be more frequent now, 'cause we do as a community need to be a family, so.
>
> —*Interviewee, Washington, D.C.*

> Participant 1: Well, people—all right. They have a park up the street. I'm like near the highway. And people in the neighborhood, when it's summertime, they come out and they barbeque for the kids on the block. I've seen some things like that, which is nice. Or people bring their family out. Or someone comes out and barbeques or do something, and the kids, and people outside on the block, they invite everybody over. And it turns into like a neighborhood thing. And they have this little basketball tournament they throw over there. It's kind of good. So far. So far.

> Participant 2: Once in a while, I don't really—in the summertime, I think I saw two cookouts, and I think the lady did it just for the kids. Like, I be in and out, so—I just observe as I'm walking in and out. If somebody invited me, I'm like, all right. I'll see if I'm going to come, you know.
>
> —*Focus Group, New York, NY*

While many participants described strong communities where families, friends, and neighbors provided social support for each other, just as many women told stories about the negative aspects of their social networks and neighborhoods. Family and neighborhood connections were not always positive influences for the participants. Some women reported having negative experiences with family members, like the situations described by these women:

> My mother passed away when I was nine years old, my father got incarcerated, my brother got taken away. I literally had to drop out of school in the fifth grade because I had no place to live, and nobody would give me an address for me to register myself for school. Like, I didn't even want to live with them. I was hustling, I was doing my thing, I was making my money, and I had my man that was doing for me, as well, too, I just needed an address to go back to school, and nobody in my family would even do that, and I don't blame them now.
>
> —*Focus Group Participant, New York, NY*

> Well, it used to really upset me. But today it don't affect me at all because I don't look at her like she's my mother today. I look at her like she's just a woman in the street. She ain't nobody to me today. It was affecting me to the point it used to make me want to kill myself. When I was younger I used to try to kill myself. But now that I'm grown with my own kids, I say I'll get even and put it in God's hands by being a better mother to my kids.
>
> —*Interviewee, Raleigh/Durham, NC*

> I do agree with you about having people to nickel and dime off of, but at the same time y'all helping each other 'cause us Black women, all we have is each other to help 'cause the men ain't nothing. If they're something they're gone from being nothing, and I ain't saying depending on my parents' money 'cause I got parents, but they're not dependable. Everybody on drugs and they wanna do their own thing. They don't care.
>
> —*Focus Group Participant, Raleigh/Durham, NC*

Sometimes, family members were not entirely out of the participants' lives but the relationships were difficult, resulting in an unreliable source of support. Examples of this come from these women's stories:

> Since my husband and I separated, you know, it's been me as far as taking care of the children and making sure they have what they need. I can get stuff from my parents. You know, they'll help me but I have to be like "can I?" You know, if I don't get on the phone and say that, then I don't get no help. They don't know unless I say it and I try not to do that too often. I like doing it on my own. But it's a struggle sometimes.
>
> —*Interviewee, Raleigh/Durham, NC*

> My dad helps me with my kids, but he wasn't there for me, but he helps me with my kids and like some people just do things, but I'm not going to do 'em.
>
> —*Focus Group Participant, Atlanta, GA*

> I don't ask anybody. I don't ask my mom for nothing. [Laughs] You can call her right now and she'd tell you! But I don't ask. Like when I really actually need it, I'll probably ask a friend. How I ask, I don't never say "look, can I borrow" 'cause if you say you borrow, it

> means you've got to give it back. So, I ask the people that can actually give and not ask for it in return.
>
> —*Interviewee, Raleigh/Durham, NC*

Other women preferred or relied on social support from small networks rather than family members. This woman discussed keeping people at arm's length, with the exception of an intimate partner on whom she could rely:

> Interviewee: I really don't get along with my family … I don't have friends.
> Researcher: So, you don't have any friends.
> Interviewee: Mm-mm [no]. I have associates. My boyfriend is my best friend.
>
> —*Interview, Raleigh/Durham, NC*

Social isolation and a lack of any support, whether from friends or family, were also described by some of the participants. This woman described an abusive childhood and the grief resulting from the deaths of well-liked family members:

> That's—I don't like violence. You understand, I hate it—my father used to be an alcoholic—I used to get beaten and whatnot, you understand me? (inaudible) on drinking. And I said "that's on over with." You know. (inaudible) he's passed and my mother had passed. You know, here I still grieve on—by losing my mother and whatnot. And at points in time, I'll shut myself down. You know. From the whole fucking world. I put it as like—you know, why? If there is a mighty God up there, why they had to take my mother? My aunt, my sister, my brother. And whatnot. So next question.
>
> —*Interviewee, New York, NY*

Similarly, this woman described a limited network on which she could rely and a lack of overall support:

> I'm all right. I'll be all right. I have friends. Somebody will give me a cigarette if I need it, but that's about as far as it goes. If they're like I need $10, I don't ask nobody to borrow no money, because that's a problem. Because then your friends will become your enemies, family members will want to cut you and kill you.
>
> —*Interviewee, New York, NY*

The women described that the negative effects of a neighborhood spread beyond individual households and situations and were a larger influence overall, concerning them regarding children's futures. These negative effects of a neighborhood or street life were sometimes a stronger influence than good parenting, as described by these participants:

> I feel it starts at home, but once again it takes a village to raise a child, so I think all of us. We're all obligated. Even if that's not our child we need to pull them aside and say, "Look, you don't need to be doing that."… like I said before, it does take a community to raise a child. It don't necessarily have to start at home though 'cause a person can be treating and teaching their child the right way 100 percent, but once they get out there and they see something different they'll be like, "Oh, I wanna do this and I wanna do that." My baby daddy, he grew up and was raised in a household holy roly. He got out here to this block on the street and he wanted to be doing this and doing that. He wanna be a kingpin and now look at him, clean, clean. That's what I gotta say.
>
> —*Focus Group Participant, Raleigh/Durham, NC*

> Be better than your environment. Learn from your environment. Like that's a big one, because it takes—I mean, it takes a bigger, stronger person to want to go against the grain.

> And I feel like a lot of the kids nowadays, they want to follow the crowd. That's why there's a lot of the gang thing. Everybody's in a gang now. Everybody and their aunts, uncles, mama, cousin, everybody want to be a Blood or a Crip or whatever falls in between, because no one in those categories is being strong enough to go against the grain. Everybody wants to follow the leader or be with the in crowd. You've really just got to, you know, take the initiative and be strong for the one that's, you know, to go against the majority, because the majority is like tearing the community down. Nothing that they're doing is really building a community up to teach the children anything better. You know, it's teaching negativity.
>
> —*Focus Group Participant, Raleigh/Durham, NC*

> I'm not saying I'm from there, but I have lived in the area, and the kids really don't have no respect and it ain't their fault, it's their parents' fault, and part of the community's fault, 'cause it takes the community to raise a child. They, "Wow, pop that booty, uh, uh," the same rap songs, but don't know their ABC's, don't know how to spell their name or tie a shoe, but in order to get to the kids you gotta get through to the adults, their parents, to let them know what they're doing wrong or what they could be doing right.
>
> —*Focus Group Participant, Raleigh/Durham, NC*

One woman expressed concern over the influence that the neighborhood's culture had on children, whom she felt were observant and impressionable:

> I mean, they in the 'hood, they doing 'hood things. They watching, observing the 'hood, learning the 'hood lifestyle. They out there. They seeing the drug dealers. They idolizing them, because that's the only people that they see out there getting any kind of money, even though it's dirty money. They out there watching the girls prostituting, watching the bums walking up and down the street. I mean, they out there. They observing what's going on around them.
>
> —*Focus Group Participant, Raleigh/Durham, NC*

This woman identified that single mothers are overburdened when trying to provide for their household, leaving the "wrong crowd" to influence their children:

> The majority of what I notice in the neighborhood with these young kids, the majority of them, they come from families that don't have a father; they don't have both parents, and the mother is struggling. So what they do is they go out there to start selling drugs, because the mothers are either on welfare on that SSI; she can't afford to buy them the sneakers that they'll want … $100 sneakers. So what happens? They start going out, hanging out with the wrong crowd, to start making money, and that's where the cycle begins.
>
> —*Focus Group Participant, New York, NY*

Some participants see problems like the one mentioned above as a call to action, addressing respect and behavioral issues if they feel like the parents are not:

> Interviewee: See with me, with everybody else's kids—I'm sitting there and I see them doing something. I'll be like, "Ohh, oh oh, what are you doing?" They'll be like, "What Miss XX"—what Miss XX—nuh uh. Well, mama …" I don't care what mama allows you to do, but as long as I'm around you will not be doing that. Where's your mama? Come on, let's go on in here and go talk to your mama real quick. "But my …" I don't care what your mom said. I'll be like—he'll be like—(whimper). It's not funny, it's not cute, it's not a joke. You know what I'm saying? Because you're laughing and joking about it, the way that I take it—the only reason I came here is because I know you. Somebody else in the street is not going to take the same time out to do what I did. I'll knock your child across the street somewhere and you'll be looking for your child. You know what I'm saying? But not everybody is like that because some parents—whoever it is—they're afraid. They're afraid of what? Shit. Somebody brought you in here, somebody can definitely take you out if you're out of line.

Researcher: The parents—you were saying that the parents are afraid?
Interviewee: Yeah, you got—come on now, you act like you don't know. You know that there are some parents that are afraid of children. Don't be playing with me, you know—yes they are. Not me, ain't afraid of none of them. Because I tell them, "Your mama might have brought you into this world, but be careful if I don't take you out, somebody else will." So be careful what you say. You know? But the parents—it's supposed to be the one that are supposed to lead their children and guide them, and protect them. If you don't do it, then who else would you expect to do it? They need to walk out on the street and be bothered by somebody else that will teach them the wrong way to do things—you know what I'm saying—or half-assed do things, halfway do things.

—*Interview, New York, NY*

A lack of parenting and its consequent negative child behavior was a common theme. Many women talked about "kids raising themselves" or a hands-off approach to parenting, which they thought had negative consequences. One woman noted:

Obviously, they didn't teach their selves. Their parents taught them that. And they all—Or they had lack of parenting that taught them that.

—*Focus Group Participant, New York, NY*

These women described similar situations:

… because I see too many kids basically raising themselves … There's no structure in the household. I mean, and I mean they just let the kids run wild and everything and it's like, well, where's your mom or your dad and everything, and I mean, what's sad is especially, in a lot of the households now a days, you know, there is no father figure there. So I mean, 'cause I have six boys and thank God that there's a man in the household and everything and what not to show them how to be a man, go to work every day, take care of your family, be at home at night and what not and everything. Not out running in the streets and everything because it's like, you're not going to be able to stop the cycle if you just let it continue on and on and on and on … I just wish some of these people would actually start taking more interest in their children and being parents …

—*Focus Group Participant, Atlanta, GA*

Researcher: So, What else do you see when you look out of your window?
Interviewee: Nothing [laughs]. Just a lot of people just sitting around wasting time, not doing anything. Pretty much just drinking and pretty much listening to music, not doing anything with their time. Just—they ain't got a care in the world! No ambition anymore. It's not like I was little and you might look out and people were having cookouts, they're doing things, they're interacting with their kids and stuff. Or it's just now just too loud, noisy, and [inaudible] and, like I said, little girls don't look like little girls no more 'cause they're like grown women 'cause they're sexually active too. So, I see a lot of things going on like fast—this. And I think the parents need to stop acting like children and be more like adults and teach their children so when they're out on the street they're children won't become a victim to what y'all are trying to educate me about, you know?

—*Interview, Raleigh/Durham, NC*

Some women expressed regret over the past, taking a pensive look at their actions and wondering whether they could have done things differently for their children:

You know, I have suffered with chronic depression believe it or not, and I medicated it in ways, you know, crack, ways to keep me up and upbeat and stuff, and I would just tell my son, you know he's 22 now, but he like that weed. It's too late for him you know pretty

> much. But he likes the weed and everything but if I had it to do all over again I think I would have kept him a little closer just so he can learn a lesson sooner. You know I think I would have, you know, because my sister, it worked with my sister and my sister she ain't have no kids to this day because when I was doing my little run she took care of my son and because she saw what it did to me she didn't use drugs. So, I'm thinking if I would have kept my son a little closer he probably would have gotten that same kind of, you know, lesson.
>
> —*Focus Group Participant, Washington, D.C.*

To compensate for negative influences, women who were concerned for children's (their own and others) futures discussed ways they took action to try to be a good example. One woman described being proactive about sex education with her daughter and her daughter's friends:

> What I do, because my daughter's 18 years old, and she's proud of, you know, the community, you know, her community. And a lot of the community is run by the adolescents, you know? So that's where, predominantly, all the, the ... say the, the venereal diseases and all that stuff is happening at now. Because I know, because I was there, I was a teenager, so what I did was when my daughter was in the house with a bunch of her friends, I ... I, you know, I did a presentation of safer sex use with condoms. And I showed them how to use a condom, I showed them how to—like, if it itches if they use a condom, a particular condom with spermicide, and if itches them every time they use it, it most likely is because they're allergic to spermicide and Nonoxynol 9, and that they would have to use a water based condom. You know, and how to check for the date—the expiration date, and things like that. And, you know, I'm just letting them know it's better to be safe than sorry.
>
> —*Focus Group Participant, New York, NY*

Another woman said that she made sure to encourage education among her children since she recognized that being educated could serve as a protector against some negative effects:

> The most important thing to me is education. I mean without education—I mean, I never you know—I don't have a high school diploma. I'm trying to get my GED now. And I have a daughter, and she's 25, and I made sure she got her high school diploma. And I see where that made a difference, because—I mean now she's going to school. She wants to be a cosmetologist. And I have one that's 13 and one that's 9. Now my 9-year-old—she has a learning disability. And with them going so far out, to different schools that's not in your area, it's hard to get to them and be involved in their schoolwork. But see, now she's closer to me, and I can walk to her school, have lunch with her. It's being there, and making sure they get that education. Letting them know that without that, it's gonna be harder. All that stuff comes into play. Drugs. Unprotected sex. Pregnancy too young. All that stuff—without that education.
>
> —*Focus Group Participant, Raleigh/Durham, NC*

This woman told a similar story of encouraging her son to continue with his schooling:

> I think it's education, like, that's what I really pull strong on my kids for, because I realize that a lot of kids that don't grow up with that education that kind of makes them feel like they're forced to sell drugs, or to rob people, or to do these things that, you know, that drive us crazy in our neighborhoods. So I try to really, you know, tell my son, "You know, school's good, and keep that education, so at least once you get older you feel like you have something. You don't have to go sell drugs, or rob somebody, or stick somebody up, or rob a store, anything like that."
>
> —*Focus Group Participant, New York, NY*

Many women expressed wanting things to be different and/or better for children, imparting these wishes and thoughts during the interviews:

> Don't be like them … Be like something better than them … Do not be a streetwalker. Do not be a dope dealer. Do not do all those things you see them other people doing. You do what you're supposed to do. Graduate from high school and go to college.
>
> —*Focus Group Participant, Atlanta, GA*

> I'm trying to get my son a mentor just so they can lead him in the right direction because I don't want my son, like I tell all of my children, I don't want to be one of them parents to get the phone call that I got to come out and identify you'll bodies because I'm not, no, I gave you all too much for that.
>
> —*Focus Group Participant, Washington, D.C.*

> Participant 1: They're hardheaded ….
> Participant 2: All you could do is hope that some of what you say is sinking in.
> Participant 1: Exactly, that's why I say, you can just tell 'em and point them in the right direction and just hopefully they're listening.
>
> —*Focus Group, Atlanta, GA*

> I tell mine you know I don't want you to make the same mistakes I made … Don't be like me. Be better than me.
>
> —*Focus Group Participant, Atlanta, GA*

## Policy Implications

Enhancing modes of social support is crucial to the well-being of women living at or below the poverty line. To be poor generally means that one is dependent on bureaucratic institutions such as the welfare systems, public housing authority, and healthcare system, which often fail the populations they attempt to support (Chaskin, 2001). Policies that target ways to support women and their families, networks, and neighborhoods can help alleviate the negative impact of poverty on women in the USA. This can be accomplished by building capacity in existing community-based organizations (CBOs), developing additional CBOs, and strategically integrating programs into these CBOs that attend specifically to the needs of women in poverty. We offer several policy recommendations that can be implemented to enhance social support and promote better outcomes.

There are three key policy recommendations that will be elaborated on in the following sections: (1) developing and utilizing organizations and programs focused on bridging community integration, (2) CBO and school-based services focused on family strengthening, and (3) CBO programs focused on developing coping mechanisms.

### *Bridging Community Integration*

As previously described, women in poverty likely have a greater need for social support–based initiatives. This is particularly the case because many women are the primary caregivers of not only children but adult family members and friends as well. There is a need for the funneling of resources into existing CBOs to build capacity and the development of additional programs to meet community needs.

Members of communities in poverty are often disorganized and disconnected from one another (Thompson, Wells, & Coats, 2012). Policy change that encourages community responsibility and leadership and is harmonious with local knowledge and ideas already in motion is imperative. One recommendation to achieve this is the development of programs that focus on policing, crime reduction, and drug-use prevention strategies through the leadership of women in the community. Promoting meaningful community participation and empowerment in this process is key.

Building social capital is also vitally important. Policy changes that require local businesses and organizations to support programs that employ women in the community to focus on enhancing community safety, as well as promoting connectedness, cohesion, and support mobilization, are important options. It is also crucial that these businesses and organizations are led by and/or have women from the community integrated into these efforts. This would have a dramatic impact on community integration.

It is critical to encourage ways of coming together in a manner that supports the common good. CBOs, including service providers, local businesses, and local branches of larger institutions such as banks, schools, major retail establishments, block clubs, social organizations, and faith settings, should all play a role in these efforts. Historically, faith settings in particular have been at the forefront of community mobilization. Reengaging these community organizations would provide additional resources. Regulations that mandate that these organizations hire and invest in the women living and working in the communities they serve would increase integration and promote economic independence. Specific strategies to accomplish this include programs focusing on leadership and organizational development, community organizing, and fostering collaborative relations among organizations (Chaskin, 2001; Voisin, 2007). Additionally, a primary focus of some of these CBOs can be on programmatic approaches such as job training and placement, structuring access to financial opportunities, or more procedural things like voter registration, and block club organization (Servon & Bates, 1998). Interagency collaborations among employers, healthcare providers, social workers, police, government officials, and educators to form programs (Anyon et al., 2013; Voisin, 2007) would ameliorate the effects of poverty on women in the USA.

## *Family Strengthening*

Women in poverty often both depend on and provide resources to familial networks. Thus, strengthening the family is of critical importance. It is important to note, however, that women in poverty are often dealing with the issue of caring for their children independent of aid. Economic stressors and mass incarceration, both of which have severe impacts on family structure, likely impact this. Policies that provide alternatives to incarceration and support reintegration for those who have been imprisoned would likely maintain and enhance family structure. This may boost economic development of families as well. Partner relationships are often strained or broken by economic stress and incarceration. Divorce and separation are particularly common in families where men provide very low or sporadic income (Vacha & McLaughlin, 2000).

Over time, family structure has changed in the USA as a whole. There is now a higher percentage of children who live in single-parent families (Vacha & McLaughlin, 2000). In communities heavily impacted by poverty, this often places the burden of caring for children and providing income to support themselves and their families on the shoulders of women. Because of the necessity of work outside of the home, there is an increasing demand for after-school care for children. It is important to support quality education and childcare for the children of women living in poverty. Women with children are more willing to gain employment when they know that they have available, affordable, quality care for their children (Sarampote, Bassett, & Winsler, 2004; Vacha & McLaughlin, 2000). Supporting these childcare efforts would contribute to family strengthening via the increased earning power of the women.

## *Childcare and School Resources*

In general, after-school care can be categorized into four types: (1) relative care, (2) nonrelative care, (3) after-school programs, and (4) self-care (Sarampote et al., 2004). Extended day programs can be operated in school buildings or local community centers within the communities of women living in poverty. Nationally, the average cost for extended care is approximately $286 per month (Sarampote et al., 2004). Nearly half of all working women with a child under the age of 13 spend about 9 % of their monthly earnings on childcare expenses. For working women whose incomes are below the federal poverty level, however, childcare costs typically comprise up to 23 % of monthly earnings (Sarampote et al., 2004).

Children of families from a lower SES experience strong positive effects from participating in formal after-school programs in comparison to other categories of after-school care (Sarampote et al., 2004). Formal after-school programs have been associated with better behavior in school, better grades, better adjustment, and better peer relations (Sarampote et al., 2004). Increasing the number of, and access to, after-school programs would provide much needed support of families in poverty.

Schools and community centers should offer programs that are consistent with the needs and characteristics of the families in their communities. Policies that provide resources to support quality extended care will certainly provide much-needed support. If these resources are based in the communities that need them the most, there is also a chance that networks of additional support could emerge among women with children in these programs. If these programs are housed within schools, additional provision of academic aid to children may also be a possibility. For children attending CBOs for extended care it is also important to note the need for safe and reliable transportation to these programs.

An additional resource for women might be school-based health centers which can promote health and also address some of the behavioral and physical needs of children and adolescents living in poverty. These school-based health centers can also be a service to connect low-income women with the support needed to overcome challenges related to accessing available resources, linkage to quality healthcare, and educational and job training opportunities (Anyon et al., 2013).

## *Building Coping Mechanisms*

Decades of research find poverty to be a correlate of psychosocial distress and diagnosable mental disorders. High levels of depressive symptoms were found to be common among women without confidants, child-rearing assistance, or employment. These symptoms were also found in women experiencing chronic stressful conditions, particularly those reflecting economic problems and community violence (Anakwenze & Zuberi, 2013). Poverty often takes a toll on a woman's support system and serves as a conduit of stress. Existing programs and organizations can integrate mental health services into their existing programs. CBOs can also develop networks of support and create safe spaces for women and their children living in poverty.

Policies supporting mental health professionals to help train teachers, police officers, and pastors to be aware of the implications of economic stress and exposure to violence, and to help support mental health and coping strategies, are recommended. Programs should address risks but also improve resiliency. Making routine assessments of mental health can also aid in identifying those that may need support to manage coping. Additionally, linkage to resources and counselors for care is vitally important. One strategy can be to engage urban clergy and lay ministers to provide short-term counseling and referrals for longer-term mental health care, building on the central role of the church as an institution with the capability of address both body and spirit (Anakwenze & Zuberi, 2013; Carling, 1990).

School programs focusing on safety training as well as public announcements delineating how to avoid dangerous situations can provide support to these women's children. Strategies can also include screening for exposure to violence, which is associated with negative psychological outcomes among youth, increased school and academic problems, heightened drug use, and other HIV-related risk behaviors (Anakwenze & Zuberi, 2013; Carling, 1990). Youth exposed to community violence are vulnerable to disturbances in self-esteem, trust, emotional regulation, as well as difficulties in interpersonal relationships and isolation from positive peer groups (Anakwenze & Zuberi, 2013). Exposure to violence also increases likelihood of committing serious criminal behaviors (Carling, 1990). This contributes to the cycle of poverty.

## Conclusion

The lives of women in poverty can be improved if their access to social support resources is increased. Policies that focus on fostering community integration through regulations that encourage the employment and integration of women in the community are crucial to developing resources from the inside out. Additionally, the funneling of resources into programs and organizations focusing on strengthening families and reducing incarceration would provide more resources and strength to these women and their families. Lastly, addressing the profound effects that violence and poverty have on the mental health and well-being of women is needed and should be integrated in individuals' daily lives and interactions.

At a minimum, every individual has the right to live in conditions that support their growth. Promoting mechanisms of social support for women living in suboptimal conditions is an important human justice imperative. Developing and reaffirming the roles that clinics, faith institutions, schools, and business have are crucial to change the face of poverty in the USA.

## References


Anakwenze, U., & Zuberi, D. (2013). Mental health and poverty in the inner city. *Health & Social Work, 38*(3), 147–157. doi:10.1093/Hsw/Hlt013.

Anyon, Y., Moore, M., Horevitz, E., Whitaker, K., Stone, S., & Shields, J. (2013). Health risks, race, and adolescents' use of school-based health centers: Policy and service recommendations. *The Journal of Behavioral Health Services & Research, 40*(4), 457–468. doi:10.1007/s11414-013-9356-9.

Berlin, G. L. (2007). Rewarding the work of individuals: A counterintuitive approach to reducing poverty and strengthening families. *Future of Children, 17*(2), 17–42. doi:10.1353/foc.2007.0013.

Carling, P. J. (1990). Major mental-illness, housing, and supports—The promise of community integration. *American Psychologist, 45*(8), 969–975. doi:10.1037//0003-066x.45.8.969.

Chaskin, R. J. (2001). Building community capacity—A definitional framework and case studies from a comprehensive community initiative. *Urban Affairs Review, 36*(3), 291–323. doi:10.1177/10780870122184876.

Cohen, S., & Wills, T. A. (1985). Stress, social support, and the buffering hypothesis. *Psychological Bulletin, 98*(2), 310.

DeGuzman, P. B., Merwin, E. I., & Bourguignon, C. (2013). Population density, distance to public transportation, and health of women in low-income neighborhoods. *Public Health Nursing, 30*(6), 478–490.

Evans, G. W., & Kim, P. (2013). Childhood poverty, chronic stress, self-regulation, and coping. *Child Development Perspectives, 7*(1), 43–48. doi:10.1111/Cdep.12013.

Ford, J. L., & Rechel, M. (2012). Parental perceptions of the neighborhood context and adolescent depression. *Public Health Nursing, 29*(5), 390–402. doi:10.1111/j.1525-1446.2012.01015.x.

Greenberg, M., Dutta-Gupta, I., & Minof, E. (2007). *From poverty to prosperity: A national strategy to cut poverty in half.* Retrieved from Washington, DC: http://cdn.americanprogress.org/wp-content/uploads/issues/2007/04/pdf/poverty_report.pdf.

Haney, T. J. (2007). "Broken windows" and self-esteem: Subjective understandings of neighborhood poverty and disorder. *Social Science Research, 36*(3), 968–994.

Hill, T. D., Burdette, A. M., Jokinen-Gordon, H. M., & Brailsford, J. M. (2013). Neighborhood disorder, social support, and self-esteem: Evidence from a sample of low-income women living in three cities. *City & Community, 12*(4), 380–395. doi:10.1111/Cico.12044.

House, J. S., Landis, K. R., & Umberson, D. (1988). Social relationships and health. *Science, 241*(4865), 540–545.

House, J. S., Williams, D. R., & Kessler, R. C. (1985). *Unemployment, social support and health.* Paper presented at the Social support, Health and Disease. Sixth International Berzelius Symposium, Malmö, Sweden.

Juon, H. S., Evans-Polce, R. J., & Ensminger, M. (2014). Early life conditions of overall and cause-specific mortality among inner-city African Americans. *American Journal of Public Health, 104*(3), 548–554. doi:10.2105/AJPH.2013.301228.

Kalil, A., & Ryan, R. M. (2010). Mothers' economic conditions and sources of support in fragile families. *Future of Children, 20*(2), 39–61.

Keene, D., Bader, M., & Ailshire, J. (2013). Length of residence and social integration: The contingent effects of neighborhood poverty. *Health & Place, 21*, 171–178. doi:10.1016/j.healthplace.2013.02.002.

Kim, J. (2010). Neighborhood disadvantage and mental health: The role of neighborhood disorder and social relationships. *Social Science Research, 39*(2), 260–271. doi:10.1016/j.ssresearch.2009.08.007.

Mair, C., Roux, A. V. D., & Morenoff, J. D. (2010). Neighborhood stressors and social support as predictors of depressive symptoms in the Chicago Community Adult Health Study. *Health & Place, 16*(5), 811–819. doi:10.1016/j.healthplace.2010.04.006.

Monroe, P. A., Tiller, V. R., O'Neil, C. E., & Blalock, L. L. (2007). "We Make our Ends Meet Good": Coping strategies of former welfare-reliant women. *Journal of Loss & Trauma, 12*(3), 199–221.

Moskowitz, D., Vittinghoff, E., & Schmidt, L. (2013). Reconsidering the effects of poverty and social support on health: A 5-year longitudinal test of the stress-buffering hypothesis. *Journal of Urban Health: Bulletin of the New York Academy of Medicine, 90*(1), 175–184. doi:10.1007/s11524-012-9757-8.

Mulia, N., Schmidt, L., Bond, J., Jacobs, L., & Korcha, R. (2008). Stress, social support and problem drinking among women in poverty. *Addiction, 103*(8), 1283–1293. doi:10.1111/j.1360-0443.2008.02234.x.

Prins, E., Toso, B. W., & Schafft, K. A. (2009). "It Feels Like a Little Family to Me" social interaction and support among women in adult education and family literacy. *Adult Education Quarterly, 59*(4), 335–352. doi:10.1177/0741713609331705.

Rabkin, J. G., Ferrando, S. J., Jacobsberg, L. B., & Fishman, B. (1997). Prevalence of axis I disorders in an AIDS cohort: A cross-sectional, controlled study. *Comprehensive Psychiatry, 38*(3), 146–154.

Ross, C. E., Reynolds, J. R., & Geis, K. J. (2000). The contingent meaning of neighborhood stability for residents' psychological well-being. *American Sociological Review, 65*(4), 581–597. doi:10.2307/2657384.

Sarampote, N., Bassett, H., & Winsler, A. (2004). After-school care: Child outcomes and recommendations for research and policy. *Child and Youth Care Forum, 33*(5), 329–348. doi:10.1023/B:CCAR.0000043039.79476.e9.

Saydah, S., & Lochner, K. (2010). Socioeconomic status and risk of diabetes-related mortality in the US. *Public Health Reports, 125*(3), 377.

Schulz, A. J., Israel, B. A., Zenk, S. N., Parker, E. A., Lichtenstein, R., Shellman-Weir, S., & Klem, A. B. L. (2006). Psychosocial stress and social support as mediators of relationships between income, length of residence and depressive symptoms among African American women on Detroit's eastside. *Social Science & Medicine, 62*(2), 510–522. doi:10.1016/j.socscimed.2005.06.028.

Servon, L. J., & Bates, T. (1998). Microenterprise as an exit route from poverty: Recommendations for programs and policy makers. *Journal of Urban Affairs, 20*(4), 419–441. doi:10.1111/j.1467-9906.1998.tb00430.x.

Thompson, V. S., Wells, A., & Coats, J. (2012). Dare to be sick: Poverty and health among vulnerable populations. In C. C. Yeakey (Ed.), *Living on the boundaries: Urban marginality in national and international contexts: Vol. 8. Advances in education in diverse communities: research, policy and praxis* (pp. 23–47). Bingley, UK: Emerald Group. doi:10.1108/S1479-358x(2012)0000008007.

Vacha, E. F., & McLaughlin, T. F. (2000). The impact of poverty, fear of crime, and crime victimization on keeping firearms for protection and unsafe gun-storage practices—A review and analysis with policy recommendations. *Urban Education, 35*(4), 496–510. doi:10.1177/0042085900354006.

Voisin, D. R. (2007). The effects of family and community violence exposure among youth: Recommendations for practice and policy. *Journal of Social Work Education, 43*(1), 51–66.

Wadsworth, M. E., & Santiago, C. D. (2008). Risk and resiliency processes in ethnically diverse families in poverty. *Journal of Family Psychology, 22*(3), 399–410. doi:10.1037/0893-3200.22.3.399.

# Chapter 8
# Partner Concurrency and Relationship Dynamics

**Kimberly A. Parker, Laura Riley, Stephanie Lykes, and Jessie R.M. Legros**

*"You'd do better just staying with what you're dealing with and just going on with your life."*

## Introduction

In 2010, the National Vital Statistics System (NVSS) reported the marriage rate for the entire US population as 6.8 per 1000 people and reported the divorce and annulment rate as 3.8 per 1000 people (National Marriage and Divorce Rate Trends, 2014). During the prior decade, the marriage and divorce and annulment rates for 2000 were 8.2 and 4.0 per 1000, respectively (National Marriage and Divorce Rate Trends, 2014). Between the years 2006 and 2010, only 36 % of females were married at least once, a decrease from previous decades in which the rate for females

K.A. Parker (✉)
Department of Health Studies, Texas Woman's University, Denton, TX, USA
e-mail: kparker6@mail.twu.edu

L. Riley
Department of Behavioral Science and Health Education, Rollins School of Public Health, Emory University, Atlanta, GA, USA

S. Lykes
ICAP, Mailman School of Public Health, Columbia University, New York, NY, USA

J.R.M. Legros
Atlanta, GA, USA



A. O'Leary, P.M. Frew (eds.), *Poverty in the United States*,
DOI 10.1007/978-3-319-43833-7_8

married at least once was as high as 44 % (Copen, Daniels, Vespa, & Mosher, 2012). Although the decline in marriage rates may infer one's desire to remain single, cohabitation rates concurrently increased as marriage rates waned. In 2010, 11 % of women reported cohabitating, an upsurge from 3 % in 1982 (Copen et al., 2012).

In a report published by the Pew Research Center, marriage remained an attainable goal for many (Cohn, 2013). When asked about aspirations of marriage, 61 % of both men and women who have never wed stated that they would like to be married (Cohn, 2013). This same survey also found that among those who have never married, 27 % of men have no desire to do so compared to only 8 % of women (Cohn, 2013). The difference in gender rates for those who do not wish to marry may appear small, but the probability of a woman being married by the age of 30 has decreased from 73 % in 2002 to 68 % in 2010 (Copen et al., 2012). For males, the probability of being married by the age of 30 lessened from 61 % in 2002 to 56 % in 2010 (Copen et al., 2012). Both men and women often express a longing to be married. Subsequently, the appeal is much higher for women compared to men.

The HPTN 064 study collected qualitative data to assess partnership concurrency and relationship dynamics among women living in the USA. Female participant interview and focus group data was used to examine discourse surrounding heterosexual relationships and socioeconomic status (SES), the construction and reinforcement of gender norms, and partner concurrency. This chapter explores the benefits associated with heterosexual partnering and the value ascribed to coupling. We also examine the gender-ratio imbalance and its effect on meeting the supply and demand of available male partners. The chapter provides a brief overview of health implications associated with sexual concurrency and concludes with implications for policy recommendations.

## Relationship Status

The benefits of marriage and coupling have been well documented and include an increase in mental and physical well-being for those within the nucleus of the relationship (Choi & Marks, 2013; De Henau & Himmelweit, 2013; Rabir, 2004), larger income and access to greater wealth (Choi & Marks, 2013; Miller, Hollist, Olsen, & Law, 2013; Rabir, 2004; Strike, 2012), and an elevated standard of living compared to those who are single (Choi & Marks, 2013; Miller et al., 2013; Rabir, 2004). Couples have access to more resources associated with a higher quality of life and frequently enjoy the perceived shield offered by a partner, enhancing a sense of security and psychological well-being (Choi & Marks, 2013; Miller et al., 2013; Waite, 2009). Although the nature of this causality is unknown, the overall income and financial stability of married households are greater than the totality of unmarried men and unmarried women with the same earning potential (Lincoln, 2008; Miller et al., 2013; Sassler & Miller, 2011). Serious, committed relationships may be appealing to both genders, but the benefits of marriage are often incommensurate; marital and relationship assets for men surmount those of women (Lincoln, 2008; Miller et al., 2013; Sassler & Miller, 2011). Men wield more decision-making power based on greater economic contributions; furthermore, married men experience greater health benefits than married women (Cohn, 2013; Hettinger, Hutchinson, & Bosson, 2014; Lincoln, 2008). Married men also benefit from the marital wage premium, a phenomenon which posits that marriage allows for added work productivity by reducing the amount of time devoted to housework, often afforded to women (De Henau & Himmelweit, 2013; Lincoln, 2008; Lincoln & Chae, 2010).

Whereas the benefits of relationships are bestowed upon those intimately involved, romantic partnerships may dissolve, and often do so for various reasons. Some of the most common reasons that lead to the relationship disbanding include arguing, unrealistic expectations of a partner, and lack of planning or preparation for a long-term commitment (Hawkins, Willoughby, & Doherty, 2012; Lincoln & Chae, 2010). Financial disputes, domestic violence, and conflict may also contribute to the separation of partners, as well as a simple lack of attraction and infidelity (Amato & Hohmann-Marriott, 2007; National Marriage and Divorce Rate Trends, 2014; Hawkins et al., 2012). Approximately 42 % of divorced couples reported at least one incident of sexual intercourse outside of the marriage and infidelity has been labeled as one of the most detrimental tribulations present in relationships (Hawkins et al., 2012; Marín, Christensen, & Atkins, 2014). Infidelity threatens the underpinning of trust within relationships, particularly if one partner is more willing to reconcile once infidelity has been discovered (Marín et al., 2014; Sassler & Miller, 2011). Infidelity may lead to distrust, anxiety, and depressive symptoms, but may also impact the physical health of those involved due to sexual concurrency (Marín et al., 2014).

Sexual concurrency is defined as the overlapping of sexual partners (Adimora et al., 2004; Adimora, Schoenbach, & Doherty, 2007; Andrasik et al., 2012; Waldrop-Valverde et al., 2013). Commonly used to designate occurrences of infidelity or adultery, sexual concurrency should not be used as a synonym for the subjective term "cheating." Sexual concurrency is denoted by sexual intercourse with one partner while engaging in synchronous sexual acts with an additional partner. Sexual concurrency is also used to describe a sexual relationship that has not dissolved prior to engaging in sexual intercourse with another person (Doherty, Schoenbach, & Adimora, 2009; Nunn et al., 2011; Waldrop-Valverde et al., 2013). Sexual concurrency may also take place within a sexual network and among multiple partners; therefore, sexual concurrency does not occur solely within established, romantic relationships (Doherty et al., 2009; Kalichman & Grebler, 2010). The correlation between time and sexual intercourse with more than one person, or simultaneous sexual relationships with at least two people is used to ascertain sexual concurrency and to characterize concurrent sexual partners (Adimora et al., 2004; Doherty et al., 2009; O'Byrne, Holmes, & Woodend, 2008). Before we address the impact of partner concurrency, we must first examine the factors that influence heterosexual relationship dynamics and the perceived benefits associated with being in a relationship.

Heterosexual relationships, defined as emotional, serious relationships between a man and a woman, provide a reflective image of male and female dynamics present in today's society. This chapter focuses on the dynamics of heterosexual relationships to illustrate the interconnectedness of constructs such as power, influence, gender norms, and sexual taboos to characterize partner concurrency and relationship dynamics. Although these concepts may be found in same-sex relationships, a woman's direct connection and affiliation with a male partner serves as the impetus within the nature of hegemonic relationships and the consequences related to women's health. Additionally, the HPTN 064 study focused on the manner in which heterosexual dynamics impact a woman's health; all female participants reported engaging in sexual intercourse with a male at least 6 months prior to enrolling in the study.

The etymology of the term "heterosexual" emphasizes the befuddling views many have towards relationships, gender roles, and concurrency. The first known use of the term "heterosexual" in the USA dates back to a medical journal published in 1892 (Katz, 1996). Once used as a lexicon to describe deviant behavior, heterosexual and homosexual referred to the sexual and erotic desires exhibited as a form of sexual immorality (Katz, 1996). By the 1920s, heterosexuality began its metamorphoses into the nomenclature used today to describe any emotional or sexual relationship between a man and woman (Katz, 1996).

Gender typing, or the display of gender roles, begins at birth and by 5 years of age, most children have developed their stereotypic attitudes and beliefs about masculine and feminine roles (Hill, 2002). These culturally ascribed roles influence socialization and communication style, play patterns and behaviors, and rudimentary views of relationship expectations (Sherman & Zurbriggen, 2014). One major role which resonates with many in today's society is the goal to be married. Marriage symbolically represents prestige and for centuries society preserved the institution of marriage as an expectation of adulthood.

## *Hegemonic Aspects of Heterosexual Relationships*

Based on societal customs, women are often forced to withstand gender norms inequitable to those prescribed for men; this impartiality leads to the hegemonic space of heterosexual relationships through which women are forced to navigate (Collins, 2005; Tong, 1998). Before we address the impact of gender dominance within heterosexual relationships, we must define the limited terrain which hinders parity for women. The tenets of feminist theory highlight the power and control of mind and body; the mind is an honored and valued structure often associated with man, while the body is objectively denigrated and associated with woman (Kolmar & Bartowski, 2005). Women are thereby oppressed due to their complex, subordinate position in society (Kolmar & Bartowski, 2005; Sassler & Miller, 2011; Tong, 1998). Feminist theory comprises three operative components. First, feminist theory purports a conscious stand in opposition to the defamation and mistreatment of women (Tong, 1998). Misogyny and the classification of women as "other" influence feminist epistemologies, or the method by which one obtains knowledge. Feminist theory also addresses the beliefs that sexes are cultural forms of societal representation and identifies women as the defective sex (Tong, 1998). Finally, notions that oppress women transcend across accepted value systems and place women in the margins of society (Jones, 2004; Tong, 1998).

Societal norms, differential earning potential, and constant marginalization of women grant sexual partiality for men. These same variations are also present within heterosexual relationship dynamics and limit women's abilities to influence relationship outcomes (Kolmar & Bartowski, 2005; Wingood & DiClemente, 2000a, 2000b). The theory of gender and power serves as a common theoretical framework which offers three major structures to explicate power imbalances often seen in heterosexual relationships: the sexual division of labor, the sexual structure of power, and the structure of the cathexis (Kolmar & Bartowski, 2005; Wingood, Camp, Dunkle, Cooper, & DiClemente, 2009; Wingood & DiClemente, 2000a, 2000b). Sexual division of labor refers to the allocation of jobs and career options based on an individual's gender (Kolmar & Bartowski, 2005; Wingood et al., 2009; Wingood & DiClemente, 2000a). Due to the occupational choices of women and wage discrepancies, women often earn less than their male counterparts. Sexual division of labor may also manifest within the segregation of unpaid work such as housework and child care, tasks often assigned to women (Lincoln, 2008; Wingood & DiClemente, 2000a). Reduced earning potential and lower wages often correlate with educational limitations and diminished access to resources. As the economic disparity between men and women continues to expand, women are often confronted with tangible consequences based on a direct and indirect financial degree of dependence (Wingood et al., 2009; Wingood & DiClemente, 2000a).

Power, or control embedded within authority or coercion, serves as a fundamental element of all human relationships (Emerson, 1990; Jones, 2004). Men generally wield more power in heterosexual relationships due, in part, to culturally bound gender roles (Hettinger et al., 2014; Wingood et al., 2009; Wingood & DiClemente, 2000a). Since women are more likely to be psychologically, economically, and socially dependent in relationships, men are able to exhibit control by providing beneficial assets for both to use. Power dynamics and lack of control may negatively impact a woman's health as explained by Wingood and DiClemente (1998):

> Power … is manifested in heterosexual relationships in the difficulty women have in negotiating safer sex with male partners, in women having little self-control or skills in using condoms, and in women perceiving themselves to have little control of their partner's use of condoms. This influence of power is also observed in the pervasive societal norms that allow men to have more sexual freedom than women resulting in men's resistance to condom use (p. 33).

The third aspect of the theory of gender and power addresses the development and reinforcement of societal norms that regulate sexual behavior for both men and women. The structure of the cathexis, or emotional significance assigned to a person, produces the standards, customs, taboos, and prohibitions that define normal behavior within heterosexual relationships (Wingood et al., 2009; Wingood &

DiClemente, 2000a). Social roles and gender norms are often created by authoritative institutions and dictate values imposed upon both men and women that equate to normalcy (Sassler & Miller, 2011; Wingood et al., 2009; Wingood & DiClemente, 2000a). These views may prescribe the notion that women should aspire towards motherhood and a family-centered household while value is placed on the earning potential of men (De Henau & Himmelweit, 2013; Hettinger et al., 2014; Wingood & DiClemente, 1998). Sexual intercourse and negotiating safer sex practices are also governed by the structure of the cathexis; a woman's failure to negotiate safer sex practices may indicate a trusting, intimate relationship, while this perspective may be discordant among her male partners (Adimora et al., 2007; Akers, Fortenberry, Adimora, & Ford, 2007; Wingood & DiClemente, 2000b).

Heterosexual relationships and sexual behavior function as a dyadic interaction that is influenced not only by the level of power each individual possesses, but also by the relationship between those negotiating power (Emerson, 1990; Gutiérrez, Oh, & Gillmore, 2000). Since the amount of resistance on the part of one individual can potentially be weakened by another, power is often expressed through decision-making dominance and the unintentional—or intentional—ability to govern one's behavior or actions (Emerson, 1976, 1990; Hettinger et al., 2014). Power is awarded to the primary decision maker; the person with less power becomes more dependent upon the relationship. Due to the privilege of power afforded to men, a structure of dominance is essential to the functionality of a heterosexual relationship (Emerson, 1976, 1990; Hettinger et al., 2014). Because of the perceived benefits associated with being in a heterosexual relationship and gender roles that encourage behavior among women to prioritize relationship maintenance, women may accept sexual concurrency on the part of their male partners to keep a relationship intact.

According to Gutiérrez et al. (2000), "the power to negotiate, struggle, and accept, despite the larger social context, is an integral component of health practices. Inequalities within a society silence women and [their] expression of sexuality which in turn may endanger health and well-being" (p. 584). Addressing the inequities associated with power is essential to the sexual health of women; variables representing heterosexual relationship dynamics, including the duration of the relationship and sexual decision-making control and safer sex practices, correlate with the amount of power a woman has to influence dyadic change (Doherty, Padian, Marlow, & Aral, 2005; Wingood & DiClemente, 2000b). This influence serves as the underpinning of several outcomes in heterosexual relationships, including financial management, employment options, personal concerns, and more importantly sexual health. Hegemonic power influences sexual health choices such as safer sex practices and condom use. Traditional gender roles often dictate the sexual passivity of women, allowing men to be the initiator of sexual encounters. Women, therefore, function in the sexual space occupied by an overpowering external locus of control, thus contributing to precarious safer sex practices (Doherty et al., 2009; Dolcini & Catania, 2000; Jones, 2004; Logan, Cole, & Leukefeld, 2002). Subsequently, women who question the fidelity of a male partner or request the use of a condom during sexual intercourse challenge the expectations of power and pleasure held within societal norms (Doherty et al., 2005; Jones, 2004; Logan et al., 2002).

## *Concurrency Within Relationships*

As defined earlier in this chapter, sexual concurrency refers to the overlapping of sexual partners (Adimora et al., 2004, 2007; Andrasik et al., 2012; Waldrop-Valverde et al., 2013). Although the benefits associated with being in a heterosexual relationship and the negative aspects of concurrency are present in all races, the corollaries of sexual concurrency are often exacerbated with the dynamics of African-American heterosexual partnering. African-American men and women are often linked historically, romantically, and socially. Same-race coupling, inherently, foretells the unique conditions African-American women confront if sexual concurrency occurs within a relationship. These conditions are mainly influenced by the male–female sex ratio imbalance (Adimora et al., 2004, 2007; Doherty et al., 2009; Logan et al., 2002; McNair & Prather, 2004).

Ratios represent the relationship or numerical affiliation of two or more variables (Kane & Kyyrro, 2001). The male–female ratio represents the number of men identified in a setting compared to the number of women. Male–female ratios frequently illustrate a disproportionate relationship in which an inequitable association hinders one group while the other group excels. For instance, U.S. Census data from 2000 to 2010 reported that 49.1 % of the population were male and 50.9 % were female. Simply stated, the ratio of men to women in the USA was 1:1 (Howden & Meyer, 2011). A slight gender imbalance emerges in looking at the male–female ratio among college students, which is 43.6–56.4; approximately 44 % of those who attend college are male and 56 % are female (Fry & Cohn, 2010). Another diverging ratio is the male–female wage gap. In the USA, men earn $1 for every $0.77 earned by women, on average (Choi & Marks, 2013; Fry & Cohn, 2010), heightening the level of power unjustly allotted to men. Another imbalance frequently encountered within romantic relationships among African-American men and women is the race-specific sex ratio which gives rise to the difficulty of power reallocation based on the number of eligible African-American men (Logan et al., 2002; McNair & Prather, 2004; Nunn et al., 2011; VanderDrift, Agnew, Harvey, & Warren, 2013).

The sex ratio imbalance witnessed in the African-American community does not refer to a smaller number of African-American men living in the USA; this ratio refers to the percentage of eligible or available African-American men compared to the number of eligible or available African-American women (Logan et al., 2002; McNair & Prather, 2004; Nunn et al., 2011). If national population Census data for the USA is to mimic that of African-Americans, we could postulate a similar sex ratio indicative of a 1:1 ratio among African-Americans. However, societal, institutional, and personal determinants uniquely and precariously contribute to the diminished number of available African-American men represented in society. The larger number of available African-American women compared to African-American men often results in fewer available male partners, therefore lessening women's interpersonal power in relationships (Adimora et al., 2007; Dolcini & Catania, 2000; Logan et al., 2002; McNair & Prather, 2004). Lower levels of interpersonal power interfere with a woman's ability to exercise a level of authority needed to initiate safer sex practices, such as condom use, due to apprehension of dissolving the relationship. To better understand this phenomenon, we must first examine the status of African-American men within the context of racial and cultural norms and behavioral patterns.

African-American men have more options for sustaining meaningful and emotional relationships compared to African-American women because African-American women outnumber African-American men in the general population. An examination of historical factors helps to explain the impact of this disproportionate ratio. First, African-American men are incarcerated at rates much higher than any other gender and race in the USA (Alexander, 2012; Reddick & Heilig, 2012). In 2013, the Pew Research Center reported that African-American men were six times more likely to be incarcerated at all levels of the penal system (local prisons, and state and federal jails) than their white counterparts (Alexander, 2012; Glaze, 2011; Drake, 2013) and many believe that the origins of African-American male incarceration can be seen within the school-to-prison pipeline (Glaze, 2011; Drake, 2013; Reddick & Heilig, 2012). Through the sanctions of "zero-tolerance" approaches to school discipline, African-American males are heavily represented among those receiving disciplinary actions for misconduct or behavioral infractions (Alexander, 2012; Drake, 2013; Reddick & Heilig, 2012). As disciplinary actions are heaped upon African-American boys, rates of suspension and expulsion increase due, in part, to harsher penalties not necessarily heaved upon their white counterparts. Lower educational achievement rates and the correlate of crime among youth are often elevated for African-American males, leading to increasingly higher rates of school drop-out, incarceration, and death (Alexander, 2012; Glaze, 2011; Drake, 2013; Reddick & Heilig, 2012).

Higher incarceration rates experienced by African-American males can also be explained by the severe and punitive consequences of drug-related offenses, particularly those associated with crack cocaine. In the late 1970s and early 1980s, trends that benefited highly educated individuals stymied the earning potential for African-American men (Alexander, 2012; Drake, 2013). Concurrently, increased drug activity associated with both use and trade spiked, and crack cocaine became known as the drug of choice for African-Americans due to its affordability and noticeable profit margin (Alexander, 2012). Although the distribution and use of crack were not exclusive to African-Americans, the newly demonstrative "war on drugs" did more to incarcerate African-Americans than any other criminal infraction in the history of the USA (Alexander, 2012). Mandatory crack-related federal sentences and unfair racially based mandates, such as the federal "Three Strikes" law, contributed to an insurmountable increase in the number of convicted African-American men since the former First Lady Nancy Reagan first uttered the phrase "Just Say No!" Drug convictions account for approximately two-thirds of those serving time in federal prisons and people of color represent 90 % of all drug convictions (Alexander, 2012). The disproportionate incarceration rate of African-American men reduces their representation in society, reducing their overall availability to establish or maintain heterosexual relationships.

The ethnic and racial landscape of America has evolved and miscegenation, or interracial coupling, appears to be commonplace in today's society. However,

African-Americans have the lowest rate of interracial dating compared to other ethnic groups and only 5 % of interracial marriages included a person identified as African-American (D'Souza, 2010; Fisman, Iyengar, Kamenca, & Simonson, 2008). Interracial relationships are less likely to lead to marriage, have a shorter duration compared to same-race relationships, and are more likely to dissolve (D'Souza, 2010). Studies have shown that some African-Americans retain negative attitudes towards interracial relationships due to historical race relations associated with discrimination and marginalization. Formidable bonds among African-American men and women strengthened by Americans' racially oppressive history are often counterintuitive to interracial dating (D'Souza, 2010; Fisman et al., 2008). Although interracial dating is less likely to occur among African Americans, African-American women hold stronger views and preferences towards same-race relationships than African-American men. Therefore, African-American women are less likely to engage in interracial dating compared to African-American men (Fisman et al., 2008; Wang, 2012). African-American men are at least two times more likely to be married to someone of a different race compared to African-American women (D'Souza, 2010), and approximately 24 % of black male newlyweds married someone of a different race while only 9 % of black women reported the same marriage pattern (Wang, 2012). Subsequently, the dating practices of African-American men further reduce their eligibility and availability for African-American women.

The presence of African-American men within society is also diminished due to rates of death and homicide. African Americans experience higher rates of homicide compared to other races. According to the statistics provided by the Centers for Disease Control and Prevention, homicide rates for non-Hispanic African-American males between the ages of 10 and 24 were 48.4 per 100,000 homicide rates for whites and Hispanics within the same age range were 2.3 and 12.4, respectively (Centers for Disease Control and Prevention, 2014).

The sex ratio imbalance is not exclusive to African Americans and some speculate that this phenomenon may disproportionately affect whites in the near future (Banks, 2011). However, the dating preferences of African Americans, and members of their sexual networks, are oftentimes racially homogenous (Adimora et al., 2007; D'Souza, 2010; Ragnarsson, Townsend, Thorson, Chopra, & Ekström, 2009). A diminutive decrease in the number of eligible African-American men compared to African-American women affords these men the dominant role of determining relationship progression (Sassler & Miller, 2011). This dominance serves as the cornerstone of sexual concurrency. An imbalance in the male–female sex ratio implies that when one sex outnumbers the other, members of the scarcer sex have a bargaining advantage within heterosexual relationships. Thus, the advantage afforded to African-American men leads to more options for alternative relationships (Adimora et al., 2007; Ragnarsson et al., 2009; Sassler & Miller, 2011). In other words, supply and demand dictate the value of the item fewer in number. The value of fewer African-American males dictates power due to demand. Gender roles within society place a strong emphasis on identifying as a part of a relationship, and the benefits of coupling often offset the desire to dissolve a committed union. With fewer options and a reduced dating pool, African-American women must often vacillate between functioning in a space void of personal power by remaining in a relationship and jeopardizing the status of the relationship by challenging the structure of power. Thus, sexual concurrency is disproportionately seen among African-American relationships and occurs at the intersection of power and demand.

## Relationship Dynamics and Poverty

The decision to enter into a heterosexual union can offer many benefits for both men and women. Heterosexual unions can provide social support and emotional support, additional financial stability, an increased sense of physical well-being, as well as decreased social stigma often attached to being single in a society that favors coupling (Kennedy et al., 2007; Rabir, 2004). Relationships can provide a better sense of mental health for both partners, as each can experience lower levels of depression, anxiety, along with other forms of psychological distress, less physical health problems, and chronic conditions (Choi & Marks, 2013; Miller et al., 2013). This can be attributed to an increased need for emotional and social support often associated with living in poverty. According to the U.S. Census Bureau, the poverty rate "is an economic indicator that measures the percentage of people within the poverty threshold" (Galea et al., 2011). As discussed earlier in this chapter, women, on average, earn less than their male counterparts and have limited access to resources which improve their quality of life. Several of the adverse effects of poverty are related to the lower SES of women and correlations among social determinants of health.

Social determinants of health are "the complex integrated and overlapping social structures and economic systems that are responsible for most health inequities" (Galindo, Walker, Hazelton, & Arnold, 2012). Overlapping structures within social determinants of health include access to wealth and opportunities to gain valuable resources to improve quality of life, conditions of one's geographical or physical location, and causal inequities produced by the marginalization of gender (Centers for Disease Control and Prevention, 2012b). The percentage of those living in poverty has gradually increased over the past decade, and poverty rates in the USA have remained constant between 2011 and 2012 (Galindo et al., 2012). Poverty is a global issue which disproportionately impacts women at higher rates than men across a life span. In the USA, women are more likely to suffer from poverty and lower SES due to societal power structures. Consequently, the diversity of race and ethnicity further marginalizes women, exacerbating the effects of poverty (Centers for Disease Control and Prevention, 2012b; Pre-Exposure Prophylaxis, 2012).

Households led and maintained by a female, or households with no husband or male present, report lower income earning and households led by women of color fare worse than other racial and ethnic groups (Pre-Exposure Prophylaxis, 2012). Women, especially women of color, living in poverty have lower education rates and suffer from forced segregation into lower income housing. Also, the nonmarital birth rate is the highest among black women and those living in a single-parent household are more likely to live in poverty (Pre-Exposure Prophylaxis, 2012). As the cycle begins, the symbiotic relationship is reinforced; women in poverty experience lower SES and nonmarital births extending the effects of poverty by habitually influencing the choices and consequences of their children. Children born into poverty continue to operate within the space of the limited resources needed to improve their quality of life (Aral, Adimora, & Fenton, 2008).

The budgetary restraints many women face while living in poverty precipitate negative health outcomes. For instance, research has found that women dependent upon others for economic resources report lower levels of self-esteem along with more depressive symptoms and mental health issues (Aral et al., 2008; Kennedy et al., 2007; Salazar et al., 2005). Conversely, coupling or marriage has also been shown to shield the negative effects of poverty (Centers for Disease Control and Prevention, 2012a). Chronic exposure to stressors such as inadequate housing, lack of financial resources, and oppression is common to all women living in poverty, especially black women who also face the underpinnings of racism based on their economic disadvantage in society (Centers for Disease Control and Prevention, 2012a; Centers for Disease Control and Prevention, 2012b; Pre-Exposure Prophylaxis, 2012). Social support is the tenet of social relationships and social networks. These relationships and networks may offer emotional, instrumental, informational, and appraisal support, and value is ascribed based on the availability of assistance received and proximity of those within a social network (Golub, Gamarel, Rendina, Surace, & Lelutiu-Weinberger, 2013). Therefore, social support offers women living in poverty the benefit of being in a trusting and loving relationship (emotional support), access to additional income and resources (instrumental support), informational support (advise and suggestions), and appraisal support (affirmations and constructive feedback) (Centers for Disease Control and Prevention, 2012a; Golub et al., 2013).

## Health Implications Associated with Concurrency

Coupling provides mutual benefits to both partners and these benefits include a sense of security, greater health benefits, financial stability, and a higher quality of life (Choi & Marks, 2013; Miller et al., 2013; Sharpe et al., 2012). Within the hegemonic nature of heterosexual relationships, men are afforded more power than women and serve as the primary decision maker within the partnership. For women living in poverty, the need to remain in a relationship is often greater than the desire to dissolve to union. Concurrency occurs when sexual relationships overlap and is disproportionately experienced among African-American women. The power exhibited by men and the desire to be in a relationship diminish the capacity by which women often function within a relationship.

Those involved in a sexually concurrent relationship subsequently comprise a sexual network. Sexual networks are groups of individuals directly or indirectly connected to each other by their sexual encounters (Adimora, Schoenbach, Taylor, Khan, & Schwartz, 2011; Doherty, Shiboski, Ellen, Adimora, & Padian, 2006; Kalichman & Grebler, 2010). According to Doherty et al. (2010), "societal determinants of sexual networks pertain to the underlying social, economic, cultural and political forces, as well as technological advances, in a county, region, or smaller community that have macro effects on network formation" (p. 542). The space and location in which a sexual network develops, and the sexual health and risk behaviors of those within the network, impact the sexual health of those identified as a part of the sexual network (Adimora et al., 2004; Doherty et al., 2006). Therefore, sexual concurrency, and concurrent sexual partners, can facilitate the spread of HIV along with other sexually transmitted diseases (STDs) (Doherty et al., 2006; Frye et al., 2013; Golub & Gamarel, 2013).

Concurrency, as defined, does not increase the risk per se; rather it is their partners' concurrency that results in increased risk. In other words, those who become infected are likely to transmit pathogens to other concurrent partners. From a behavioral standpoint, both men and women engage in sexually concurrent relationships. However, women bear the brunt of the health implications associated with having concurrent sexual partners. Sexually transmitted diseases are infections acquired through an act of anal, oral, or vaginal sex. Within the context of social norms and physical space, the risk of transmitting and acquiring an STD increases for an individual whose partner has sex with multiple partners or an individual who engages in concurrent sex with an infected partner (Doherty et al., 2006). Women within a sexual network are impacted differently by STDs than men, and unfortunately the risk associated with acquiring an STD is higher for women (Adimora et al., 2007; Jackson et al., 2013). First, the vagina is a more suitable environment for bacteria growth making the lining of the vagina susceptible to infections (Karim, Kashuba, Werner, & Karim, 2011). Also, women are less likely to notice the symptoms of certain STDs compared to men due to anatomical differences. Ulcers or sores that develop on the penis are more noticeable than those that may develop within the lining of vagina and women may not realize that they are infected, resulting in a lower likelihood to seek treatment (Karim et al., 2011). Therefore, the discovery of an STD among women may take place only once the disease has progressed.

The use of condoms is crucial in reducing the spread of certain STDs. However, the lack of power most women display within sexual relationships, and engaging in sexual intercourse with a concurrent partner, places women at greater risk for acquiring HIV (Adimora et al., 2004; Golub & Gamarel, 2013; Wingood et al., 2007; Wingood & DiClemente, 2000b). Condom negotiation encompasses the ability and efficacy by which a woman can successfully ask her sexual partner to use or wear a condom. Factors such as perceived sexual monogamy or lack of knowledge about a partner's sexual health may not warrant the use of a condom during sexual intercourse (Adimora et al., 2007; Frye et al., 2013; Golub & Gamarel, 2013). Those who perceive themselves to be in serious, committed relationships, such as marriage, may not see the need to wear condoms during sexual intercourse.

## Partner Concurrency and Relationship Dynamics

### *Relationship Views and Desires: "She Wants to Be in a Relationship."*

As discussed in the previous section, both men and women experience benefits from coupling. Female participants in the HPTN 064 study agreed with this notion and provided examples to support these views based on personal experience and community perceptions. The benefits associated with being in a relationship included intangible and tangible assets, both of equal value. Intangible assets included esteem and social support and will be discussed later in this section. According to the participants, financial security serves as the primary benefit of being in a relationship. One participant described an acquaintance's desire to be in a relationship for monetary support in the following manner:

> I say we are both looking for [a relationship] sometimes. With her, she's looking for guys with money. Oh, they gotta have money … I told her, it's not all about the money sometimes … and her expectations are real high and I'm like that's why you keep getting hurt.
>
> —*Interviewee, Atlanta, GA*

The participants also provided insight into the advantages of financial support and coupling. Monetary support from male partners was often used to take care of basic needs such as clothing and food, and these needs were heightened if children were a part of the nuclear family. Phrases such as "I didn't want for nothing" and "if I needed something, my husband would go out and get it" were supported by this description of a participant whose financial support was jeopardized when her partner was incarcerated:

> I remember at one point, I didn't have no money and my baby daddy was locked up 'cause for the most part, he does take care of me … and my baby, but I didn't have no money for pampers or anything like that. So what I did was … [popped open] a pack of pampers and took some pampers out and walked out of the store, put [them] in the baby bag, but I only did that 'cause I needed it.
>
> —*Focus Group Participant, Raleigh/Durham, NC*

Others listed items such as clothing, food, and rent as the primary tangible resources received while coupling and another participant stated that she often dated married men "for support [and] the convenience." Additionally, financial support from male partners was used to pay bills and monthly expenses:

> He supports me and the kids. No, he don't ever see us hungry … and I don't worry about eating. I'm [going to] eat. So, I don't pay no bills, he pays my cell phone. I don't pay no rent, I don't pay no cable bill.
>
> —*Interviewee, Washington, D.C.*

Men frequently benefit more than women within the realms of society and the realms of heterosexual relationships. Women recognized the hegemonic views of male and female relationships and substantiated this perception in their responses related to reasons for concurrency. Male sexual concurrency was seen as a normal part of male sexual behavior that oftentimes cannot be changed or altered.

> It's in [men], it's their nature … now I done got numbers from guys just to see if I can do it. I'll go out 'betcha I can get ten numbers tonight' something like that but … most of [men] it's just in their nature.
>
> *—Interviewee, Washington, D.C.*

An interview participant in Atlanta described how her boyfriend had multiple sexual encounters with other women while in a relationship with her; though she initially accepted his sexual infidelity as a normal behavior, she finally made the decision to dissolve the relationship:

> I was just going through his cell phone and I found different numbers and I asked him about it but he never did say that he was messing with that person. So, I kind of figured and put two and two together that he was and I used to call the female and ask and she said yes. So I was hurt, I was really hurt and I just … I did forgive him, I did go back but it's just a certain point in time when you just stop forgiving that person because he's going to keep doing it over and over again and obviously he don't care about your feelings and so I just left it alone and moved on.
>
> *—Interviewee, Atlanta, GA*

A similar response was provided by a focus group participant from D.C.:

> I'm going to tell you the honest to God truth, I don't know if he cheating but my thing is I [will experience it] with the next one and still go through the same bullshit that I just left. So, I might as well just stay there and try to work on that instead of going somewhere else and starting all over again and still end up going through the same thing.
>
> *—Focus Group Participant, Washington, D.C.*

If male sexual concurrency was a natural act, then female sexual concurrency was unnatural and occurred as a reaction instigated as an emotional or a vengeful response to male behavior. Female sexual concurrency also resulted as a means for benefit or gain.

> I ain't even going to lie, I used to be just like that. I just used to treat men how they treated women but the only thing about me is I always thought about it before I went, always. I never caught nothing, none of that. Men don't think, I'm going to think. I used to be just like that. You treat me like that, I'm going to treat you and your men like that.
>
> *—Focus Group Participant, Washington, D.C.*

The view of sexual concurrency as a common behavior for men lends itself to the power dynamics often seen on heterosexual behaviors. If male sexual concurrency does take place, women in heterosexual relationships are at the mercy of an act considered to be a normal or standard way of life, and must decide to either accept the concurrent behavior or dissolve the relationship as a result of it.

## *Sexual Concurrency: "There's a Little Bit of Cheating in Everybody."*

Concurrency was an expected and unavoidable occurrence among several of the HPTN 064 participants. A number of women expressed a high level of commitment and fidelity to their partner; yet, they still experienced acts of sexual concurrency by their partners. One of the participants illustrated the commonality of sexual concurrency in this manner:

> Right now, what seems to be going on with these dudes … they don't even try to cheat on you. They gonna let you know from the get-go, 'I'm gonna have you … I'm gonna have you … I'm bored, I'm gonna have me two or three women.'
>
> —*Focus Group Participant, Raleigh/Durham, NC*

Women, therefore, have now been conditioned to accept concurrency as a part of heterosexual coupling. Subsequently, this level of acceptance often came with a price. Women were relegated to confirming their perceived level of importance among the number of women in their partner's sexual network as a method of validation. Although an unfortunate reality, one participant expressed her displeasure with this demeaning consequence of wanting to remain in a relationship:

> [Women] look at it like this, "I'm wifey, he's getting what he wants, and I'm going to be his number one. No matter what, he's going to come home to me tonight." But, I hate when girls say that but don't seem to realize…your saying that, but at the end of the day, your man is sharing something that's supposed to be yours.
>
> —*Focus Group Participant, New York, NY*

One reason for the acceptance of concurrency is the imbalanced male–female ratio. Statements such as "I feel like if there [were] enough men out here for … us women, it might be easier" and "if we had the equal amount of men for women I think we'd all be happy" corroborated the idea that females often outnumber males in the general population and the scarcity of men afforded their male partners the benefit of engaging in concurrent relationships with multiple women. Additionally, men and women may have dissimilar relationship expectations which lead to sexual concurrency; women are more willing to settle down and establish serious committed relationships, while men do not express the same sentiment:

> It might be harder for [females] than for [males] because you have a lot of single men out here that's just … fun-filled and … just want to try a lot of different things. They are just open to experiencing everything. Most females now are like ready to settle down but [there] are a lot of males out here that are just hopping."
>
> —*Interviewee, Atlanta, GA*

One woman explained how her and her partner's discordant relationship expectations led to a more lenient view of commitment within their relationship and her acceptance of his sexually concurrent behavior:

> I don't mind him looking at a female. We can talk about other females and everything … and sometimes, we might bet bored with each other … because the reason why me and this young gentlemen had an open relationship [was] because he said he wasn't ready for a girlfriend.
>
> —*Interviewee, Atlanta, GA*

The revelation or discovery of unexpected sexual concurrency in a serious committed relationship is usually devastating, but does not always lead to the end of the partnership. Women are forced to navigate through a hegemonic society which benefits men, and remaining in a relationship buffers the harsh realities faced by this marginalized group. The view that women remain in relationships for fear of being alone was mentioned several times using phrases indicating "a lot of women can't be by themselves" and "[women] have to be with a man" because they do not want to be single. Establishing a relationship is often viewed as a timely process, and once the mutual benefits of social support are developed and cultivated, a woman is less likely to terminate a relationship.

> I think a lot of it has to deal with you just [not wanting to] go through the commotion of meeting somebody else all over again, dealing with that person, dealing with their personality, all over again. You feel like you don't have time for that. You'd just do better staying with [who] you're dealing with and just going on with your life.
>
> —*Focus Group Participant, Raleigh/Durham, NC*

Some of the participants speculated that women were less likely to dissolve the relationship due to the benefits of social support and self-esteem. A lack of self-esteem may be evident among women with "baggage" such as small children and the burdens associated with previous relationship conflict. Consequently, a woman may not be seen as attractive if she has baggage from prior relationships, which may negatively impact her self-esteem with each repeated episode. One participant stated that her mother remained with her father after she discovered infidelity within the relationship because of "self-esteem issues," adding that her mother would often state "I got four kids. Three of them still live with me. [Who's] gonna want to deal with a 40-year old women with three kids?" *Focus Group Participant, Raleigh/Durham, NC*. Another example of remaining in a concurrent relationship because of low self-esteem is described below:

> … it's self-esteem. Whether the person knows it or not, they feel like they can't get somebody that's going to be faithful, or somebody that's going to love them, so they might as well be with everybody and get as much from as many people as they can to make [themselves] feel better.
>
> —*Focus Group Participant, New York, NY*

## *Health Implications: "… Even Though A Woman's Not Promiscuous, If Her Partner Is, You're Putting Yourself At Risk"*

Although sexual concurrency among men served as the prominent theme among the participants, women bore the brunt of the disproportionate consequences of a male partner's expanded sexual network. Subsequently, the women in the HPTN 064 study were aware of this uncontrollable factor and its health implications. If a woman is willing to remain in a sexual concurrent relationship with her partner, she is exposed to sexual health risk associated with the sexual behavior exhibited by the male. A participant described the intersectionality associated with a partner's risky sexual behavior and dynamic relationship factors many face when dealing with infidelity and multiple sex partners:

> "Yeah, well my friends, she been with her boyfriend for 10 years. They met in middle school and they have two kids together … when … she recently found out over half of those years he had other girlfriends, she was hurt by it, but she … [has] two kids by him, and she's going to stick by him and I told her you need to move on. Y'all been together for 10 years but what if he [brings] you something back? And y'all are not using protection [because] y'all have two kids.
>
> —*Focus Group Participant, Atlanta, GA*

One of the health risks of sexual concurrency is higher rates of STDs. Some of the more commonly known STDs recognized as the result of concurrent partners included gonorrhea, syphilis, chlamydia, and HIV/AIDS:

> I've caught a transmitted disease from that person. He gave me gonorrhea. I got clean, everything's alright now … I've been sexually active almost 15 years of my life and I've never had an STD and this one man … I really starting to feel for him in my heart and he was in the closet, and he was the first on to fucking give me a STD. That's a shame!
>
> —*Focus Group Participant, New York, NY*

Another participant shared the disappointment and anguish she experienced once she learned that she had contracted STDs from her boyfriend who was having unprotected sex with multiple sexual partners:

> I have an ex-boyfriends, I was 18. He gave me [several STDs] … he gave me herpes, genital warts, chlamydia, [trichomoniasis] and gonorrhea … he stays in the house, me, like a dummy … I stay with him, try not to have sex with him, take my medicine, knowing he's still dirty because he doesn't go to the hospital, have sex with him again and get it again. Finally, I had to make him go to the hospital because he wasn't going trying to go. It was crazy, I was 18 - so called 'in love.'
>
> —*Focus Group Participant, New York, NY*

Those who do contract an STD from their male partner experience shame and guilt associated with the diagnosis, and, as evident in the previous statement, may have unprotected sex and become repeatedly reinfected. A woman may also experience shame, fear, and anger upon a confirmed diagnosis of an STD. A focus group participant from New York stated that she "was scared" and expressed her anger with the diagnosis by exclaiming "I was like how fucking dare you! … the one motherfucker I was truly faithful to, you give me this shit!"

Several STDs can be prevented with the use of condoms. However, rates of condom use among women who perceive themselves to be in committed heterosexual relationships are low. Many women do not assess themselves at risk for contracting an STD, although a number of them are aware of the potential for acquiring a disease due to partner infidelity. Therefore, condom use is rare and infrequent:

> When I'm with a partner or whatever … a couple a years or a couple of months … and they move in and out and shit. You don't think 'oh, put a condom on,' you're just like 'whatever.'
>
> —*Focus Group Participant, New York, NY*

Another explanation for the lack of condom use among women in relationships in which sexual concurrency is known is the fear or concern of their partner's reaction. Men may become offended at the request and express a sense of displeasure with the level of distrust implied by recommending a condom be used during a sexual encounter:

> I also think once you didn't use a condom with a certain person and all, that it's like hard to tell them oh, you want to use a condom because you didn't use a condom with him before … you are going to start thinking differently, like why [do] you want to use a condom [now]?
>
> —*Focus Group Participant, New York, NY*

Intimate partner violence (IPV) often occurs within relationships and many women are fearful of being physically assaulted by their male partners. This fear may hinder a woman's ability to negotiate the use of a condom if sexual concurrency has occurred in the past or if her partner is currently having sex with multiple women. One woman's personal account of IPV is detailed below:

> When he was with another woman and then started being violent towards me. I still stayed because I promised his father I would, you know. Plus, I had nowhere to go … I gave my life up to take care of him, I gave my life up because, I could have easily went somewhere else and stayed with somebody else until I got on my feet. But, I gave my life up to take care of him because I felt sorry for him … ten years of my life. And then, the thanks I got for it was the violence-verbally and physically … so, I just gave up, I couldn't do it no more.
>
> —*Interviewee, Atlanta, GA*

## Policy Implications

Many women experience sexual concurrency within their relationships for several reasons, and although it may not be possible to enact policies to prevent the expansion of sexual networks, we may be able to address the contextual factors associated with the negative outcomes and consequences inherently rooted in sexually concurrent relationships. Additionally, it is not possible to offer a "quick fix" to address aspects which influence the hegemonic nature of today's society. For instance, women, especially women of lower SES, may be more reliant upon the social support and multiple income resources afforded to them by remaining in a relationship. Policies may be proposed to increase employment opportunities for women, or implement changes to drug sentencing laws to decrease the number of minor drug violators or offenders in prison who are overwhelmingly minority males. Both of these policy implications are necessary to increase the quality of life for marginalized groups, but sexual concurrency is directly related to subjective variables (i.e., feelings and emotions) and we may experience difficulty in addressing the very nature in which one may place a heterosexual relationship in such high regard.

## References

Adimora, A. A., Schoenbach, V. J., & Doherty, I. A. (2007). Concurrent sexual partnerships among men in the United States. *American Journal of Public Health, 97*(12), 2230–2237.

Adimora, A. A., Schoenbach, V. J., Taylor, E. M., Khan, M. R., & Schwartz, R. J. (2011). Concurrent partnerships, nonmonogamous partners, and substance use among women in the United States. *American Journal of Public Health, 101*(1), 128–136.

Adimora, A., Schoenbach, V., Martinson, F., Donaldson, K., Stancil, T., & Fullilove, R. (2004). Concurrent sexual partnerships among African Americans in the rural South. *Annals of Epidemiology, 14*(3), 155–160.

Akers, A. Y., Fortenberry, J. D., Adimora, A. A., & Ford, C. A. (2007). Longitudinal variation in sexual behaviors among young, urban women. *Journal of Adolescent Health, 40*(2), S21.

Alexander, M. (2012). *The New Jim Crow: Mass incarceration in the age of colorblindness*. New York: The New Press.

Amato, P. R., & Hohmann-Marriott, B. (2007). A comparison of high-and low-distress marriages that end in divorce. *Journal of Marriage and the Family, 69*, 621–638.

Andrasik, M. P., Chapman, C. H., Clad, R., Murray, K., Foster, J., Morris, M., … Kurth, A. E. (2012). Developing concurrency messages for the black community in Seattle, Washington. *AIDS Education & Prevention, 24*(6), 527–548.

Aral, S. O., Adimora, A. A., & Fenton, K. A. (2008). Understanding and responding to disparities in HIV and other sexually transmitted infections in African Americans. *Lancet, 372*(9635), 337–340.

Banks, R. (2011). *Is marriage for white people? How the African American marriage decline affects everybody*. New York: Penguin Group.

Glaze, L. (2011). Correctional Populations in the United States, 2010. http://www.bjs.gov/content/pub/pdf/cpus11.pdf.

Centers for Disease Control and Prevention. (2012a). Check interim guidance for PrEP in men, women. *Contraceptive Technology Update, 33*(10), 113–114.

Centers for Disease Control and Prevention. (2014). Youth Violence: National Statistics, 2013.

Centers for Disease Control and Prevention. (2012b). Interim guidance for clinicians considering the use of preexposure prophylaxis for the prevention of HIV infection in heterosexually active adults. *MMWR. Morbidity and Mortality Weekly Report, 61*, 586–589.

Choi, H., & Marks, N. (2013). Marital quality, socioeconomic status, and physical health. *Journal of Marriage and Family, 75*(4), 903–919.

Cohn, D. V. (2013). *Love and marriage*. Retrieved April 12, 2014, from http://www.pewsocialtrends.org/2013/02/13/love-and-marriage/.

Collins, P. H. (2005). *Black sexual politics: African Americans, gender, and the new racism*. New York: Routledge.

Copen, C., Daniels, K., Vespa, J., & Mosher, W. (2012). *First marriages in the United States: Data from the 2006–2010 National Survey of Family Growth*. National Canter for Health Statistics: Hyattsville, MD.

D'Souza, R. A. (2010). A multilevel analysis of interracial relationship characteristics among young adults. *Race and Social Problems, 2*(2), 92–100.

De Henau, J., & Himmelweit, S. (2013). Unpacking within-household gender differences in partners' subjective benefits from household income. *Journal of Marriage and Family, 75*(3), 611–624.

Doherty, I. A., Padian, N. S., Marlow, C., & Aral, S. O. (2005). Determinants and consequences of sexual networks as they affect the spread of sexually transmitted infections. *Journal of Infectious Diseases, 191*, S42–S54.

Doherty, I. A., Schoenbach, V. J., & Adimora, A. A. (2009). Sexual mixing patterns and heterosexual HIV transmission among African Americans in the southeastern United States. *Journal of Acquired Immune Deficiency Syndromes, 52*(1), 114–120.

Doherty, I. A., Shiboski, S., Ellen, J. M., Adimora, A. A., & Padian, N. S. (2006). Sexual bridging socially and over time: A simulation model exploring the relative effects of mixing and concurrency on viral sexually transmitted infection transmission. *Sexually Transmitted Diseases, 33*(6), 368–373.

Dolcini, M. M., & Catania, J. A. (2000). Psychosocial profiles of women with risky sexual partners: The National AIDS Behavioral Surveys (NABS). *AIDS and Behavior, 4*(3), 297–308.

Drake, B. (2013). *Incarceration gap widens between whites and blacks*. Washington, DC: Pew Research Center.

Emerson, R. M. (1976). Social exchange theory. *Annual Review of Sociology, 2*, 335–362.

Emerson, R. M. (1990). Social exchange theory. In M. Rosenberg & R. H. Turner (Eds.), *Social psychology: Sociological perspectives* (pp. 30–65). Piscataway, NJ: Transaction.

Fisman, R., Iyengar, S., Kamenca, E., & Simonson, I. (2008). Racial preferences in dating. *Review of Economic Studies, 75*, 117–132.

Fry, R., & Cohn, D. V. (2010). *A social and demographic trend report*. Washington, DC: Pew Research Center.

Frye, V., Williams, K., Bond, K. T., Henny, K., Cupid, M., Weiss, L., ... Koblin, B. A. (2013). Condom use and concurrent partnering among heterosexually active, African American men: A qualitative report. *Journal of Urban Health, 90*(5), 953–969.

Galea, J. T., Kinsler, J. J., Salazar, X., Lee, S. J., Giron, M., Sayles, J. N., ... Cunningham, W. E. (2011). Acceptability of pre-exposure prophylaxis as an HIV prevention strategy: Barriers and facilitators to pre-exposure prophylaxis uptake among at-risk Peruvian populations. *International Journal of STD & AIDS, 22*(5), 256–262.

Galindo, G. R., Walker, J. N. J., Hazelton, P., & Arnold, E. (2012). Community member perspectives from transgender women and men who have sex with men on pre-exposure prophylaxis as an HIV prevention strategy: Implications for implementation. *Implementation Science, 7*(1), 116.

Golub, S. A., & Gamarel, K. E. (2013). The impact of anticipated HIV stigma on delays in HIV testing behaviors: Findings from a community-based sample of men who have sex with men and transgender women in New York City. *AIDS Patient Care and STDs, 27*(11), 621–627.

Golub, S. A., Gamarel, K. E., Rendina, H. J., Surace, A., & Lelutiu-Weinberger, C. (2013). From efficacy to effectiveness: Facilitators and barriers to PrEP acceptability and motivations for adherence among MSM and transgender women in New York City. *AIDS Patient Care and STDs, 27*(4), 248–254.

Gutiérrez, L., Oh, H. J., & Gillmore, M. R. (2000). Toward an understanding of (em)power(ment) for HIV/AIDS prevention with adolescent women. *Sex Roles, 42*(7–8), 581–611.

Hawkins, A. J., Willoughby, B. J., & Doherty, W. J. (2012). Reasons for divorce and openness to marital reconciliation. *Journal of Divorce & Remarriage, 53*(6), 453–463.

Hettinger, V. E., Hutchinson, D. M., & Bosson, J. K. (2014). Influence of professional status on perceptions of romantic relationship dynamics. *Psychology of Men & Masculinity, 15*, 470–480.

Hill, S. A. (2002). Teaching and doing gender in African American families. *Sex Roles, 47*(11), 493–506.

Howden, L., & Meyer, J. (2011). *Age and sex composition: 2010*. Washington, DC: U.S. Census Bureau.

Jackson, T., Huang, A., Chen, H., Gao, X., Zhang, Y., & Zhong, X. (2013). Predictors of willingness to use HIV pre-exposure prophylaxis among female sex workers in Southwest China. *AIDS Care, 25*(5), 601–605.

Jones, R. (2004). Relationships of sexual imposition, dyadic trust, and sensation seeking with sexual risk behavior in young Urban women. *Research in Nursing & Health, 27*(3), 185–197.

Kalichman, S., & Grebler, T. (2010). Reducing numbers of sex partners: Do we really need special interventions for sexual concurrency? *AIDS and Behavior, 14*(5), 987–990.

Kane, E. W., & Kyyrro, E. K. (2001). For whom does education enlighten? Race, gender, education, and beliefs about social inequality. *Gender & Society, 15*(5), 710–733.

Karim, S. S., Kashuba, A. D., Werner, L., & Karim, Q. A. (2011). Drug concentrations after topical and oral antiretroviral pre-exposure prophylaxis: Implications for HIV prevention in women. *Lancet, 378*(9787), 279–281.

Katz, J. (1996). *The invention of heterosexuality*. New York: Penguin.

Kennedy, B. M., Ard, J. D., Harrison, L., Jr, Conish, B. K., Kennedy, E., Levy, E. J., & Brantley, P. J. (2007). Cultural characteristics of African Americans: Implications for the design of trials that target behavior and health promotion programs. *Ethnicity and Disease, 17*(Summer), 548–554.

Kolmar, W., & Bartowski, F. (2005). *Feminist theory: A reader*. Boston: McGraw Hill.

Lincoln, A. E. (2008). Gender, productivity, and the marital wage premium. *Journal of Marriage and Family, 70*(3), 806–814.

Lincoln, K., & Chae, D. (2010). Stress, marital satisfaction, and psychological distress among African Americans. *Journal of Family Issues, 31*(8), 1081–1105.

Logan, T. K., Cole, J., & Leukefeld, C. (2002). Women, sex, and HIV: Social and contextual factors, meta-analysis of published interventions, and implications for practice and research. *Psychological Bulletin, 128*(6), 851–885.

Marín, R. A., Christensen, A., & Atkins, D. C. (2014). Infidelity and behavioral couple therapy: Relationship outcomes over 5 years following therapy. *Couple and Family Psychology: Research and Practice, 3*(1), 1–12.

McNair, L. D., & Prather, C. M. (2004). African American women and AIDS: Factors influencing risk and reaction to HIV disease. *Journal of Black Psychology, 30*(1), 106–123.

Miller, R. B., Hollist, C. S., Olsen, J., & Law, D. (2013). Marital quality and health over 20 years: A growth curve analysis. *Journal of Marriage and Family, 75*(3), 667–680.

National Marriage and Divorce Rate Trends (2014). http://www.cdc.gov/nchs/nvss/marriage_divorce_tables.htm. Retrieved April 14, 2014.

Nunn, A., Dickman, S., Cornwall, A., Rosengard, C., Kwakwa, H., Kim, D., … Mayer, K. H. (2011). Social, structural and behavioral drivers of concurrent partnerships among African American men in Philadelphia. *AIDS Care, 23*(11), 1392–1399.

O'Byrne, P., Holmes, D., & Woodend, K. (2008). Understanding human sexual networks: A critique of the promiscuity paradigm. *Critical Public Health, 18*(3), 333–345.

Pre-Exposure Prophylaxis (PrEP). (2012). Prevention. Using PrEP cost-effective in high-risk MSM groups. *AIDS Policy & Law, 27*(7), 1.

Rabir, D. (2004). *What do social scientist know about the benefits of marriage?: A review of quantitative methodologies.* Institution for the Study of Labor, Discussion Paper no. 998, January 2004.

Ragnarsson, A., Townsend, L., Thorson, A., Chopra, M., & Ekström, A. M. (2009). Social networks and concurrent sexual relationships—A qualitative study among men in an urban South African community. *AIDS Care, 21*(10), 1253–1258.

Reddick, R., & Heilig, J. V. (2012). The current and dire state of African American male crime and education in the Central Southwest: Are mentoring constellation a promising strategies. *Journal of African American Males in Education, 3*(1), 29–46.

Salazar, L. F., Crosby, R. A., DiClemente, R. J., Wingood, G. M., Lescano, C. M., Brown, L. K., … Davies, S. (2005). Self-esteem and theoretical mediators of safer sex among African American female adolescents: Implications for sexual risk reduction interventions. *Health Education & Behavior, 32*(3(Print)), 413–427.

Sassler, S., & Miller, A. J. (2011). Waiting to be asked: Gender, power, and relationship progression among cohabiting couples. *Journal of Family Issues, 32*(4), 482–506.

Sharpe, T. T., Voûte, C., Rose, M. A., Cleveland, J., Dean, H. D., & Fenton, K. (2012). Social determinants of HIV/AIDS and sexually transmitted diseases among black women: Implications for health equity. *Journal of Women's Health, 21*(3), 249–254.

Sherman, A., & Zurbriggen, E. (2014). 'Boys Can Be Anything': Effect of Barbie play on girls' career cognitions. *Sex Roles, 70*(5/6), 195–208.

Strike, A. (2012). *What is the source of the male marital wage premium?* Cedar Falls, IA: University of Northern Iowa.

Tong, R. (1998). *Feminist thought: A more comprehensive introduction* (2nd ed.). Boulder, CO: Westview Press.

VanderDrift, L. E., Agnew, C. R., Harvey, S. M., & Warren, J. T. (2013). Whose intentions predict? Power over condom use within heterosexual dyads. *Health Psychology, 32*(10), 1038–1046.

Waite, L. (2009). Marital happiness and marital stability: Consequences for psychological well-being. *Social Science Research, 38*(1), 201–212.

Waldrop-Valverde, D. G., Davis, T. L., Sales, J. M., Rose, E. S., Wingood, G. M., & DiClemente, R. J. (2013). Sexual concurrency among young African American women. *Psychology, Health & Medicine, 18*(6), 676–686.

Wang, W. (2012). *The rise of interracial marriage.* Washington, DC: Pew Research Center.

Wingood, G. M., Camp, C., Dunkle, K., Cooper, H., & DiClemente, R. J. (2009). The theory of gender and power: Constructs, variables, and implications for developing HIV interventions for women. In R. J. DiClemente, R. A. Crosby, & M. C. Kegler (Eds.), *Emerging theories in health promotion practice and research* (2nd ed., pp. 393–414). San Francisco, CA: Jossey-Bas.

Wingood, G. M., & DiClemente, R. J. (1998). Partner influences and gender-related factors associated with noncondom use among young adult African American women. *American Journal of Community Psychology, 26*(1), 29–51.

Wingood, G. M., & DiClemente, R. J. (2000a). Application of the theory of gender and power to examine HIV-related exposures, risk factors, and effective interventions for women. *Health Education & Behavior, 27*(5), 539–565.

Wingood, G. M., & DiClemente, R. J. (2000b). Reconceptualizing women's HIV risk. *Health Education & Behavior, 27*(5), 570–571.

Wingood, G. M., Diclemente, R. J., Mikhail, I., McCree, D. H., Davies, S. L., Hardin, J. W., … Saag, M. (2007). HIV discrimination and the health of women living with HIV. *Women & Health, 46*(2–3), 99–112.

# Chapter 9
# The Logic of Exchange Sex Among Women Living in Poverty

**Kari R. Olson, Jessica E. Justman, Yunmi Chung, Kimberly A. Parker, Carol E. Golin, and Stephanie Lykes**

*"I think that's why we're poor and that's why women are selling they asses ... Because we poor! We cannot feed our kids!"*

## Introduction

Exchange sex, defined as having sex in exchange for money or for commodities such as food, shelter or drugs, is linked to poverty and HIV risk. Exchange sex falls on a spectrum of economically motivated transactional sexual practices, landing somewhere between commercial sex work and the exchange of gifts between

K.R. Olson • J.E. Justman (✉)
ICAP, Mailman School of Public Health, Columbia University,
New York, NY, USA
e-mail: jj2158@mail.cumc.columbia.edu

Y. Chung
Division of Infectious Diseases, Department of Medicine, School of Medicine,
Emory University, Atlanta, GA, USA

K.A. Parker
Department of Health Studies, Texas Woman's University, Denton, TX, USA

C.E. Golin
Cecil G. Sheps Center for Health Services Research,
University of North Carolina at Chapel Hill, Chapel Hill, NC, USA

Department of Health Behavior, Gillings School of Global Public Health,
University of North Carolina at Chapel Hill,
Chapel Hill, NC, USA

Division of General Medicine and Clinical Epidemiology,
School of Medicine, University of North Carolina at Chapel Hill, Chapel Hill, NC, USA



A. O'Leary, P.M. Frew (eds.), *Poverty in the United States*,
DOI 10.1007/978-3-319-43833-7_9

romantic partners (Dunkle et al., 2010, Whyte 2006). Women who engage in exchange sex most often do so out of a need for money, food, shelter or drugs, and many point to a history of trauma and sexual abuse as a critical factor in their initial engagement in exchange sex (Mallory & Stern, 2000; Weeks et al., 1998). Although it is a survival tactic, exchange sex presents a host of dangers and risks. Despite the many potential adverse outcomes, for those who live in poverty, lack alternatives for income generation, or are involved in drugs, it is a logical way to meet immediate needs or basic life necessities.

## Exchange Sex, Poverty, and HIV Risk in the USA

In the United States, exchange sex is associated with poverty and HIV risk behaviors (Arnold, Risher & McFarland, 2011; Collins, von Unger, Sweetland, & Wright, 2008; Davey-Rothwell & Latkin, 2008; Decker, Raj, Gupta, & Silverman, 2008; Dunkle, Wingood, Camp, & DiClemente, 2010; German & Latkin, 2012; Jenness et al., 2011; Rudolph, Linton, Dyer, & Latkin, 2013; Warf et al., 2013; Weir, Bard, O'Brien, Casciato, & Stark, 2007; Whyte, 2006). A national random digit dial telephone survey of unmarried women and a convenience sample from the Southeastern United States found that among African-American women, 13 % and 15 %, respectively, reported having had exchange sex in the past year (Dunkle et al., 2010; McLellan-Lemal et al., 2012). By comparison, rates reported by white women and Hispanic women were 3 % (Dunkle et al., 2010) and 8 % (McLellan-Lemal et al., 2012), respectively. In addition, 33 % of the women in the random digit dial sample reported having stayed in a relationship longer than they wanted for economic reasons and 22 % started relationships due to economic considerations (Dunkle et al., 2010), while another convenience sample found that 8 % of African-American women had sex to avoid loss of shelter (Whyte, 2006). In these studies, increased survival sex behaviors correlated with decreased income (Dunkle et al., 2010; Whyte, 2006). Not surprisingly, women living in high poverty and HIV areas report higher rates of exchange sex in the past year, ranging from 21 to 41 % (Arnold et al., 2011; Jenness et al., 2011). Low-income heterosexual men also frequently buy or sell sex, or both, with rates ranging from 15 to 28 % (Arnold et al., 2011; Jenness et al., 2011). These findings underscore the basic economics of exchange sex for women and men living in poverty.

In addition to poverty and race, exchange sex is correlated with HIV infection and HIV risk factors, including multiple sexual partners, unprotected sex, and high-risk sexual partners (Collins et al., 2008; Davey-Rothwell & Latkin, 2008; Decker et al., 2008; Dunkle et al., 2010; German & Latkin, 2012; Jenness et al., 2011; McLellan-Lemal et al., 2012; Rudolph et al., 2013; Warf et al., 2013; Weir et al.,

S. Lykes
ICAP, Mailman School of Public Health, Columbia University, New York, NY, USA

2007; Whyte, 2006). Men who engage in exchange sex report higher rates of sexual risk behaviors than non-exchangers (Arnold et al., 2011; Decker et al., 2008; Jenness et al., 2011). A New York City survey indicated that over half of the men who had exchange sex reported unprotected sex with both exchange partners and non-exchange partners, and men who both bought and sold sex were significantly more likely to have unprotected sex (Jenness et al., 2011). A number of other factors that correlate with HIV risk are also associated with exchange sex, including substance abuse, mental illness, sexually transmitted infections, homelessness, and housing instability (Collins et al., 2008; Davey-Rothwell & Latkin, 2008; Dunkle et al., 2010; German & Latkin, 2012; Gollub et al., 2010; Jenness et al., 2011; Rudolph et al., 2013; Warf et al., 2013; Weir et al., 2007; Whyte, 2006).

Qualitative research details the relationships among engagement in exchange sex, economic hardship, and involvement with drugs (Mallory & Stern, 2000; McLellan-Lemal et al., 2013; Sharpe, 2001; Sherman, Lilleston, & Reuben, 2011; Sterk, Elifson, & German, 2000; Wahab, 2004; Weeks, Grier, Romero-Daza, Puglisi-Vasquez, & Singer, 1998). Women interviewees describe gradually falling into exchange sex or exotic dance due to financial need and the perception of having few or no alternatives for earning income (Mallory & Stern, 2000; Sherman et al., 2011). Some respondents connected their early history of sexual abuse to low self-esteem, drug use, and their entry into exchange sex (Mallory & Stern, 2000; Weeks et al., 1998). Women who worked in exotic dance clubs described the pressure from the managers to engage in exchange sex on the job because it would be lucrative for the women and for the club (Sherman et al., 2011). If they were not already using drugs and alcohol, engagement in exchange sex frequently led to regular substance use as a coping mechanism, which increased the likelihood of unsafe sex (Mallory & Stern, 2000; Sherman et al., 2011).

The interviewees discussed the many risks inherent in exchange sex, including arrest, rape, physical assault, unwanted pregnancy, and HIV and other STIs (Mallory & Stern, 2000; Sherman et al., 2011; Wahab, 2004; Weeks et al., 1998). Some portrayed an ongoing battle between survival and risk, and a sense of powerlessness to end the cycle of exchange sex and drug use (Mallory & Stern, 2000; Sharpe, 2001; Sherman et al., 2011; Weeks et al., 1998). By contrast, others revealed a sense of control and agency during exchange sex. A number of respondents reported that they insisted on condom use, assessed their partners for STIs before sex, took measures to protect themselves from rape and assault, carefully selected their sex exchange partners, and chose regular exchange partners, based on which men they deemed safe (Sherman et al., 2011; Sterk et al., 2000; Wahab, 2004; Weeks et al., 1998).

Many women interviewees desired a steady partnership with a man who would provide emotional and economic support, and yet many bemoaned the lack of such available men (McLellan-Lemal et al., 2013; Sterk et al., 2000). A convenience sample of African-American and Hispanic women felt that, regardless of whether they engaged in exchange sex, they often had to tolerate infidelity, and sometimes violence, if they wanted a steady male partner (McLellan-Lemal et al., 2013). Among these women, only 12 % of whom reported exchange sex, sex was described as a currency, which held economic or emotional value and could be offered or withheld as a way to obtain a desired outcome (McLellan-Lemal et al., 2013). Women who regularly engaged in exchange sex felt that they had little negotiating power in a steady relationship and that their partners would inevitably have sex with other women (Sterk et al., 2000). Despite this, women sex exchangers were likely to have unprotected sex with regular male partners as a symbol of trust and commitment (Weeks et al., 1998). If a male partner cheated but provided financially, a woman might stay with him, and have unprotected sex with him, to avoid losing his economic support (McLellan-Lemal et al., 2013). If her primary partner did not provide financial support, she might continue to engage in exchange sex as a way to feed her children or make ends meet, but still maintain the relationship for consistency, connection, or emotional support (Weeks et al., 1998). Thus, desired gender norms of wife, lover, or mother for women, and of provider or partner for men, contributed to the complex logic of survival and risk as related to exchange sex (McLellan-Lemal et al., 2013; Sharpe, 2001; Sterk et al., 2000; Weeks et al., 1998).

## Exchange Sex Among Women Living in Poverty: HPTN 064 Interview and Focus Groups Results

Despite the relatively high percentage (37 %) of women in the HPTN 064 cohort who reported having exchange sex at least once in the past 6 months (Justman et al., 2015), the subsample of women participating in interviews and focus groups only rarely spoke of having exchange sex themselves. When they mentioned exchange sex, it was usually to describe the behavior of other women. They spoke of reasons why women had exchange sex, and reasons for avoiding exchange sex. Women also outlined the conditions under which exchange sex was deemed acceptable or unacceptable, and discussed the topic of men and exchange sex. These topics are described below and are illustrated with relevant quotes from the interviews and focus groups.

### *Reasons for Having Exchange Sex*

The women interviewed in individual interviews and focus groups described a number of reasons why they or other women have exchange sex, including the need for money for food, drugs, rent, and payment of the household bills.

One woman described her past employment as a stripper. Although she spoke of it lightly with humor, she indicated that she viewed her body and her sexuality as her primary means of generating income:

> Well, I have manipulation. I have my looks to get me what I want. A lot of women, you know, such as myself, what I used to do, you know what I mean—when I used to strip dance, yeah, I was able to be seductive, and I would (inaudible) him, let him read me, (laughter) you know what I mean, and make that money, you know what I mean? I had to make … I mean, nowadays there's no money in a strip club. What's that, $2–300 a night? … I was making $1500 a night. Are you crazy? I'm going to go and make my money. I'm not going to sit there with $500 or $600 and say that's OK. You want to see these nipples, you have to pay those nipples. (laughter) It's $200 a nipple! (laughter)
>
> —*Focus Group Participant, New York, NY*

A basic need for food was a common reason given for having exchange sex. One woman expressed dismay that grown women in her community were having oral sex for small amounts of money to buy food:

> You got grown women still do it. You got a grown woman out here claiming to go to school and somebody supposed to be giving them money and at the same time they running around sucking dick for $20 just so that they can have something to eat.
>
> —*Focus Group Participant, Washington, D.C.*

Poverty and the need to feed their children were also reasons given to explain why women were having exchange sex:

> I think that's why we're poor and that's why women are selling they asses in my [location]! Because we poor! We cannot feed our kids!
>
> —*Focus Group Participant, New York, NY*

One woman indicated that when men were doing well financially due to criminal activity, they were generous in the community and might pay a woman's rent and buy things for her children. When the man was caught and arrested, the woman was perceived as having few means for survival, and she may have to resort to stripping to get by:

> Like, they're very lovable, and even to the women in the neighborhood they look forward to these people paying their rent. "I'm gonna pay your rent, I'm gonna do this right here for you. Just let me stash this gun in your crib. Let me keep this dope over here." Can't do nothing for your kids, "Don't worry. I got 'em. Here go a pair of shoes. Here go this and that." So everybody starting to be dependent on this one person 'cause he coming through, he looking out for everybody in the community. Everybody. Then it's like now everybody is falling because there's one person that got knock off and now they can't eat no more. Now they can't sleep no more. Now they gotta walk around bummy all over again … When he got locked up what was everybody doing? They said, "Girl, I don't know, girl. Might have to go strip." It's sad though.
>
> —*Focus Group Participant, Raleigh/Durham, NC*

Exchange sex was also a way to obtain drugs. One woman spoke of her concern that her children would resort to exchanging sex for drugs if she did not provide them with everything they wanted and needed:

> And, I don't want my kids nothing like I was when I was young. That's why I try so hard, see I give my kids everything even if I know they don't deserve it I still give it to them because I hear some crazy stuff little girls do for like weed. Having sex with weed, giving head for weed.
>
> —*Focus Group Participant, Washington, D.C.*

Another participant described her exhaustion from her life of using drugs and "tricking" (having sex) to get drugs or money for drugs, yet being unable to bring herself to stop:

> And I just be sitting in the hallway like the other people with my head up against the wall tired of tricking, tired of smoking for that moment. All I want to do is take a bath and lay down and go to sleep, you know, wake up as I usually do, my routine when I do this and eat … But people do get tired because I'm tired of getting high so. But I don't understand that I'm tired and why I don't want no help. I'm tired and my sister told me, "You may be tired but you just not ready to stop; you saying you want to stop but you ain't ready to stop."
>
> —*Interviewee, Washington, D.C.*

In addition, some women said that they had exchange sex with men who, in turn, paid their household bills. One woman spoke of her expectation that having sex with a man who spent time at her home meant that he would contribute to paying her bills:

> You are not going to just get what you want out of me and I leave broke. Like, no. (inaudible), sorry … I'm like, "Yeah, my electricity bill need to be paid." … And my cable. You can come—to my house and watch cable, right? You saw that fight pay-per-view.
>
> —*Focus Group Participant, New York, NY*

Another woman described an arrangement she had with a male friend who paid her bills, but who did not live with her, which was a convenient arrangement for both of them:

> My friend is paying the bills for me—my friend is paying the bills for me. (laughter)
> (What kind of friend?)
> We can't get into that friend. My male friend. He's paying the bills for me …. No, he don't live—no, he don't live with me. Process of elimination.
> (How did you come to this arrangement with the male friend?)
> Oh, very easily—very easily—this is what I need. OK. Do you have a problem with it? No, all right then. End of conversation. I love it.
>
> —*Interviewee, New York, NY*

In this case, the woman was initially reluctant to discuss the arrangement she had with her male friend, saying, "We can't get into that friend." She went on to describe how easily she got into the arrangement, stating, "—this is what I need." Yet, her words reveal a sense of defensiveness about her situation. Ambivalence about exchange sex was evident among some of the women. Exchange sex was something that they felt was necessary, and yet they may have felt uncertain about engaging in it, or self-conscious when talking about it during interviews.

## *Reasons for Not Having Exchange Sex*

The interviewees also mentioned a number of deterrents to exchange sex. An awareness of AIDS and fear of contracting AIDS were the reasons given for avoiding exchange sex:

> Participant 1: They was making money, now it's a recession men ain't paying for no sex no more. They just like, why pay for you when I can get her to get with me and ain't nobody using no condoms. Young girls getting pregnant don't know who their baby father is …
> Participant 2: Or AIDS?
> Participant 1: Yeah, and AIDS and then that's high, that rate is real high.
>
> —*Focus Group, Washington, D.C.*

> There's this one girl, she always be up there on [name of location] right there by the store in a dirty looking—it looked like it may have been pink at point in time—prom dress, and she be tricking. She always tell me, "You look pretty!" You won't catch me out there with you, honey. I swear to god before I sell my body I sell drugs. Not trying to catch the AIDS.
>
> —*Focus Group Participant, Raleigh/Durham, NC*

A participant stated that she educated other women about AIDS when they said that they were going to have exchange sex:

> [Sighs] When I see women saying how they're gonna go make some money and stuff like that and I be like, I guess now 'cause I'm thinking about it, "Y'all really don't need to do that. 'Cause, I mean, there's jobs out here and it's AIDS out here and y'all need"—I don't know. When people say they're gonna go make some money, that's when I tell them about that.
> (So, when the women tell you that they're gonna make some money, what are they really talking about?)
> They're gonna go prostitute.

*—Interviewee, Raleigh/Durham, NC*

Another reason given for not having exchange sex was finding a different way to meet their needs. One woman mentioned that she had found a church program that would provide her with food, and so she was able to stop having sex in exchange for food:

> Sometime, sometime I don't have nothing to eat, but then I be like, I go to ... well, the church I go to and then they be like, well, how you doing? And they be like you don't have to do nothing but ask, but then I use to think that ... I use to go and stay with this man, just so me to have me something to eat, you know, and have sex with him. Taking a chance, I don't know what he doing, you know, just to get food, but I don't have to do that no more.
> *—Interviewee, Atlanta, GA*

Some women said that they did not engage in exchange sex, but were able to get things they needed or wanted from men in other ways. One woman suggested that she would try to talk a man out of his money or other favors, but determined that she would not do "certain things," such as having exchange sex:

> Participant 1: And ... Some people say girl you better do this and you better do that, and I'm like, I'm not going to do certain things, it's just point blank. I ain't fixing to do certain things. If I can't talk you out of it, I don't need it.
> Participant 2: Morals.
> Participant 1: So I'm not just going to do certain things, I'm, some women have to trick off to get their bills paid.

*—Focus Group, Atlanta, GA*

Another woman described how she was able to fool men into thinking that she would have sex with them at another time in order to get them to give her things, including food:

> Participant: I never had sex or nothing like that, but I do have guy friends I might call and tell a couple lies to and get what I need, you know? [Laughter] I get what I need, yes I do, but I'm having it. I might give them a call. I might give 'em a coupon to come back later for. I'm being honest. Little [Participant] gonna eat ...
> (Would he have the impression that he could exchange that coupon for sex?)
> Participant: Sometimes he might. I ain't gonna lie. Sometimes he might think, "I'm gonna take this coupon. I done did this and got this coupon, so I'm gonna take this coupon and see what Miss [Participant] talking about." Miss [Participant] fools 'em all the time though. I am telling you!

*—Focus Group, Raleigh/Durham, NC*

Although this woman spoke of using her sexuality to get what she wanted from men, she, along with other women in the study, harshly judged women who engaged in exchange sex, unless it was done to feed one's children.

## Evaluating Exchange Sex Among Women

Although nearly two-fifths of the sample reported having engaged in exchange sex, for the most part, the women condemned the practice, depicting it as an act of shameful desperation, or judging it as a weak or selfish action. One woman expressed her disgust with the prostitutes on her block and especially the idea that the local men associated all of the women in the area with the prostitutes:

> The shelters, like those women, they make—oh, I can't stand them. They make the whole block nasty, because they come out there and they solicit themselves, and then these guys come and they think everybody in the building is doing it.
>
> —*Focus Group Participant, New York, NY*

However, if a woman was thought to be having exchange sex to feed her kids or herself, it was judged very differently than if she was perceived to be doing it to enrich herself. Exchange sex was condoned when it was considered to be a woman's only way to obtain food. The participant quoted below described the situation in her community as similar to a war zone, with a sense of desperation and urgency leaving young women to resort "to any and everything" to get food and feed their children:

> There's girls out here that I know that you would never imagine in your wildest dreams that they would do the type of things they do. But crunch times, you got your kids, you got to feed your baby. You got to feed yourself. They out here streaking or whatever you want to call it just to make sure that they good and they baby good, because at the end of the day, if they ain't watching out for their kids, ain't nobody else gone do it. I mean, people is resorting to any and everything at the end of the day, just to make sure they're getting—they're gonna eat, and their baby's gonna eat.
>
> —*Focus Group Participant, Raleigh/Durham, NC*

The woman quoted earlier who fooled men into thinking that she would have sex with them at a later time stated that she could understand if a woman had exchange sex to feed her children. However, if a woman had exchange sex and did not tend to her children's needs, she judged the situation differently:

> Participant 1: Well, you know what? See, it goes back to me saying you have to take care of yours. Now if you're seeing a woman that does what she does and as far as children, I look at that, but if I see you doing what you do and you're sitting there getting hotter and [inaudible] and doing this and that and not taking care of your kids, now you got a problem. That's a situation right there to me. There is some women like that in our neighborhood community that is like that and the kids still running to [Participant 2] and [Participant 3], [Participant 4] and [Participant 1] for us to do that.
>
> (So you're saying there's some people who do whatever is necessary because they need to take care of their kids and there's some people who do it just to -?)
>
> Participant 1: Just 'cause they got a—I call it a disease. That's what it is. It's a disease. It's a problem.

—*Focus Group, Raleigh/Durham, NC*

Thus, interviewees did not harshly judge women who engaged in exchange sex to obtain food for their children; yet they disparaged women who exchanged sex for personal gain. By contrast, men were almost universally condemned for engaging in exchange sex.

## *Men and Exchange Sex*

The women interviewees estimated that more men than women engaged in exchange sex, and assumed that men did it secretly without letting others know:

> Participant 1: My name is [Participant 1]. The men do—they're worse than the damn women nowadays.
> Participant 2: They worse. Yes, they are.
> Participant 1: They jumping in and out of cars too.
> Participant 2: Yeah, they are.
> Participant 1: They are—keeping it real—they are. They're under covers.

—*Focus Group, Raleigh/Durham, NC*

Another woman emphasized that men were having exchange sex for the ease and convenience of getting cash immediately, while women tried other means first:

> Well, you know men is just nasty. They're going to be nasty, so let me see. Sixty percent of women will do and forty percent of women won't do. They're going to use their mom before they use the streets. Men, they're going to do it … eighty percent of men will do it because they see it as easy cash, no taxes, and you don't have to cash the check to get it right then and there.
>
> —*Interviewee, New York, NY*

Some women expressed their suspicion that men in their communities were having exchange sex with both men and women:

> Participant 1: The men, they are doing the same thing. They might not be sleeping with men—maybe; I don't know.
> Participant 2: They are sleeping with women.

—*Focus Group, New York, NY*

One woman struggled to articulate the ramifications for women when men both bought and sold sex, had multiple exchange partners, and had both female and male partners:

> I think it's just o- like women are exploited. Because just like you said, a girl could go sleep with a guy for some money … the money he gave her, he could have slept with another girl to get. It's like some people, you might think you are in a relationship, and you are spending money. Like I am in a relationship; I spend—he locked up—I mean, I don't know if he gay, I don't know what he do the deed.
>
> —*Focus Group Participant, New York, NY*

Another participant expressed her distress when, out of economic desperation, her male partner had had exchange sex with a man:

> It upsets me 'cause he ain't have to do it. I mean we were homeless and we ain't had no money. And before, he would want me to trick or whatever, he would, he stepped out and did it first but it was with a man. And it just made me sick. Not much to say about that.
>
> —*Interviewee, Raleigh/Durham, NC*

## Discussion

Over one-third (37 %) of the participants in the study reported at baseline having had exchange sex in survey responses; yet during the in-depth interviews and focus groups, few interviewees described their own experiences of exchange sex. When participants described their own exchange sex, they sometimes used humor, spoke defensively, or alluded to it in an indirect way. By contrast, when exchange sex was explicitly described, it was usually referred to as something engaged in by other women. Very likely this was due to the heavy stigma against exchange sex within society, despite its prevalence within this population (Sharpe, 2001; Sterk et al., 2000; Wahab, 2004). In a study of sex workers Wahab (2004) found that respondents felt that they were automatically judged by outsiders as exploited victims in need of therapeutic care. Yet some respondents in that study stated that they enjoyed the flexibility and performance aspects of their work, and saw themselves as educators and caregivers who provided an important service (Wahab, 2004). Nonetheless, it is understandable that given the negative stereotypes attached to exchange sex (Sharpe, 2001; Sterk et al., 2000; Wahab, 2004), many of the interviewees in this study seemed reluctant to directly describe their own experiences.

The participants depicted a life of poverty, drug use, and food scarcity that led them and other women in their community to have sex in exchange for basic necessities for living, including food and payment of household bills. Participants evaluated exchange sex negatively, using terms such as "nasty," "disease," "dirty," "problem," and "crazy," to describe the activity. However, having sex in exchange for food or support for one's children was condoned as something the women could justify within their context of severe deprivation. Other studies of women and exchange sex concur that women make logical calculations, despite the risks. The authors of one study state that as women made decisions about exchange sex, "Underlying the process was women's practical decisions to bear a set of risks in exchange for economic survival" (Mallory & Stern, 2000, p. 585). Similarly, although they were aware of the risks and dangers of exchange sex, including HIV, a number of women in this study articulated their assessment that the risk of leaving their children without food and resources outweighed the risks associated with exchange sex.

By contrast, the interviewees had very negative views of women and men who seemingly exchanged sex for their own personal gain. In the calculation of risk and survival, personal enrichment was not considered an acceptable reason for exchange sex, and men were judged most harshly. This may have been due to gender norms of men as providers and protectors. Exchange sex was not viewed as an acceptable means of income generation for men, and it also meant that men were placing their female partners at risk. The participants felt that men engaged in exchange sex more often than women, and suspected them of having sex with both men and women, buying and selling sex, and having multiple and concurrent sexual partners. Their estimation of the additional risks that these men introduced into the sexual equation by engaging in these activities was accurate, as shown by surveys of men who engage in exchange sex and their increased risk behaviors and high-risk outcomes (Arnold et al, 2011; Decker et al., 2008; Jenness et al., 2011).

An in-depth understanding of the circumstances under which women and men engage in exchange sex can benefit the development of behavioral interventions aimed at reducing the frequency or increasing the safety. Personal motivation for change is an essential component to the success of any behavioral intervention. From qualitative interviews conducted with women who engaged in survival sex, Mallory and Stern (2000) describe the process of "awakening" in which an event or a crisis that is spiritually or emotionally laden occurs in a woman's life and serves as a catalyst for change. "Awakening describes a process by which the women come to a new understanding about the nature of risk and survival and make concomitant changes in their behavior that serve to reduce their risk for exposure to HIV" (Mallory & Stern, 2000, p. 585). The authors suggest that interventions that can serve as such a catalyst for change, or can harness the energy that such an event generates, will be successful.

Other authors have explored the sexual scripts among African Americans and Hispanics and how they contribute to sexual risk behaviors (McLellan-Lemal et al., 2013; Sterk et al., 2000). These studies have found that African-American women, due to a desire to keep a steady man in their life and in the lives of their children, will forgo condoms despite their assumption of their partner's infidelity. "As long as women think or know that a man is not in favor of using condoms, then women will make allowances for men not wanting to use them … emphasis needs to be on figuring out what would increase their importance for women" (McLellan-Lemal et al., 2013, p. 11). Condoms have been available for a long time and yet they are seldom used within steady sexual partnerships, and only slightly more often used within exchange partnerships. Therefore, increased options for female-controlled methods of HIV prevention are needed, which will open up options for women to avoid HIV risks without risking the loss of a steady male partner (Abdool Karim & Baxter, 2010).

## Policy Implications

What constitutes a successful behavioral intervention that can reduce exchange sex and other risk behaviors? How do we create economic opportunities for those living in poverty or who lack alternatives to generate income to reduce the risk of resorting to exchange sex?

Various theories attempt to understand and explain behavior change through key variables such as external environmental factors and personal factors that influence change (i.e., social cognitive theory) (Bandura, 1986), individual attitudes and norms that shape one's intention and determine one's behavior (i.e., theory of planned behavior) (Ajzen, 1991), and different stages of change from change in intention to change in action (i.e., transtheoretical model) (Marshal & Biddle, 2001; Prochaska, Johnson, & Lee, 1998). Although the processes which these major theories and models use to explain behavior change vary, all of them point to the multiplicity and complexity of explanatory factors. For example, previous research has evaluated the efficacy of a social skill intervention versus education and delayed education on sexual risk behavior among mostly low-income African-American women (DiCemente & Wingood, 1995). Findings show that education or dissemination of risk-reduction information alone is not enough to influence sexual risk behavior or increase risk-reduction knowledge (DiClemente & Wingood, 1995). Other studies with interventions targeting high-risk women have found that multiple interventions were more effective than a single intervention, and interactive interventions were superior to passive interventions in reducing sexual risk behavior (Billings et al., 2015; Raj et al., 2001; Uhl et al., 2002). Interventions were also more effective when they were tailored to the individual or the target population.

However, knowledge dissemination and behavior change interventions are not sufficient to reduce the high prevalence of exchange sex. For people without the feeling of hope who are caught in the vicious cycle of poverty, the only way out is to eliminate the most significant environmental factor: poverty. Since 1964, when President Lyndon B. Johnson declared "War on Poverty" with the goal of providing better education, skills, jobs, and access to various economic resources for people and ultimately to reduce poverty (The Council of Economic Advisers, 2014), the United States has continued to increase its welfare spending. The United States currently spends approximately a trillion dollars per year on federal welfare programs, which is approximately 16 times greater than the spending since the 1960s (Boccia, 2014; United States Senate Budget Committee, 2013). The prevalence of poverty ("poverty rate") has decreased from 25.8 % in 1967 to 15.0 % in 2014; however, there were still over 47 million people living below the federal poverty level in 2014 (Kaiser Family Foundation, 2014; The Council of Economic Advisers, 2014). The poverty rate for female-headed households with children is about 33 %, much higher than the national average (Haskins, 2015). Child poverty rates have also remained relatively high at around 21 % (Haskins, 2015). Studies have shown that parents' income level affects their children's future income as unequal economic opportunities hinder upward economic mobility (i.e., ability for children to improve their economic status compared to their parents) (Haskins, 2015; The Pew Charitable Trusts, 2012). Not only are women in poverty ensnared in their situation, but they are also more likely to pass the burden on to their children.

Strategies to tackle poverty have ranged from reducing the number of single-parent families through sexual education, promoting contraceptive use, and publicly funded family planning services to reducing unplanned births (Guttmacher

Institute, 2015), to shrinking the education attainment gap, and to reducing jobless rates through policy changes such as welfare reform and the work support system (Haskins, 2015). Some improvements have been observed in reducing unintended pregnancy rates at the national level over the last several decades (Tapales & Finer, 2015); however rates are still high at around half of all pregnancies (Kost, 2015). Among young minority women living in poverty, unintended pregnancy rates are five times that of women with the highest income level (Finer & Zolna, 2014). The overall national education level has increased over time as well, but the educational achievement gap between children living in poverty and those that are not has also increased (Reardon, 2011). Despite these efforts to reduce poverty through work incentives and support systems among many other policies and programs, significant poverty in the United States persists.

Interventions aimed at reducing exchange sex must be constructed with consideration for the underlying economics of the behavior. A focus on researching, testing, and implementing evidence-based risk-reduction behavior interventions is crucial and should continue. However, without addressing the fundamental causes of exchange sex (i.e., poverty and unequal access to resources) through policy changes that bring about improved economic opportunities within poor communities, individual or group behavioral interventions aimed at people living in poverty will not be effective. As long as other opportunities for income generation are lacking, as they currently are for this population of women, for some, exchange sex will remain a logical choice for survival.

## References


Abdool Karim, S., & Baxter, C. (2010). Microbicides and their implications in HIV prevention. *Indian Journal of Medical Research, 132*, 656–659.

Ajzen, I. (1991). The theory of planned behavior. *Organizational Behavior and Human Decision Processes, 50*(2), 179–211.

Arnold, M. P., Risher, H. R., & McFarland, W. (2011). Socioeconomic position and HIV risk-relevant behavior among lower-income heterosexuals in San Francisco. *AIDS and Behavior, 15*, 499–506.

Bandura, A. (1986). *Social foundations of thought and action: A social cognitive theory*. Upper Saddle River, NJ: Prentice-Hall.

Billings, D. W., Leaf, S. L., Spencer, J., Crenshaw, T., Brockington, S., & Dalal, R. S. (2015). A randomized trial to evaluate the efficacy of a web-based HIV behavioral intervention for high-risk African American women. *AIDS and Behavior, 19*(7), 1263–1274.

Boccia, R. (2014). Federal Spending by the Numbers, 2014: Government spending trends in graphics, tables, and key points (including 51 examples of Government Waste). Retrieved from http://www.heritage.org/research/reports/2014/12/federal-spending-by-the-numbers-2014.

Collins, P. Y., von Unger, H., Sweetland, A., & Wright, E. R. (2008). Relationship of stigma to HIV risk among women with mental illness. *American Journal of Orthopsychiatry, 78*(4), 498–506.

Davey-Rothwell, M. A., & Latkin, C. (2008). An examination of perceived norms and exchanging sex for money or drugs among women injectors in Baltimore, MD, USA. *International Journal of STD & AIDS, 19*, 47–50.

Decker, M. R., Raj, A., Gupta, J., & Silverman, J. G. (2008). Sex purchasing and associations with HIV/sexually transmitted infections among a clinic-based sample of US men. *Journal of Acquired Immune Deficiency Syndromes, 48*(3), 355–359.

DiClemente, R. J., & Wingood, G. M. (1995). A randomized controlled trial of an HIV sexual risk-reduction intervention for young African–American women. *Journal of the American Medical Association, 274*(16), 1271–1276.

Dunkle, K. L., Wingood, G. M., Camp, C. M., & DiClemente, R. J. (2010). Economically motivated relationships and transactional sex among unmarried Africa American and white women: Results from a U.S. national telephone survey. *Public Health Reports, 125*(4), 90–100.

Finer, L. B., & Zolna, M. R. (2014). Shifts in intended and unintended pregnancies in the United Sates, 2001–2008. *American Journal of Public Health, 104*(S1), S44–S48.

German, D., & Latkin, C. (2012). Boredom, depressive symptoms, and HIV risk behaviors among urban injection drug users. *AIDS and Behavior, 16*, 2244–2250.

Gollub, E. L., Armstrong, K., Boney, T., Mercer, D., Chhatre, S., Fiore, D., … Mackey, K. (2010). Correlates of Trichomonas prevalence among street-recruited, drug using women enrolled in a randomized trial. *Substance Use & Misuse, 45*, 2203–2220.

Guttmacher Institute. (2015). Unintended pregnancy in the United States. *Guttmacher Institute*. Retrieved from http://www.guttmacher.org/pubs/FB-Unintended-Pregnancy-US.html#.

Haskins, R. (2015). *How to reduce poverty and increase economic mobility*. Retrieved from http://www.brookings.edu/research/testimony/2015/10/27-reduce-poverty-increase-economic-mobility-haskins.

Jenness, S. M., Kobrak, P., Wendel, T., Neaigus, A., Murrill, C. S., & Hagan, H. (2011). Patterns of exchange sex and HIV infection in high-risk heterosexual men and women. *Journal of Urban Health: Bulletin of the New York Academy of Medicine, 88*(2), 329–341.

Justman, J. Befus, M., Hughes, J., Wang, J., Golin, C.E., Adimora, A. A. Kuo, I., Haley, D. F., del Rio, C., El-Sadr, W. M., Rompalo, A., Mannheimer, S., Soto-Torres, L., Hodder, S. (2015, July) Sexual behaviors of US women at risk of HIV acquisition: A longitudinal analysis of findings from HPTN 064. AIDS and Behavior 19(7):1327–37. PMCID: PMC25626889

Kaiser Family Foundation. (2014). *Distribution of total population by federal poverty level*. Retrieved from http://kff.org/other/state-indicator/distribution-by-flp/.

Kost, K. (2015). Unintended pregnancy rates at the state level: Estimates for 2010 and trends since 2002. *Guttmacher Institute*. Retrieved from http://www.guttmacher.org/pubs/StateUP10.pdf?utm_source=Master+List&utm_campaign=e5cff5fe20-State_Unintended_Pregnancy_2010&utm_medium=email&utm_term=0_9ac83dc920-e5cff5fe20-244293949.

Mallory, C., & Stern, P. N. (2000). Awakening as a change process among women at risk for HIV who engage in survival sex. *Qualitative Health Research, 10*(5), 581–594.

Marshal, S. J., & Biddle, S. J. (2001). The transtheoretical model of behavior change: A meta-analysis of applications to physical activity and exercise. *Annals of Behavioral Medicine, 23*(4), 229–246.

McLellan-Lemal, E., O'Daniels, C., Marks, G., Villar-Loubet, O., Doherty, I. A., Simpson, C., … Borkowf, C. B. (2012). Sexual risk behaviors among African–American and Hispanic women in five counties in the southeastern United States: 2008–2009. *Women's Health Issues, 22*(1), e9–e18. doi:10.1186/1472-6874-13-27.

McLellan-Lemal, E., Toledo, L., O'Daniels, C., Villar-Loubet, O., Simpson, C., Adimora, A. A., & Marks, G. (2013). "A man's gonna do what a man wants to do": African American and Hispanic women's perceptions about heterosexual relationships: A qualitative study. *BMC Women's Health, 13*, 27. doi:10.1016/j.whi.2011.06.002.

Prochaska, J., Johnson, S., & Lee, P. (1998). The transtheoretical model of behavior change. In S. Schumaker, E. Schron, J. Ockene, & W. McBee (Eds.), *The handbook of health behavior change* (2nd ed.). New York, NY: Springer.

Raj, A., Amaro, H., Cranston, K., Martin, B., Cabral, H., Navarro, A., & Conron, K. (2001). Is a general women's health promotion program as effective as an HIV-intensive prevention program in reducing HIV risk among Hispanic women?. *Public Health Reports, 116*(6), 599.

Reardon, S. F. (2011). The widening academic achievement gap between the rich and the poor: New evidence and possible explanations. In *Whither opportunity* (pp. 91–116). New York: Russell Sage Foundation Press.

Rudolph, A. E., Linton, S., Dyer, T. P., & Latkin, C. (2013). Individual, network, and neighborhood correlates of exchange sex among female non-injection drug users in Baltimore, MD (2005–2007). *AIDS and Behavior, 17*, 598–611.

Sharpe, T. T. (2001). Sex-for-crack-cocaine exchange, poor black women, and pregnancy. *Qualitative Health Research, 11*(5), 612–630.

Sherman, S. G., Lilleston, P., & Reuben, J. (2011). More than a dance: The production of sexual health risk in the exotic dance clubs in Baltimore, USA. *Social Science & Medicine, 73*, 475–481.

Sterk, C. E., Elifson, K. W., & German, D. (2000). Female crack users and their sexual relationships: The role of sex-for-crack exchanges. *Journal of Sex Research, 37*(4), 354–360.

Tapales, A., & Finer, L. (2015). Unintended pregnancy and the changing demography of American women, 1987–2008. *Demographic Research, 33*, 1257–1270.

The Council of Economic Advisers. (2014). *The war on poverty 50 years later: A progress report.* Retrieved from https://www.whitehouse.gov/sites/default/files/docs/50th_anniversary_cea_report_0_final_post_embargo.pdf.

The Pew Charitable Trusts. (2012). *Pursuing the American dream: Economic mobility across generations.* Retrieved from http://www.pewtrusts.org/~/media/legacy/uploadedfiles/pcs_assets/2012/pursuingamericandreampdf.pdf.

Uhl, G., Miner, M., Bockting, W. O., Scheltema, K. E., Rosser, B. S., & Westover, B. (2002). Evaluation of a sexual health approach to prevent HIV among low income, urban, primarily African American women: Results of a randomized controlled trial. *AIDS Education and Prevention, 14*(3 Supplement), 81.

United States Senate Budget Committee. (2013). *CRS report: Welfare spending the largest item in the federal budget.* Retrieved from http://www.budget.senate.gov/republican/public/index.cfm/files/serve/?File_id=34919307-6286-47ab-b114-2fd5bcedfeb5.

Wahab, S. (2004). Tricks of the trade: What social workers can learn about female sex workers through dialogue. *Qualitative Social Work, 3*(2), 139–160.

Warf, C. W., Clark, L. F., Desai, M., Rabinovitz, S. J., Agahi, G., Calvo, R., & Hoffman, J. (2013). Coming of age on the streets: Survival sex among homeless young women in Hollywood. *Journal of Adolescence, 36*, 1205–1213.

Weeks, M. R., Grier, M., Romero-Daza, N., Puglisi-Vasquez, M. J., & Singer, M. (1998). Streets, drugs, and the economy of sex in the age of AIDS. *Women & Health, 27*(1/2), 205–229.

Weir, B. W., Bard, R. S., O'Brien, K., Casciato, C. J., & Stark, M. J. (2007). Uncovering patterns of HIV risk through multiple housing measures. *AIDS and Behavior, 11*, S31–S44.

Whyte, J. (2006). Sexual assertiveness in low-income African American women: Unwanted sex, survival, and HIV risk. *Journal of Community Health Nursing, 23*(4), 235–244.

# Chapter 10
# Physical Safety and Neighborhood Issues

**Kimberly A. Parker, Danielle F. Haley, Lauren Bishop, and Dorothy Bota**

*"I don't feel safe, and that's not cool for a young lady ..."*

## Introduction

In the spring of 2014, the CBS affiliate in San Francisco, California, aired an intriguing exposé about a new form of post-traumatic stress disorder (PTSD) having an impact on children living in poverty-stricken neighborhoods (Tokuda, 2014). This new form of PTSD was referred to in the news segment by the controversial moniker "hood disease" and the effects were often seen in those from impoverished areas with increased rates of crime and violence. Based on Tokuda's report, children residing in certain areas of East Oakland, California, were exposed to conditions comparable to those of war zones, and unlike solders in battle, many were unable to escape the circumstances producing these violent conditions. The story sparked the interest of a number of people across the country, mainly, those unaware of the determinants that plague many disadvantaged and impoverished neighborhoods.

K.A. Parker (✉)
Department of Health Studies, Texas Woman's University, Denton, TX, USA
e-mail: kparker6@mail.twu.edu

D.F. Haley
FHI 360, Durham, NC, USA

Department of Behavioral Sciences and Health Education, Rollins School of Public Health, Emory University, Atlanta, GA, USA

L. Bishop
Division of Infectious Diseases, Department of Medicine, School of Medicine, Emory University, Atlanta, GA, USA

D. Bota
Department of Behavioral Sciences and Health Education, Rollins School of Public Health, Emory University, Atlanta, GA, USA

 
A. O'Leary, P.M. Frew (eds.), *Poverty in the United States*,
DOI 10.1007/978-3-319-43833-7_10

According to the Centers for Disease Control and Prevention (CDC), homicide is the leading cause of death for those between the ages of 10 and 24, and violence among youth is one of the leading causes of nonfatal injuries for this same age group (CDC, 2013). The destructive consequences of youth violence span the USA and the undesirable mental, physical, social, economic, and environmental consequences often serve as a harbinger of problems for future generations.

Residents of disadvantaged or impoverished neighborhoods—communities burdened by the lack of financial resources and economic stability—are exposed to higher levels of crime and violence compared to those residing in more affluent communities (Peterson & Krivo, 2012; Sun, Cenzer, Kao, Ahalt, & Williams, 2012). Although exposure to criminal and violent acts may vary, disadvantaged neighborhoods have remained racially homogenous over time (Peterson & Krivo, 2010, 2012). These communities are more likely to contain poorly performing schools, have limited access to basic needs and services, and have a lower proportion of residents who have amassed the wealth needed for homeownership (Echeverria, Luan Kang, Isasi, Johnson-Dias, & Pacquiao, 2014; Garo, 2013; Willits, Broidy, & Denman, 2013). Impoverished neighborhoods are also characterized by the glaring racial-spatial divide encapsulated within the creation and reinforcement of structural racism and discriminatory practices (Peterson & Krivo, 2009, 2012; Rahier, 1998). Over time, systemic, discriminatory practices have limited access to wealth for nonwhites. This limitation often leads to segregation based on socioeconomic status (SES), available resources, and creation of poor and economically unstable neighborhoods. Subsequently, neighborhoods that experience higher rates of crime and violence are more likely to be comprised of low-income minorities (Kirk & Papachristos, 2011; Walton, 2010; Zuberi, 2009). Although race is not used as a predictor of violent behavior, a person's race serves as the correlate for lower income, poverty, and exposure to crime and violence (Brenner, 2013; Hill, Burdette, Jokinen-Gordon, & Brailsford, 2013).

The HPTN 064 study collected and analyzed qualitative data related to neighborhood safety from female participants residing in four metropolitan areas located in the eastern portion of the USA. Both qualitative and quantitative data were used to identify and assess predictor variables associated with poverty and poor health outcomes among women. This chapter examines the correlation between poverty, violence, and race, and the implications for personal safety among women living in poverty. This chapter also explores health risk factors observed in disadvantaged neighborhoods and offers recommendations for policy implementation.

## The Creation of Poverty

In this portion of the chapter, we explore social and structural phenomena that create and support the development of poverty and of impoverished neighborhoods. The National Poverty Center defines poverty as the minimal amount of cash, income, or monetary provision needed to support families of varying sizes (NPC, 2014). Whereas the term "poor" is considered a subjective indicator, it will be used in this chapter to identify the condition in which a family's pre-tax earnings are below the amount identified as the poverty income threshold. In 2010, the poverty threshold for a single-parent household with one child was an annual income of \$15,030 and the threshold for a family comprising one parent and two children was \$17,568 (NPC, 2014). If a child lived with both parents, the family would be considered poor if the totality of annual earnings was below \$17,552 (NPC, 2014). The relationship between poverty and the accrual of wealth is causal; a person's earning potential and income afford him or her access to the resources needed to improve his or her quality of life. As one accumulates wealth, the prosperities associated with an enhanced quality of life may linger for generations, leading to the continuance of accessing and managing wealth. Those who are considered poor are unable to accrue wealth due to the dearth of opportunities needed to promote economic mobility (Klein & Merritt, 2014; Western, Bloome, Sosnaud, & Tach, 2012).

Economic mobility is defined as one's ability to increase his or her earning potential and climb the proverbial socioeconomic ladder (Corak, Curtis, & Phipps, 2010). Most see economic mobility as the ultimate undertaking for achieving the "American Dream," but the resources needed to initiate the arduous journey may not be readily accessible to those living in disadvantaged neighborhoods. Subsequently, placement at the lower rung of the economic mobility ladder may make the climb a bit more strenuous for some (Muller, Riegle-Crumb, Schiller, Wilkinson, & Frank, 2010; Western et al., 2012). Socioeconomic status is an amalgamated calculation of a person's economic, work, and social status (CDC, 2014), and social status is determined by education and exposure to different experiences that expand knowledge. Economic status is ascertained by income earned and the ability to amass wealth while occupational choices are governed by a person's social status and job selection (CDC, 2014; NPC, 2014; Peterson & Krivo, 2012). Subsequently, work status is influenced by educational choices, exposure to various learning opportunities, and economic status.

Residents living in low-income neighborhoods find themselves concentrated in these areas as a result of segregation based on limited fiscal earnings and economic hardship (Bruinsma, Pauwels, Weerman, & Bernasco, 2013; NPC, 2014; Peterson & Krivo, 2012). Neighborhoods with higher concentrations of low-income families are created based on the level of affordability offered by these areas. Resources for education and school systems located in low-income communities are associated with the earning potential of those residing in the neighborhoods these systems serve because local income taxes are used to fund schools. Therefore, education and school systems are unable to provide adequate learning opportunities based on the reduction of available resources (Tran, 2012; Walton, 2010; Willits et al., 2013). Lower levels of education achievement and the abatement of learning opportunities reduce the number of occupational choices from which a person can select. Ultimately, one with limited education and occupational choices will not possess the earning potential needed to foster economic mobility (Peterson & Krivo, 2012; Western et al., 2012). As communities become more economically segregated, the racial composition of neighborhoods homogenizes, which supports a racial divide among income levels and access to resources for wealth. Although the racial makeup of these neighborhoods does not explicate increased violence and crime rates, the diminished wealth and limited opportunities among minorities living in racially homogenous neighborhoods do propagate the endurance and perpetuation of crime. The historical context of structural racism provides substantial insight into the disproportionate crime rates among impoverished neighborhoods more commonly populated by minorities, especially African Americans. This will be discussed further in the next section.

## Racial Divide and Poverty

Racism is commonly referred to as the unfair or unequal treatment of a person based on his or her race (Peterson & Krivo, 2012; Tatum, 2003; Walton, 2010; West, 1994). To fully understand the inequities caused by racism, however, we must understand how unfair treatment based on race serves as a detriment to those oppressed simply due to the color of one's skin. The classification of race does not lead to racism; it is the advantage afforded to those based on the structural context of privilege that gives rise to racism and racial oppression (Mendez, Hogan, & Culhane, 2014; Ross & Leigh, 2000). The classification of race readily identifies and organizes groups based upon a hierarchical divide (Hudson, 2010; Peterson & Krivo, 2009; Tatum, 2003; West, 1994). The dominant groups within the hierarchy profit from a superior position, which is sustained by the status quo, and those excluded from the dominant group customarily lack the power to alter or modify the systems that sustain racial division (Hudson, 2010; Peterson & Krivo, 2009, 2012). Therefore, the intentional or unintentional rift created by the division of race is strengthened and manifested in political, social, and economic structures. Structural racism, commonly referred to as institutional racism, occurs when policies, laws, or practices are implemented to fortify the subordination of certain groups based on race (Mendez et al., 2014; West, 1994). Although one would like to believe that the effects are unintentional, these overt and covert practices have led to the forced segregation of minorities by restricting access to opportunities for wealth attainment and economic gains (Mendez et al., 2014; Peterson & Krivo, 2009; Reedus, 2011; Ross & Leigh, 2000).

Historically, minorities have had limited earning power based on fewer employment opportunities, which reduce the amount of disposable income needed to integrate into white neighborhoods and communities (Peterson & Krivo, 2009; Ross & Leigh, 2000). Unfair housing practices and housing market discrimination have also led to the racialization of communities and neighborhoods in many urban cites across the USA (Mendez et al., 2014; Peterson & Krivo, 2009; Ross & Leigh, 2000). African Americans and Latinos are more likely to have their application for a mortgage loan denied compared to white applicants. If the loan application is approved, practices such as redlining, or systematically denying home loans in certain geographic areas based on race, force minorities to purchase homes and property in areas that impede integration into more affluent communities (Mendez et al., 2014; Peterson & Krivo, 2009, 2010). As whites secure home loans at rates higher than minorities, the sheer volume of home ownership favors those who benefit from this type of structural advantage and allows for the continued practices of racially stratifying neighborhoods. Those living in neighborhoods with fewer minorities can indirectly influence real estate purchasing trends in areas with higher property values by forcing minorities to reside in areas with lower property values based on lower earnings that correlate with affordability. Additionally, the interest rates for home loans awarded to whites were lower compared to interest rates for loans awarded to minorities. Mortgages that carry a higher interest rate compared to those awarded for conventional financing are known as subprime loans, borrowers possessing subprime loans are more likely to face foreclosure (Hernandez, 2009).

As the spatial gap among minorities and whites widens, property values in minority-concentrated areas decrease (Peterson & Krivo, 2010; Shoff & Yang, 2012). Neighborhoods mostly populated by minorities have higher poverty and unemployment rates as well as higher foreclosure rates based on the disproportionate number of subprime loans held by minorities (Lo, 2010; Mendez et al., 2014; Peterson & Krivo, 2010; Pinchevsky & Wright, 2012). Homeownership-property value and established home equity serve as one of the primary methods for acquiring wealth and those living in neighborhoods occupied by more minorities often find themselves living in areas vulnerable to financial instability; it is this financial instability that leads to a diminished assessment of property value (Lo, 2010; Mendez et al., 2014; Peterson & Krivo, 2009; Shoff & Yang, 2012). Businesses frequently make decisions on where to invest based on a community property value. If an area is valued highly, businesses are more likely to establish fiscal footing in these economically prosperous communities, further enhancing the social and economic prosperity of a community (Lo, 2010; Peterson & Krivo, 2009, 2010). Consequently, income and revenue generated by community residents directly dictate with a community's economic stability. The expansion and growth brought on by reinvestment of resources in more affluent neighborhoods also foster the racial segregation seen in many communities. Regrettably, the segregated racial structure of a neighborhood serves as the underpinning for patterns of violence and crime experienced in disadvantaged communities which is further discussed in the chapter on housing issues (Chen, 2013; Emerick, Curry, Collins, & Fernando Rodriguez, 2014; Peterson & Krivo, 2009; Regoeczi & Jarvis, 2013; Wilson-Genderson & Pruchno, 2013).

## Crime and Violence in Disadvantaged Neighborhoods

The intersection of poverty and disadvantage has produced an increased level of crime within communities of color. After the CBS affiliate in San Francisco used the term "hood disease" to represent a type of PTSD characterized by the repercussions of violence in East Oakland, many expressed concern about using such a negative term that only highlighted the plight of disadvantaged, minority neighborhoods (Chen, 2013; Emerick et al., 2014; Peterson & Krivo, 2009; Regoeczi & Jarvis,

2013; Wilson-Genderson & Pruchno, 2013). Although PTSD is not isolated to the confines of disadvantaged or impoverished neighborhoods, economically challenged neighborhoods do, however, report higher rates of crime and violence that may lead to PTSD (Peterson & Krivo, 2009, 2010; Regoeczi & Jarvis, 2013; Zuberi, 2009). Subsequently, crime rates are higher in areas with high concentrations due to the racial segregation caused by limited economic opportunities (Brenner, 2013; Dias & Whitaker, 2013; Peterson & Krivo, 2009; Pitner, Yu, & Brown, 2012; Reedus, 2011; Walton, 2010).

The National Neighborhood Crime Study (NNCS) collected and examined crime data from neighborhoods comprised of different racial and ethnic groups to offer insight into the racial-spatial divide critical to understanding neighborhood racialization as well as crime and violence rates (Peterson & Krivo, 2009, 2010; Pitner et al., 2012). Among over 9000 neighborhoods in 91 large US cities, violent crime rates were higher in neighborhoods occupied by minorities compared to other residential areas (Peterson & Krivo, 2010, 2012). Violent crimes are defined as murder, nonnegligent homicide, and aggravated assault; those living in African-American communities were five times more likely to experience a violent crime compared to those residing in predominantly white areas (Peterson & Krivo, 2009, 2010; Violent Crime, 2011). Furthermore, Latinos were 2.5 times more likely to be exposed to violent crimes within a residential area compared to those occupied by whites (Peterson & Krivo, 2009, 2010) and the rates of property crime were higher in African-American neighborhoods than those for Latino and white communities (Kirk & Papachristos, 2011; Peterson & Krivo, 2009, 2010). While crime may be present in all neighborhoods regardless of racial makeup, the probability of residing in a neighborhood marred by violence is higher for minorities, especially African Americans.

Economically disadvantaged neighborhoods experience higher crime rates for two primary reasons. First, disadvantaged communities experience more social disorder. Secondly, impoverished neighborhoods commonly lack the resources needed to deter criminal activity based on social disorganization and social control (Cohen, Farley, & Mason, 2003; Peterson & Krivo, 2009; Reedus, 2011). The social disorganization theory posits that criminal activity is elevated in neighborhoods exhibiting higher levels of instability due to a lack of shared common goals, social control, and community organization (Sampson, Raudenbush, & Earles, 1997). Neighborhoods that lack social organization and control are unable to effectively thwart acts of violence and crime which weakens social networks and social cohesion (Bruinsma et al., 2013; Hill et al., 2013; Klein & Merritt, 2014; Peterson & Krivo, 2009, 2012). Disadvantaged neighborhoods have limited access to opportunities allowing for the accrual of wealth. In an effort to secure basic needs and resources, disadvantaged neighborhoods are more likely to experience higher rates of criminal activity including theft, prostitution, and shoplifting, as well as the violence associated with retaliation and protection (Peterson & Krivo, 2012; Regoeczi & Jarvis, 2013; Sun et al., 2012). In addition, frequent turnover of residents coupled with fear of violence may inhibit the ability of residents to develop informal social relationships needed to regulate violent crimes (Browning, 2002;

Sampson et al., 1997). Those who experience crime may eventually view their living conditions as a socialized behavior frequently modeled by other residents. As crime and violence rates increase due to the modeled behavior, the ability to discourage criminal activity decreases and structures for controlling crime, such as law enforcement, are perceived as ineffective (Bruinsma et al., 2013; Menard & Morris, 2012; Pitner et al., 2012; Shoff & Yang, 2012; Willits et al., 2013; Wright & Benson, 2011). Crime is therefore sustained through a cyclical pattern, further decaying the physical and moral conditions of disadvantaged neighborhoods. Those residing in the areas buffer the effects of criminal wrongdoing and misconduct through social isolation (Chen, 2013; Cohen et al., 2003; Peterson & Krivo, 2012; Pitner et al., 2012; Willits et al., 2013).

African Americans are more likely than not to reside in racially homogenous neighborhoods (Peterson & Krivo, 2009, 2012; Pitner et al., 2012). Poverty rates and unemployment are higher in African-American neighborhoods and the percentage of African – Americans residing in disadvantaged neighborhoods is higher than that of whites or Latinos (Peterson & Krivo, 2009, 2010, 2012). In fact, approximately 13 % of white neighborhoods examined in the NCCS were labeled as having some characteristic denoting extreme disadvantage while approximately 97 % and 96 % of African-American and Latino neighborhoods reported at least one extreme characteristic of extreme disadvantage, respectively (Peterson & Krivo, 2010, 2012). Statistics reported by the Federal Bureau of Investigation (FBI) indicate that crimes are committed by all races and that whites account for approximately 69 % of all offenses charged ("Arrest Rates by Race, 2011," 2014). Subsequently, economically disadvantaged neighborhoods segregated by race report higher rates of crime. Factors such as structural racism, reduced access to income, and wealth and social disorganization influence the rates at which crimes occur. Minorities, especially African Americans, are more likely to reside in impoverished communities and it is this pattern of racialization that influences crime rates among those living in poverty.

## Neighborhood Safety Issues and Women

In the USA, women are more likely to be poor compared to men (Robbins & Rohlich, 2013) and women of color experience higher poverty rates than the national average and 25 % of African-American women and Hispanics are considered poor (Robbins & Rohlich, 2013). Lower wages and the burden of childcare contribute to increased poverty rates among women; 41 % of single-parent households led by women fall below the poverty threshold (NPC, 2014; Robbins & Rohlich, 2013). Based on inequities of poverty and higher rates of women living under the poverty threshold, women are more likely to live in impoverished communities and raise children in disadvantaged neighborhoods compared to their male counterparts (NPC, 2014; Robbins & Rohlich, 2013).

Women living in economically disadvantaged neighborhoods are susceptible to adverse outcomes associated with elevated crime rates and social disorganization (Bosch & Cervantes, 2013; Zuberi, 2009). Depressive symptoms linked to neighborhood violence and safety perceptions have been seen in adults living in impoverished communities (Wilson-Genderson & Pruchno, 2013). Residents in low-income areas are also exposed to more physical and psychological stressors in their lifetime such as residential instability, food insecurity, racism, and environmental health hazards (Brenner, 2013; Caetano, Ramisetty-Mikler, & Harris, 2010). Levels of social cohesion diminish as those living in impoverished communities attempt to safeguard themselves through isolation and seclusion, exacerbating the adverse effects related to poverty (Booth, Ayers, & Marsiglia, 2012; Brenner, 2013). Protective barriers such as chronic alcohol and drug use and social seclusion may offer some reprieve, but the coping behaviors used by many may also cause secondary stressors such as powerlessness, additional psychological distress, and heightened levels of distrust (Booth et al., 2012; Brenner, 2013). Macrosystemic factors may impact all who live in low-income neighborhoods; however, women bear the brunt of this ecological distress (Kiss et al., 2012; Robbins & Rohlich, 2013).

Recent studies have indicated that poverty serves as one of the primary correlates for intimate partner violence (IPV) (Caetano et al., 2010; Goodman, Smyth, Borges, & Singer, 2009; Kiss et al., 2012). The lifetime rate of women experiencing IPV and receiving some type of financial assistance may range from 35 to 50 %, and can be as high as 74 % (Goodman et al., 2009). Previous victimization and past experience with violence, including violence fostered in economically unstable communities, leads to subsequent episodes of victimization and options for impoverished women wishing to escape abusive relationship are scarce (Edwards, Mattingly, Dixon, & Banyard, 2014; Goodman et al., 2009; Kiss et al., 2012). On average, women earn lower wages than men while assuming the bulk of childrearing duties. Those in economically disadvantaged areas have access to fewer employment options based upon crumbling economic structures, lowering the chances for economic mobility. Therefore, women living below the poverty threshold are often forced to remain in the structural and physical environments that breed violent behaviors (Goodman et al., 2009). Accordingly, women who are able to escape violent environments are faced with homelessness and continued needed for financial and child care assistance (Caetano et al., 2010; Goodman et al., 2009). Coupled with the psychological and physical distress of poverty, victims of IPV may be unable to obtain gainful employment or maintain their current level of employment.

Since employment and earning potential serves as a primary method for reducing poverty, the cycle of poverty and violence reinforces powerlessness and social isolation among women (Caetano et al., 2010; Goodman et al., 2009; Kiss et al., 2012; Pinchevsky & Wright, 2012). Children represent 36 % of those living below the poverty threshold and, unfortunately, they are not immune to the unfavorable effects of hardship and distress (Goodman et al., 2009; NPC, 2014). Those exposed to the elevated rates of crime in disadvantaged neighborhoods are at an increased risk of the adverse effects associated with living in impoverished communities. Minorities, especially Africans Americans, are more likely to live in racially homogenous and economically unstable neighborhoods created by repression that restricts opportunities for wealth attainment and economic gains. The underpinnings for patterns of violence and crime experienced in disadvantaged communities lie within the formation of racially segregated neighborhoods. It is within these macrosystems that women are disproportionally burdened by the persistent effects of poverty.

## Physical Safety and Neighborhood Among HPTN 064 Participants

### *Characteristics of Impoverished Neighborhoods*

Disadvantaged neighborhoods are often burdened by the scarcity of financial resources and economic stability and elevated crime rates. Therefore, characteristics of low-income areas create unfavorable assessments of one's living conditions, as described by this focus group participant:

> The part I don't like about where I stay besides the crime rate and the violence is that it don't have to be labeled the projects, but it's just labeled the projects because of the people that's inside the bricks and how they treat each other.
>
> —*Focus Group Participant, Raleigh/Durham, NC*

Another woman shared similar statements while characterizing her neighborhood based on criminal activity and the mentality of those residing in her community:

> Where I live it's very, very rough out in the projects. Crime rates sky high, gang rates sky high, police get shot, kids might get shot. It don't even matter. People robbing banks running through the neighborhood in the people's houses. We're on the news around there. It's bad, it really is. I'm trying to move up out of there. All jokes aside, it's like the worst.
>
> —*Focus Group Participant, Raleigh/Durham, NC*

Many of the participants regularly witnessed various types of criminal activity and described it as a part of their everyday lives. Participant location varied, but women from each of the HPTN 064 study sites reported seeing at least one type of criminal behavior, including drug sales, homicide, and prostitution:

> Yeah, where I live is, there's a spot right across the street from my house and there's always shootouts, everything. Every single day, there's fights every single day. I hear it every day … sometimes, I even find drugs, I even find drugs on the—on the floor, you know? I want to get out, I really want to get out, and I feel kind of miserable there because I'm tired of sirens—this is what I hear every day. That, that noise—the ambulance every single day. You hear the shootouts.
>
> —*Focus Group Participant, New York, NY*

Many of the women regularly witness various acts of crime in their communities and the reproduction of this modeled behavior; many begin to feel discouraged by the constant barrage of such social ills and a sense of hopelessness and powerlessness envelops those within the surrounding areas. Although efforts have been made to revitalize the community, the negative attributes related to living in poverty remain:

> I live in [name of quadrant] over there off of [name of street] and it's terrible over there too. The neighborhood looks nice. All that look good ain't good, that's what that is, so they done took [name of street] down, [name of street] put new houses up there called [name of housing] and … all of that look really nice but once the lights go down and sometimes … it's about where you live that, yeah, it's terrible. I live right on the outskirts of [name of neighborhood] and it's terrible. I mean it's so bad that they shoot guns that I feel like they coming through my living room window. So, it's just terrible.
>
> —*Interviewee, Washington, D.C.*

## *Elevated Rates of Crimes*

Many of the HPTN 064 participants expressed growing concern for their safety based on crime, including homicide and aggravated assault. An interviewee from New York, NY, stated that she had witnessed both men and women engaging in aggravated assault to resolve arguments, or "beefing." Also, many indicated that innocent people or bystanders were victims of aggravated assault and homicide because of the violent behavior exhibited in their communities. One woman shared these statements when describing topics such as gun violence and safety in her neighborhood:

> In the summer time this year it's going to get a little worse than [last] year, because, like, last year they were, it was like 10 people got shot on the same corner in like 2 weeks and that's ridiculous. Like, you can't after a certain time at night, walking outside is not even an option. Walking in the backyard not even an option because I know people I could do it, but my company and people that come visit, you can't do that.
>
> —*Interviewee, Washington, D.C.*

In addition to witnessing violent crimes in their neighborhoods, a majority of women have also been directly impacted by such behavior. One participant described her life growing up and the impact that knowing someone who has committed armed robbery at a young age has had on her life. One participant described the actions taken by her childhood sweetheart and how her ex-boyfriend was arrested and sentenced to life in prison:

> [My childhood sweetheart] and his best friend robbed somebody in broad daylight and shot and killed the man. And because he was an adult at the time and he didn't turn himself in, he ran and all that other stuff. Then … they finally caught him [and] he's doing a life sentence. I wish him well though. I write to him every now and then. I do write to him and let him know how I'm doing. Or I'll be asking about how his family doing or whatever 'cause me and his family was, like, really close.
>
> —*Interviewee, Washington, D.C.*

Participants had observed other acts of crime including robbery and theft, shoplifting, loitering, and drug activity. Many frequently stated seeing sex workers in their neighborhoods which accompanied robbery and drug use. Sex work as a source of income impacts community morale. Sex work may also place someone at an increased risk of victimization and contracting sexually transmitted infections

(STIs) and HIV. A woman responding to the use of condoms to prevent the spread of HIV and STIs explained her concern:

> I have a friend, she prostitutes herself, she doesn't know that I know, but I know. You know, you see, just see little things and I try to talk to her … but she's in denial and she's young: she's only 26, you know. And she's … she has a lot of different men and … she's crazy, she's like one of them girls that she sees a guy on the street, and if he look good, she starts slobbering him down the street. I tell her, "You can't be doing that. You know, that's not cool."
>
> —*Focus Group Participant, New York, NY*

## *Social Disorganization*

As neighborhood crime rates increase, so does the level of instability due to lack of social control and community organizations. Social control decreases because those exposed to higher amounts of crime become distrustful of the systems often used to prevent crime. Law enforcement agencies such as the police were created to combat violence and safety issues, but those living in low-income areas are more likely to lose faith in these institutions (Bruinsma et al., 2013; Kaylen & Pridemore, 2013; Latkin & Curry, 2003). Participants still viewed the police as the most effective way to address crime and safety issues, and many of the participants have either relied on law enforcement to address victimization or have witnessed the police handle other matters related to personal security or well-being. However, perceived lack of crime prevention effectiveness has sullied the image of this social structure. One interviewee in Washington, D.C., believes that the increased police presence seen in her neighborhood is more of nuisance. From her perspective, the police focus on minor disputes and spend a great deal of time harassing children playing in the neighborhood. Another participant said that because she lives in an identified high-crime area, the police constantly harass people for unfounded reasons:

> Like, one time the cops came around there with big guns and everything and I'm just walking. You gonna stop me and search me and yell at me. What am I doing? They talking about some, "You signaled them to leave" and all that. And I'm like, "I don't have nothing to do with that." I seen police officers with big guns and I'm leaving, you know. And they stopped my old best friend. She got into it with the female police officer 'cause the female police officer called her a "B." They don't care about people who live in the ghetto, I believe so … My area is red zone. They have cameras on the light post and stuff. It's terrible, I can't wait until I move.
>
> —*Interviewee, Washington, D.C.*

An interviewee expressed her concerns with the unprofessional behavior of the law enforcement agents:

> And the police are the biggest gang out here. But I could just talk about how much I don't like them all day. But I just think sometimes—there's some good cops out here sometimes. Don't get me wrong. But I haven't seen one yet. My kids will never grow up to think the police are their friends. That's just something that's never going to happen. And even staying up North, I've seen cops kill people for no reason and they can get away with it

because of that badge. But it's—I don't like it. I don't talk to them. I don't want anything to do with them.

—*Interviewee, Raleigh/Durham, NC*

Another participant shared her concern about the lack of police involvement in stopping crime and alluded to the police's lack of concern about neighborhood safety due to possible criminal involvement with actual offenders:

They just made it look a little better 'cause they put like this little mobile [precinct] on the corner, but that doesn't stop anything or anybody, 'cause I've seen with my own eyes drug transactions in front of the cops, and literally, the cops would just look and turn away. And I'm like, God forbid, if I was to (inaudible) a stop sign or something, like they'd be on top of me like white on rice, but he's just dealing in front of them, and it's like they're in cahoots with each other. It's ridiculous.

—*Focus Group Participant, New York, NY*

Several participants stated that they engage in some form of social isolation as a buffer and coping mechanism to shield themselves from the effects of living in these communities. Statements such as "I feel safe because I stay in my house and mind my business" show that participants think that this helps protect them from criminal activity. Another participant conveyed her family's concerns about her safety due to her late work hours and the conditions of the neighborhood she lives in, and her use of social isolation as a form of protection:

I have a couple of cousins, a couple of aunts, and like, my aunt she worries about me because sometimes I do walk out at night because I just feel like the Lord on my side. If something is going to happen, it's going to happen but I don't be in nobody business for anything to happen to me. But my aunt worries because she, like, a stray bullet can come or whatever but like I told my aunt I can't stay locked up in my house. I'll do, I work at night so nine times out of ten I'm going to see something coming home because I don't get off until twelve or one o'clock in the morning. So, when they're in the midst of doing whatever they're doing I'm just coming home. So it, I just, that's why I try to stay to myself. I speak, you know, if they speak to me I speak back and I leave at that.

—*Interviewee, Washington, D.C.*

## *Personal Safety and Victimization*

The most common form of victimization reported by the participants was IPV. The correlation between poverty and rates of IPV and victimization has been documented in previous research studies and was also a factor that impacted the personal safety of some of the HPTN 064 participants. As reflected in Chap. 5, there is a compounding effect of interpersonal violence and experiences of neighborhood violence. Physical abuse at the hands of a male partner was the most common form of IPV reported by those who experienced some form of victimization. These women reported being beaten or hit; one stated that she was struck by her boyfriend after accusing him of speaking to another woman:

We argued a lot but nothing like crazy would happen but we argued a lot. I heard him talking to a girl and he said he wasn't talking to a girl. So, I'm ready to just go to work. We go to the door and he's like, he gets in front of the door, closes the door and he's like, "What

> do you think I said?" I was like I heard you talking to her. He gets mad and then he's just looking [at] me and then he just started hitting me and he didn't stop.
>
> —*Interviewee, Atlanta, GA*

A participant from New York, NY, stated that while she was working as a prostitute, she was repeatedly physically assaulted by her pimp if she did not reach her quota. Also, an interviewee from Atlanta, GA, attributed her male partner's verbal and physical abuse towards her to alcohol use. The verbal abuse impacted her esteem: "with the verbal abuse I can say I lost some self-confidence, some, but I gained it back with him not being around me. His physical abuse, it just made me stronger," and the abuse stopped after she had him arrested for domestic violence.

Women who experience some form of victimization while suffering from the physiological distress of poverty may sense a level of helplessness, forcing them to remain in the structural and physical environment that cultivates violence. The desire to keep her family intact forced a participant from Washington, D.C., to remain with her abusive partner. She recounted how the IPV impacted her health and the health of her unborn twins, and that his drinking made him violent towards her:

> … one night he had came home from work, he was drunk and I was like seven and a half months pregnant with the twins. I was in the kitchen cooking food to eat. And so we was living out there off of [name of street] at the [name of apartment complex]. He had came in, he went to the bathroom, our phone had rang it was my …
>
> And I guess he thought it was, I don't know, whatever clicked in his head he thought it was another man … and the next thing you know he just came across my face with his fist real hard. You can see right there it's on one side, right here; I think it's right here. He split my eye right here. And I had to go to the hospital for that. Still stuck by him.
>
> I was trying to raise our family; keeping our family together … I was in so much distress [the babies] came early. He had beat me … and ever since the twins was born when I did came back to my senses and seen him then I just told him, "You have to go, I can't deal with it."
>
> —*Interviewee, Washington, D.C.*

## *Generational Concerns of Physical Violence and Safety*

Women living below the poverty threshold are more likely to raise their children in disadvantaged neighborhoods, and the meager resources in those communities limit economic mobility. Consequently, children raised in poverty will be exposed to the same adverse outcomes that plague women living in poverty, reinforcing the cyclical pattern of violence, hopelessness, social isolation, and negative modeled behavior. Many of the women interviewed for this study were extremely concerned about the safety of their children and the need to disrupt the pattern of structural detriment.

> I have kids. I have two, actually, both under the age of five. And I can't, like—I just—I feel uncomfortable coming out early, late—any time of the day, I just feel like anything could happen, and then it's like, it's worrying. It's—that's the only thing I have a problem with:

> that somebody start shooting, my kids—something like that. So that's my problem with where I live.
>
> —*Focus Group Participant, New York, NY*

The need to protect their children from a destructive environment is the primary concern for many of the participants:

> [Neighborhood conditions] affects my life because I have two small children growing up in this city … I'm seeing these 10-year-old, 13-year-olds with guns. I'm really afraid. And … you could teach your child. But it always seems like [based on outside influences].
>
> You can feel like, I did everything in my power and—I don't know, it's just kids. But it affects everybody because we're living in it today. We could walk out of here right now, ain't got nothing to do with nothing, and—anything can happen
>
> *Focus Group Participant, New York, NY*

## Policy Implications

Issues pertaining to physical safety and neighborhood violence are dynamic and complex. The policies needed to address this social health issue will need to be comprehensive in nature in order to provide structural change at multiple levels. Economically stratified neighborhoods bear the history of racial oppression which stems from years of unjust practices such as structural racism. Policies should first act to increase opportunities for economic mobility by providing those living in disadvantaged neighborhoods with the supplemental resources needed to improve the quality of life. Resources should be used to improve school systems, encourage economic development, and reduce barriers to employment. Expanding access to employment and training opportunities will provide those living in impoverished areas with the skills and personal development needed to increase earning capacity. Additionally, home ownership is essential to the accrual of wealth; financial institutions must engage in fair and just practices that increase the purchasing power of minorities. Also, federal, state, and local governments must be committed to continue funding aid and service programs to increase wages for women.

Residents of disadvantaged neighborhoods are often plagued with a level of distrust stemming from social disorganization and a pattern of learned and reinforced violent behavior. Changing the mindset of individuals who have experienced the lingering effects of generational policy may be difficult without structural policy change. The development and implementation of policies to support social cohesiveness will instill a sense of community pride while reducing social isolation seen by those living in low-income neighborhoods. Since women disproportionately suffer the burden of misfortunes related to social disorganization, and more often serve as the head of single-family households, policies that address the adverse outcomes of gendered inequality should be essential to any strategy implemented to reduce the lingering effects of unjust generational policy. Access to healthcare services for women and children and support from law enforcement entities will lead to incremental change which, over time, will diminish the level of economic instability that women living below the poverty threshold may experience. Poverty should be approached as a chronic condition and policies implemented to address physical safety and neighborhood concerns should be constructed and implemented to address mico- and macro-levels of systemic change.

## References

Booth, J., Ayers, S. L., & Marsiglia, F. F. (2012). Perceived neighborhood safety and psychological distress: Exploring protective factors. *Journal of Sociology and Social Welfare, 39*(4), 137–156.

Bosch, S., & Cervantes, J. M. (2013). Sacred advocacy: Helping at-risk boys and girls find meaning in violent, unjust communities. In J. A. Kottler, M. Englar-Carlson, & J. Carlson (Eds.), *Helping beyond the 50-minute hour: Therapists involved in meaningful social action* (pp. 73–85). New York, NY: Routledge/Taylor & Francis Group.

Brenner, A. (2013). *Does where we live matter? Neighborhood context and implications for stress and health*, ProQuest Information & Learning. Retrieved from http://ezproxy.twu.edu:2048/login?url=http://search.ebscohost.com/login.aspx?direct=true&db=psyh&AN=2013-99160-335&site=ehost-live&scope=site. Available from EBSCOhost psyh database.

Browning, C. (2002). The span of collective efficacy: Extending social disorganization theory to partner violence. *Journal of Marriage and Family, 64*, 833–850. doi:10.1111/j.1741-3737.2002.00833.x.

Bruinsma, G. J. N., Pauwels, L. J. R., Weerman, F. M., & Bernasco, W. (2013). Social disorganization, social capital, collective efficacy and the spatial distribution of crime and offenders. *British Journal of Criminology, 53*(5), 942–963.

Caetano, R., Ramisetty-Mikler, S., & Harris, T. R. (2010). Neighborhood characteristics as predictors of male to female and female to male partner violence. *Journal of Interpersonal Violence, 25*(11), 1986–2009.

CDC. (2013). *Injury. Youth violence national and state statistics at a glance*. Retrieved April 14, 2014, from http://www.cdc.gov/VIOLENCEPREVENTION/youthviolence/stats_at-a_glance/.

CDC. (2014). *Social determinants of health*. Retrieved July 27, 2014, from http://www.cdc.gov/socialdeterminants/Definitions.html.

Chen, J. C. (2013). *No crime left behind: Exposure to neighborhood violence and school performance in New York City*. ProQuest Information & Learning. Retrieved from http://ezproxy.twu.edu:2048/login?url=http://search.ebscohost.com/login.aspx?direct=true&db=psyh&AN=2013-99220-314&site=ehost-live&scope=site. Available from EBSCOhost psyh database.

Cohen, D. A., Farley, T. A., & Mason, K. (2003). Why is poverty unhealthy? Social and physical mediators. *Social Science & Medicine, 57*(9), 1631–1641.

Cohen, D. A., Mason, K., Bedimo, A., Scribner, R., Basolo, V., & Farley, T. A. (2003). Neighborhood physical conditions and health. *American Journal of Public Health, 93*(3), 467–471.

Corak, M., Curtis, L., & Phipps, S. (2010). Economic mobility, family background, and the well-being of children in the United States and Canada. *Discussion Paper Series*, Ottawa, ON: University of Ottawa.

Crimes in the United States 2011 (C. J. I. S. Division, Trans.). (2014). *Arrest by Race, 2011*. US Department of Justice-Federal Bureau of Investigation.

Dias, J. J., & Whitaker, R. C. (2013). Black mothers' perceptions about urban neighborhood safety and outdoor play for their preadolescent daughters. *Journal of Health Care for the Poor and Underserved, 24*(1), 206–219.

Echeverria, S. E., Luan Kang, A., Isasi, C. R., Johnson-Dias, J., & Pacquiao, D. (2014). A community survey on neighborhood violence, park use, and physical activity among urban youth. *Journal of Physical Activity & Health, 11*(1), 186–194.

Edwards, K., Mattingly, M., Dixon, K., & Banyard, V. (2014). Community matters: Intimate partner violence among rural young adults. *American Journal of Community Psychology, 53*(1/2), 198–207. doi:10.1007/s10464-014-9633-7.

Emerick, N. A., Curry, T. R., Collins, T. W., & Fernando Rodriguez, S. (2014). Homicide and social disorganization on the border: Implications for Latino and immigrant populations. *Social Science Quarterly, 95*(2), 360–379. doi:10.1111/ssqu.12051.

Garo, L. A. (2013). Children's exposure to neighborhood poverty and violence: Implications for Black student middle school literacy in Charlotte, North Carolina. *Vulnerable Children and Youth Studies, 8*(1), 60–96.

Goodman, L. A., Smyth, K. F., Borges, A. M., & Singer, R. (2009). When crises collide: How intimate partner violence and poverty intersect to shape women's mental health and coping? *Trauma, Violence & Abuse, 10*(4), 306–329. doi:10.1177/1524838009339754.

Hernandez, J. (2009). Redlining revisited: Mortgage lending patterns in sacramento 1930–2004. *International Journal of Urban and Regional Research, 33*(2), 291–313. doi:10.1111/j.1468-2427.2009.00873.x.

Hill, T. D., Burdette, A. M., Jokinen-Gordon, H. M., & Brailsford, J. M. (2013). Neighborhood disorder, social support, and self-esteem: Evidence from a sample of low-income women living in three cities. *City & Community, 12*(4), 380–395. doi:10.1111/cico.12044.

Hudson, D. L. (2010). *Race, socioeconomic position and depression: The mental health costs of upwardmobility*. ProQuest Information & Learning. Retrieved from http://ezproxy.twu.edu:2048/login?url=http://search.ebscohost.com/login.aspx?direct=true&db=psyh&AN=2010-99140-256&site=ehost-live&scope=site. Available from EBSCOhost psyh database.

Kaylen, M. T., & Pridemore, W. A. (2013). Social disorganization and crime in rural communities. *British Journal of Criminology, 53*(5), 905–923.

Kirk, D. S., & Papachristos, A. V. (2011). Cultural mechanisms and the persistence of neighborhood violence. *American Journal of Sociology, 116*(4), 1190–1233.

Kiss, L., Schraiber, L. B., Heise, L., Zimmerman, C., Gouveia, N., & Watts, C. (2012). Gender-based violence and socioeconomic inequalities: Does living in more deprived neighbourhoods increase women's risk of intimate partner violence? *Social Science & Medicine, 74*(8), 1172–1179.

Klein, S., & Merritt, D. H. (2014). Neighborhood racial & ethnic diversity as a predictor of child welfare system involvement. *Children & Youth Services Review, 41*, 95–105. doi:10.1016/j.childyouth.2014.03.009.

Latkin, C. A., & Curry, A. D. (2003). Stressful neighborhoods and depression: A prospective study of the impact of neighborhood disorder. *Journal of Health and Social Behavior, 44*(1), 34–44.

Lo, S. Y. (2010). *Neighborhood environment, social mobility, and health: A longitudinal examination of individual and neighborhood factors*. ProQuest Information & Learning. Retrieved from http://ezproxy.twu.edu:2048/login?url=http://search.ebscohost.com/login.aspx?direct=true&db=psyh&AN=2010-99220-262&site=ehost-live&scope=site. Available from EBSCOhost psyh database.

Menard, S., & Morris, R. (2012). Integrated theory and crimes of trust. *Journal of Quantitative Criminology, 28*(2), 365–387. doi:10.1007/s10940-011-9142-x.

Mendez, D. D., Hogan, V. K., & Culhane, J. F. (2014). Institutional racism, neighborhood factors, stress, and preterm birth. *Ethnicity & Health, 19*(5), 479–499. doi:10.1080/13557858.2013.846300.

Muller, C., Riegle-Crumb, C., Schiller, K. S., Wilkinson, L., & Frank, K. A. (2010). Race and academic achievement in racially diverse high schools: Opportunity and stratification. *Teachers College Record, 112*(4), 1038–1063.

NPC. (2014). *2010 Poverty thresholds, selected families*. Retrieved May 5, 2014, from http://www.npc.umich.edu/poverty/.

Peterson, R. D., & Krivo, L. J. (2009). Segregated spatial locations, race-ethnic composition, and neighborhood violent crime. *Annals of the American Academy of Political and Social Science, 623*(1), 93–107.

Peterson, R. D., & Krivo, L. J. (2010). National Neighborhood Crime Study (NNCS), 2000. Ann Arbor, MI: Inter-university Consortium for Political and Social Research (ICPSR) [distributor].

Peterson, R. D., & Krivo, L. J. (2012). *Divergent social worlds: Neighborhood crime and the racial–spatial divide*. New York: Russell Sage Foundation.

Pinchevsky, G. M., & Wright, E. M. (2012). The impact of neighborhoods on intimate partner violence and victimization. *Trauma, Violence & Abuse, 13*(2), 112–132. doi:10.1177/1524838012445641.

Pitner, R. O., Yu, M., & Brown, E. (2012). Making neighborhoods safer: Examining predictors of residents' concerns about neighborhood safety. *Journal of Environmental Psychology, 32*(1), 43–49.

Rahier, J. M. (1998). Blackness, the racial/spatial order, migrations, and Miss Ecuador 1995–96. *American Anthropologist, 100*(2), 421.

Reedus, L. R. (2011). *The increasing significance of race: The effects of race and immigration on violent and property crime for white, black, and Latino neighborhoods*. ProQuest Information & Learning. Retrieved from http://ezproxy.twu.edu:2048/login?url=http://search.ebscohost.com/login.aspx?direct=true&db=psyh&AN=2011-99130-489&site=ehost-live&scope=site. Available from EBSCOhost psyh database.

Regoeczi, W. C., & Jarvis, J. P. (2013). Beyond the social production of homicide rates: Extending social disorganization theory to explain homicide case outcomes. *Justice Quarterly, 30*(6), 983–1014. doi:10.1080/07418825.2011.639793.

Robbins, K. G., & Rohlich, L. (2013). National snapshot: Poverty among women & families, 2012. In *Poverty & family supports* (p. 4). Washington, DC: National Women's Law Center.

Ross, C. L., & Leigh, N. G. (2000). Planning, urban revitalization, and the inner city: An exploration of structural racism. *Journal of Planning Literature, 14*(3), 367.

Sampson, R., Raudenbush, S., & Earles, F. (1997). Neighborhoods ad violent crimes: A multilevel study of collective efficacy. *Science, 277*, 918–924.

Shoff, C., & Yang, T.-C. (2012). Untangling the associations among distrust, race, and neighborhood social environment: A social disorganization perspective. *Social Science & Medicine, 74*(9), 1342–1352. doi:10.1016/j.socscimed.2012.01.012.

Sun, V. K., Cenzer, I. S., Kao, H., Ahalt, C., & Williams, B. A. (2012). How safe is your neighborhood? Perceived neighborhood safety and functional decline in older adults. *Journal of General Internal Medicine, 27*(5), 541–547.

Tatum, B. D. (2003). *"Why are all the Black kids sitting together in the cafeteria?": And other conversations about race*. New York :Basic Books, 2003. Print.

Tokuda, W. (2014). *Inner-City Oakland youth suffering from post-traumatic stress disorder*. Retrieved June 14, 2014, from http://sanfrancisco.cbslocal.com/2014/05/16/hood-disease-inner-city-oakland-youth-suffering-from-post-traumatic-stress-disorder-ptsd-crime-violence-shooting-homicide-murder/.

Tran, V. C. (2012). *How neighborhoods matter, and for whom: Disadvantaged context, ethnic cultural repertoires and second-generation social mobility in young adulthood*. ProQuest Information & Learning. Retrieved from http://ezproxy.twu.edu:2048/login?url=http://search.ebscohost.com/login.aspx?direct=true&db=psyh&AN=2012-99060-056&site=ehost-live&scope=site. Available from EBSCOhost psyh database.

Violent Crime. (2011). *Uniform Crime Report: Crime in the United States, 2010*. US Department of Justice-Federal Bureau of Investigation.

Walton, E. (2010). *Exploring the effects of residential segregation on health outcomes among racial and ethnic minority groups*. ProQuest Information & Learning. Retrieved fromhttp://ezproxy.twu.edu:2048/login?url=http://search.ebscohost.com/login.aspx?direct=true&db=psyh&AN=2010-99150-073&site=ehost-live&scope=site. Available from EBSCOhost psyh database.

West, C. (1994). *Race matters*. New York: Vintage Books, 1994. Print.

Western, B., Bloome, D., Sosnaud, B., & Tach, L. (2012). Economic insecurity and social stratification. *Annual Review of Sociology, 38*, 341–359.

Willits, D., Broidy, L., & Denman, K. (2013). Schools, neighborhood risk factors, and crime. *Crime & Delinquency, 59*(2), 292–315. doi:10.1177/0011128712470991.

Wilson-Genderson, M., & Pruchno, R. (2013). Effects of neighborhood violence and perceptions of neighborhood safety on depressive symptoms of older adults. *Social Science & Medicine, 85*, 43–49.

Wright, E. M., & Benson, M. L. (2011). Clarifying the effects of neighborhood context on violence 'Behind Closed Doors'. *Justice Quarterly, 28*(5), 775–798. doi:10.1080/07418825.2010.533687.

Zuberi, A. L. (2009). *Neighborhood safety and moving to opportunity: Understanding gender and life course differences using a mixed-methods approach.* ProQuest Information & Learning. Retrieved from http://ezproxy.twu.edu:2048/login?url=http://search.ebscohost.com/login.aspx?direct=true&db=psyh&AN=2009-99210-471&site=ehost-live&scope=site. Available from EBSCOhost psyh database.

# Chapter 11
# Housing and Health: Exploring the Complex Intersections Between Housing Environments and Health Behaviors Among Women Living in Poverty

**Danielle F. Haley, Kimberly A. Parker, Emily F. Dauria, Christin Root, Lorenna Rodriguez, Erin Ruel, Deirdre Oakley, Jing Wang, Larissa Jennings, Lydia Soto-Torres, and Hannah L.F. Cooper**

*"I wish I could move, but … I can't afford nowhere else to live."*

## Introduction

The associations between the location, quality, and reliability of housing and physical and mental health are well documented. Poorer home and neighborhood conditions are associated with negative physical and mental health and well-being (Boardman, Finch, Ellison, Williams, & Jackson, 2001; Cohen et al., 2003; Curry, Latkin, & Davey-Rothwell, 2008; Hill & Angel, 2005; Jones-Webb, Snowden, Herd, Short, & Hannan, 1997; Krieger & Higgins, 2002; Kruger, Reischl, & Gee, 2007; Latkin, Curry, Hua, & Davey, 2007; Latkin, Williams, Wang, & Curry, 2005; Osypuk & Acevedo-Garcia, 2010; Ruel, Oakley, Wilson, & Maddox, 2010; Schroeder et al., 2001; Stiffman, Hadley-Ives, Elze, Johnson, & Doré, 1999; Theall

D.F. Haley (✉)
FHI 360, Durham, NC, USA

Department of Behavioral Sciences and Health Education, Rollins School of Public Health, Emory University, Atlanta, GA, USA
e-mail: danielle_haley@med.unc.edu

K.A. Parker
Department of Health Studies, Texas Woman's University, Denton, TX, USA

E.F. Dauria • H.L.F. Cooper
Department of Behavioral Science and Health Education, Rollins School of Public Health, Emory University, Atlanta, GA, USA

C. Root
Rollins School of Public Health and Center for AIDS Research, Emory University, Atlanta, GA, USA



A. O'Leary, P.M. Frew (eds.), *Poverty in the United States*,
DOI 10.1007/978-3-319-43833-7_11

et al., 2009; Wen, Hawkley, & Cacioppo, 2006; Williams & Latkin, 2007; Wilson-Genderson & Pruchno, 2013). Financial resources (or lack thereof) and availability of affordable housing may restrict housing choice and mobility (Dickson-Gomez, Cromley, Convey, & Hilario, 2009; McClure, 2010; United States Office of Community Planning and Development, 2007). Women, and unmarried women with children in particular, experience greater poverty rates than other groups, and, as a result, are particularly vulnerable to the ill effects of precarious housing conditions (Heggeness & Mykyta, 2012; Popkin & Cove, 2007).

The home environment can be viewed as the neighborhood and social environment where housing is situated, the conditions of the physical housing structure, and the consistency and reliability of housing. A richer understanding of how neighborhood social and built environments, housing conditions, and reliability of housing interact to produce health behaviors among women living in poverty can inform our understanding of how housing affects health. This chapter explores interview and focus group themes as they relate to women's experiences of their housing environment. The aims of this chapter are to:

- Describe the physical attributes of housing where women reside, and the social and built characteristics of the neighborhoods where this housing is situated.
- Explore how poverty affects housing choice and mobility.

## Intersections Between Social and Built Environments, Physical Condition and Reliability of Housing, and Health

As noted earlier, the types and attributes of the places where women live can be framed as the neighborhoods and social environments where housing is situated, the conditions of the physical housing structure itself, and the consistency and reliability of housing.

L. Rodriquez
Bronx Lebanon Hospital, New York, NY, USA

E. Ruel • D. Oakley
Department of Sociology, Georgia State University, Atlanta, GA, USA

J. Wang
Fred Hutchinson Cancer Research Center, Seattle, WA, USA

L. Jennings
Bloomberg School of Public Health, Johns Hopkins University, Baltimore, MD, USA

L. Soto-Torres
Kelly Government Solutions, Contractor to DAIDS/NIAID/NIH, Rockville, MD, USA

## *Social and Built Environment*

Decay of a neighborhood's physical environment, such as broken windows, poorly maintained buildings, and vacant housing, may contribute to a host of poor outcomes, including increased crime rates and violence, lower social capital, fewer employment opportunities, increased depressive symptoms, substance and alcohol use, and as a result reduced opportunities to engage in healthful behaviors (Boardman et al., 2001; Cohen et al., 2003; Curry et al., 2008; Hill & Angel, 2005; Jones-Webb et al., 1997; Kruger et al., 2007; Latkin et al., 2005, 2007; Schroeder et al., 2001; Stiffman et al., 1999; Theall et al., 2009; Wen et al., 2006; Williams & Latkin, 2007; Wilson-Genderson & Pruchno, 2013). The pathways linking neighborhood social and built environments and health outcomes are many and varied. For example, off-site alcohol outlets may contribute to higher levels of alcohol consumption on a community level, and create more opportunities for unregulated consumption of alcohol, high-risk sexual behavior, purchase of drug-related paraphernalia, and interaction with substance using networks (Cohen et al., 2003; Truong & Sturm, 2007). Similarly, neighborhood environments with poor lighting and few areas for walking and other physical activities are associated with obesity and other chronic disease outcomes (Coughenour, Coker, & Bungum, 2014).

## *Physical condition*

The physical condition of buildings has important implications not only for neighborhood social disorder, but also for overall physical and mental health. Living in housing in physical disrepair (e.g., mold, insect, and rodent infestation) has been associated with a multitude of poor health outcomes such as injury, asthma, respiratory infections, lead poisoning, and poor mental health (Krieger & Higgins, 2002; Ruel et al., 2010). Children are particularly vulnerable to environmental causes of illness (e.g., lead poisoning and asthma) and may suffer from emotional problems and cognitive development delays as a result of home and neighborhood characteristics (e.g., exposure to violence, quality of schools) (Cohen et al., 2003; Krieger & Higgins, 2002; Popkin et al., 2002; Popkin, Levy, et al., 2004). Consequently, the impact of substandard housing and resulting neighborhood characteristics may be amplified for women who are concerned about their children's safety, health, and long-term development (Krieger & Higgins, 2002; Popkin & Cove, 2007; Ruel et al., 2010).

## *Stability and Reliability*

Similarly, the stability and reliability of housing arrangements can have short- and long-term health effects for women. From 2007 to 2009, the USA saw an increase in homelessness, particularly among female-headed families, largely attributable to the economic recession (United States Office of Community Planning and Development, 2007). Homelessness has been associated with increased risk of substance use, mortality, risky sexual behaviors, susceptibility to violence, sexually transmitted infections (STIs), and HIV (Barrow, Herman, Córdova, & Struening, 1999; Dickson-Gomez, McAuliffe, Convey, Weeks, & Owczarzak, 2011; Kushel, Hahn, Evans, Bangsberg, & Moss, 2005; Wenzel et al., 2004). A number of socio-structural factors contribute to risk of homelessness among women, including incarceration, mental illness, substance use, availability of affordable housing, and challenges in accessing and keeping government subsidies (Baillargeon, Binswanger, Penn, Williams, & Murray, 2009; Baillargeon, Hoge, & Penn, 2010; Baillargeon, Penn, et al., 2010; Kushel et al., 2005; Riley, Gandhi, Hare, Cohen, & Hwang, 2007). These challenges may be exacerbated for women living in poverty, who may have less resilient financial safety nets, particularly if their families and social networks are also experiencing similar financial strain.

In addition to more visible forms of homelessness such as living in a shelter or on the street, women are also vulnerable to precarious living arrangements, such as living with or moving frequently among family or friends ("couch surfing"), or exchanging sex or remaining in a sexual partnership for shelter (Davey-Rothwell, Villarroel, Grieb, & Latkin, 2012; Riley et al., 2007). In 2010, 23 % of single mothers living in poverty lived in someone else's household with their own children (Heggeness & Mykyta, 2012). Women may also be considered marginally housed if they are living in boarding houses, low-cost motels, or single-room-occupancy hotels (SROs), all of which may be in physical disrepair, expensive, or provide intermittent shelter during periods of acute homelessness. These types of arrangements may not provide adequate facilities for cooking and storing food, which may lead to added food costs and increased consumption of fast food or other prepackaged options. Overcrowding, poorly maintained physical conditions, and frequent in- and out-migration of housing residents may also contribute to health and safety concerns (Knight et al., 2014; Lazarus, Chettiar, Deering, Nabess, & Shannon, 2011; Riley et al., 2007). Furthermore, marginal housing arrangements may perpetuate long-term housing instability and limited financial assets. For example, women who do not have sufficient resources for a rental security deposit may be able to pay the nightly cost of a motel on a short- or longer-term basis. The cumulative cost, however, of such arrangements may exceed typical monthly rental payments and inhibit a woman's ability to accumulate sufficient savings for a future security deposit.

## Understanding the Role of Housing for Women Living in Poverty: HPTN 064 Interview and Focus Group Results

A number of salient themes related to housing and housing environments emerged in the qualitative interviews and focus groups (Fig. 11.1). Women recounted how life circumstances, such as financial hardships or a need for access to public

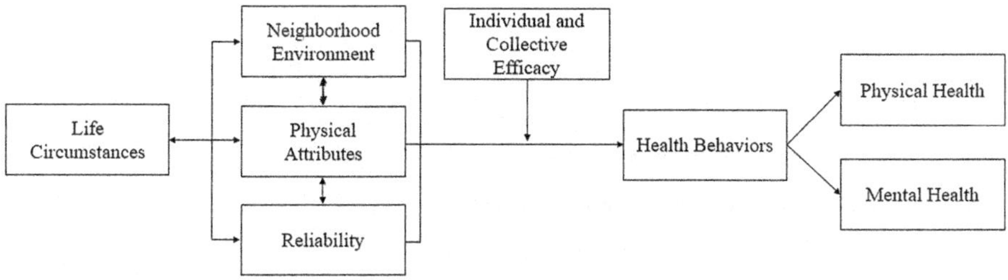


**Fig. 11.1** Major themes related to housing

transportation, influenced their current housing situation. They also described how the neighborhood social and built environment, the physical attributes of their housing, and the reliability of their housing (e.g., long-term vs. temporary housing arrangements) interacted to produce health behaviors (e.g., sexual risk behaviors, feelings of stress). Additionally, women described how they sought to create better living situations, either independently or in collaboration with other community members (individual and collective efficacy). These themes, as well as salient quotes, are illustrated below.

## *Life Circumstances*

The length of time that women lived in their homes and neighborhoods varied, as did the life circumstances which both led to and perpetuated their current housing situation. In some cases, women had recently relocated (less than one month), and in others, women had lived in their home or neighborhood for the majority of their lives. Notably, the majority of women reported wanting to move out of their current housing situation but were unable to do so, predominantly due to financial constraints. Although a small but significant proportion of women indicated that they were living on the street or in homeless shelter, many women reported that they were living in a state of transition, including living in rooming or halfway houses, "couch surfing," or being in a state of limbo with respect to upcoming public housing relocation or related housing policies. An understanding of why and for how long women stay in their housing situation, particularly when they express a desire to move, is critical in understanding how housing impacts the physical and mental health of women living in poverty. The reasons that women cited both in producing and perpetuating their current housing situation were many. The most prevalent themes included financial constraints, housing policies, proximity to public transport and other resources, and a desire to live independently.

## Financial Constraints

Financial constraints frequently dictated women's living arrangements. Women often felt trapped in their situation due to the cost of moving and an inability to pay higher rent and utility bills as exemplified by this woman:

> I wish I could move, but … I can't afford nowhere else to live.
>
> —*Focus Group Participant, Washington, D.C.*

A number of women described living with friends or with family members, usually a parent. In many cases, this was seen as a temporary situation brought on by financial hardship or the loss of Section 8 housing benefits (a government subsidy program for very-low-income families, the elderly, and the disabled where public housing authorities pay rent directly to the landlord on behalf of the recipient; the recipient identifies the housing and pays any difference between the cost of rent and the subsidy) (U.S. Department of Housing and Urban Development, 2014). Women who moved in with family members for financial reasons described the emotional burden that this created for themselves and their family members and expressed the desire to live independently as quickly as possible. This sentiment was particularly salient for women with children, as one woman expressed:

> Right now I currently stay with my mom and my step-dad and my two kids…I actually did have a voucher, a Section 8 voucher for housing … but I lost it … it's kind of hectic because she only has two bedrooms and, you know, it's only one bed in that other room. So, I let my kids sleep on the bed … I did actually sign up for like a couple of churches that does transitional housing, but I'm on a list with them. So, I'm just praying and you know hoping that something come up soon because my mom is helping me [financially] ….
>
> —*Interviewee, Raleigh/Durham, NC*

## Housing Policy

Of the women who stated that they lived in Section 8 or some kind of public housing, many expressed a desire to move, but cited lack of available Section 8 housing or housing policies that prevented them from doing so. These circumstances left women feeling trapped in a state of limbo. One woman described the poor conditions of her apartment and complex, the experience of being on waiting lists, and the financial and emotional strain the poor housing conditions created for her and her family, as follows:

> Everything about the hallway and coming in the building, mice infestation in our apartment … And it's not just my apartment, it's the whole complex and all kind of stuff … cold come in my house then I got to pay a big electric bill … trying to take care of my babies … Seven years … I didn't want to stay seven years but it just … I mean I put my name on other waiting lists and I'm never, you know like one of them I called, every time I call they say they don't have any vacancies … I can't get out.
>
> —*Interviewee, Washington, D.C.*

Women who lived in public housing scheduled for demolition risked losing their housing if they moved before instructed to do so. One woman noted the changes occurring in her neighborhood, the horrible state of her own apartment, her inability to move due to the risk of losing her benefits, and a lack of other alternatives:

> They tore down all the other projects. It's like we're like the last one ... What's the holdup already? And they tell us, "Don't move. If you move, you're on your own." So, I'm kind of waiting around so I can get some financing help to move 'cause I really want to move ... My apartment ... It's just falling apart. The pipes is a mess. The heat is too hot. I have bugs ...
>
> —*Interviewee, Raleigh/Durham, NC*

### Proximity to Public Transportation and Other Resources

Proximity of housing to public transportation, job opportunities, retail locations, and public resources such as the library was of particular importance to women. Proximity to daily activities or public transportation may be a necessity for women who do not own vehicles. Women with children, in particular, noted the importance of areas for children, such as a private yard or nearby parks.

> There's multiple parks. I have a baby, so parks in walking distance ... It's close to downtown, like places to eat, on the bus line.
>
> —*Focus Group Participant, Raleigh/Durham, NC*

### Desire to Live Independently

Many women valued living on their own, and saw this as a measure of success. Living in substandard housing was sometimes seen as the required trade-off given the realities of limited financial resources:

> I had to get out of my parent's house. I had to. But then once I got over there I'm like, "Oh, God. Why did I move here [to a bad neighborhood]?"... Well, where I stay at my rent is not that much ... I like my space. I like my privacy ... It's mine.
>
> —*Interviewee, Raleigh/Durham, NC*

Living independently was particularly important for women with children, who felt that it was a symbol of being a responsible mother able to provide for one's children. One woman discussed the instability she experienced as a child, and the need to secure housing for herself and her son as a means of providing him with greater stability:

> I first came to [city] as a child with my mother, I did travel with my mother throughout the problems we was having so we had to move ... so once I had my son I knew I had to take care of myself and my son. That's how I got on the list to have the subsidized housing.
>
> —*Interviewee, Washington, D.C.*

## *Neighborhood Attributes*

The neighborhood environments where women lived fell into three overarching categories: (1) neighborhoods with highly visible levels of social disorder ("*the projects*"); (2) neighborhoods in transition; and (3) "*nice, quiet*" neighborhoods.

## Highly Visible Social Disorder, "the Projects"

As described in Chap. 10 [Physical Safety and Neighborhood Issues], a number of women described living in "the projects" or "the ghetto." In these communities, the actual buildings women were living in, as well as the neighborhood block, were in a state of disrepair, both inside and out, and communities were characterized by high levels of social disorder. Social disorder is operationalized in this chapter as environments with overt visual evidence of substance use, violence, physical decay of surroundings, and loitering. Women attributed a lack of opportunities as contributing to a community-wide "ghetto mentality," which included responding to conflict with violence, a lack of investment in the general upkeep of the surroundings, spending days loitering and listening to loud music late into the night, and using alcohol and drugs:

> I see don't nobody care. They ain't got no job. They ain't got nothing to do with their time. So, that's pretty much why they're drinking.
>
> —*Interviewee, Raleigh/Durham, NC*

Women regularly witnessed illegal activity in the forms of drug dealing, prostitution, and violence, and often avoided interactions with the people participating in these activities for safety reasons. As one woman described:

> I done seen a whole lot and I try to act like I don't see it … it's dangerous out here … I can hear them [drug dealers, prostitutes] at night.
>
> —*Interviewee, Washington, D.C.*

These concerns were amplified for women with children, who attempted to shield their children from violence, but found it difficult to do so. One mother explained:

> People die, the drugs, the apartment building, the whole building breaking down. If it's not something in your house tearing up, it's something in the building or somebody been caught having sex in the steps. Somebody OD'd on the elevator. It's just a lot of stuff and I got girls and you know what I'm saying. You can't really hide certain stuff because once they see it, they're like, "Well mommy, why is this this way?" and I have to explain.
>
> —*Focus Group Participant, Washington, D.C.*

## Neighborhoods in Transition

In contrast, some women described living in neighborhoods where either their own building or other buildings had undergone or were currently undergoing improvements, such as regular yard upkeep, new paint, or addition of outdoor lighting. Women often expressed immediate improvements in their emotional state as a result of enhancements to their own housing and hoped that these environmental changes would transform the neighborhood culture over time. As one woman recounted:

> When I first moved into my building, it was, like I said, loud, rowdy, everything … on the first of this month, they repainted it … They put cameras in two days ago … they did the

> front door locks... That should make it better ... It's now, like, when you go out stairs, you walk out and you think you're someplace else. I just feel, oh my goodness, so clean ... it's a total relief.
>
> —*Focus Group Participant, New York, NY*

Women who had experienced improved building exteriors and neighborhood environments for longer periods of time, however, often felt that these changes were not sufficient for lasting, meaningful, social change within their community. One woman demonstrated this sentiment in the following:

> I stay in the [housing complex] community that they just remodeled ... they made it over to look good, but it's still the 'hood. It's still the same. It's drugs, drug dealers, prostitutes, bums, everything still coming in and out of the neighborhood. But as far as the look goes, you would never think so driving through the neighborhood.
>
> —*Focus Group Participant, Raleigh/Durham, NC*

Women living in neighborhoods undergoing transition sometimes described choosing to live there because they thought that the building exteriors were indicative of more desirable neighborhoods, only to later find that their housing was "bad at night," leaving them committed to a lease and unhappy with their living situation:

> I'm kinda stuck between a rock and a hard place ... Yeah, the day it was so pretty. I thought it was so quiet ... Summer time all them [people doing drugs] came out like roaches.
>
> —*Focus Group Participant, Atlanta, GA*

### "Nice, Quiet" Neighborhoods

A minority of women described living in "nice, quiet" neighborhoods. Those who did often lived with other family members. In these instances, women described their own housing and neighborhood as well maintained and peaceful. These homes are often in a different part of town than the "projects," and had yards or more spacious interiors. In contrast to the types of housing described previously, many women describe the notable absence of noise due to sirens, gunshots, and late-night music as compared to their previous neighborhoods. One woman depicted her surroundings as follows:

> A quiet street, trees, people working in their yards ... Other than that, it's quiet ... not a lot of people walking up and down the street. No music played at night when you go to sleep.
>
> —*Interviewee, Raleigh/Durham, NC*

Women's feelings about living in these types of neighborhoods varied. Women who chose to live in these types of neighborhoods, either out of their own volition or in an effort to secure a safer environment for their children, enjoyed the sense of peace these neighborhoods provided. In contrast, women who had moved to these types of neighborhoods because financial hardship had forced them to move in with family members expressed a desire to move out of their current situation and into their own apartment, regardless of where that apartment may be located.

## Physical Condition of Housing

There were numerous accounts of women living in apartments or homes in physical disrepair, with cockroach or rodent infestations, mice, and poor pipes, especially if they were also living in more socially disordered neighborhoods. The minority of women described living in good-quality housing conditions, and of these, the majority lived in "nice, quiet" neighborhoods. Women expressed concerns for their own physical and mental health as a direct result of their living environments. One woman living in a rooming house exemplified this as she described challenges with overcrowding, a lack of sanitation, and resulting worries for her own health and well-being as follows:

> It's like the roaches. And people don't clean up behind themselves. And you got to go in the bathroom. You got to be concerned about the air. Just took a shower. Do I need to mop the floor before I get in the shower? Do I got to bleach the toilet before I can use the bathroom? Like, I stand up to use the bathroom. It's got to be a dire emergency for me to sit down.
>
> *—Focus Group Participant, Raleigh/Durham, NC*

## Reliability of Housing

As described earlier, the life circumstances which had either led to their housing arrangement or inhibited women's ability to alter their housing often left women feeling trapped in a state of limbo. The most salient examples of precarious housing emerged for women who were homeless or were living in other transitional living situations (e.g., rooming houses). Of the women who did describe being homeless, many described long-term homelessness, including one woman's experience of living on the street for more than 8 years and another living in a homeless shelter for more than 5 years. As already described, being homeless has important implications for overall health and well-being. Homeless women may be particularly susceptible to violence, substance use, and sexual risk (Barrow et al., 1999; Dickson-Gomez et al., 2011; Kushel et al., 2005; Wenzel et al., 2004). These vulnerabilities are exemplified by one focus group participant who described how each morning a pimp waited outside the women's homeless shelter, hoping to recruit desperate women for prostitution:

> I live in a homeless shelter right now, so like, it's like these pimps … trying to talk to the girls that live inside the shelter. It seems like every day, you come out, there's a different set of guys waiting for a desperate girl or, you know, a girl that's lonely and try to talk to them and stuff.
>
> *—Focus Group Participant, New York, NY*

In addition to being acutely homeless, some women described informal living arrangements with male sex partners who provided them with necessities, such as food and shelter. One woman recounted:

> I used to go stay with this man, just … to have me something to eat, you know, and have sex with him.
>
> *—Interviewee, Atlanta, GA*

This same participant acknowledged that she was "taking a chance" by having sex with a man who might also be having sex with other women or engaging in other activities that may place her at heightened risk, but that this trade-off was necessary in order to fulfill her basic necessities.

### *Individual and Collective Efficacy*

In the main, exposure to neighborhood social disorder and substandard housing conditions were chronic and many women perceived that improvements of these conditions were out of their direct control. Some women attempted to improve the condition of their homes (the interior and exterior), only to be met by unresponsive building maintenance or landlords:

> The maintenance workers never fix anything. It takes months and months and months …
>
> —*Focus Group Participant, New York, NY*

A number of women, however, were determined to make the best of their situation, as exemplified by one woman:

> … to me, it's what you make of it. It's the ghetto, so it's what you make of it.
>
> —*Interviewee, Raleigh/Durham, NC*

Women demonstrated both individual and collective efficacy as they described developing relationships with select women in their community as a way to improve their living situation. For example, one woman described joining forces with another woman in her housing complex in order to convince the management to install more outdoor lighting. Another woman described swapping meals with neighbors. Women with children, in particular, discussed forming micro-communities with other mothers. Women described how they looked out for other children in the neighborhood, and, in cases where women lived in neighborhoods with social disorder, shielded their children from neighborhood violence by spending recreational time outside of their home in other more desirable communities or by associating only with other women with children, as described here:

> We normally don't stay in the neighborhood, like the majority of times we plan picnics and we'll go, you know, out of the neighborhood … If we stay … it's mainly a kids thing. We just really play with the kids.
>
> —*Interviewee, New York, NY*

## Policy Implications

Overall, the HPTN 064 data depict a complex picture of the housing status of women living in poverty in the USA. Although the literature associating health, housing, and poverty is well established, HPTN 064 provides qualitative insight into how this process unfolds for women. The stories of the participants highlight chronic, marginal living situations, which are often the product of limited housing choice and financial constraints. Women were keenly aware of how their life circumstances and housing environments were in constant interplay, and that these intersections affected their overall health and the well-being of their families. Women's stories were filled with trade-offs they made on a daily basis, trade-offs that have immediate and long-term health implications: choosing between staying in pest-infested public housing or losing their benefits, staying with a man and having sex or going hungry, or choosing their children's needs over their own.

During the interviews and focus groups, a number of women described receiving Section 8 housing vouchers or living in public housing. HPTN 064 data collection took place during a time when public housing policy shifted from geographically concentrating public housing residents (e.g., high rises, campuses) to dispersing people living in these public housing complexes, often by placing them in privately owned voucher-subsidized rental units that may be situated across neighborhoods within a city (Cooper et al., 2013; Goetz, 2003; Keating & Flores, 2000; Popkin et al., 2002). Research has documented that public housing residents, who by definition must be living in poverty in order to qualify for this benefit, have the worst health outcomes of any population in the USA (Ruel et al., 2010). A recent study documented that recipients of public housing enter this housing in poor health (Ruel et al., 2010). This population may represent a complex nexus of ongoing poverty, inequality, and health disparity. A 2010 review of available evidence linking neighborhood-level housing interventions (e.g., housing programs or policies) to health outcomes determined that only one intervention, the Housing Choice Voucher Program, a federally funded program which assists very-low-income families, the elderly, and the disabled to afford safe and decent housing in the private market, had sufficient evidence for implementation or expansion. The evidence suggested that voucher holders were less likely to experience overcrowding, malnutrition due to food insecurity, and concentrated neighborhood poverty than non-voucher holders (Lindberg et al., 2010). However, voucher units still tend to be in poorer neighborhoods, and the availability of suitable housing and ability of women to successfully secure housing using vouchers in the private market are unclear (Blankenship, Smoyer, Bray, & Mattocks, 2005; Harris & Miller, 2003; McClure, 2010; McClure, Schwartz, & Taghavi, 2014; Popkin, Cunningham, & Gustafson, 2004).

Regardless of whether women lived in public housing, in secured housing through the private market, or with family or friends, women in HPTN 064 expressed feeling "trapped" in their current housing situation, frequently because they felt that they would be unable to find affordable housing elsewhere, were on waiting lists, or were required to remain in their housing because of a preexisting lease or housing authority policy. It is unclear whether this perception was due to inadequate supply of affordable housing or if women faced challenges finding and securing available affordable housing. Of concern, reports suggest that the amount of publicly subsidized housing is decreasing and that up to 40 % of the 4.8 million housing units currently subsidized may be lost within the next decade (Joint Center for Housing Studies of Harvard University, 2014). In addition, the geographic location of housing is particularly important for women with limited financial resources. Women in the interviews and focus groups identified transportation as a priority and often remained in housing situations they deemed unsuitable in exchange for access to needed resources. The spatial proximity of housing to community infrastructure, such as public transportation, health care facilities, and healthy food options has been linked to a range of health-related outcomes such as body mass index and use of primary health care services, and should be considered in the development of future housing policies (Bonney et al., 2012; Carroll-Scott et al., 2013; Cooper et al., 2012). Collectively, these findings suggest that women would benefit from additional support in identifying eligible and affordable rental units, and in navigating the transition and integration into new housing, particularly if moving brings women to new communities. In addition, it is possible that interventions targeting potential landlords may be needed both to reduce the stigma associated with renting to low-income women and to ensure that affordable housing units are well maintained.

A number of women described being homeless or living in other types of marginal housing, such as a rooming house. Notably, some women discussed chronic, multiyear homelessness, suggesting that they had somehow "fallen through the cracks." Given the strong association between homelessness and adverse health outcomes, and the emergence of similar themes in the qualitative data, immediate alleviation of homelessness requires further dedicated attention and resources. In addition, there is a need for an increased focus on how policies create chronic poverty and place women at increased risk of homelessness. Notably, a number of women recounted experiences of being single mothers. This may be a reflection of public assistance policies that encourage female-headed households or the lack of available male partners due to incarceration or premature death. Programs designed to increase women's financial assets and resilience may help to prevent homelessness.

Although community revitalization efforts, such as exterior upgrades to buildings, improved women's general sense of well-being, deeper changes are required for lasting cultural shifts. Community-based interventions designed to enhance the collective efficacy of neighborhood residents may be a promising approach to alleviating poverty and improving neighborhood conditions. A number of federally funded neighborhood revitalization projects are currently under way (Miller, Pollack, & Williams, 2011). Women in HPTN 064 were highly aware of the challenges facing their community and, as a result, should be involved in generating appropriate solutions. Women, particularly those with children, formed partnerships with other women in their community as a way to improve their living situation. Mothers sought out safe play areas for their children in other communities. The development of community resources such as playgrounds as well as the provision of social services housed within the community or provided through mobile units could enhance individual and community efficacy. It is possible that successful interventions could identify "change agents" within communities. Of course, such changes require allocation of funding both for immediate change and long-term financial commitments to maintenance and ongoing improvements. Otherwise, these physical structures ultimately contribute to social disorder. Approaches to future housing policies and development will benefit from active community engagement and input, which is likely to generate a host of new, innovative ideas.

## References


Baillargeon, J., Binswanger, I. A., Penn, J. V., Williams, B. A., & Murray, O. J. (2009). Psychiatric disorders and repeat incarcerations: The revolving prison door. *The American Journal of Psychiatry, 166*(1), 103–109. doi:10.1176/appi.ajp.2008.08030416.

Baillargeon, J., Hoge, S. K., & Penn, J. V. (2010). Addressing the challenge of community reentry among released inmates with serious mental illness. *American Journal of Community Psychology, 46*(3–4), 361–375. doi:10.1007/s10464-010-9345-6.

Baillargeon, J., Penn, J. V., Knight, K., Harzke, A. J., Baillargeon, G., & Becker, E. A. (2010). Risk of reincarceration among prisoners with co-occurring severe mental illness and substance use disorders. *Administration and Policy in Mental Health, 37*(4), 367–374. doi:10.1007/s10488-009-0252-9.

Barrow, S. M., Herman, D. B., Córdova, P., & Struening, E. L. (1999). Mortality among homeless shelter residents in New York City. *American Journal of Public Health, 89*(4), 529–534.

Blankenship, K. M., Smoyer, A. B., Bray, S. J., & Mattocks, K. (2005). Black-white disparities in HIV/AIDS: The role of drug policy and the corrections system. *Journal of Health Care for the Poor and Underserved, 16*(4 Suppl B), 140–156. doi:10.1353/hpu.2005.0110.

Boardman, J., Finch, B., Ellison, C. G., Williams, D. R., & Jackson, J. (2001). Neighborhood disadvantage, stress, and drug use among adults. *Journal of Health and Social Behavior, 42*(2), 151–165.

Bonney, L. E., Cooper, H. L., Caliendo, A. M., Del Rio, C., Hunter-Jones, J., Swan, D. F., … Druss, B. (2012). Access to health services and sexually transmitted infections in a cohort of relocating African American public housing residents: An association between travel time and infection. *Sexually Transmitted Diseases, 39*(2), 116–121. doi: 10.1097/OLQ.0b013e318235b673.

Carroll-Scott, A., Gilstad-Hayden, K., Rosenthal, L., Peters, S. M., McCaslin, C., Joyce, R., & Ickovics, J. R. (2013). Disentangling neighborhood contextual associations with child body mass index, diet, and physical activity: The role of built, socioeconomic, and social environments. *Social Science & Medicine, 95*, 106–114. doi: 10.1016/j.socscimed.2013.04.003.

Cohen, D. A., Mason, K., Bedimo, A., Scribner, R., Basolo, V., & Farley, T. A. (2003). Neighborhood physical conditions and health. *American Journal of Public Health, 93*(3), 467–471.

Cooper, H. L. F., Hunter-Jones, J., Kelley, M. E., Karnes, C., Haley, D. F., Ross, Z., … Bonney, L. E. (2013). The aftermath of public housing relocations: Relationships between changes in local socioeconomic conditions and depressive symptoms in a cohort of adult relocaters. *Journal of Urban Health, 91*(2), 223–241. doi: 10.1007/s11524-013-9844-5.

Cooper, H. L., Wodarski, S., Cummings, J., Hunter-Jones, J., Karnes, C., Ross, Z., … Bonney, L. E. (2012). Public housing relocations in Atlanta, Georgia, and declines in spatial access to safety net primary care. *Health Place, 18*(6), 1255–1260. doi: 10.1016/j.healthplace.2012.08.007.

Coughenour, C., Coker, L., & Bungum, T. J. (2014). Environmental and social determinants of youth physical activity intensity levels at neighborhood parks in Las Vegas, NV. *Journal of Community Health, 39*, 1092–1096. doi:10.1007/s10900-014-9856-4.

Curry, A., Latkin, C., & Davey-Rothwell, M. (2008). Pathways to depression: The impact of neighborhood violent crime on inner-city residents in Baltimore, Maryland, USA. *Social Science & Medicine, 67*(1), 23–30. doi:10.1016/j.socscimed.2008.03.007.

Davey-Rothwell, M. A., Villarroel, M. A., Grieb, S. D., & Latkin, C. A. (2012). Norms, attitudes, and sex behaviors among women with incarcerated main partners. *Journal of Urban Health, 90*(6), 1151–1165. doi:10.1007/s11524-012-9749-8.

Dickson-Gomez, J. B., Cromley, E., Convey, M., & Hilario, H. (2009). How much choice is there in housing choice vouchers? Neighborhood risk and free market rental housing accessibility for active drug users in Hartford, Connecticut. *Substance Abuse Treatment, Prevention, and Policy, 4*, 5. doi:10.1186/1747-597X-4-5.

Dickson-Gomez, J., McAuliffe, T., Convey, M., Weeks, M., & Owczarzak, J. (2011). Access to housing subsidies, housing status, drug use and HIV risk among low-income U.S. urban residents. *Substance Abuse Treatment, Prevention, and Policy, 6*, 31. doi:10.1186/1747-597X-6-31.

Goetz, E. G. (2003). *Clearing the way: Deconcentrating the poor in urban America*. Washington, DC: The Urban Institute.

Harris, O., & Miller, R. R. (Eds.). (2003). *Impacts of incarceration on the African American family*. Washington, DC: Library of Congress.

Heggeness, M. L., & Mykyta, L. (2012). *Changing the face of poor lone mothers: Understanding how alternative poverty definitions change the composition of lone mother families living in poverty*. Social, Economic, and Housing Statistics Division.

Hill, T. D., & Angel, R. J. (2005). Neighborhood disorder, psychological distress, and heavy drinking. *Social Science and Medicine, 61*, 965–975.

Joint Center for Housing Studies of Harvard University. (2014). *The state of the nation's housing* (pp. 40). Harvard University.

Jones-Webb, R., Snowden, L., Herd, D., Short, B., & Hannan, P. (1997). Alcohol-related problems among black, Hispanic, and white men: The contribution of neighborhood poverty. *Journal of Studies on Alcohol, 58*(5), 539–545.

Keating, L., & Flores, C. (2000). Sixty and out: Techwood homes transformed by enemies and friends. *Journal of Urban History, 26*(3), 275–311.

Knight, K. R., Lopez, A. M., Comfort, M., Shumway, M., Cohen, J., & Riley, E. D. (2014). Single room occupancy (SRO) hotels as mental health risk environments among impoverished women: The intersection of policy, drug use, trauma, and urban space. *The International Journal on Drug Policy, 25*(3), 556–561. doi:10.1016/j.drugpo.2013.10.011.

Krieger, J., & Higgins, D. L. (2002). Housing and health: Time again for public health action. *American Journal of Public Health, 92*(5), 758–768.

Kruger, D. J., Reischl, T. M., & Gee, G. C. (2007). Neighborhood social conditions mediate the association between physical deterioration and mental health. *American Journal of Community Psychology, 40*(3–4), 261–271. doi:10.1007/s10464-007-9139-7.

Kushel, M. B., Hahn, J. A., Evans, J. L., Bangsberg, D. R., & Moss, A. R. (2005). Revolving doors: Imprisonment among the homeless and marginally housed population. *American Journal of Public Health, 95*(10), 1747–1752. doi:10.2105/AJPH.2005.065094.

Latkin, C. A., Curry, A. D., Hua, W., & Davey, M. A. (2007). Direct and indirect associations of neighborhood disorder with drug use and high-risk sexual partners. *American Journal of Preventive Medicine, 32*(6 Suppl), S234–S241.

Latkin, C., Williams, C. T., Wang, J., & Curry, A. D. (2005). Neighborhood social disorder as a determinant of drug injection behaviors: A structural equation modelling approach. *Health Psychology, 24*(1), 96–100.

Lazarus, L., Chettiar, J., Deering, K., Nabess, R., & Shannon, K. (2011). Risky health environments: Women sex workers' struggles to find safe, secure and non-exploitative housing in

Canada's poorest postal code. *Social Science & Medicine, 73*(11), 1600–1607. doi:10.1016/j.socscimed.2011.09.015.

Lindberg, R. A., Shenassa, E. D., Acevedo-Garcia, D., Popkin, S. J., Villaveces, A., & Morley, R. L. (2010). Housing interventions at the neighborhood level and health: A review of the evidence. *Journal of Public Health Management and Practice, 16*(5 Suppl), S44–S52. doi:10.1097/PHH.0b013e3181dfbb72.

McClure, K. (2010). The prospects for guiding housing choice voucher household to high-opportunity neighborhoods. *Cityscape: A Journal of Policy Development and Research, 12*(3), 101.

McClure, K., Schwartz, A., & Taghavi, L. (2014). Housing choice voucher location patterns a decade later. *Housing Policy Debate, 25*(2), 208–214. doi:10.1080/10511482.2014.921223.

Miller, W. D., Pollack, C. E., & Williams, D. R. (2011). Healthy homes and communities: Putting the pieces together. *American Journal of Preventive Medicine, 40*(1 Suppl 1), S48–S57. doi:10.1016/j.amepre.2010.09.024.

Osypuk, T. L., & Acevedo-Garcia, D. (2010). Beyond individual neighborhoods: A geography of opportunity perspective for understanding racial/ethnic health disparities. *Health & Place, 16*(6), 1113–1123. doi:10.1016/j.healthplace.2010.07.002.

Popkin, S., & Cove, E. (2007). *Safety is the most important thing: How HOPE VI helped families* (Metropolitan Housing and Communities Center: HOPE VI: Where do we go from here? Vol. 2). Washington, DC: Urban Institute.

Popkin, S., Cunningham, M., & Gustafson, J. (2004). *A decade of HOPE VI: Research findings and policy challenges*. Washington, DC: The Urban Institute.

Popkin, S. J., Levy, D. K., Harris, L. E., Comey, J., Cunningham, M. K., & Buron, L. F. (2004). The HOPE VI program: What about the residents? *Housing and Policy Debate, 15*(2), 385–414. doi:10.1080/10511482.2004.9521506.

Popkin, S., Levy, D., Harris, L. E., Comey, J., Cunningham, M., Buron, L., & Woodley, W. (2002). *HOPE VI panel study: Baseline report*. Washington, DC: Urban Institute.

Riley, E. D., Gandhi, M., Hare, C., Cohen, J., & Hwang, S. (2007). Poverty, unstable housing, and HIV infection among women living in the United States. *Current HIV/AIDS Reports, 4*(4), 181–186.

Ruel, E., Oakley, D., Wilson, G. E., & Maddox, R. (2010). Is public housing the cause of poor health or a safety net for the unhealthy poor? *Journal of Urban Health, 87*(5), 827–838. doi:10.1007/s11524-010-9484-y.

Schroeder, J. R., Latkin, C. A., Hoover, D. R., Curry, A. D., Knowlton, A. R., & Celentano, D. D. (2001). Illicit drug use in one's social network and in one's neighborhood predicts individual heroin and cocaine use. *Annals of Epidemiology, 11*, 389–394.

Stiffman, A. R., Hadley-Ives, E., Elze, D., Johnson, S., & Doré, P. (1999). Impact of environment on adolescent mental health and behavior: Structural equation modeling. *American Journal of Orthopsychiatry, 69*(1), 73–86.

Theall, K. P., Scribner, R., Ghosh-Dastidar, B., Cohen, D., Mason, K., & Simonsen, N. (2009). Neighbourhood alcohol availability and gonorrhea rates: Impact of social capital. *Geospatial Health, 3*(2), 241–255.

Truong, K. D., & Sturm, R. (2007). Alcohol outlets and problem drinking among adults in California. *Journal of Studies on Alcohol and Drugs, 68*(6), 923–933.

U.S. Department of Housing and Urban Development. (2014). *Housing choice vouchers fact sheet*. Retrieved September 26, 2014, from http://portal.hud.gov/hudportal/HUD?src=/topics/housing_choice_voucher_program_section_8

United States Office of Community Planning and Development. (2007). *The annual homeless assessment report to congress* (pp. v.). Washington, DC: U.S. Dept. of Housing and Urban Development, Office of Community Planning and Development.

Wen, M., Hawkley, L. C., & Cacioppo, J. T. (2006). Objective and perceived neighborhood environment, individual SES and psychosocial factors, and self-rated health: An analysis of older adults in Cook County, Illinois. *Social Science & Medicine, 63*(10), 2575–2590. doi:10.1016/j.socscimed.2006.06.025.

Wenzel, S. L., Tucker, J. S., Elliott, M. N., Hambarsoomians, K., Perlman, J., Becker, K., … Golinelli, D. (2004). Prevalence and co-occurrence of violence, substance use and disorder, and HIV risk behavior: A comparison of sheltered and low-income housed women in Los Angeles County. *Preventive Medicine, 39*(3), 617–624. doi: 10.1016/j.ypmed.2004.02.027.

Williams, C. T., & Latkin, C. (2007). Neighborhood socioeconomic status, personal network attributes, and use of heroin and cocaine. *American Journal of Preventive Medicine, 32*(6 Suppl), S203–S210.

Wilson-Genderson, M., & Pruchno, R. (2013). Effects of neighborhood violence and perceptions of neighborhood safety on depressive symptoms of older adults. *Social Science & Medicine, 85*, 43–49. doi:10.1016/j.socscimed.2013.02.028.

# Chapter 12
# Descriptions of Gun Violence

**Ann O'Leary, Lisa Diane White, Lynne Anderson, and Lauren Bishop**

*"Because somebody always dying."*

## Introduction

Guns small enough to be portable were invented at approximately the time that Europeans were settling in the New World. Guns have played an important part throughout the history of the USA, including during the Revolutionary War and the westward expansion. In the early days of our country, guns were also often used for hunting.

The right for free men to possess guns had been codified in English Common Law. In 1789, the USA adopted the Second Amendment asserting the "right to keep and bear arms," and in 1868 adopted the Fourteenth Amendment, which guaranteed basic rights for all on the basis of commonly agreed and lived rights. Because of these laws, gun ownership has been available to the general US population throughout the country's history.

Inherent racism has been present in gun laws since their inception (Cramer, 1993). Slave owners feared the rebellion of their slaves and thus prohibited them from carrying guns, even after they had been freed. Now homicide—the vast majority of it from gunfire—is the leading cause of death for black males aged 15–34 (Hennekens, Drowos, & Levine, 2013). Most often, both the victim and perpetrator are young black men.

A. O'Leary (✉)
Atlanta, Georgia, USA
e-mail: aoleary@cdc.gov

L.D. White
SisterLove, Inc., Atlanta, GA, USA

L. Anderson
School of Public Health, Georgia State University, Atlanta, GA, USA

L. Bishop
Division of Infectious Diseases, Department of Medicine, School of Medicine,
Emory University, Atlanta, GA, USA



A. O'Leary, P.M. Frew (eds.), *Poverty in the United States*,
DOI 10.1007/978-3-319-43833-7_12

After a great deal of gang-related and racially-driven violence during the 1920s and '30s, then-National Rifle Association president Karl T. Frederick said, "I do not believe in the general promiscuous toting of guns. I think it should be sharply restricted and only under licenses" (Winkler, 2011). The result was the National Firearm Act (NFA) of 1934. The act's intent was to make it difficult for gangsters to obtain their weapons of choice, which included machine guns and short-barreled long guns. The NFA increased taxes on the manufacture and distribution of specified firearms. It also required the registration of the entire production and distribution system, from the manufacturer to the buyer, with the Attorney General (Krouse, 2012). The law was highly successful.

During the late 1960s, political assassinations, civil unrest, and race riots swept the country. African Americans, long-tired of discrimination, inequality, and police brutality, rioted in cities across the nation. The Black Panther Party for Self-Defense formed in California, and membership soon spread nationwide. The Panthers, who opposed gun control, policed their communities by openly carrying weapons as permitted by a new law, introduced by the California state legislature in 1967. This elicited strong negative reactions from whites, including Don Mulford, a conservative Republican member of the state legislature. He proposed to change the law to a prohibition of guns in all cities within the state. In fewer than three months, then-California Governor Ronald Reagan signed into law the Mulford Act, which mandated a five-year sentence to anyone carrying a loaded gun on a public street.

After a lengthy period of gun rights restrictions, pro-gun rights efforts have been ascendant; in response, Congress has gradually weakened gun control laws. In 1986, Congress passed the Firearm Owners Protection Act, which weakened regulation, oversight, and accountability of federally licensed gun owners. Further, penalties for violating gun sale laws were reduced. Gun control efforts were further stymied when the Supreme Court decided in *District of Columbia vs Heller* that the Second Amendment explicitly grants the constitutional right of the individual to keep and bear arms, and not just members of a state-sanctioned militia, as had previously been interpreted throughout Supreme Court history.

The National Rifle Association, now a powerful lobby against gun control, is financed in large part by gun manufacturers. Its most generous gun industry backer is MidwayUSA, a distributor of high-capacity magazine clips. Others include Barrett Firearms and Freedom Group; the latter owns Bushmaster, the company that made the AR-15 military-style rifle used by Adam Lanza at Sandy Hook. We shall return to the topic of policy concerning gun control in the last section of this chapter.

## Connection to Youth

Gun violence in this country is very much an epidemic of youth. In 2003, US homicide rates were 6.9 times higher than homicide rates in other high-income countries, while homicide rates among US 15–24-year-olds were 42.7 times higher (Richardson

& Hemenway, 2011). The Centers for Disease Control and Prevention has reported that the highest homicide mortality for all races and age groups occurred among Hispanic blacks/African Americans aged 20–24 years (109.4 per 100,000 population) (Logan, Smith, Stevens, & Centers for Disease Control & Prevention (CDC), 2011). There are certain factors that make adolescence a time of great vulnerability to violence. One factor is adolescents' stage of development. Throughout adolescence there is an increase in the volume of white matter in children's brains (Paus, 2005). These myelinated fibers are responsible for rapid communication between different parts of the brain. A paucity of white matter is thought to be responsible for adolescents' poor decision-making abilities and low regulatory competence (Paus, 2005), which can lead to snap judgements resulting in violent outcomes.

The second factor linking youth to violence is exposure to violence through video games and other mass media. Correlational studies have not yet distinguished between two possibilities: exposure to violence causes violent behavior or violent tendencies are associated with higher use of violent media. Longitudinal studies also have not resolved this dichotomy, with some finding null results (Ferguson, Miguel, Garza, & Jerabeck, 2012) and others supporting the causal role of environmental exposure (Willoughby, Adachi, & Good, 2012). In any case, the prevalence of guns and other criminal activities in low-income neighborhoods make gun violence particularly an epidemic of poor youth.

## The HPTN 064 Data

We identified several themes in the HPTN 064 participants' descriptions of gun violence in their communities. Women discussed the frequency with which gun violence occurs in their living environment, including occasions when the violence occurred in close proximity to where they were, e.g., just outside one of their windows at home. The women also used war analogies to describe their neighborhoods. They often included reasons for shootings in their narratives, as well as their methods to avoid harm.

## Frequency

Gun violence was described as a near-constant aspect of women's lives in their neighborhoods.

> … because I know in the summer time this year it's going to get a little worse than [last] year because, like, last year they were, it was like 10 people got shot on the same corner in like two weeks and that's ridiculous. Like you can't, after a certain time at night, walking outside is not even an option. Walking in the backyard not even an option.
>
> —*Interviewee, Washington, D.C.*

Well, I where I used to live—(location). I mean, like I watched my cousin die right—like I was like, two blocks away from—and I watched him die last year. Like, right after that, around—I think it was sometime this month last year, too, his best friend died, too. Like it was just like, back to back, so it's like, you know, like I am really distraught from that. Like I'm very, very distraught from that, you know? So I'm still trying to grieve over that. So, you know?

*—Focus Group Participant, New York, NY*

Yeah. I'm used to it. Since I've been in D.C., I been hearing about people getting killed and fights. It's real, I can I say it, dangerous on [name of street]. Well, it's dangerous everywhere but what I know mostly [name of street] 'cause that's where I live, it's very dangerous around there.

*—Interviewee, Washington, D.C.*

Wow, the neighborhood where I live at now it's, it's bad, it's bad, it's every other night, every other day, all you hear is just gun shots and that's another reason why I can't live around here because I don't want to raise my daughter around there.

*–Interviewee, Washington, D.C.*

Not in the household but on the street every day … Every day I see a fight when I come home. Or I see the yellow tape out where somebody done got shot … On the bus.

*—Interviewee, Washington, D.C.*

Shooting occurs around there every bit of every other day … Every other day, yeah every other day. It's getting to the point; stop, drop and roll is just how it is in my house, it's crazy. It really, really is crazy around there with the gun fire. And it seem like anybody can get a gun these days. It's like anybody can get a gun these days. 'Cause it's like one minute you hear one gun sound and you wait a little bit longer and you hear a completely different gun coming from a completely different area. So I think that's the main thing I'm worried about is probably getting shot. I think that's the main thing I'm worried about.

*—Interviewee, Washington, D.C.*

Yeah, it's been like an enormous amount of deaths in the building I mean it's. I mean when you have no choice but to be in a certain area until you can better yourself I think that's what cause a lot of conflict with the people in the building as well so …. I mean I've witness a death. My mom has witnessed a death.

*—Interviewee, Washington, D.C.*

The last couple of years I've had family members who've gotten shot. I had one who got killed. I've had friends who've gotten killed. 'Cause I grew up in a rough neighborhood so the ones I'm talking about they all were still in that neighborhood. And it's like it's always something every time I turn around.

*—Interviewee, Washington, D.C.*

You say what has happen to them? I told you one of my cousins got killed. I think that was in 2008 or '7. And like a couple of months ago two of my cousins, my uncle and my cousin they got shot; one of them almost died. And then last year it was the same thing; it's just always something caused with violence in our family, well, in my family … Getting shot. The one of the buses that I catch to get the girls, a guy got on the bus and shot someone. So that's around the same time that I be traveling back and forth.

*—Interviewee, Washington, D.C.*

## *Proximity*

Many women described hearing or seeing gunshots very close to them, suggesting that shooting is ubiquitous.

Participant 1: Ambulance, the ambulance every single day. You hear the shootouts. Once I was in my apartment, and I had the lights off, and the shooting was so close to my—to my room, that my whole room lit up because of the gunshots ... and I never experienced something like that in my life, that my room lit up with the—it must have been like right in front of my house.

Participant 2: Yeah, the other day, it was in front of my building. And my brother was telling me—"No, no, I'm telling—" he's telling me, "Yes, Yes, it's right in front!" I said, "No, it can't be. Why would it be right in front?" And it was. And somebody died right, right between my building and the hole—in the passageway to the other building.

Participant 3: My daughter doesn't even like to take my grandkids no more to my house. Some of the shootings, they hear in the back, in the front, everywhere.

*—Focus Group, New York, NY*

Who, she don't say nothing to me, I don't feel safe there because somebody got killed in front of my son window so that's why.

*—Focus Group Participant, Washington, D.C.*

## *War Analogies*

The participants described their neighborhoods using war analogies: either original analogies or ones they had heard other residents use to describe their living environment.

Wow. World War I, II, and III all in one, my neighborhood .... I live in the projects but at the end of the project. And I hear a lot of shooting, a lot of fighting, just a lot of carrying on. A ruckus of people getting killed, people getting hurt.

*—Interviewee, Washington, D.C.*

I mean I only been around there for a couple of years so I don't know nobody or anything like that, I just know what I've heard about the neighborhood, which they call Vietnam.

[Okay, why do they call it that?]

Because somebody always dying.

*—Interviewee, Washington, D.C.*

# Reasons for Gun Violence

Among the reasons given by participants for the gun violence were sexual assault, drug use or drug sales, retribution or prevention of disclosure of criminal activity, by accident, and for no apparent reason.

## *Sexual Assault*

And, um, he just snatched me in the clothesline and had a gun and told me do not say anything, if I tell it after he did what he did, he told me, if you tell it, if I tell anybody, he was going to kill my mother and my mother mean the world to me.

*—Interviewee, Washington, D.C.*

So where she was walking at it was two boys that came up and they shot her boyfriend in the head and raped her and then sent her on her way. I remember weren't there to see it happen but when she was—we just found out because was crying and she was so hysterical she was just knocking on everybody door.

*—Interviewee, Washington, D.C.*

When I was fourteen my mother boyfriend molested me. I got raped when I got out of high school. And I did three years in jail 'cause I shot him for second degree manslaughter.

*—Interviewee, Washington, D.C.*

With the one that hit me with the gun. After we got past the police car he put the gun to my head. He put the clip back in the gun. He took me over somebody's apartment and made me give him oral sex while blood was coming out of my mouth and then he called a cab and we went to a hotel. But that's how I ended up calling my P.O. I waited until he just, I just did what he said until he just passed out and once he went to sleep I called my mom.

*—Interviewee, Washington, D.C.*

## Drug Related

[And is that how your friend [name of friend], so it wasn't, people weren't necessarily aiming at him they were just randomly shooting?]

I think it was for him because they shot him in his head twice … I heard they dismissed the case because when they took him to the morgue they found drugs and money, so …

*—Interviewee, Washington, D.C.*

There's always somebody arguing over drugs. Like right now, we're actually—well, people say it's like war, because the people that's coming out of jail, wants their territory back, so right now, like, there's people fighting and shooting every night. They just killed somebody two days ago in front of my building.

[So how safe do you feel?]

I don't feel safe at all.

*—Interviewee, New York, NY*

Just like I know a person that sold PCP to people and the people that they sold it to either got killed or got killed or killed somebody else just by them giving them that. So it's just self-, like Ward [number] is self-destructive.

*—Interviewee, Washington, D.C.*

## Accidental

A nearly universal response expressed by participants was their fear of stray gunshot bullets.

I just hope I don't walk out and be in a fire of like somebody shooting or anything. But when I walk out I just make sure that ain't nobody out there arguing or whatever.

*—Interviewee, Washington, D.C.*

I'm really kind of scared for my life 'cause it's a lot of innocent people get shot.

*—Interviewee, Washington, D.C.*

Participant 1: You know, you can feel like, I did everything in my power and—I don't know, it's just kids. But it affects everybody because we're living in it today. We could walk out of here right now, ain't got nothing to do with nothing, and—

Participant 2: Get shot.

Participant 1: Anything can happen, so—

Participant 3: Stray bullet.

Participant 2: Yup.

Participant 1: It plays a big part in our lives living here.

*—Focus Group, New York, NY*

## *Retribution/Prevention of Disclosure of Criminal Activity*

Some respondents reported incidents of people being killed because they had harmed the shooter in some way. Others killed to prevent the victim from disclosing something about the shooter that was threatening to the shooter, such as criminal activity.

> He used to like hang out with the drugs boys and from the rumors that was like circulating that they did something or he was acquitted for a murder or something one time before but the person who like committed the murder or whatever must of, I don't know, he must have knew too much about what they do in the little gang or whatever. And when he start distancing himself for school, 'cause he was going to school to be a paramedic, one of the dudes lured him out at like two o'clock in the morning. And when he got in the car with him the next thing we heard that they found him shot in the back of the head slumped over a trash can. And this was back in 2002.
>
> *—Interviewee, Washington, D.C.*

Sometimes retribution is for the death of a friend or loved one, as described below in the context of funerals.

> A lot, regardless. It's like—just like she said, she—the person got shot right in front of her building. And I don't know her, but I'm trying to figure out who, because I know everybody over there, and I went to every funeral, and I got a T-shirt for everybody over there. And it's like, it can bring people together, and then it can pull people apart in the neighborhood. Because like, one of my friends who was—like two of them got killed at the same time, same day, and it was like a big thing in my... But then it was like, then you go to the funeral, and everybody's all distraught. Some girls is just extra, and then it turns into, "I'm going to punch in her face because she didn't even know him like that," and ... It's just there's a pro and a con to everything. Like, so, violence, it kind of makes you violent.
>
> *—Focus Group Participant, New York, NY*

The story related below was told by a participant who had left her male partner and taken their children with her. This occurred when he arrived to pick the child up from a visit to her mother.

> So he pushed me in the car and I was like, "oh my God, I'm in the fucking car now, like what am I going to do." So he said, "bitch, I'm a take you out there in Virginia," mind you I was staying in [neighborhood]. He say, "bitch, I'm a take you out there in Virginia and I'm a blow your brains out and I'm a dump your body in the woods." Now remind you, I'm in the

car so as he driving he got the gun towards me like this and this, the swear, I'm not even lying to you, the swear to God truth. And he said, "bitch, I'm a take you out there in Virginia and I'm shoot you in the head and dump your body out there." Let me tell you we was five minutes from Virginia at least 'cause we been left my mother's house. So where we was at when he stopped we was like if he would have went down the hill some more and turned we'd a been in Virginia. So the closer we got going towards Virginia I'm begging for my life. I'm like, "man, we got kids," this, that and the other, "we got kids, why you doing this?"
*—Interviewee, Washington, D.C.*

## *Over Little or Nothing*

No, they was outside of our old house where we used to live at in [name of area]. They was out there drinking and they was arguing over my, my Gameboy. 'Cause my God brother had it but my brother wanted it back because he paid for it. And he had asked my God brother where was it, got in an argument with that. My brother used to smoke PCP also my God brother did too and they was out there drinking. So one thing led to another, my God brother hit my brother in the head with the Remy bottle the next thing you know they start fighting. My God brother came back, he said, "alright, stay right here, I be back, I got something for you." My God brother came back with a gun and shot him. My brother shot back, shot my God brother in the stomach and the leg. Somehow, I don't know how it all happened because I had left like thirty minutes prior to that time; they said that my God brother just slinked over my brother and just starting shooting him back. ...My brother died but not my God brother, he's locked up, he's locked up now.
*—Interviewee, Washington, D.C.*

Like, my side is not that bad, but I have done—since I've lived there, I've done seen somebody murdered somebody in front of my building. Like a person that I know. It was the first person that I met when I moved over there, so it's like—and he wasn't even no type of drug dealer or no nothing. He was the type of person that that just listen to his little music, come through, sit in front of the building ... He got killed for no reason, so like, once that happened, and then I hear shooting every day, and the kids is saying, "They shooting outside," it's like, it's not safe. It's not.
*—Focus Group Participant, New York, NY*

## *Funerals*

The frequency with which respondents attended funerals is reminiscent of the frequency of deaths during the AIDS epidemic in sub-Saharan Africa.

... and it gets to the point you are tired of going to funerals. You are just like, "I'm not going to this one, because I went to one last week." It is so annoying, and it just makes you a different person. It's not—you don't even have time to mourn now because you are so angry, because you are tired of it.
*—Focus Group Participant, New York, NY*

## Fear and Concern About Loved Ones

... maybe my God ... She's my cousin but she's my God-baby too. [She's] a Crip OG baby. Like, how can I say OG—a leader of a gang that's his child. So, yeah, that's his child. So, yeah, if anybody has a problem with him and they can't get to him they're going to go to her. And if we're nowhere around, like when she start going to school, they could easily shoot her when she gets off the bus or something. That's just all I be worried about. Sometimes but, she's only one so she's got four more years before she's got to go to school ...'Cause growing up up north, you could just walk around the corner and there's a dead body laying there. And some days the Bloods were shooting at Crips, Crips shooting at Bloods and people cutting off people's fingers.

*–Interviewee, Raleigh*/Durham, *NC*

Another woman reported:

Mm-Mmm. Yeah, because like, even though it's a lot of things going on [name of street] I know a lot of people on [name of street]. So, like, the majority of the shootings is one of my friends getting shot or killed. And as far as my friends, like, my old friends that I used to have, they used to have a little disagreement with a group of friends down the street so they'll come up here and fight. But I won't fight, I don't like fighting and I'm not going to fight unless I'm feeling threatened. So they'll fight.

*—Interviewee, Washington, D.C.*

I'm scared for my family 'cause when my friend [name of friend] got shot they shot off and they shot through windows. And I'm glad my mother apartment is like not towards the street, it's inside of a court, so when they shoot they really can't shoot. But my little brother windows, their window is kind of like sideways to the street, like the window's right here and the street is right here. So it's kind of like if somebody's coming down the street and they shoot, it could fly through the window like this. That's what I'm scared of.

*—Interviewee, Washington, D.C.*

I'm so scared that one day the bullets going to come through my window. And the way my son and my nephew like to be in the window one of them could be shot.

[So you have a fourteen year old son?]

Participant: Mm-Mmm. And my nephew comes over on weekends and he's fourteen too and they like to be in the window.

*—Interviewee, Washington, D.C.*

Before, I would hang out with them but as far as like the gun shooting on the 4th of July and stuff like that, I disliked that because bullets come up. They gotta come down so little kids outside. I didn't like the shooting.

*—Interviewee, Atlanta, GA*

## Methods for Avoiding Danger

Women reported limiting their movements due to their fear of stray gunfire. They also emphasized the importance of avoiding windows. As one reported:

3:00 in the afternoon. And I see him getting shot, and my kids—when they heard the gunshots, they throw themselves in the floor. I'm like, keep everybody down. I look out the window and I hear that every—so when I look out the window, I see the guy throwing up blood. And when—and his clothes is all full of blood, like he's bleeding through everywhere.

So that was a very … very shocking, to see something like that. I was in shock, I was in—my nerves were wrecked for like four hours. I still think about it, I get nervous.

*—Interviewee, New York, NY*

Another woman remarked:

I will take everybody to the park every day if I have to. If they want to go outside and play. But I will not allow them to play outside my building. Because there's a lot of—you don't know when there's going to be gunshots in front of my building, in my block. This is the first time I saw somebody get shot and killed right—that he was dying, didn't die right there, and (inaudible) out of the hospital—but it was the first time that I saw somebody get shot right there. But every other day there's gunshots. You don't know when one of these—a stray bullet could get one of your kids. So when I'm going toward my block, it's like I'm walking as fast as I can to get inside my building, to try and get inside my apartment and close the door. And just staying indoors.

*—Interviewee, New York, NY*

So I really worry—I'm … I worry a lot. I'm very conscious, when I walk outside in the streets, with my kids, because I worry a lot that any little thing happens to them. I—when I walk outside, my husband tells I'm crazy, because I'm walking with my five kids, I count my kids. I count them, to make—because if I'm talking, and I like lose concern—like, the sight of my kids, I start looking for them. Counting that I have five with me.

*—Interviewee, New York, NY*

I do have a child and it could be one day we're walking out for an appointment or, you know, an event or something and we get caught in a crossfire. That's what I'm really afraid of, you know? It's like before I leave the house I look out my window, see who's outside, how long they've been out there, what's going on, who's selling (inaudible). And even when I'm outside with her I have to watch which ways I walk. Because if there's a crowd you never know what could be going before you get to the scene. So I have to like, detour, go certain areas just to get to my building. It's, it's sad.

*—Interviewee, New York, NY*

At least one woman reported fear of answering the telephone in case it was bad news:

I be, sometimes it be to the point where I'm scared to answer my phone in the middle of the night 'cause I'm always thinking that it's going to be some bad news, somebody calling with something. I don't know, I think my family just got bad luck or something, the boys anyway.

*—Interviewee, Washington, D.C.*

[And so what do you do when you hear shots?]

Go in the closet.

[Really? And how often is that?]

Maybe two or three days out of a week … I think my son say I feel asleep one time in the closet 'cause it was just like madness going on.

*—Interviewee, Washington, D.C.*

If I have to go get my baby some medicine at 2:00 in the morning and I'm going to the store, them—these Jamaican guys is fighting, and I know how they give it up. Like they just want to shoot. So I'm mad scared. I'm hiding behind the corner, like, "Is it safe for me to go to the store?" You know, like I'm scared. I can't even just walk. I have to ask somebody to walk with me, like—

*—Focus Group Participant, New York, NY*

Some women reported avoiding particular establishments, streets, etc.

There's a lot of shootouts at night and so on. And I know they sell a lot of drugs on the corner store, I never go there. My boyfriend said, "Don't you ever go there, just go around to [street], don't go to [street]." Go straight (inaudible)? There's a lot of killings, drug related, killings in that store. So I don't ever go there.

—*Focus Group Participant, New York, NY*

I live right there where [name of neighborhood] I live right on the outskirts of [name of neighborhood] and it's terrible. I mean it's so bad that they shoot guns that I feel like they coming through my living room window. I be telling my kids get down, they get in the middle of the floor, they've been getting in the floor. So, everybody just get down on the floor. So, it's just terrible. I mean, I don't feel safe at night when I sleep because where my bedroom window is it feel like somebody could just come through there shooting or my house been burglarized already.

—*Focus Group Participant, Washington, D.C.*

Yes, my nephew got shot on the playground out there on the playground .... But ever since he got shot I don't—

[Did he die?]

No, no. Luckily, whew, I don't know how he didn't because he got shot up like five or six times.

—*Interviewee, Washington, D.C.*

But ever since that happened like I don't take them outside. If they want to go outside we'll get suited and booted for the weekend and we'll go over my sister house 'cause she has a house. I'll let them go out to the backyard.

—*Interviewee, Washington, D.C.*

Some women reported monitoring their children closely to be sure that they were safe.

Like I said, I tell my kids every day. You call me. I don't care if you're going to the store, call me .... When you're coming back from the store, call me, because like I said, I'm facing a project and I'm behind a project, and God only knows.

—*Focus Group Participant, New York, NY*

What I dislike is because I have kids. I have two, actually, both under the age of five. And I can't, like—I just—I feel uncomfortable coming out early, late—any time of the day, I just feel like anything could happen, and then it's like, it's worrying. It's—that's the only thing I have a problem with: that somebody start shooting, my kids—something like that. So that's my problem with where I live. (laughter)

—*Focus Group Participant, New York, NY*

## *Defensive Fatalism*

Several women reported that they were becoming desensitized to the danger and fear that they had been experiencing.

You know what, to be quite honest with you, I'm beginning to get ... to get numb to it already. I'm getting numb to it, you know, it's like a part of my life already. You know and that's sad to say, you know? When I go to another neighborhood, like with someone saying about—what letter are you? C?—C says about Soho—when I go to Staten Island to my family's house, I could look up at the sky and it's all quiet and I just like, I'll just take a deep breath and I just feel so calm. Even the air smells different, you know, and coming back over here it's like detention. It's like boom, boom, boom.

—*Focus Group Participant, New York, NY*

Another woman commented:

> And, then they get immune to it, so it don't hurt their feelings no more, you understand what I'm saying. You go through it so much it don't bother you like that.
> *—Focus Group Participant, Washington, D.C.*

Some women adopted the attitude that when God means for you to go, you will; it's in his hands.

> I have a couple of cousins, a couple of aunts and like my aunt she worries about me because sometimes I do walk out at night because I just feel like the Lord on my side. If something is going to happen, it's going to happen but I don't be in nobody business for anything to happen to me.
> *—Interviewee, Washington, D.C.*

Some women wished to avoid talking about traumatic events.

> Yes my friend [name of friend] got killed in my face
> [Oh no.]
> –so it was kind of.
> [Really? Do you feel comfortable talking about that like more about that like what happened and when and stuff?]
> Not really.
> *—Interviewee, Washington, D.C.*

## *Role of Police*

While some women reported positive feelings toward the police, much more common was the belief that they were either useless or harassing residents.

> Say, like my street I'm on [name of intersection] and at the end of [name of street] two people got shot on the corner. The police would be at the top of [name of street] and the bottom of [name of street] but never catch it in the middle and like they would come and leave and the same thing will happen a couple of hours later and they still don't want to understand why it's happening. I mean you all not doing anything. I mean, you just got to understand, these, the young kids out here on a whole different level, like they into this type of stuff, the guns and the drugs and who got the most money and all of that.
> *—Interviewee, Washington, D.C.*

Police were reported to drop murder cases when the victim had drugs or money on their person.

> Yeah. I think it's pretty common, like, if somebody get murdered, most of the time they going to have drug or money on them. And if they see it's drug related they probably like, well, these people they killing the drug dealers, let them do our job, you know. So that's probably, I think that's what the situation is. I really don't like the cops … Like, one time the cops came around there with big guns and everything and I'm just walking. You gonna stop me and search me and yell at me. What am I doing? They talking about some, "you signaled them to leave" and all that. And I'm like, "I don't have nothing to do with that." I seen police officers with big guns and I'm leaving, you know. And they stopped my old best friend. She got into it with the female police officer 'cause the female police officer called her a "B." They don't care about people who live in the ghetto I believe so.
> *—Interviewee, Washington, D.C.*

Regardless of participants' attitudes toward police and the correctional system in general, it is clear that enforcement of gun-related laws is woefully inadequate to protect many American citizens.

## Policy Implications

As the sociohistorical introduction demonstrated, gun control policies have gradually become less restricted and are more relaxed today than they have ever been historically. Gun control advocates today espouse policy efforts such as requiring background checks to prevent gun ownership by individuals designated as mentally ill or convicted criminals, and banning the possession of guns capable of quickly firing multiple rounds of ammunition, which can cause many deaths in mass shootings. These highly salient events typically spark dialogue concerning gun control. In fact, following the murder of 26 people at Sandy Hook Elementary School in December 2012, many of them first-grade students, President Barack Obama issued 23 Executive Orders restricting types of guns, requiring background checks, and bolstering mental health services. Only some of these were made into law, and only at the level of individual states. What this chapter illustrates, however, is that many more deaths are attributable to gun violence. Between 2007 and 2011, 68,720 Americans were murdered as a result of gun violence (Institute of Medicine and National Research Council, 2013). This figure is higher than the number of Americans killed in the Vietnam (58,220), Iraq (4476), and Afghanistan (2279) wars (Defense Manpower Data Center).

Until we can get firearms, particularly military-style weapons, out of the hands of our young people, we will continue to see the premature ending of children's lives.

## References


Cramer, C. E. (1993). The racist roots of gun control. *Kansas Journal of Law & Public Policy, 42*(2), 9.

Defense Manpower Data Center. *Defense casualty analysis system.* Retrieved October 2013, from https://dmdc.osd.mil/dcas/pages/casualties_oef.xhtml

Ferguson, C. J., Miguel, C. S., Garza, A., & Jerabeck, J. M. (2012). A longitudinal test of video game violence influences on dating and aggression: A 3-year longitudinal study of adolescents. *Journal of Psychiatric Research, 46*(2), 141–146. doi:10.1016/j.jpsychires.2011.10.014.

Hennekens, C. H., Drowos, J., & Levine, R. S. (2013). Mortality from homicide among young black men: A new American tragedy. *American Journal of Medicine, 126*(4), 282–283. doi:10.1016/j.amjmed.2012.07.007.

Institute of Medicine and National Research Council. (2013). Priorities for research to reduce the threat of firearm-related violence. Washington, D.C.: The National Academies Press.

Logan, J. E., Smith, S. G., Stevens, M. R., & Centers for Disease Control and Prevention (CDC). (2011). Homicides—United States, 1999-2007. *MMWR Surveillance Summaries, 60*(Suppl), 67–70.

Krouse, W. J. (2012). *Gun control legislation* (pp. 113). Washington, D.C.

Paus, T. (2005). Mapping brain maturation and cognitive development during adolescence. *Trends in Cognitive Sciences, 9*(2), 60–68. doi:10.1016/j.tics.2004.12.008.

Richardson, E. G., & Hemenway, D. (2011). Homicide, suicide, and unintentional firearm fatality: Comparing the United States with other high-income countries, 2003. *Journal of Trauma, 70*(1), 238–243. doi:10.1097/TA.0b013e3181dbaddf.

Willoughby, T., Adachi, P. J. C., & Good, M. (2012). A longitudinal study of the association between violent video game play and aggression among adolescents. *Developmental Psychology, 48*(4), 1044–1057. doi:10.1037/A0026046.

Winkler, A. (2011). Gunfight: Over the Right to Bear Arms in America. New York, New York, United States: WW Norton and company. Retrieved October 16, 2013.

# Afterword
# Policy and Human Rights Implications of Women's Poverty and Vulnerability in the USA

**Sten H. Vermund, Wafaa El-Sadr, Carlos del Rio, and Gina M. Wingood**

## Context of the HPTN 064 Study

The HIV Prevention Trials Network (HPTN) mission is to conduct randomized clinical trials (RCT) to assess the efficacy of HIV prevention strategies and technologies to reduce HIV transmission among adolescents and/or adults (Sista et al., 2011).[1] The ultimate goal of the HPTN is to identify strategies that demonstrate public health impact by significantly reducing the risk of HIV transmission. In preparation for such RCTs, developmental vanguard studies may be conducted in order to garner answers to questions that stand in the way of design and/or implementation of these RCTs. Vanguard studies may explore the feasibility of recruitment and retention of certain populations, measure anticipated HIV incidence in a specific

[1] HPTN is not the only HIV/AIDS network supported by the NIH. Other NIH networks support HIV/AIDS research in other areas: AIDS Clinical Trials Group (ACTG); International Network for Strategic Initiatives in Global HIV Trials (INSIGHT); International Maternal Pediatric Adolescent AIDS Clinical Trials (IMPAACT); HIV Vaccine Trials Network (HVTN); Microbicide Trials Network (MTN); Adolescent Medicine Trials Network for HIV/AIDS Interventions (ATN); AIDS Malignancy Consortium (AMC); International Epidemiologic Databases to Evaluate AIDS (IeDEA); and others. Beyond the NIH, other US agencies like the Centers for Disease Control and Prevention (CDC) and international organizations support other networks for analogous research purposes.

S.H. Vermund (✉)
Vanderbilt Institute for Global Health, Vanderbilt University School of Medicine, Nashville, TN, USA
e-mail: sten.vermund@vanderbilt.edu

W. El-Sadr
ICAP, Mailman School of Public Health, Columbia University, New York, NY, USA

C. del Rio
Hubert Department of Global Health, Rollins School of Public Health, Emory University, Atlanta, GA 30322, USA

G.M. Wingood
Mailman School of Public Health, Columbia University, New York, NY, USA



A. O'Leary, P.M. Frew (eds.), *Poverty in the United States*,
DOI 10.1007/978-3-319-43833-7_13

population to inform feasibility of design of efficacy trial and statistical power analyses, and evaluate the feasibility of implementation of a proposed intervention(s). The HPTN has a broad prevention research agenda, especially highlighting the use of antiretroviral drugs to prevent HIV transmission between adults, both by reducing infectiousness among HIV-infected persons taking combination antiretroviral therapy (ART) and seeking new approaches to reduce susceptibility among HIV-uninfected persons through antiretroviral drugs for preexposure prophylaxis (PrEP). Ultimately, the HPTN aims to design integrated strategy studies that include biomedical, behavioral, and structural interventions that are tailored to the population at risk. The epidemic of HIV in the USA among women of color has been an area that has been understudied but that is of special concern as currently one in five new HIV infections are among women, and women of color are disproportionately affected by HIV.

This book has been spearheaded by investigators and leaders of the HPTN 064 study, one of HPTN's flagship vanguard studies. While pivotal efficacy trials to test HIV-specific prevention strategies and technologies are the main HPTN priority, HPTN 064 was deemed a high network priority given the dearth of recent data on HIV incidence among women-at-risk in the USA (El-Sadr, Mayer, & Hodder, 2010; Vermund et al., 2010).

The study used novel methods to select at-risk women, first by selecting the communities where the study would be conducted based on prevalence of both HIV and poverty; these were the antecedent criteria before personal and partner risk assessments determined individual study eligibility, giving the investigators the strongest possible chance of working with the women who were most at risk for HIV acquisition (Haley, Golin, et al., 2014). HPTN 064 study aimed to document HIV incidence in this population of women as determined by the geography of their residence as well as the nature of their personal behaviors and exposures (Haley, Golin, et al., 2014).

Incidence rates in HPTN 064 were 2.5 per 1000 women, far higher than for women in general in the USA, validating the selection strategy that sought women participants into the study from communities in the USA who were most in the path of HIV infection (Hodder et al., 2013, 2016). This may represent the lower limit of the probable "real-world" rate since participation in the study included participants' receiving substantial educational guidance as to how to avoid HIV, along with peer support elements and were also provided with condoms (Haley, Lucas, et al., 2014). Another novel aspect of the study is that HIV incidence was also estimated using a validated multiassay algorithm that used cross-sectional data to estimate HIV incidence based on specific characteristics of the immune response that differ between recently and chronically infected persons (Eshleman et al., 2013).

The core insights from the HPTN 064 study are steeped in sociocultural context, structural challenges at the community level, and individual circumstances that influence behaviors. ***Poverty in the United States: Women's Voices*** is an evidence-driven exploration of women's experiences in the context of living in inner city and rural regions in the USA experiencing scarcities. Low income, high unemployment, high male incarceration rates, limited educational opportunities, and other markers of poverty in the USA are the context for these book chapters. The summary of the behavioral and contextual factors underpinning the experiences of women in HPTN 064 sets the stage for the deepening of the understanding of women's risk of HIV in the USA (Adimora et al., 2014; Jennings et al., 2015; Kuo et al., 2014) and helps us realize the enormous challenges these woman face.

## The Context of Poverty in America

Drivers of poverty among US women are complex and can be attributed in part to access to educational, health, employment, and housing opportunities. These poverty mitigators are typically more readily available to women overall and particularly to lower income women in other Western democracies. The Gini Index is defined by the World Bank as measuring, "... the extent to which the distribution of income or consumption expenditure among individuals or households within an economy deviates from a perfectly equal distribution" (World Bank, 2014). Economists use the Gini Index to judge the degree of economic and attendant disparities within a nation. The higher the Gini Index, the lower equity is noted in income distribution. The Organization for Economic Co-Operation and Development (OECD) website database lists both historic (1983–1985) and the most recent (2010–2012) Gini Index calculations for larger economy nations with larger economies, including the larger high-income nations (OECD, 2014). It is notable that yearly trends are in the direction of less and less equity over time (Table 1). The USA is considerably less equitable as measured by the Gini Index than most of its larger economy counterpart nations, on average (Table 1). This results in a huge challenge for low-income women in the USA, namely the widening of income disparities over time with trends that are unfavorable over the past three decades (Frew et al., 2016).

Poverty can breed desperation. Whether food insecurity and hunger (O'Leary et al., 2016a, 2016b), substance use (Kuo et al., 2016), or exchange of goods or money for sex (Olson et al., 2016), lack of resources affects the lives of women in profound and negative ways. At the community level, housing insecurity and poor housing stock is demoralizing and disruptive for job and school opportunities (Haley et al., 2016). Both community-level gun violence (O'Leary et al., 2016b) and other compelling personal and family safety issues (Parker et al., 2016a) loom large in women's concerns. This is highlighted especially by religious groups, as with Bishops Against Gun Violence (Bishops Against Gun Violence, 2016). Furthermore, high incarceration rates in the USA, by far the highest compared to any OECD nation (Figure; Kearney, Harris, Jácome, & Parker, 2014), may disrupt family and social networks. Women living in poverty who are trying to support families in single-parent households are disadvantaged in the context of family income, companionship, and supervision of children (Frew et al., 2016). Men are often absent from the homes and lives of their partners and children due to incarceration, or may have been estranged as a result of prior incarceration. As a result, in impoverished

**Table 1** Income distribution and poverty as assessed by Gini Index: high-income nations in 1983–1986 and 2010–2012

| Measure | Gini Index (at disposable income, post-taxes, and transfers) | | | | | |
|---|---|---|---|---|---|---|
| Year | 1983 | 1984 | 1985 | 2010 | 2011 | 2012 |
| **Country** | | | | | | |
| Australia | .. | .. | .. | 0.33 | .. | 0.32 |
| Austria | .. | .. | .. | 0.27 | 0.28 | .. |
| Belgium | .. | .. | .. | 0.26 | .. | .. |
| Canada | 0.30 | 0.30 | 0.29 | 0.32 | 0.32 | .. |
| Chile | .. | .. | .. | .. | 0.50 | .. |
| The Czech Republic | .. | .. | .. | 0.26 | 0.26 | .. |
| Denmark | .. | .. | 0.22 | 0.25 | 0.25 | .. |
| Estonia | .. | .. | .. | 0.32 | 0.32 | .. |
| Finland | .. | .. | .. | 0.26 | 0.27 | 0.26 |
| France | .. | .. | .. | 0.30 | 0.31 | .. |
| Germany | .. | .. | 0.25 | 0.29 | 0.29 | .. |
| Greece | .. | .. | .. | 0.34 | 0.34 | .. |
| Hungary | .. | .. | .. | .. | .. | 0.29 |
| Iceland | .. | .. | .. | 0.25 | 0.25 | .. |
| Ireland | .. | .. | .. | 0.31 | 0.30 | .. |
| Israel | .. | .. | 0.33 | 0.38 | 0.38 | .. |
| Italy | .. | 0.29 | .. | 0.32 | 0.32 | .. |
| Japan | .. | .. | 0.30 | .. | .. | .. |
| Korea | .. | .. | .. | 0.31 | 0.31 | 0.31 |
| Luxembourg | .. | .. | .. | 0.27 | 0.28 | .. |
| Mexico | .. | 0.45 | .. | 0.47 | .. | 0.48 |
| The Netherlands | .. | .. | 0.27 | 0.28 | .. | 0.28 |
| New Zealand | .. | .. | 0.27 | .. | 0.32 | .. |
| Norway | .. | .. | .. | 0.25 | 0.25 | .. |
| Poland | .. | .. | .. | 0.31 | 0.30 | .. |
| Portugal | .. | .. | .. | 0.34 | 0.34 | .. |
| Slovak Republic | .. | .. | .. | 0.26 | 0.26 | .. |
| Slovenia | .. | .. | .. | 0.25 | 0.25 | .. |
| Spain | .. | .. | .. | 0.33 | 0.34 | .. |
| Sweden | 0.20 | .. | .. | 0.27 | 0.27 | .. |
| Switzerland | .. | .. | .. | .. | 0.29 | .. |
| Turkey | .. | .. | .. | 0.42 | 0.41 | .. |
| UK | .. | .. | 0.31 | 0.34 | 0.34 | .. |
| USA | 0.34 | 0.34 | 0.34 | 0.38 | 0.39 | 0.39 |

Data extracted on 17 September 2014 17:30 UTC (GMT) from OECD. Stat, the Organisation for Economic Co-Operation and Development (OECD) website database: http://stats.oecd.org/Index.aspx?DataSetCode=IDD#

neighborhoods, women may find themselves with multiple partners to enhance financial security, improve opportunities for their children, or alleviate loneliness, to name just a few motives (Parker et al., 2016b) (Fig. 1).

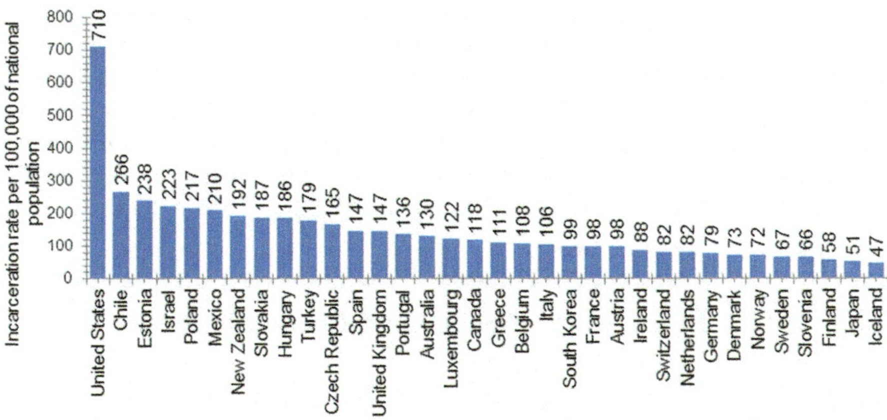


**Fig. 1** Incarceration rates: OECD countries, 2012–2013. *Source*: Kearney MS, Harris BH, Jácome E, Parker L. *Ten Economic Facts about Crime and Incarceration in the United States*. Washington, D.C.: The Brookings Institution/The Hamilton Project Policy Memo, May 2014

Throughout this book, its authors have sought to present insights and suggestions for policy reform, as informed by the qualitative findings, that would benefit the lives of poor women in the USA. Notably, criminal sentencing guidelines that disproportionately incarcerate minority men and women for terms that are beyond reason given the nature of offenses disrupt communities and individual lives. Lack of male role models will inevitably jeopardize the lives of future generations. Partners, wives, and mothers all suffer alongside the incarcerated men. Reform in this arena could be transformative. Educational opportunities and job training, whether for adults or children, can improve substantially the jobs for which they can compete either now for the women and men or in the future for their children. The linking of property taxes to school financing condemns poor neighborhoods to have underfunded schools. High-volume, low-documentation gun sales in some states are guaranteed to fuel gun distributions to poor, crime-ridden neighborhoods even beyond these states' borders, often to other states that themselves have strong gun-control policies. Politically motivated attacks and limitations on food stamp programs will increase food insecurity. Trends in the USA in 2014 are negative ones for women in poverty; government policy trends are increasing disparities and stress in poor communities and families.

Revitalization of traditional social support programs and nurturing of peer support networks among women can help address the social isolation reported by so many of our interviewees in HPTN 064 (Archibald et al., 2016). Expanded primary health care services for reproductive health in general and for sexually transmitted infections, and HIV in particular, can help women avoid these conditions and ensure that they get the care they need and deserve (Olson et al., 2016; Parker et al., 2016b). Substance-use services that focus on prevention, early detection, and evidence-based treatment rather than incarceration can give women with and without addictions a second chance to live drug-free lives (Kuo et al., 2016). The book's policy implications should not be dismissed as a "bleeding-heart" liberal agenda. Rather, they represent smart business practice. To sacrifice a generation of Americans to the squalor and desperation of poverty is shortsighted and will hamper the country's global competitiveness while at the same time serving as a drain to our social and economic capital. The authors of ***Poverty in the United States: Women's Voices*** have taken an HIV prevention feasibility study and turned it into a landmark exploration of poverty among vulnerable women in the USA.

## Integrating a Framework of Social and Economic Rights

The book's authors have eloquently outlined the complex factors that drive the HIV epidemic—poverty, lack of access to health care, high incarceration, lack of stable housing, and violence—and have argued that these factors are particularly powerful for women (Dean & Fenton, 2013; Hodder et al., 2010, 2013; Golin, et al., 2016). To end HIV among women in the USA, this consensus tells us, we must create meaningful structural change that would raise women's economic status, decrease incarceration rates, and increase access to stable housing and provide access to quality health care. Given the goal of creating meaningful structural change, it is time to integrate a framework of social and economic rights into existing HIV prevention efforts to stop the epidemic (Shinn, 1999; Whelan, 1998). The framework below on social and economic rights for women at risk and living with HIV is based on the international models project on women's rights (Carpenter, 2012).

Social and economic rights are acknowledged in international legal discourse as a key part of the basic package of fundamental human rights (Carpenter, 2012). These include rights to shelter, health care, work opportunities, and adequate nutrition, all of which require government action. These rights, also known as positive rights, are commonly contrasted with negative rights, which include rights to be free from government interference. Negative rights include the civil and political rights familiar to all Americans, such as the rights to freedom of speech and private property.

In the context of responding to the HIV epidemic, the USA is a clear outlier on social and economic rights (Liptak, 2012). U.S. Supreme Court Justice Ruth Bader Ginsburg noted that if she were to recommend a model for drafting a modern constitution, she would probe modern constitutions that recognize a broad commitment to human rights, such as the Canadian Charter of Rights and Freedoms and the South African Constitution (Liptak, 2012).

In the international community, there is a consensus that HIV/AIDS implicates such rights and that the epidemic cannot be stopped without systemic changes that attack economic and gender inequality (Office of the United Nations High Commission for Human Rights & UNAIDS, 2006). For those who advocate incorporating a social and economic rights framework into US-based HIV prevention efforts, an ultimate goal is the recognition and enforcement of legal claims to social and economic rights, particularly rights to a minimum level of economic support, health, and housing. The shorter term objective is to integrate a vision of social justice and systemic change into the policy discourse around the HIV epidemic, which in turn may build support for efforts to enact legislative and policy changes that begin to address the interrelated problems of poverty, violence, and gender inequality. Such reforms would include economic support, housing, and health care access for low-income women, their families, and their communities. A commitment to social and economic rights offers three key benefits. These benefits may be characterized as descriptive, pragmatic, and aspirational (Carpenter, 2012).

## *Descriptive Benefit of a Rights-Based Framework*

HIV is a public health problem that requires traditional public health responses. Yet, HIV is also driven by systemic forces and thus by political power. A major benefit of a rights-based framework is that it accurately identifies the epidemic as a problem with legal and political dimensions and one that implicates the fundamental interests of those affected (Carpenter, 2012). The language of rights is inevitably the language of entitlements and of power. As a historical matter, rights claims implicate the political power of the group claiming the right, the role of the legal system in assessing and enforcing the right, and, insofar as social and economic rights describe the basic social goods that all people need to thrive, fundamental human needs.

A diverse set of diseases are distributed in highly disparate patterns and have their most devastating impact on and pose the highest risk to the least politically and economically powerful groups in America. Whether diabetes or HIV, hypertension or tuberculosis, these diseases can be perpetuated and exacerbated by poverty and inequality and thus requires systemic responses that necessitate state action. Many disease conditions have clear political dimensions in that the greatest impact of the disease is felt among those groups who have the least and most diffuse political power. Women at risk for HIV represent some of the most marginalized segments of our society in terms of economic strength, political force, social status, and access to the legal system (Carpenter, 2012). To state that the rights of women are violated when they are placed at risk for HIV and other health problems for reasons beyond their control is to recognize the broad and severe impact of the problem, to identify the complex structural forces at play, and to recognize a role for legal justice remedies.

## *Practical Benefit of a Rights-Based Framework*

Historically, state courts have been reluctant to enforce social and economic rights guarantees due to concerns about institutional competence and a view that within the federal system, the U.S. Supreme Court adjudicates what may be recognized as constitutional rights (Hershkoff & Loffredo, 2011; Pascal, 2008; Rava, 1998; Usman, 2010). However, in recent years, advocates and legal scholars have begun developing a jurisprudence of social and economic rights through state constitutional law.

Legal inspiration has come from the South African Constitutional Court, which has recognized a right to housing (Neuborne, 1989; Rotunno, 1996; Usman, 2010). Many scholars have lauded the South African court's decision for its balance between the realities of limited government resources and the responsibility of government to meet the minimal needs of citizens. The court declared that the government had a duty to provide housing, and then instructed the legislature to "devise and implement within its available resources a comprehensive and coordinated program progressively to realize the right of access to adequate housing." Thus, the court recognized a right to housing while also recognizing that a full realization of the right would take time and deferring to the legislature, alleviating some concerns about the court's competence to adjudicate rights claims.

Despite historical resistance to social and economic rights claims, state constitutional law provides one pragmatic path towards promoting systemic reforms for women at risk for HIV through such rights claims. While the path towards full realization of rights in this context will be long and complex, examples such as the South African experience offer hope that social and economic rights also have a constitutional and legal basis in the US legal system.

## *Aspirational Benefit of a Rights-Based Framework*

The language of social and economic rights is aspirational in that it invokes an ideal vision of what might be possible when a government makes a commitment to protecting the basic human rights of its people. All rights claims, whether regarding positive or negative rights, begin as mere ideas, as ideals, and as expressions of fundamental values. Rights claims implicate our shared notions of justice and fundamental fairness and define the possible contours of the relationship between the state and the individual. Even where a particular articulated right is not yet legally enforceable, making the claim to that right stakes out a moral and political position that articulates an affirmative role for the state in protecting that right. To invoke the language of rights in the context of protecting women at risk for HIV is to describe an ideal that may not be fully realized, but which sets the highest possible achievable standard and thus shapes judicial interpretation, legislative actions, and advocacy conversations. Rights claims broaden our collective vision about what law and, by definition, government can achieve (Pascal, 2008; Rava, 1998). To claim a violation of fundamental rights where the government fails to protect or respond to the needs of women at risk for HIV is to offer hope for what is possible rather than a story about what is impossible.

### *Benefit of Integrating Social Capital into a Rights-Based Framework*

Actualizing the realization of social and economic rights may be obtained through building social capital within programs, institutions, and communities. An individual may acquire social capital through participating in informal networks, registered organizations, associations of different kinds, and social movements, and it represents the sum of these experiences. It is believed that through membership in different organizations and networks individuals will develop joint interests and shared norms, which in turn will lead to trust and better understanding of differences in culture, background, and lifestyle (Rocco & Suhrcke, 2012). During this process democracy might emerge and individuals might have the opportunity to capture social and economic rights and benefits. Leveraging social capital may be an important risk management strategy during times of economic distress. Understanding the efficacy of social capital in its institutional context implies that how communities manage both opportunities and risk will necessarily depend on the quality of the institutions under which they live. Suppressed civil liberties and failure to uphold the rule of law can be expected to force communities to supply privately and informally what should be delivered publicly and formally. International strategic development partners including The World Bank, OECD, European Union (EU), and the United Nations Development Programme (UNDP) tend to view social capital as the glue that holds society together. Governments need to invest adequate time and resources in building robust social and economic rights frameworks; however, they also need to involve citizens in the policy-making process. A framework that involves public consultation and participation is vital towards improving policies, revitalizing democracy, and nurturing stability (Kahssay & Oakley, 1999).

In South Africa, key factors in the success of the IMAGE (Intervention with Microfinance for AIDS and Gender Equity) program's reductions in gender-based violence and HIV risk included a combination of microfinance, leadership training, women's empowerment training towards improved self-confidence, improved social capital, and collective action (Pronyk et al., 2006). In the USA, it has been demonstrated that states with higher levels of social capital have lower rates of sexually transmitted diseases (Holtgrave & Crosby, 2003). Recently, a social intervention that focused on enhancing religious social capital among African-American women attending predominantly black churches was effective in reducing African-American women's HIV risk and improving HIV testing among female congregants (Wingood et al., 2013). Research in the field of criminal justice has also shown that social capital assists ex-inmates upon societal reentry, particularly those who reconnect with their social networks. Having stronger social networks allows ex-inmates to develop a more positive identity, be better equipped to reduce the stigma of incarceration, and have access to more resources supporting the management of their personal relationships and their finances (Rose, Clear, & Ryder, 2001). In this view, building social capital among ex-offenders may reduce vulnerability to HIV among themselves and their sexual partners.

Given the emerging consensus in the field of public health that such diverse epidemics as diabetes or HIV among US women can be traced directly to the impact of economic and social inequality and cannot be stopped without structural interventions, ending health disparities will require lifting women and their families out of poverty, offering women the economic means and security to leave violent relationships, providing secure stable housing, ending the so-called war on drugs by transforming strategies from failed interdiction into addition prevention and rehabilitation, securing access to health care, and enhancing their social capital. Doing all of these things is not as hard as most think or as expensive as some may believe, given the economic benefits of fuller employment, lower incarceration, and better health within a more educated populace. It is the right thing to do and doing so will make the USA a better nation.

## References


Adimora, A. A., Hughes, J. P., Wang, J., Haley, D. F., Golin, C. E., Magnus, M., … HPTN 064 Protocol Team. (2014). Characteristics of multiple and concurrent partnerships among women at high risk for HIV infection. *Journal of Acquired Immune Deficiency Syndromes, 65*, 99–106.

Archibald, M., Stewart, J., Vo, L., Diallo, D.D., Shabazz, W. ... Randall, L. (2016). The Role of Social Support for Women Living in Poverty. In A. O'Leary & P. Frew (Eds.), *Poverty in the United States: Women's Voices*. New York: Springer.

Bishops Against Gun Violence. (2016). Website, retrieved September 12, 2016, from http://bishopsagainstgunviolence.org/

Carpenter, A. (2012). *Women and HIV/AIDS: Towards a jurisprudence of social and economic rights*. International Models Project on Women's Rights (IMPOWR). Retrieved January 20, 2015, from http://www.impowr.org/journal/women-and-hivaids-toward-jurisprudence-social-and-economic-rights

Dean, H. D., & Fenton, K. A. (2013). Integrating a social determinants of health approach into public health practice: A five-year perspective of actions implemented by CDC's national center for HIV/AIDS, viral hepatitis, STD, and TB prevention. *Public Health Reports, 128*(Suppl 3), 5–11.

El-Sadr, W. M., Mayer, K. H., & Hodder, S. L. (2010). AIDS in America—Forgotten but not gone. *New England Journal of Medicine, 362*, 967–970.

Eshleman, S. H., Hughes, J. P., Laeyendecker, O., Wang, J., Brookmeyer, R., Johnson-Lewis, L., … Hodder, S. (2013). Use of a multifaceted approach to analyze HIV incidence in a cohort study of women in the United States: HIV Prevention Trials Network 064 Study. *Journal of Infectious Diseases, 207*, 223–231.

Frew, P., Parker, K.A., Vo, L., Haley, D.F., McGovern, T., Owens, L., ... Randall, L. (2016). The Intersection of Women's Health and Poverty. In A. O'Leary & P. Frew (Eds.), *Poverty in the United States: Women's Voices*. New York: Springer.

Golin, C., Amola, O., Dardick, A., Montgomery, B., Bishop, L., ... Owens, L. (2016). Poverty, Personal Experiences of Violence, and Mental Health: Understanding Their Complex Intersections Among Low-Income Women. In A. O'Leary & P. Frew (Eds.), *Poverty in the United States: Women's Voices*. New York: Springer.

Haley, D. F., Golin, C., El-Sadr, W., Hughes, J. P., Wang, J., Roman Isler, M., … Hodder, S. (2014). Venue-based recruitment of women at elevated risk for HIV: An HIV Prevention Trials Network Study. *Journal of Women's Health, 23*, 541–551.

Haley, D. F., Lucas, J., Golin, C. E., Wang, J., Hughes, J. P., Emel, L., … HPTN 064 Study Team. (2014). Retention strategies and factors associated with missed visits among low income women at increased risk of HIV acquisition in the US (HPTN 064). *AIDS Patient Care STDS, 28*, 206–217.

Haley, D. F., Parker, K., Dauria, E. F., Root, C., Rodriguez, L., Ruel, E., ... Cooper, H. L. F. (2016). Housing and Health: Exploring the Complex Intersections Between Housing Environments and Health Behaviors Among Women Living in Poverty. In A. O'Leary & P. Frew (Eds.), *Poverty in the United States: Women's Voices*. New York: Springer.

Hershkoff, H., & Loffredo, S. (2011). State courts and constitutional socio-economic rights: Exploring the underutilization thesis. *Penn State Law Review, 115*, 923.

Hodder, S. L., Justman, J., Haley, D. F., Adimora, A. A., Fogel, C. I., Golin, C. E., ... HIV Prevention Trials Network Domestic Prevention in Women Working Group. (2010). Challenges of a hidden epidemic: HIV prevention among women in the United States. *Journal of Acquired Immune Deficiency Syndromes, 55*(Suppl 2), S69–S70.

Hodder, S. L., Justman, J., Hughes, J. P., Wang, J., Haley, D. F., Adimora, A. A., ... Women's HIV SeroIncidence Study Team. (2013). HIV acquisition among women from selected areas of the United States: A cohort study. *Annals of Internal Medicine, 158*, 10–18.

Hodder, S., Spiegel, H., Soto-Torres, L., & Haley, D.F. (2016). Women and Poverty in the USA. In A. O'Leary & P. Frew (Eds.), *Poverty in the United States: Women's Voices*. New York: Springer.

Holtgrave, D. R., & Crosby, R. A. (2003). Social capital, poverty, and income inequality as predictors of gonorrhoea, syphilis, chlamydia and AIDS case rates in the United States. *Sexually Transmitted Infections, 79*, 62–64.

Jennings, L., Rompalo, A. M., Wang, J., Hughes, J., Adimora, A. A., Hodder, S., ... HIV Prevention Trials Network (HPTN 064) Women's HIV SeroIncidence Study (ISIS). (2015). Prevalence and correlates of knowledge of male partner HIV testing and serostatus among African-American women living in high poverty, high HIV prevalence communities (HPTN 064). *AIDS and Behavior, 19*(2), 291–301.

Kahssay, H. M., & Oakley, P. (Eds). (1999). *Community involvement in health development: A review of the concept and practice* (Public Health in Action, No. 5). Geneva: World Health Organization.

Kearney, M. S., Harris, B. H., Jácome, E., & Parker, L. (2014, May). *Ten economic facts about crime and incarceration in the United States* (Figure 6, p. 10). Washington, DC: The Brookings Institution/The Hamilton Project Policy Memo.

Kuo, I., Golin, C. E., Wang, J., Haley, D. F., Hughes, J., Mannheimer, S., ... HPTN 064 Study Team. (2014). Substance use patterns and factors associated with changes over time in a cohort of heterosexual women at risk for HIV acquisition in the United States. *Drug and Alcohol Dependence, 139*, 93–99.

Kuo, I., Turner, M., Trezza, C., Peterson, J. (2016). Substance Use Among Women in Poverty. In A. O'Leary & P. Frew (Eds.), *Poverty in the United States: Women's Voices*. New York: Springer.

Liptak, A. (2012, February 6). 'We the People' loses appeal with people around the world. *The New York Times*. Retrieved January 20, 2015, from http://www.nytimes.com/2012/02/07/us/we-the-people-loses-appeal-with-people-around-the-world.html?_r=1

Neuborne, B. (1989). Foreword: State constitutions and the evolution of positive rights. *Rutgers Law Journal, 20*(881), 893–901.

O'Leary, A., Raskind, I. G., Turner, M.. (2016a). Food Insecurity Experienced by Women Living in Poverty. In A. O'Leary & P. Frew (Eds.), *Poverty in the United States: Women's Voices*. New York: Springer.

O'Leary, A., White, L. D., Anderson, L., Bishop, L. (2016b). Descriptions of Gun Violence. In A. O'Leary & P. Frew (Eds.), *Poverty in the United States: Women's Voices*. New York: Springer.

Office of the United Nations High Commission for Human Rights and UNAIDS. (2006). *International guidelines on HIV/AIDS and human rights* (Consolidated Version). Geneva: Office of the United Nations High Commissioner for Human Rights. Retrieved January 20, 2015, from http://www.ohchr.org/Documents/Publications/HIVAIDSGuidelinesen.pdf

Olson, K. R., Justman, J. E., Chung, Y., Parker, K., Golin, C., Lykes, S. (2016). The Logic of Exchange Sex Among Women Living in Poverty. In A. O'Leary & P. Frew (Eds.), *Poverty in the United States: Women's Voices*. New York: Springer.

Organisation for Economic Co-Operation and Development (OECD). (2014). Retrieved January 20, 2015, from http://stats.oecd.org/Index.aspx?DataSetCode=IDD#

Parker, K. A., Haley, D., Bishop, L., Bota, D. (2016a). Physical Safety and Neighborhood Issues. In A. O'Leary & P. Frew (Eds.), *Poverty in the United States: Women's Voices*. New York: Springer.

Parker, K. A., Riley, L., Lykes, S., Legros, J. R. M. (2016b). Partner Concurrency and Relationship Dynamics. In A. O'Leary & P. Frew (Eds.), *Poverty in the United States: Women's Voices*. New York: Springer.

Pascal, E. (2008). Welfare rights in state constitutions. *Rutgers Law Journal, 39*, 863–864.

Pronyk, P. M., Hargreaves, J. R., Kim, J. C., Morison, L. A., Phetla, G., Watts, C., … Porter, J. D. (2006). Effects of a structural intervention for the prevention of intimate partner violence and HIV in rural South Africa: A cluster randomized trial. *Lancet, 368*, 1973–1983.

Rava, W. C. (1998). State constitutional protections for the poor. *Temple Law Review, 71*, 543–551.

Rocco, L., & Suhrcke, M. (2012). *Is social capital good for health?* Copenhagen: WHO Regional Office for Europe.

Rose, D. R., Clear, T. R., & Ryder, J. A. (2001). Addressing the unintended consequences of incarceration through community-oriented services. *Corrections Management Quarterly, 5*, 69–78.

Rotunno, N. (1996). State constitutional social welfare provisions and the right to housing. *Hofstra Law Policy Symposium, 1*(111), 128–133.

Shinn, C. (1999). The right to the highest attainable standard of health: Public health's opportunity to reframe a human rights debate in the United States. *Health and Human Rights, 4*, 114–129.

Sista, N. D., Abdool Karim, Q., Hinson, K., Donnell, D., Eshleman, S. H., & Vermund, S. H. (2011). Experience in international clinical research: The HIV Prevention Trials Network. *Clinical Investigation, 1*, 1609–1618.

Usman, J. O. (2010). Good enough for government work: The interpretation of positive constitutional rights in state constitutions. *Albany Law Review, 73*, 1459.

Vermund, S. H., Hodder, S. L., Justman, J. E., Koblin, B. A., Mastro, T. D., Mayer, K. H., … El-Sadr, W. M. (2010). Addressing research priorities for prevention of HIV infection in the United States. *Clinical Infectious Diseases, 50*(Suppl 3), S149–S55.

Whelan, D. (1998). Human rights approaches to an expanded response to address women's vulnerability to HIV/AIDS. *Health and Human Rights, 3*, 20–22.

Wingood, G. M., Robinson, L. R., Braxton, N. D., Er, D. L., Conner, A. C., Renfro, T. L., … DiClemente, R. J. (2013). Comparative effectiveness of a faith-based HIV intervention for African American women: Importance of enhancing religious social capital. *American Journal of Public Health, 103*, 2226–2233.

World Bank. (2014). *GINI website*. Retrieved January 20, 2015, from http://data.worldbank.org/indicator/SI.POV.GINI

# Index




A. O'Leary, P.M. Frew (eds.), *Poverty in the United States*,
DOI 10.1007/978-3-319-43833-7

CPSIA information can be obtained
at www.ICGtesting.com
Printed in the USA
LVOW02*1709230517
535544LV00002BA/9/P

9 783319 438313